THE CATALOGUE OF AMERICAN CATALOGUES

by Maria Elena de La Iglesia

THE CATALOGUE OF CATALOGUES:
The Complete Guide to
World-wide Shopping by Mail

THE CATALOGUE OF AMERICAN CATALOGUES
How to Buy Everything by Mail
in America

Maria Elena De La Iglesia

THE CATALOGUE OF AMERICAN CATALOGUES

How to Buy Practically Everything by Mail in America

Random House • New York

 Published in the United States by Random House, Inc., New York, New York, and simultaneously in Canada by Random House of Canada Limited, Toronto.

Library of Congress Cataloging in Publication Data

De La Iglesia, Maria Elena.
The catalogue of American catalogues.
1. Mail-order business—Directories. I. Title.
HF5466.D44 380.1′025 73-5047
ISBN 0-394-48690-0
ISBN 0-394-70982-9 (pbk.)

Designed by Hermann Strohbach

Manufactured in the United States of America

9 8 7 6 5 4 3 2

CONTENTS

ACKNOWLEDGMENTS

A great many people helped me with this book and I would like specially to thank Susan Samelson, who worked with me, and Clement Meadmore, Mike Rockliffe, Calvin Trillin and Mary Ann Spencer, who gave advice and told me about some of the most interesting stores.

INTRODUCTION

More is bought by mail in America than in any other country, and has been bought that way ever since the colonists, who ordered everything from Europe from seeds to looking-glasses. The mail-order business in this country is now very large and sophisticated. To people who don't order *anything* by mail, the process conjures up pictures of junk brochures and scrubby catalogues hawking gimcrack novelties, whereas to "catalogue freaks," as they sometimes call themselves (and I know several), mail order has the magic of limitless possibilities, and catalogues are treasures to be anticipated, pored over, hoarded and only incidentally bought from. Such aficionados speak rapturously of the marvels of L. L. Bean or Sears, Roebuck, where boundless equipment is laid out in great profusion.

Between the extremes of those who buy everything by mail and those who buy nothing stand most people, ordering rather haphazardly certain things that they need and can't get, or don't want to get, locally, from firms they already know about or through advertisements in newspapers and magazines. It is for these people I hope this book will be useful as a guide to the whereabouts of good sources that are often hard to find and inconvenient to reach.

Shopping by mail gives you a far wider choice than is possible in all but the largest cities, and even then, much that is in this book is unavailable even in New York. Increasingly, stores have come to limit what they sell to the most popular or, to be more to the point, fastest-moving items. "Merchandise managers" have to determine what makes the most dollars per cubic foot of store space. As a result, the out-of-the-way items, the one of a kind, the bargains, in short, many worthwhile things, tend to disappear from an increasing number of stores. Just as items disappear, so do the stores themselves. Spiraling rents downtown, the lack of rent control, all combine to squeeze out the old stores that used to supply the variety and interest to the city's streets. To survive, stores relocate elsewhere and start to sell by mail, or stay in town but seek a national clientele which will give them the turnover they need. There are New York stores listed in this book which do as little as 2 percent of their business locally, the rest comes from customers all over the country. As a result, mail-order buying may be the only way to obtain many of the products listed in this book. For example, some of the bookstores or craft shops are the only sources in the country for certain items.

Linked to this change has been the back-to-the-land movement of the 1960's. The *Whole Earth Catalog* suggested the extent of this phenomenon, but more than youngsters are involved. I have found interesting examples of people who picked up and went to the country, some as early as the 1930's, starting farms or stores or simply carrying on with their same work but away from the cities. Natural food and handicrafts are only a few of the results of this attempt to start afresh, and here again, mail order is the way to keep going. The interest in crafts goes beyond the traditional do-it-yourself. Hobbyists and collectors have always ordered by mail, so have those seeking craft supplies or electronic parts, for example. More companies are now deliberately manufacturing components. Whether it's the dulcimer or the down-filled sleeping bag or eiderdown, there are dozens of sources in this book of parts or partially completed goods that you can buy for far less than the finished product.

A word about the unexpected. Just as in shopping, you often end up taking home something that was on the shelf next to the item you originally intended to buy, so in these catalogues the most fascinating objects have often been the least expected. You may find bargains or exceptionally well designed or useful items under the categories that at first glance seem unlikely. I've tried to give some cross references, and the index is as comprehensive as I could make it. But the entries themselves may still contain a few surprises. For instance, I found that some of the best kitchen utensils came from suppliers of camping equipment. Museums turn out to be excellent sources of needlework kits. Some of the best, most useful and least expensive clothing for everyday use is sold by suppliers who specialize in outfitting expeditions and mountain climbers but sell a flannel shirt or a pair of trousers that is more durable, better made and cheaper than I could find in our best department stores. Books are sold in the most unexpected places; a whole library is tucked into the end of an archery catalogue, and all sorts of specialized catalogues have extensive offerings of books, maps, pictures and other printed matter.

The convenience of buying by mail is not just that you can buy from excellent shops that are far away, not only that you can buy things that are not available in retail shops, and not only that you can very comfortably buy from your own home, comparing costs and buying at the lowest price, but also that you can get far more information and advice about what you are buying from most catalogues than you would get from any retail store. Which shop assistant would be able to take time off to give you the gardening instructions of the White Flower Farm, the advice about hi-fi components of Stereo Warehouse, the lecture on early American interiors of the Craft House, Williamsburg, or the descriptions of methods and basic necessities given by the firms selling hobby equipment?

The shops listed in this volume come from several sources. Some of them I knew about before settling down to write this book, others were recommended by friends and acquaintances, and the rest I got from advertisements, guides and directories. I wrote to over five thousand stores, looked through quantities of catalogues and chose the ones that seemed of most interest. I have tried to make the book comprehensive by choosing shops that *sell by mail* in every area, so that people who don't like shopping in person, or who can't because they live in isolated areas or are housebound, or even who simply are at work when the shops are open, will be able to find most things they need in most price ranges. But I am still haunted by the thought of the ones that got away: good, small firms that hardly advertise and are not widely known. I would be especially interested to hear about them for my next edition. If you know of any, please write to me c/o Random House, 201 E. 50th Street, New York, N.Y. 10022.

In trying to be comprehensive, I have assumed that people who read this book do not necessarily want to buy by mail from abroad, so I have included imports that should really be bought from abroad. But I must add here that on certain brand-name items you can save up to a third of the price so relatively easily that it is folly to buy them in America. Stereo components and photographic equipment from Hong Kong, glass and china from England and Scandinavia, cashmere sweaters from Scotland and perfume from France are the main foreign mail-order businesses, and well worth trying. What to buy from abroad and how to go about it was the subject of my earlier book, *The Catalogue of Catalogues: The Complete Guide to World-Wide Shopping by Mail,* which was published last year by Random House, in paperback and hardcover.

Finally, I should add that this book is just a guide to the shops listed, not an endorsement of them, and my descriptions are intended to give just an idea of prices and goods; *both will change* so it is important to write for catalogues before ordering.

M.E.I.
March 1973

HOW TO BUY

CATALOGUES

Please do not order directly from this book; write for catalogues first, as prices and goods change. Most catalogues are, theoretically at least, always available, although they may go out of print periodically while new ones are being prepared. Where shops change a large part of their stock seasonally and publish new catalogues regularly, the time of publication is included in the catalogue listing herein. When you send coins to pay for a catalogue, always wrap them and tape them to the letter, and to be on the safe side you should pay for the more expensive catalogues with a check. Where listings say that the price of the catalogue is refundable, it means that it is credited toward a purchase.

ORDERING

When you buy by mail you sometimes get the advantage of trying things out in your own home. Charles W. Jacobsen, Inc., for instance, will send you several carpets on approval, while Scanda Duo allows a thirty-day trial of their down-filled comforter. Many shops offer money-back guarantees with no questions asked, but others, such as some of the firms that sell furniture, will only accept returns if there is something wrong with the merchandise, so read catalogues carefully. Most firms ask for payment with the order; many now accept credit cards. When buying out of state, you don't need to pay sales tax.

SHIPPING

Some firms include shipping costs in the price of their goods, others tell you what to add or send zone rates so that you can calculate the cost yourself. Each firm has its own regular shipping methods, usually one of the following:

PARCEL POST

Parcels up to 40 lbs. in weight and not more than 84 inches in length and girth can be delivered in any part of the country (length and girth means that the length of the parcel is measured in the usual way but the width is measured with the tape measure right around it). Larger parcels of up to 70 lbs. and 100 inches in length and girth can be delivered to small towns with second-class post offices. Parcels going by "priority mail" (what used to be called first class) can be of any size, but of course it is expensive to mail large parcels this way.

UNITED PARCEL SERVICE

UPS and similar firms usually take parcels of up to 50 lbs. and are quicker than parcel post. However, they must be given a receipt when they deliver, so if no one is there when they come, after three attempts to deliver they take the parcel back to the sender.

REA EXPRESS

Rea Express and similar firms handle mainly goods of 50 to 500 lbs. with door-to-door delivery either by truck or by air freight, or "Air Express" in the case of REA. Air freight is fast, and goods should take one day to arrive unless you live far from an airport, in which case they will take two to three days. On short distances with goods that weigh under 100 lbs., air freight is usually less expensive than truck, although there is a minimum charge of $10.

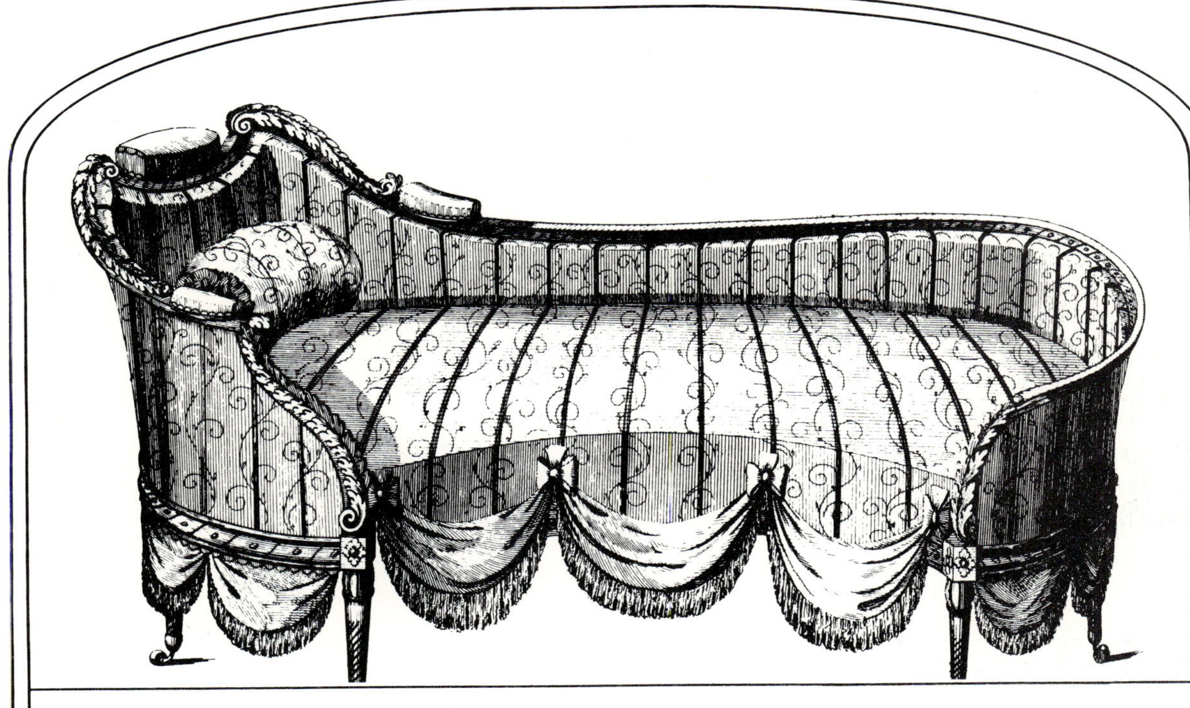

1
ANTIQUES

ADVERTISING CURIOS

Palmetto Antiques, U.S. Highway 301 and 321, Ulmer, S.C. 29849
44-page catalogue, 48 cents in stamps.

In keeping with the new nostalgia craze in this country, this general antique shop specializes in old advertising items. The bulk of the items in their catalogue are Coca-Cola pieces, all well described and many accompanied by pictures. A Coke cigarette lighter from the 1940's costs $2.50, while a Coke serving tray from the '50's runs to $12.50.

Some of the descriptions mention that the item is an original, some say that it is an "official reproduction," while many are left in question. An interesting array of advertising objects, as well as a few political goodies (buttons from the 1960's, $1.75 each) and military (Nazi uniform ribbon bars, $2.95 each) thrown in.

For more old advertising curios, see Propinquity in the Household Objects and Gifts section.

AUTOMATA

Stephen Leonard, 60 E. 12th Street, Apt. 6E, New York, N.Y. 10003
6-page catalogue, $2.

Stephen Leonard, who sounds very much like a one-man operation, sells antique phonographs and other mechanical music items. A messy and outrageously overpriced catalogue has blurry photographs of an Edison Standard Model (2-minute player, in mint condition, is priced at $175). A musical pocket watch, Swiss-made, $375, and a few other things, including the pièce de résistance, a grand roller organ, with seventeen music rolls, the original table, and the original bill of sale dated 1894 ($650). As Leonard urges, "Hedge against inflation . . . buy and save rare items!"

Mekanisk Musik Museum, P.O. Box 1669, Beverly Hills, Calif. 90210
52-page catalogue, $1.

This Danish firm, dealing in automatic musical instruments, has done so much business with the United States that it has established warehousing and shipping facilities in California. Player pianos are the most famous of these instruments, but there are others, called orchestrions, symphonions, etc., as well as the classic music box. The Museum also sells books, records and souvenirs, for people interested in this field.

Mekanisk Musik catalogue is a fascinating introduction to the world of mechanical musical instruments as well as a description of the various machines currently available. Prices vary enormously; a classic nickelodeon costs $475, while a Wurlitzer-style 15 Mandolin Pianorchestra with unique twelve-roll automatic changer, the only one in existence, costs $15,000. Machines that can be attached to any upright, or grand piano, can be had for $195, including fifty music rolls. If you see an instrument in the catalog that you wish to reserve, a 10 percent deposit is required. Phone numbers in California and Copenhagen are given so that you can call and discuss your purchase, if you wish. MMM is also interested in buying automatic instruments or collections.

In addition to these major pieces, MMM sells books, records, hand organs, music boxes, mechanical singing birds in cages, and nineteenth-century mechanical musical figures.

MMM's directors, an American, Q. David Bowers, and a Dane, Claes O. Friberg, are obviously enthusiasts, eager to discuss their interest with fellow collectors and proud of the openness and friendliness with which they deal with their customers. The catalogue exudes their enthusiasm and interest.

Player Piano Co., Inc., 620 E. Douglas, Wichita, Kans. 67202
60-page catalogue, $1.

If you have a player piano, or are planning to buy one from Mekanisk Museum, or elsewhere, maintenance can obviously be a problem, since the few player-piano repairmen around probably don't make house calls. For these, the Player Piano catalogue is a godsend, since, as the firm's owner says, "most all of the prices are bargains, because the component parts are not available anywhere else." The catalogue "offers a complete selection of supply of parts and materials . . . to repair or rebuild a player piano." The catalogue is aimed at the hobbyist, who is forced to do it himself, rather than at professional piano repairers.

CLOCKS, ICONS, PORCELAIN AND SILVER

Bull and Bear Antiques, P.O. Box 261, Evanston, Ill. 60204
Price list, free. Three per year. Black-and-white photographs, free. Color photographs, $1 each.

Three-year-old Bull and Bear sells English, Russian and Chinese antiques, but specializes in antique clocks and icons. The list I looked at had Russian and English silver spoons, wine goblets, pastry tongs, teapots, beakers, jugs, with most prices between $200 and $500.

Russian and Greek icons are from $85 for a "small Russian bronze tryptich of St. George, blue enamel background, 18th century," to $1,400 for a "Russian icon of St. Nicholas of Mosaisk." The saint is shown holding a sword in his right hand and a church in his left, the icon has a silver *riza* (cover) hallmarked Moscow and dated 1808.

Of the clocks the Bull and Bear says that it makes every effort to see that they leave the shop in running condition, but as the clocks are old and relatively fragile, the firm won't accept responsibility for any breakdowns. The clocks, which are mainly English, cost from $200 to $600; there are many bracket clocks as well as a few skeleton, mantel and grandfather clocks.

1

2

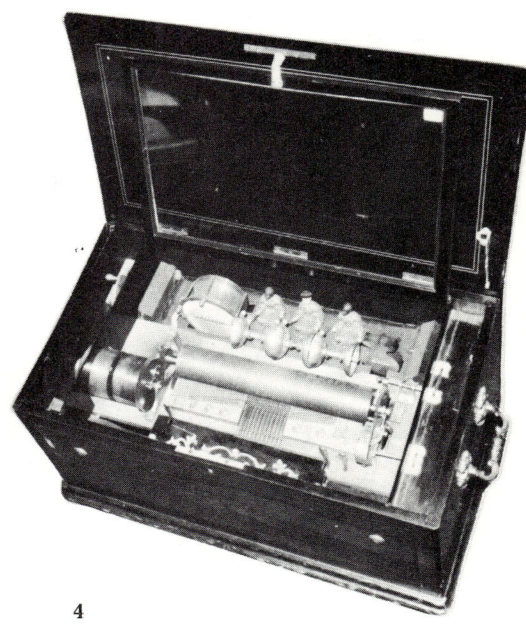

4

1 • *Propinquity* (see Household Objects and Gifts section) Tray, $10, made for the Coca-Cola Company in 1950. Propinquity specializes in Coca-Cola memorabilia and always keeps a stock of trays made between 1905 and 1950.

2 • *Propinquity* (see Household Objects and Gifts section) Pulver gum machine. $150.

3 • *Mekanisk Musik Museum* 10′-high Wurlitzer Mandolin Pianorchestra Orchestrion from the 1910 era. The "motion picture scene" on the front is a backlighted translucent painting. Orchestrions are available for from $5,000 to $25,000.

4 • *Mekanisk Musik Museum* Swiss music box with mandarin figures as bell strikers, c. 1895-1900. Typical of the many music boxes available.

5 • *Bull and Bear Antiques* Russian icon of the Mother of God of Vladimir, which belongs to the group of icons of the Mother of God called *umileniye* (loving kindness). Eighteenth century. Egg tempera on wooden panel 12″ by 9″. $1,000.

3

5

DOLLS

Blue Barn Antiques, P.O. Box 295, Mount Airy, N.C. 27030
8-page catalogue, 25 cents, plus double-stamped self-addressed envelope. Six per year.

This mimeographed catalogue is strictly for serious collectors of dolls. The prices range from $4 for a souvenir doll from the Seminole Indians to $895 for an old French bisque doll. All the listings are photographed, but since most of the prices are well over $100, you really have to know what you are doing.

Ann Ford, The Little Match Girl, 4218 Atlantic Avenue, Sea Gate, New York Harbor, N.Y. 11224
No catalogue.

Ann Ford, like many people who sell collector's items or antiques, has made a business out of a hobby. Her shop is well known to collectors of old dolls and dollhouses, and they write to her and ask for special things they are looking for—wallpaper for an antique dollhouse, or "a secretary made by the Lynnfield Company with a Governor Winthrop desk base and a bookcase with glass on top, scaled one inch to the foot." For the less specialized who want antique toys for decorative effect, Ann Ford stocks toy theaters, old toys, hand-colored prints, and puppets, which can be made to order too.

Antique dolls are also sold by the New York Doll Hospital, in the Toys and Games section.

GENERAL

Sotheby Parke Bernet Los Angeles, 7660 Beverly Boulevard, Los Angeles, Calif. 90036

Sotheby Parke Bernet Inc., 980 Madison Avenue, New York, N.Y. 10021
List of annual subscription rates for catalogues and price lists, free.

The renowned firm of Parke-Bernet was started in 1937, and bought by Sotheby's of London in 1964. They appraise and auction thousands of other people's rare possessions each year, and in spite of the astronomical prices that hit the headlines, they claim that over 70 percent of the lots sold fetch an average price of $250 and that the solid core of their business consists of the sale of "worthy, but unspectacular items."

Anyone too far away or too busy to attend the auctions, or who would simply like to keep up with prices, can subscribe to a year's worth of catalogues, ask Parke-Bernet for an estimate of what particular lots will fetch as a help to his bidding, bid by mail or telephone, and subscribe to price lists that arrive later telling what everything went for.

Categories covered include antiquities and ethnographical art, books, manuscripts and autographs, paintings, drawings, sculpture, prints, furniture, jewelry, coins and medals, as well as "decorative objects," which covers a myriad of things such as porcelain, clocks, rugs, minerals, scientific instruments, and Art Nouveau and art deco.

6

7

6 • *Ann Ford, The Little Match Girl* Typical examples of black-and-white or hand-colored reproductions of old doll and toy prints for $5 to $25.

7 • *Ann Ford, The Little Match Girl* Typical of the antique dolls for sale at various prices. *photo Sy Katsoff*

The catalogues are fully illustrated, in black-and-white with occasional photographs in color. Prices for a year's subscription to New York catalogues *and* price lists go from $20 for categories such as Art Nouveau, art deco or coins to $105 for impressionists and modern paintings, drawings and sculpture. All the categories together from New York cost $525, whereas from Los Angeles, where there are fewer auctions, subscription to all categories costs only $45 per year.

8 • *Ann Ford, The Little Match Girl* Modern George and Martha Washington Parian dolls made from the original Emma C. Clears molds, with clothes designed and made by Ann Ford. $300 the pair.
photo Multipics Studios

Adam A. Weschler and Son, Inc., 905–9 E Street, N.W., Washington, D.C. 20005
Mailing list for auction announcements, free. Each catalogue for large auctions, $6.50; each catalogue for smaller auctions, $3.

Auctioneers and appraisers since 1891, Adam A. Weschler specializes in fine art, antiques and general estate appraisals and auctions. The firm has three to four large auctions per year, for which it puts out illustrated catalogues, and three to four smaller auctions, for which it publishes unillustrated catalogues. People who can't be present can buy the catalogues and bid by telephone, though the bid should be confirmed by mail. The unillustrated catalogues are really for gamblers or people who know what they are looking for, as the listings are of the briefest: "Petitpoint and grospoint picture by Lucy A. Hopkins "A sleeping girl with reclining protective dog," "Antique silver on copper samovar height 16″," "Mexican sterling five-gallon punch bowl," etc. But the goods in the catalogues for the bigger sales are often photographed and are described better. About a third of the goods goes for less than $200, and almost everything goes for less than $2,000. In the catalogue that I looked at, an early-nineteenth-century elaborately carved teak hinge-top sewing box ("Lion's-paw feet. Origin West Coast of India") went for $100. An antique Sèvres hinge-top jewel box (turquoise ground, against which are painted various landscape and figural medallions, contained within gold enameled framework, with ormolu mounts) was $130, and Rhode Island walnut captain's desk c. 1790 (illustrated), $775.

MILITARY AND NAUTICAL

N. Flayderman and Co., Inc., Squash Hollow, R.F.D. 2, New Milford, Conn. 06776
Subscription to two 96-page military and nautical antiques catalogues, and one book catalogue per year, $2. Book catalogue alone, 25 cents.

Mr. Flayderman has an impressive list of official positions as adviser to various institutions. His firm has been publishing catalogues longer than any other firm in the antique-arms, military and nautical business, and the stock of firearms, edged weapons and arms literature is well known to people in the field. But what would be of interest to less dedicated people, who are simply trying to decorate their homes, is that amid the scrimshaws and muskets are some fascinating pieces of Americana. Most things are just described in the catalogues, but in the ones I looked at there were, among many others, pictures of a brilliantly colored American Revolutionary-era poster of a drummer for $80, and

9

10

11

12

9 ● *Sotheby Parke Bernet* George III silver soup tureen and cover, Sheffield 1815 (Kirkby, Waterhouse and Co.). 15½″ long. Sold in 1972 for $2,200.

10 ● *Sotheby Parke Bernet* Federal inlaid mahogany serpentine front chest of drawers, Boston or Salem, Massachusetts, c. 1800. 37½″ high, 44¼″ long. Sold in 1973 for $1,600.

11 ● *Sotheby Parke Bernet* Antique Tabriz rug, nineteenth century, 4′ by 4′9″. Sold in 1973 for $525.

12 ● *Sotheby Parke Bernet* "Winter Hawk," hand-colored engraving and aquatint after the watercolor by Audubon, 1831. Sold in 1972 for $950.

Wild West watercolors painted for covers of 1920's dime novels, $125 each.

There are also one of the rarest of the Buffalo Bill posters, showing Annie Oakley, for $275; a "superb" wool 1830 embroidery of "Action between the Chesapeake and Shannon, June 1, 1813" for $395; a 6'8" figurehead model of a boxer, $3,900; a 6'10" cigar-store Indian, $2,900; a nice primitive old woodcarving of an eagle fighting a snake, $80; also old copper ship's lanterns, Indian antiques, and lots of primitive paintings of American scenes.

Peter Hlinka Historical Americana, 226 E. 89th Street, New York, N.Y. 10028
25-page catalogue, 50 cents. Two issues per year.

Hlinka deals in military and war relics, mainly medals and badges. From World War I, for example, a Belgian war-service medal costs $4.50. The large listing of Nazi items must have elicited quite a response from his customers. In a lengthy note the dealer explains, "I do not do this to memorialize the Nazis or to lend support to any theories of Hitler's system." He offers them as historical items with lessons to be learned from them.

Jacques Noel Jacobsen, Jr. Collectors Antiquities, 60 Manor Road, Staten Island, N.Y. 10310
140-page military catalogue, $1.
30-page fire and police antiques catalogue, $1.

This firm specializes in military, fire and police collector's items and has been in the field for over thirty years. The military catalogue is filled with over 2,000 listings relevant in one way or another to military history. If uniforms interest you, choose from an Indian War captain's infantry frock coat in excellent condition for $130, or an 1880's artillery officer's dress helmet for $160. If equipment weapons and insignia do (men as well as the actual objects), there are plenty of photographic records in the form of daguerreotypes, ambrotypes and tintypes. A small tintype of a Civil War soldier in shell jacket is listed for $30. Jacobsen also stocks documents, books and reports on martial subjects.

The fire and police catalogue has a similar array of collector's items. An early fire lantern costs $75, an antique brass fire nozzle for hand-drawn equipment, $35. The catalogues represent a very specialized service for collectors and museums, but they are also a lot of fun to look through.

SILVER

Edward G. Wilson, 1802 Chestnut Street, Philadelphia, Pa. 19103
One year's subscription to four lists of Souvenir and Unusual Spoons, $1.
List of antique spoons, eighteenth century to Civil War, 50 cents.
List of Silver by Southern Silversmiths, including Delaware, Kentucky and Missouri, 50 cents.
List of English and Irish Georgian silver, 50 cents.

Around ninety small pieces of silver appear on each list, with the name of each maker, when known, and approximate date. There are zillions of spoons, single or in sets: early-nineteenth-century-fiddleback teaspoons at $4 each; extraordinary souvenir spoons (one manages to cram an embossed view of the U.S. infantry camp in Cuba into the bowl, and a portrait of the army commander General Miles onto the handle; its one of the few plated pieces and costs $9); an unmarked eighteenth-century marrow scoop for $45. A shell bowl floral-engraved 1772 punch ladle is $165. The English and Irish list has, besides spoons, other usable pieces such as 1818 asparagus tongs, $125; 1814 fish slice, $85; a fine carved crystal muffinier with a silver top, $125; a 1789 chocolate pot with an ivory handle, $750, etc. Photos are available for the Irish and English silver at 25 cents each, but not for the other lists, and you can always send anything you don't like, back.

TOOLS

Iron Horse Antique, Inc., Star Route, Bomoseen, Vt. 05732
74-page catalogue, $2 a year.

Iron Horse specializes in antique tools, a fascinating area which is, as far as I know, still virgin soil for antique dealers. A particular expertise is needed, and the catalogue itself notes the difficulties in dating axes, for instance. The catalogue is divided into various kinds of tools, metalworking, agricultural, woodworking, etc., and includes pages of such specialized trades as coopers' tools, coachmakers' instruments, etc. Prices are not low, the $15-$50 range seems the most common, though you can buy a polled hatchet, c. 1850, for $7, while goosewing axes cost from $135 to $300. The catalogue is fully, though rather primitively, illustrated and contains a list of the still relatively few books that are available on this subject.

TOYS

Antiques & Amusements, 1209 Merrick Road, Copaigue, N.Y. 11726
Occasional catalogues, $1.

This small shop specializes in antique coin-operated and amusement devices ranging from wind-up toys to old pinball machines. The latter, made for the most part in the 1920's and 1930's, cost as little as $150 to $200, while later and larger machines cost from $400 to $500. A table top 1920's "Totalizer" thus costs $95, while an early Wurlitzer jukebox, made entirely of wood and with lights that go on while the record is playing, costs $450. Gum machines cost $50 and up, and pinball games range from $90 to $195. The wind-up toys include every variant that you can recall from your childhood—trains, boats, tractors, all costing much more than your relatives ever paid, and making you sorry you never kept all those discarded playthings. A "daredevil, roll-over motorcycle cop" that rides in circles, falls on the side and rights itself and starts up again, would make a perfect Christmas present, but $75 may be too much even for enthusiasts; by comparison, those pinball machines seem very reasonable.

WEAPONS

Robert Abels, Inc., P.O. Box 428, Hopewell Junction, N.Y. 12533
96-page catalogue, $2.

Abels deals in "antique firearms and edged weapons," and his catalogue is a veritable history of warfare from the sixteenth century to the present. His strongest offerings are antique pistols and his catalogue devotes some thirty-eight pages to these. You can buy a pair of Queen Anne flintlock butt pistols, made in 1750 and used in the Revolutionary War, for $2,200, or a 6″ vest-pocket pistol for $125. Prices for pistols go beyond these two examples, but most offerings are in the $300-$500 range. The rifles offered are largely American, with a number of Civil War rifles, Winchesters, Kentucky rifles and the like.

A smaller selection of swords, rapiers, daggers, knives, poleaxes, halberds and maces are also available, as are a few pieces of armor. There are also some models of cannons, costing from $165 to $650. Abels also sells a number of books, including his own on the Bowie knife and an anonymous, it appears, "*Catalog of Torture Collection.* Formerly of Nuremberg Royal Castle, 1893, most complete collection, shackles, iron maiden, racks, executioner swords, all sorts of iron masks and fiendish instruments that the writer owned a few years ago, well described, and a good reference book, $2."

14

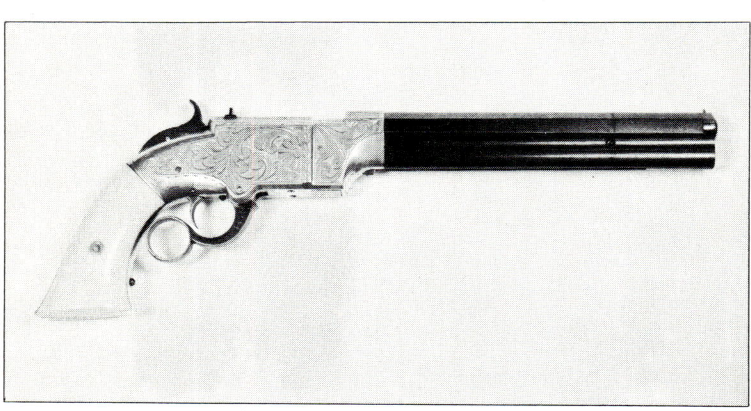

13

13 • *N. Flayderman* Large brass-frame Volcanic repeating pistol, with original floral engraving and ivory grips, 8″ barrel. American, c. 1856. $1,250. Typical of guns in stock.

14 • *N. Flayderman* An original Civil War-period recruiting poster for a unit of a Northern regiment that served with distinction in the early part of the war. Size, 19″ by 24″, in fine condition. $225. Typical of posters in stock.

2
ART

The most satisfactory art to buy by mail is that which was made to be printed and can be fairly well reproduced in catalogues, so I have concentrated on original prints in this art section. However, serious collectors and museums buy paintings and sculpture by mail, asking the galleries to let them know when certain works they are looking for become available. If you have the money and inclination to buy paintings and sculpture by well-established artists, you'll find a list of the leading New York galleries, and the artists they represent, in the Arts and Entertainment Section of the *Madison Avenue Handbook*. The Art and Entertainment Section is published annually and costs $2.14, including postage. It is available from the publisher, Peter Glenn Publications Ltd., 17 E. 48th Street, New York, N.Y. 10017.

GRAPHICS

Associated American Artists, 663 Fifth Avenue, New York, N.Y. 10022
"Introductory Kit": two catalogues, 25 cents.

The AAA was founded in 1934 to provide people with original prints for very low prices, and it offered the works of such popular artists as Thomas Hart Benton and Grant Wood for as little as $5 each. That general feeling still permeates the AAA catalogue, which continues to offer such popular artists as Benton. His two lithographs in the current catalogue sell for $250 each. AAA possesses America's largest collection of original prints, and commissions many of its prints directly from the artists, which means that some, though not all, of its offerings are very reasonably priced. The artists represented tend to be realistic in their style. There are few abstractions. AAA sells works of very famous artists, such as Soyer and Baskin, and they also offer, for as little as $15, prints by lesser-known print makers.

Frame House Gallery, 110 E. Market Street, Louisville, Ky. 40202
Two color catalogues (one of wildlife prints, one on general subjects), $1 each. Published semiannually.

Frame House Gallery is the "country's largest publisher of wildlife art"; that is to say, they publish a large number of very colorful and accurate lithographs of birds, flowers, wild animals, etc., selling these as prints, with some signed and numbered by the artist. Frame House has a rather complicated system of listing what they claim to be current market prices of earlier prints that were sold out and are listed here as collector's items. These can sometimes still be bought from them at the new prices, which are usually much higher than the original. Conversely, the Gallery says it will consider taking your prints on consignment for resale.

These two catalogues offer some very reasonably priced items. The work is largely in what you might call the *National Geographic* style, and Frame House has donated a number of its prints to help fund-raising efforts by local Audubon and conservation groups (many of the subjects were treated by Audubon himself). Prints are available from $15 and up, but the majority are in the $20-$35 range. Other prints are available on such traditional subjects as Indians, racing scenes, etc. Though these are signed and numbered, the edition sizes are 1,000 and up, and prices are in the $30-$40 range.

Lucien Goldschmidt, Inc., 1117 Madison Avenue, New York, N.Y. 10028
Occasional catalogues, about $1.50 each, but prices vary, so write and ask what is available.

Goldschmidt's quiet, dark Madison Avenue store looks like the office of some overburdened museum director, filled with treasures that need to be exhibited but in the meantime are piling up in expansive profusion. The store's basic specialty is illustrated books, but these contain so many engravings and illustrations that the store really is an art gallery. Here, for instance, are Rembrandt etchings, from $600 for a golf player (of all things!) to $1,250 for Christ driving the money changers from the temple, a perfect pair to give a golf-playing banker. Rubens, Breughel Van de Velde, are represented, names that one associates with museums rather than private collections, but unsigned etchings and engravings are available here in a very wide selection, and there is plenty to be found for under $100.

All sorts of modern artists are also offered in the Goldschmidt catalogue: six drypoints and four original lithographs by Toulouse-Lautrec cost $1,750, while a first edition of Léger's *Cirque* will set you back $2,750.

Not all of Goldschmidt's offerings are as expensive, and a number of illustrated books are available for less than $100. Many are books which famous artists illustrated and which were published in editions of various sizes. Obviously, in all these areas, you are dealing with serious art collecting and prices will vary far more than those asked for contemporary works being offered simultaneously by various galleries. Goldschmidt's catalogues have few competitors in the United States, and price comparisons ought to be made with similar English and European stores.

Harcus-Krakow Gallery, 167 Newbury Street, Boston, Mass. 02116
Color catalogue, $1.25. Price list, free.

Harcus-Krakow runs both a large Boston gallery and also publishes original graphics. Their catalogue, therefore, lists graphics that are available elsewhere and a number that they themselves have executed, including a portfolio which they published for the National Collection of Fine Arts to commemorate the establishment of the new Smithsonian collection. The portfolio of seven "images" sells for $1,300 and is limited to 144 copies signed and numbered, and includes works by Larry Rivers and Claes Oldenburg. Among the other artists available through the gallery are Milton Avery, Jim Dine, Lyonel Feininger, Josef Albers, Robert Rauschenberg, and others less famous. There is a large selection here of major works, and although some cost much more, there is a good deal at prices between $150 and $600.

Multiples, 927 Madison Avenue, New York, N.Y. 10021
Occasional catalogues and brochures, free.

Multiples was one of the first galleries to commission and sell prints, "objects and wall hangings" by contemporary American artists and the catalogue lists some of

1

2

3

4

5

1 • *Associated American Artists* Leonard Baskin, "Safari" 27″ by 15½″ lithograph in an edition of 160. $125.

2 • *Associated American Artists* Thomas Hart Benton, "Discussion," matted, 14″ by 18″, signed black-and-white lithograph in an edition of 220. $200.

3 • *Lucien Goldschmidt* Jan Van de Veld (1596-1653), "The Village Fair in Front of the Inn," 11″ by 16½″. Original etching, 1617. $145.

4 • *Frame House Gallery* Ray Harm, "Lazuli Bunting," 12″ by 15″. Lithograph in an edition of 7,500. $15.

5 • *Lucien Goldschmidt* Willem Panneels (a pupil of Rubens; born c. 1600), "David Fighting the Bear," 4″ by 5½″. An original etching after Rubens. $50.

6

the most famous exponents of these genres: Josef Albers, Frankenthaler, Robert Indiana, Claes Oldenburg, Robert Rauschenberg, Rosenquist and Andy Warhol. These artists are increasingly known for this kind of print or silkscreen, and the Multiples catalogue lists many works of art that one is already familiar with, such as Warhol's "Mao Tse Tung," a portfolio of ten silkscreens that is a companion piece to his "Marilyn Monroe," although the latter costs $800, while "Mao Tse Tung" is a bargain at $500 (ten for $4,500). Multiples sells the Albers "Homage to the Square," the Indiana "Numbers," Vasarley's "Permutations," and other prints now so popular that when I called to check prices, I discovered they were already sold out.

In addition to prints, Multiples sells a number of objects that might be called sculpture, such as a charming Steinberg Record (1966), a black enamel disk with a lithograph label in the center, an edition of twenty-five selling for $250, or an untitled string construction by Sandback, unsigned, for $75.

In addition to these more expensive items, Multiples also sells framed, unsigned silkscreens in unlimited editions by many of the same artists for $45, and silkscreened cards in boxes of ten for $8.50.

7

Kenneth Nebenzahl, Inc., 333 N. Michigan Avenue, Chicago, Ill. 60601

Various price lists, free.
The Print Collector, listing American historical prints, $1. Semiannual.
The Compass, listing maps, $1. Three-four times a year.

Nebenzahl deals in rare books, maps and manuscripts relating to the Western hemisphere, and its catalogues are among the handsomest that I've seen. The firm has several volumes devoted to rare Americana and these include some lovely but extremely expensive maps, prints, and the like. Increase Mather's early book on New England, for instance, costs $1,800 for a first edition, and a 1673 French map of the Northern Great Lakes goes for $3,200. There are less expensive items, on which prices occasionally dip below $100, but for the most part these catalogues are aimed at very wealthy collectors or institutions.

Penn Atelier Graphics, 572 Fifth Avenue, New York, N.Y. 10036

32-page annual color catalogue, $1.

Penn publishes and sells its own limited editions of original graphics by such artists as Henry Moore, Salvador Dali, Marino Marini, René Magritte, and others. Prices vary according to the market valuation of each artist, but all are rather high. For instance, an original Moore lithograph of reclining figures in an edition of seventy-five, but not signed, costs $500.

Solomon & Company, 350 Hudson Street, New York, N.Y. 10014

36-page catalogue, some color, free.

Solomon sells a handsome selection of posters and limited-edition prints, most of which are shown in color in the catalogue. The posters range in price from $5 for a Robert Motherwell announcement of a Whitney Museum exhibit to $25 for Saul Steinberg's well-known Spoleto poster. The limited-edition prints are by such varied artists as Alexander Archipenko ($500), Braque ($900) and Adolph Gottlieb ($200). Solomon

6 • *Multiples* Robert Indiana, "Black and White Love" (1971), 39″ by 32″. Silkscreen in a signed and numbered edition of 200. $300.

7 • *Multiples* Robert Indiana, "The American Dream" (1971), 39″ by 32″. Silkscreen in a signed and numbered edition of 200. $400.

also sells a "Peace Portfolio 1" by several distinguished American artists, such as Motherwell, Steinberg, Rauschenberg and others, twelve prints for $1,500 or singly at varying prices.

Spanish Refugee Aid, 80 E. 11th Street, New York, N.Y. 10003
Leaflet, free.

This may seem an unlikely name to find in this section, but Spanish Refugee Aid offers the nicest way I know to buy current prints as well as offering some of the best bargains available in the art world. Each year a number of distinguished American artists donate one of their prints to this charity, which for years now has offered help to exiled Spanish Republicans who fled Franco and are now living out their lives in great poverty in France. Among the artists who have helped most regularly are Alexander Calder, Saul Steinberg, Robert Motherwell, Frasconi and Esteban Vicente. Calder, for instance, has donated four black, blue, red and yellow designs that are among the freshest and loveliest of his that I have ever seen. Currently there is also a stark black-and-white Motherwell abstract, and a delightful Steinberg, limited to twenty-five copies. Each print is a signed and limited edition, and the Spanish Refugee Aid price of $250 for each of these three artists is far less than their going gallery price. The prints by Frasconi and Vincente are less expensive, as are a number of original drawings and paintings also available. Photos of the prints can be requested. If you like the work of these particular artists, as I do, you can have the rare experience of buying a beautiful object while knowing at the same time that all the money involved is going to a worthy cause.

The Sporting Gallery, Inc., P.O. Box 146, Middleburg, Va. 22117
16-page color Robin Hill catalogue, $1.50

This gallery specializes in American and English art from the eighteenth century on but has recently branched out into publishing prints, the first of which is a series on the extinct and endangered birds of North America. Based on the work of an Australian artist, Robin Hill, these are four-color lithographs, very nicely done in the style that has been popular since the days of Audubon. Three hundred and fifty sets of this particular series have been printed, with other subjects contemplated.

David Tunick, Inc., 441 West End Avenue, New York, N.Y. 10024
Large, illustrated catalogues, $4.00 each.

David Tunick is a young man who graduated as an art history major from Williams in 1966 and after further study set up selling old-master prints and a few modern ones. He works primarily from his catalogues but will meet clients by appointment. Tunick feels he has one of the world's largest stocks of original prints, engravings, etchings, etc., from the fifteenth to the eighteenth centuries. His handsome, well-printed catalogue averages two hundred entries selling from $50 and up, which can go pretty far up. The artists listed include the most famous; a recent catalogue offers six Dürer woodcuts ranging in price from $450 to $1,750, a Piranesi for $2,000, and some Tiepolos for a little as $200 and as much as $2,000. The moderns are even more expensive (a Matisse lithograph of a seated odalisque

8 • *Multiples* Andy Warhol, "Mao Tse-tung," 36″ by 36″. Silkscreen in a signed and numbered edition of 250. $500.

sells for $3,250), and as with other dealers in this field, the surprise is more how relatively inexpensive the older prints can be.

Yankee Publishing and Trading Co., P.O. Box 860, Chula Vista, Calif. 92012
Illustrated brochure, free.

Wesley H. Marden is another artist who has decided to sell his own works directly by mail. His lithographs are in a traditional style, focusing on harbor scenes, but of a contemporary, non-nostalgic nature. He prints 250 copies of his signed and numbered reproductions and sells them at prices that range from $14 to $20.

PICTURE FRAMES

Kulicke Frames, Inc., 43 E. 10th Street, New York, N.Y. 10003
Catalogue, $1.

Kulicke's manufactures several extremely elegant and minimal aluminum and clear acrylic picture frames which have been used by museums, are sold in museum stores and have won design awards. Their thin aluminium frames cost from about $4.50 for a complete 8″ framing kit, to about $38 for a complete kit for a 24″ by 30″ frame. There are also plastic box frames with invisible frames which were designed at the request of the Museum of Modern Art, and start, in a mass-produced version, at about $3.50, as well as standing frames designed in collaboration with Andy Warhol, and standing frames in which several small pictures or photographs can be shown at once.

Sam Milstein—Photographer, 852 Lake Avenue, Clark, N.J. 07066
Leaflet, free.

Sam Milstein sells very simple picture frames of his own design which consist of a lucite sheet fixed with very small clips to a masonite-and-wood backing. The frames, he says, give a floating-off-the-wall effect, and prices, including postage, start at $6 for an 8″ by 10″ frame.

POSTERS

Poster Originals, Ltd., 16 W. 78th Street, New York, N.Y. 10021
16-page "American Posters" color catalogue, $2. Published once a year.
16-page "European Posters" black-and-white catalogue, $2. Published once a year.

Poster Originals is a gallery devoted entirely to posters, printed here or abroad, by artists for their own shows. Posters may include the work of living artists for current shows, or feature pictures chosen by a museum or gallery for an exhibit by an artist from an earlier time. Some are in their second printing. The American catalogue, for instance, has a Linder poster for $5 and a Steinberg announcement for $10, or an Andy Warhol silkscreen for $15. Most of the posters are in this price range, and some very attractive prints are available. Some prints go up to $100, such as a Rauschenberg poster for the St. Louis orchestra, but that is for a signed edition; the unsigned costs $10.

The European posters include some lovely and, at times, familiar posters: Matisse's multicolored leaf pattern for his retrospective, at $40; and various Picasso and Chagall posters in the $20-$25 range. In addition to these contemporary artists, there are a number of very striking posters recently printed for exhibits of the classics, such as a majestic nude in beige, gray and white by Ingres for the Petit Palais exhibit, or a gorgeous Klimt poster in gold, purple, pink and turquoise for a Vienna exhibit.

The Poster Place, 32 W. 53rd Street, New York, N.Y. 10019
Price list, free.

A list, with no descriptions at all, of modern silkscreen or lithograph posters by well-known American and European artists such as Albers, Braque, Picasso and Rothko. Prices from $10 to $40 unframed, and $40 to $75 framed in box mount or plexiglass.

Triton Gallery, 323 W. 45th Street, New York, N.Y. 10036
20-page catalogue, some color, free.

This gallery sells posters for recent events—mainly theater posters. A very nice, crisp little catalogue lists several hundred posters, briefly describes some of them, and illustrates, in color, about twenty-five of the more graphically appealing ones. Prices between $3 and $10.

REPRODUCTIONS

Alva Museum Replicas, Inc., 30-30 Northern Boulevard, Long Island City, N.Y. 11101
80-page sculpture catalogue and 36-page jewelry catalogue, both for $4.

Alva is one of the firms that produces the reproductions which are on sale in many museum stores and elsewhere, and normally sells only to these shops. However, if no store exists near you, you can buy the catalogues and order direct. The choice in the catalogues is far more extensive than any I have seen in stores and includes some extremely handsome pieces. Alva was among the first firms to enter this field and it feels that its workmanship is greatly superior to that of some of its competitors.

The pieces in the sculpture catalogue come from most of the major museums in the country as well as a few foreign museums. The strongest selections are from the ancient world, though there are a number of modern pieces, primarily American, which are not seen that often. The jewelry catalogue has some lovely pieces, with the handsomest being either from the older civilizations or reproductions of African or Latin American jewelry. If you don't want to order the catalogues yourself and you live in a large city, you might see whether your local museum store has these listings and would order specially for you pieces they might not normally stock.

9

10

11

12

13

9 • *Triton Gallery* Erte, "Salome and the Dance of the Seven Veils," 24″ by 31″. Poster in white, blue, green, orange and violet on black. $5.

10 • *Triton Gallery* Vittorio Fiorucci, "Italian Film Week" poster in red, green and black on white. $6.

11 • *Triton Gallery* "Mame," 25″ by 38″ poster in orange, yellow and black on white. $5.

12 • *Buck Hill* Reproduction of a 1904 bicycle advertisement. 75 cents.

13 • *Buck Hill* Reproduction of the "Jumping Frog" poster advertising a lecture by Mark Twain. 75 cents.

Buck Hill Associates, Garnet Lake Road, Johnsburg, N.Y. 12843
Price list, 25 cents.

A humorous collection of reproductions of old American posters, handbills, broadsides, documents and prints, including Revolutionary and Civil War posters (one for recruiting announces that Cavalry is "not to be sent at once into the field"—one wonders how long the pause lasted). Reward posters, political cartoons, antique fashion posters, playbills, and a curious lot of old advertisements—a fill-your-teeth-yourself ad for a home dental outfit; a noiseless-vacuum-toothpick ad, "a boon to well-bred people"; and an 1877 telephone handbill, "Prof. Bell Speaks and Sings." Unfortunately the price list is unillustrated, but fortunately the posters cost about $1 each.

Oestreicher's Prints, Inc., 43 W. 46th Street, New York, N.Y. 10036
160-page catalogue, some color, $8.

This famous shop has an enormous collection of reproductions, both imported and American. The catalogue has over twelve thousand listings and over a thousand illustrations in color of their stock, which ranges from "antiquities to non-objective abstracts."

14 • *Philadelphia Museum of Art* (see Museums section) Edward Hicks, "Noah's Ark" (c. 1846). Reproduction, 24½″ by 28″. $15.

Omnigraphics, 1249 Washington Boulevard, Detroit, Mich. 48226
28-page catalogue, free.

This firm sells copies of famous prints, which are hand-colored and then sold either matted or framed for $15 and $30. The prints include such famous series as Daumier's illustrations of married life or Gilray's spoofs of doctors, as well as a number of nineteenth-century American prints on sports, New York, etc. The lithographs are 13½″ by 16″ and are simply reproductions, with no particular value as such, and should not be confused with the originals, some of which are still available. Some of the originals were black-and-white, which should be remembered by purists. But as decorations for offices or homes, these reproductions may please many, in particular those who enjoy the way graphic artists in the past made often very vicious and accurate fun of the professions.

Vignari Art Enterprises, Inc., 2 Main Street, Box 335, Ogunquit, Maine 03907
40-page catalogue, $1.

People who are looking for pictures of the sea or ships are almost certain to find what they want in this catalogue compiled by marine artist John T. Vignari. Besides romantic views of foam-flecked waves in open seas, there are reproductions of paintings by famous painters from Canaletto on, many of whom were not primarily marine artists but happened to paint a picture or two involving ships or sea. At prices mainly between $8 and $20, you'll find pictures by Thomas Eakins, Winslow Homer, Edward Hopper, Andrew Wyeth, various lesser known English painters and most of the French impressionists.

Allan Waller Ltd., 3580 Piedmont Road, N.E., Atlanta, Ga. 30305
12-page color catalogue, $5.

Allan Waller imports tapestry reproductions made by Éditions d'Art Rambouillet, in France. The reproductions are not woven but silkscreen-printed onto a canvas of Dacron, flax and wool made to resemble stitching as much as possible. The tapestries copied date from the fifteenth to the eighteenth centuries and are in French museums. Prices run from $360 for one of a pair of 2′2″ by 7′10″ eighteenth-century Gobelins sketched by Claud Audran to $2,000 for a 6′4″ by 8′3″ special edition Le Berger. The catalogue gives a great many interesting details on the history of tapestries, but rather too few on the manufacture of the reproductions.

3
BOOKS

There's nothing nicer than having a good neighborhood bookstore, but unfortunately very few cities in America can boast more than a handful of such shops. We've been amazed to see our once-bookless neighborhood give birth to half a dozen new shops in the last few years, most starting as paperback shops, then gradually growing to encompass hardcover books, etc. Perhaps this is a sign for the rest of the country. But in the meantime, a book buyer's lot is not a happy one. In many towns, only the most recent paperbacks and best sellers are available, and all too often department stores have closed down or skimped on their book departments. This has left many people with no good source for books, a problem compounded by the fact that there are no first-rate major bookstores equipped to do a national mail-order business. There are areas where buying by mail will help, but unfortunately there are no American equivalents of Blackwell's or Heffer's, stores which can be counted on to send you a steady stream of catalogues with the latest in a wide variety of fields.

There are, on the other hand, an amazing variety of extremely good specialized stores, shops that are often the best in the world, though they often sell largely by mail and are therefore unknown to the general public. If you are interested in Asia, or the film, or naval history, the chances are excellent that you can find just about anything that has ever been published. Likewise, a large number of stores listed elsewhere in this book will sell books that are related to their specialty. Thus you can get an extensive choice of books on archery, for instance, or on sailing from dealers in sports equipment. Museums are excellent sources of art books (and reproductions). Natural-food stores nearly always sell books on their subject, and so on. In other words, if you know the area you're interested in, you should find just the store you want (often the only one in the country) listed either in the pages that follow or under the main subject heading.

If you're interested in books in general, the problem remains. Most big bookstores or chains will "special-order" a book for you and many will supply you at Christmas time with a lavish catalogue. These, however, tend to feature the gift books that publishers are pushing at that Christmas and may therefore not really answer your needs. Still, it's worth seeing at least one of these, and among the stores you can try are Brentano's (586 Fifth Avenue, New York, N.Y. 10036), Doubleday (673 Fifth Avenue, New York, N.Y. 10022), Scribner's (579 Fifth Avenue, New York, N.Y. 10017) and Rizzoli's (712 Fifth Avenue, New York, N.Y. 10019). The first three of these are owned by leading New York publishers, the last by a major Italian publisher. Among their equivalents in other major cities are Kroch-Brentano's (29 S. Wabash Avenue, Chicago Ill. 60603) and the Pickwick Bookshops (6743 Hollywood Boulevard, Los Angeles, Calif. 90028). Any library and most bookstores stock several basic reference works that will tell you if a book is indeed available. *Books in Print*, *Paperbound Books in Print* and the *Publishers' Trade List Annual*, which is, in effect, a publishers' catalogue, gathering all the publishers' lists into one basic reference work. Since hundreds of thousands of titles are in print, you may wish to check these.

You may want to order the book from a discount bookseller. A list of these appears in each Sunday *New York Times Book Review* and related journals. These will mail you any book in print, usually with a discount of 30-33 percent on general books, and 10-20 percent on technical titles. Among these firms is Bookquick, Box B, Roseland, N.J. 07068. You can also write directly to publishers; some have very well organized mail-order services.

AEROSPACE

Hampton Books, Route #1, P.O. Box 76, Newberry, S.C. 29108

Catalogues issued irregularly, $1 each.

Hampton Books has specialties in subjects that I never expected to find together—aerospace and theater, film and TV (unless it's an obsession with stars). Whatever the rationale, they issue two unusual lists. Their last aeorspace list included over two thousand items, mostly on the modern period, but including a number of items on physics and astronomy from the sixteenth century to the present. So if you are looking for old biographies of Captain Eddie Rickenbacker or World War I aviation books from all countries, this is the catalogue to ask for. Their theater list is not quite as extensive and the items here are more expensive, but there are many more books from the eighteenth century on, in all languages, both of texts and about the theater.

AFRICA

University Place Book Shop, 821 Broadway, New York, N.Y. 10003

Price lists on African culture, Afro-American writers, free.

This bookstore always intrigued me because for years, well before the boom in Black Studies, it specialized in books on African culture and Afro-Americans. Its shelves were filled with fascinating volumes, some close to a hundred years old, that made the store something of an Afro-American reference room. Here were first editions of a W. E. B. DuBois novel (1911), pamphlets from the 1930's and '40's, books on Africa in French, Dutch and Portuguese—thousands of items in all. Obviously these are basic catalogues for those interested in these fields, but the store is also an eloquent example of the cultural importance of booksellers, who often do the work of libraries and museums well before these institutions are persuaded to follow suit.

ANTIQUES

American Reprints, 4656 Virginia Avenue, St. Louis, Mo. 63111

32-page annual catalogue, free.

This firm started off ten years ago with a reprint of a 1904 St. Louis Clock Calendar and has gone on both to reprint some twenty similar catalogues of watches, guns, knives, etc., and to sell related books for collectors. Books for watch and clock collectors, including repair books, are still their strongest point, but their catalogue also lists a large number of titles on other collectibles, such as guns, buttons, dolls, and the like. The clock section is remarkably thorough, including a number of reprints of old Seth Thomas Waterbury Clock and other catalogues. There are dozens of books on repairs of all sorts of watches and clocks, as well as books that may interest more generally inclined antique collectors, such as *English Barometers 1680–1860.*

Hotchkiss House, 18 Hearthstone Road, Pittsford, N.Y. 14534
32-page annual catalogue, free.

The Hotchkiss House catalogue is by far the most thorough compilation of books on antiques and other collectibles that I have seen. Over fourteen hundred titles are listed, "Divided and Indexed into 60 recognized categories of Antiques, Arts, Hobbies and Collecting." All this is an offshoot of John Hotchkiss starting nearly ten years ago to compile antique price guides as a hobby. Having finished twelve of these, he began to stock and sell books other than his own. The catalogue shows an author's hand in that it is extremely well organized and has a brief description of each title. Its organization also led me to discover a number of hobbies I hadn't realized existed. Familiar as I was with button collecting, I didn't know there was a *Book of a Thousand Thimbles*, nor did I realize that collecting electric barbed-wire insulators was now so common that at least a half-dozen books about them have been published. Inkwells, barbed wire, early farmer's tools, hammers, here are books on all these—of interest, I should think, not only to collectors but to graphic artists and even to social historians.

Old Drover Inn, 31 Jefferson Street, Box 6, Westfield, N.Y. 14787
Price list, free.

Old Drover Inn, "antiquarians since 1922," specializes in books about antiques. They have books on everything from "How to Repair and Dress Old Dolls" ($5.75) to books on collecting Coca-Cola bottles. Their list has books on clocks, music boxes, guns, paperweights and just about anything else you might think of collecting, along with a very thorough compilation of price guides, which apparently exist even for the most arcane subjects, not just comics and French cameo glass but milk bottles and old trunks.

A number of the books are sold below their original price, so if you splurge and spend $5.50 on *Regimental Steins of the Bavarian and Imperial German Armies*, you can make up for it by buying *Toby Jugs* for only $1 instead of the original $3.50.

ART

Hacker Art Books, 54 W. 57th Street, New York, N.Y. 10019
Reprint and sale catalogues, semiannually, free.
Rare-book and fine-binding catalogues, free.

Hacker's is one of New York's best art-book shops with an excellent stock not only of current titles but of old and rare books as well. If you know specifically what you want, Hacker's will try to find an unlisted title for you. As is so often the case, many of these books contain works of art in themselves, and the catalogues are

1 • *Hacker Art Books* Illuminated Book of Hours. Printed on vellum with fourteen large and three small miniatures in colors and gold within gold borders, colored floral page borders and hundreds of small illuminated initials in gold on blue and red ground. Seventy-four leaves, eight volumes, full old red morocco binding blind-stamped with borders and sacred monogram. Clasps and ten leaves lacking. Paris: Germain Hardouyn (1533). $1,500.

2 • *Wittenborn and Company* Paintings and drawings of Egon Schiele. $2.

filled with fascinating items. Some may be beyond your current budget, such as an early nineteenth-century survey of natural history in twenty-seven volumes, with 1,590 hand-colored copperplates for $1,375, although it is, after all, less than a dollar an engraving.

On the other hand, Hacker's sale catalogue does offer art books at very reasonable prices. Their current list includes a wide selection of the famous Skira art books at half price. These days art books are so expensive that publishers often plan to sell them at two prices, at their original price, usually at Christmas, and then at a much lower, remainder price, about a year or two later. Hacker's list is an excellent way of keeping track of some of these bargains.

Wittenborn and Company, 1018 Madison Avenue, New York, N.Y. 10021
Price list, free.

Wittenborn is one of the country's best art-book shops; the store, located in the midst of what has become the city's art district, is a marvelously crowded and endlessly tempting storehouse of art books from the world over. Wittenborn not only stocks the books and periodicals from most publishers but also sells a number of special catalogues, largely unavailable elsewhere. I think it safe to say that they could fill just about any order you might send them. Wittenborn also publishes and distributes a large number of specialized works.

ASIA

China Books and Periodicals, 125 Fifth Avenue, New York, N.Y. 10003
24-page catalogue, free.

For several years now, China Books and Periodicals has been a major source of materials from and about the People's Republic and the countries and movements associated with it. With interest in China taking a great leap forward, they have expanded their imports to include records, posters, wood-block prints, etc.

This exceptionally useful catalogue lists pages of titles on China today, over two pages of the writings of Chairman Mao, many of these published in English in China, as well as a very full selection of books on Chinese art, literature, philosophy, etc. The books imported from China are very inexpensive and include current novels, plays, and a very good selection of children's books, paperbound, but with color illustrations, for as little as 25 cents each.

The selection of records includes a number of American-made records but has a broader choice of imports, such as a three-record set of the music from *The Red Detachment of Women* at $9.95; selections of songs from the Peking Opera at $1.95 for a 10″ record; and even records of readings in English of Mao Tse-tung's most famous articles. Perhaps the most intriguing record is a 10″ LP called "Warmly Hail the Communiqué of the 12th Plenary Session of the 8th Central Committee of the Chinese Communist Party," a solo and chorus arrangement with instrumental accompaniment.

Particularly appealing are the various posters. Giant color posters (30″ by 42″) are only $1, smaller ones are three for $1, and are the very posters distributed in China.

An essential catalogue for anyone interested in China.

Orientalia, Inc., 11 E. 12th Street, New York, N.Y. 10003
Various catalogues, 25 cents each.

Founded some fifty years ago, Orientalia is one of the country's several excellent stores that specialize in the East. Catalogues are available on India, the largest single country listing; China, Korea and Japan; Oriental languages and religion; and of particular interest, the Near and Middle East, an area served, in the United States, by fewer bookstores. The listings are extensive and varied, and while in certain areas not as comprehensive as Paragon's, they do contain special areas of their own strength. A large selection of records is also listed, along with books on music, the dance, the culinary arts and other less forbidding aspects of Asian scholarship. The more specialized listings, however, are also there, such as five books on Paleosiberian in the language catalogue. As is the case with most stores of this kind, books from all over the world are listed.

Paragon Book Gallery, Ltd., 14 E. 38th Street, New York, N.Y. 10016
200- to 300-page catalogue, free. Spring, fall.

Paragon is one of New York's most intriguing bookstores, though relatively few people have ever gone into the old office building that houses the endless stacks holding over a hundred thousand books on every aspect of the Orient and Africa. It is a book lover's delight, a place filled with the unknown and unexpected, and Paragon's meticulous catalogue of books on the Orient and Africa gives mail-order buyers some inkling of its many treasures. A recent issue, which properly lists its author, Max Faerber, totaled 280 pages describing just under 3,500 items on the history, politics, philosophy, religion, literature, art and archaeology of countries from Africa to Australia and all those in between. This includes over 100 books on Tibet, 500 on art and archaeology, 140 different items on Oriental languages, etc.

Such numbers reflect much more than current publishing, and Paragon has what must be one of the most complete stocks of out-of-print books in these fields. One of my European friends whose own collection of books on the Orient is the most extensive I have ever seen was astonished when he first visited Paragon and ended up spending far more than he'd ever intended, filling the gaps in his collection. It should be mentioned that he did so for less than he would have spent elsewhere, since Paragon's prices are generally reasonable. Out-of-print books, even those published early in the century, are often priced as if they'd just been published. Reprints, including a number published by Paragon, are also priced very honestly, unlike the exorbitant amounts demanded by so many professional library reprinters who charge $12–$20 for any book. For example, a reprint of *A Record of Buddhistic Kingdoms,* an 1866 Oxford book, sells here for $6.50.

Though Paragon's stock is all-encompassing, special attention should be paid the extraordinary art and archaeology section, which art collectors, people interested in pottery and others should consult. Naturally, books from all countries and in all languages are listed, as well as grammars and dictionaries to help you with the languages (Tibetan? Tamil?) you may lack.

BELLES LETTRES

The Gotham Book Mart, Inc., 41 W. 47th Street, New York, N.Y. 10036
Various catalogues and price lists, free.

The Gotham Book Mart has long enjoyed a reputation as the country's leading literary bookstore, a place that not only sold serious fiction and poetry but acted as a gathering place for writers and a disseminator of their work. In the long run, this interest has paid off handsomely, since the store is now one of the few places in the country where one can find the small press publications, the pamphlets and hand-printed booklets, the rare and out-of-print books where so many of America's major twentieth-century authors first appeared. A visitor to the crowded shop tucked away among New York's diamond merchants may not realize at first what jewels are hidden among these dusty shelves, but a look at the store's catalogues surprises one with the variety of editions available. Who would have expected a collection of James Joyce's early reviews to have been published by a small press in Colorado Springs, or that Ezra Pound's early pamphlets on Money had all been reprinted by an English firm. These gems are from the general Gotham catalogue of rare books (code word *Sitwell,* should you wish to cable an order for these), but other lists are available on Tennessee Williams, Hart Crane, and others, as well as a specialized film catalogue, another Gotham specialty.

Obviously, so carefully constructed a collection contains no surprise bargains, but prices seemed reasonable to me and in many cases an early edition of a work was offered for less than the current paperback reprint would cost. Gotham also has a huge file of fifty thousand little magazines and periodicals, a thousand of which are listed in a current catalogue. Finally, the store offers a service I've seen nowhere else: they will attend a literary auction in New York, occasionally in London, as your agent for a 10 percent commission.

BOATING

Caravan-Maritime Books, 87-06 168th Place, Jamaica, N.Y. 11432
30-page catalogue, $1.

Caravan specializes in rare maritime material, which covers not only naval history, but books on oceanography, Arctica, ship building and ship modeling. As with many other specialized booksellers, there is a search service, which means that they will advertise for a title they do not stock, charging you $1 per volume. Prices are high, but then, most of the books listed are rare and often date back well into the nineteenth century.

International Marine Publishing Co., Camden, Maine 04843
Catalogue, free.

International Marine focuses on "real, knowledgeable boating people, commercial boatmen, yachtsmen, sailing buffs, etc.," and selling them books and prints on nautical matters, a number of which are published by the firm. Their latest catalogue features *Ferrocement*

Boat Construction, but also lists a book on the Liberty ships, a book of seafood recipes and the fifteenth edition of *Knight's Modern Seamanship*. Books on commercial fishing, shipping, boat building and design, practical boating and sailing are included, as well as picture books, books on maritime history and ship models. In addition to these very thorough listings of new books, there are a number of prints and a selection of marine equipment.

CHILDREN'S BOOKS AND BOOKS ON EDUCATION

The Bank Street Bookstore, 610 W. 112th Street, New York, N.Y. 10025
Mimeographed catalogue, 50 cents.

Its practically impossible, outside the very largest cities, to find a good children's bookstore and we unfortunately have never developed local equivalents of London's Children's Book Centre. The Bank Street Bookstore is therefore the answer to many a parent's and teacher's hopes, even though most New Yorkers don't even know of the shop's existence. Located in the new building of the Bank Street College of Education, the store is part of the famous school's education program. Its large and well-selected stock of books "reflects the college's educational philosophy and research programs, which include studies of children's responses to story material." The store catalogue lists most of the books actually in stock, not just the children's books but the many books for teachers and others interested in education.

Since the books listed have been specially selected, the catalogue can also be used as a reading list. Here are suggested first picture books, books on various subjects for each age group, science and other specialized books, both in paperback and hardcover.

For parents and teachers, there is a large selection of books on child development, early-childhood education, music, math, art and open education, as well as the college's own famous publications on teaching. A very useful guide to books that ought to be far more readily available than they are.

F. A. O. Schwarz, 745 Fifth Avenue, New York, N.Y. 10022
List, free.

In addition to its famous toy catalogue, Schwarz also publishes a list of children's books and records, listing the more popular new and perennial children's books from various American publishers.

Victoria Book Shop, 16 W. 36th Street, New York, N.Y. 10036
62-page catalogue, free. Issued three times a year.

This is another of what might be called New York's hidden bookshops. Located on the twelfth floor of an office building and visitable by appointment only, it is hardly a place you are likely to stumble across. Yet here is a stock of five thousand books, one of the largest collections in the country, of old and rare children's books as well as other illustrated volumes. The books are expensive and rare, prices running "from $5.00 to well into four figures . . . Basically our books are for collectors and institutions, although many sales are made for people seeking choice gifts." Here are various first editions of *Alice*, fetching as much as $400; or twenty-four copies of *The Boys Comic Journal* (1893) for $30; or a three-volume French 1768 *Robinson Crusoe* with fourteen engravings for $55. A fascinating list that makes one long to call for an appointment and look at the pictures.

COOKING

Corner Book Shop, 102 Fourth Avenue, New York, N.Y. 10003
20-page catalogue, free.

The Corner Book Shop is one of the small, dark, crowded bookstores on Manhattan's lower Fourth Avenue, New York's book row, and in many ways it is an example of the advantages of buying by mail. I've often walked past the store and have even gone into it a few times without beginning to suspect its riches. The store's stationery lists cinema, drama, gastronomy and textiles as its specialties, and its current 20-page catalogue on food and drink is a delight, listing a great variety of books from all countries at very reasonable prices. From *101 Practical Non-Flesh Recipes*, a vegetarian cookbook from London in 1918, to *365 Ways to Cook Hamburgers*, the catalogue shows that you can enjoy browsing at a distance and perhaps even find some books you've always wanted.

CRAFTS

Craft and Hobby Book Service, P.O. Box 626, Pacific Grove, Calif. 93950
76-page annual book list, 50 cents.

"Books for the Weaver and Needleworker" is the title of this very comprehensive listing. The books here are nearly all current American publications with a sprinkling of Scandinavian works. They also include the publications of the Shuttle Craft Guild and a number of books published by the Service itself, such as *How to Build a Loom* ($2.50) and other practical titles. Subjects covered in addition to weaving are band weaving, spinning and dyeing, needlework, patchwork, tatting, lace, knots, knitting and crochet. Each book is described in detail and I should think this catalogue would be essential to anyone seriously involved in these fields.

Museum Books, Inc., 48 E. 43rd Street, New York, N.Y. 10017
108-page price list on handicrafts, design and applied arts, 50 cents.
Price list on primitive art, graphic arts, photography, etc., free.

Museum Books is the perfect store for anyone interested in the applied arts. Though it has a large stock of books on art and art history, its major appeal is the great thoroughness with which it sells and lists books on the various handicrafts. Its huge catalogue has entries for batik, candlemaking, crewel embroidery, knitting, mosaics, rubbings, silkscreen, tatting and lacework, toys and dolls and woodworking, just to list a few.

There are twelve pages on handweaving alone, from beginner's guides to very specialized works such as *Functional Overshot* or *Sectional Warping.* Antique collectors, people interested in dolls, and others who buy rather than make objects, will also find the catalogue to be a gold mine in their fields. Those professionals involved in design and the graphic arts in New York have long known of the Museum Books stock of books on lettering, layout, display, etc., and I should think it would be safe to write to Museum for any title in these fields.

The Unicorn, Box 645, Rockville, Md. 20851
64-page catalogue, 50 cents.

The Unicorn is a new firm, with a very extensive catalogue of books for craftsmen. They try to carry all craft books in print in the United States and also import volumes from abroad. In addition to this, they publish a quarterly *Guide to Craft Books,* which is available for $2 a year. Unicorn's strongest holdings are on handweaving and needlework, including quilting, patchwork and rug hooking. The catalogue has a well-organized subject index so that you can quickly find the book on *Spruce Root Basketry* or *Papago Indian Pottery,* along with the more mundane titles.

EUROPEAN BOOKS

Adler's Foreign Books, Inc., 162 Fifth Avenue, New York, N.Y. 10010
Catalogues of books on literature, reference, etc., free.

Adler's is familiar to generations of specialists in foreign languages and foreign literature who may never have visited this store but who have seen its wares displayed at various learned meetings. Adler's forte is literature from Western Europe, though it also stocks a number of reference and scientific books, and will order any book published abroad that you may wish. The current, very thorough catalogue of German literature runs to 138 pages, from Adorno to Zwingli, and lists, for instance, two full pages of Hofmannsthal. There is also a very helpful addendum of books from the German Democratic Republic, and the much lower prices of these shows that Adler uses restraint in its markups. The French catalogue is 130 pages long, and there are catalogues listing dictionaries, books on Germanistik and the teaching of German, paperbacks in French, German and Spanish, as well as a list of Spanish and Latin American literature. Adler's also has a catalogue of the handsome foreign, mostly German, calendars that it imports.

French and European Publications, Inc., 610 Fifth Avenue, New York, N.Y. 10020
Various catalogues and brochures, free.

Many tourists have passed by the windows of this French bookstore in Rockefeller Center, to see the latest French best sellers and fashion magazines displayed there, but the main business of this store seems to be supplying schools and universities throughout

3 • *J. N. Bartfield Books* A typical collection of the books in fine bindings that are always in stock.

the country. Their catalogues, geared to the teaching of French and Spanish, are very thorough and impressive documents. Their "comprehensive bibliography" of French Language and Literature is 436 pages long, and includes a great many French as well as American textbooks. The Spanish list is nearly as long, starting with books and records for the elementary school and going through graduate school. Various catalogues from the European publishers themselves are also available, primarily for reference works and paperbacks. French and European Publications also puts out an interesting 34-page list of books on Africa and by Africans, all in French; a useful supplement to the usual African-studies emphasis on English-speaking Africa. Obviously, these services are of primary interest to teachers and educational institutions. For individuals who need only the occasional book in French and can wait a few weeks, it may be worth their while comparing prices with those charged in Paris.

GARDENING

Garden Way Publishing, Charlotte, Vt., 05445
64-page catalogue, 25 cents. January.

The Greening of Vermont, which has led to so many farms and shops being set up in that once neglected state, may soon embellish the rest of the land if Garden Way Publishing continues to prosper. Garden Way publishes its own books aimed at the encouragement of gardening and self-reliance, but its catalogue aims at offering the best books from all publishers and seeks to "give very honest reviews and recommendations, pointing out the strengths and weaknesses of the books" as well as offering various discounts. The catalogue includes sections on gardening, cooking, country living, animal husbandry, home repair and children's books. Their exhaustive list runs from the familiar and popular titles to such essential but harder-to-find items as *How to Shoe a Horse, Raising Earthworms for Profit* and *What You Should Know About the Purple Martin*, which, once you discover this swallow can eat two thousand mosquitoes a day, you may wish to know more about. The catalogue is thoroughly revised each year and strikes me as a particularly useful guide for any serious gardener or natural-food enthusiast.

NAUTICAL

Antheil Booksellers, 2177 Isabelle Court, No. Bellmore, N.Y. 11710
32-page catalogue, free. Issued every other month.

Antheil deals exclusively by mail, having a stock of some ten thousand volumes, specializing in books on maritime subjects but also stocking some books on aviation and military subjects. The books are, for the most part, out of print; they come from all over the world but seem to be primarily in English. The range is wide, from the ever-present books on Amelia Earhart to government hearings on the munitions industry, from German naval yearbooks in World War I to the official history of various Italian naval ships—who would have thought a whole volume could be devoted to the Italian submarine?

OCCULT

Shambala Booksellers, 2482 Telegraph Avenue, Berkeley, Calif. 94704
8-page newsletter-price list, $1.00 for six issues.

Shambala publishes a newsletter that includes a number of reviews of new books as well as lists of some of the titles that they sell and others that they publish. Shambala's interest encompasses Eastern philosophy and astrology, and the related fields that cover a number of the interests of the counterculture, the occult and subjects that used to be called "esoteric." Shambala offers to fill orders for books they don't list, as long as they are in print, and extend the same kind of friendly service that they apparently try to create in their store, where benches have been provided for those who want to sit and read.

Samuel Weiser, Inc., 734 Broadway, New York, N.Y. 10003
62-page catalogue, free.

For years those interested in the occult, the esoteric and the magical have found their way to Samuel Weiser's crowded and friendly store. This is, as far as I know, the only American equivalent of Watkins in London. Here are books on astrology, hypnosis, the cabala, magic, palmistry, tarot and Oriental religions. Aleister Crowley, Gurdijeff are here but also Progoff, Suzuki and others who have linked Western and Oriental psychiatry and philosophy. In addition to stocking a very full selection of books, Weiser publishes a number of new and reprinted titles on its own.

For other books on the occult, astrology, etc., see the Hobby and Professional Equipment section under Occult.

PERFORMING ARTS

The Dance Mart, Box 48, Homecrest Station, Brooklyn, N.Y. 11229
15-page price list, free.

The Dance Mart offers a very full list of books on dance techniques and studies, but this is seen to include a very broad field, including mime, acrobatics, physical fitness and kinetics, even baton twirling. You may start out, as I did, looking for books on ballet, and end up being tempted by *Baton Twirling Made Easy* ($2.75) or wondering what there is in *Strutting Confidential* that justifies a price of 50 cents for forty pages.

The Drama Book Shop, 150 W. 52nd Street, New York, N.Y. 10019
28-page quarterly Annotated Bibliography, $2.50 annual subscription, $1 per copy.

Now in its fiftieth year, this well-known store prides itself on having "the most complete stock of in-print theater material to be found anywhere." The store's catalogue, a quarterly bibliography, lists an average of five hundred new publications and is used by a number of institutions to keep in touch as well as to buy. All aspects of contemporary and classical theater are covered, as well as the dance, puppets, film, television and radio. Records of performances, spoken as well as instrumental, and magazines and learned journals about the theater are also available. As with other good specialized stores, the bibliography is a pleasure to read, far-reaching and comprehensive; it will list the novels on which famous movies were based, as well as the scripts or even the biographies of those who inspired plays.

Larry Edmunds Cinema and Theatre Bookshop, Inc., 6658 Hollywood Boulevard, Hollywood, Calif. 90028
524-page Cinema Catalogue, $2.95.

This is by far the most extraordinary catalogue of printed material that I have ever seen, documenting beyond any doubt this store's claim to having the "world's largest collection of books on the cinema." Close to fifteen thousand items are listed (and indexed), covering not simply books on the cinema, but screenplays, original scripts, film magazines and a vast array of posters, programs, lobby cards and other promotional materials that I never knew existed. In addition to these, there is a great deal of similar material on the theater, radio and television.

Started thirty-three years ago, Larry Edmunds Bookshop is well known to informed film buffs, but we were able to stun some movie-fanatic friends when we showed them this voluminous catalogue. Here is a truly comprehensive international collection, as ready to supply you with *Le Monde de Jerry Lewis* as with a study of young Hungarian film makers. In these severe (and alas unillustrated) pages is the history of the cinema as it has yet to be written, not just of the stars and the famous movies but the whole fascinating structure of the publicity and technical underpinnings that made up the "dream factory."

PSYCHOLOGY

Brunner Mazel, Inc., 64 University Place, New York, N.Y. 10003
Book lists, free.

This is probably the country's leading bookstore in the fields of psychology, psychiatry, psychoanalysis, neurology, and child development, and much of their business is conducted by mail. The store keeps a stock of over three thousand titles in these subjects and will order any book in print that you may need. Brunner Mazel also mails out, free of charge, a list of new titles which is prepared ten times a year and which includes a large number of books that are not reviewed in the general press or reviewed quite late in the professional journals. This is, however, very professionally oriented and I would not suggest your getting on the mailing list if you are just looking for an occasional title. If you are a constant book buyer in any of these areas, then Mazel's service is extremely useful and occasionally money-saving, since a number of books are offered at a small discount.

4 • *J. N. Bartfield Books* Eight volumes, full crushed levant, multiple gilt ornamental borders enclosing, of *The Posthumous Papers of the Pickwick Club.* Sixteen color plates by C. E. Brock. On the front cover a picture, in varicolored morocco, of Mr. Pickwick holding Mrs. Bardell in his arms while her son kicks him. Back gilt with fleurons, inner dentelles gilt, gilt edges by Rivière. London: Harrap (1930). $175.

5 • *J. N. Bartfield Books* Twenty-volume edition of "Secret Memoires of the Court of France" by Lamballe in pre-1929 Exhibition binding in blue morocco, with gilt tops and decorative spines. $250 the set.

6 • *Philip C. Duschnes* Manuscript leaf from the Book of Hours, France, fifteenth century. Written in black lettering (Gothic) on vellum. 7″ by 5″, mounted in a mat. The decorative initials are in burnished gold on colored background, the border of sprays is in the traditional ivy pattern in burnished gold. $25.

RARE BOOKS

Argosy Book Stores, Inc., 116 E. 59th Street, New York, N.Y. 10022

Catalogues, 50 cents.

Argosy is one of New York's best-known old bookstores, equally famous for its prints, maps and books. There is, unfortunately, no specific mail-order catalogue for what Argosy calls "by far the largest collection of old maps," many of which go back to the sixteenth century. Argosy also sells old leather bindings to decorators, for $4, and though there are no listings of these, I suppose you could order by the piece or by the yard if you felt your living room needed a leathery look.

As to books, Argosy's recent catalogue is indicative of its stock: 573 items of Americana are listed, including a number of maps and prints; a 1605 set of four maps, showing the whole world, costs $150; a 1661 colored map of New Amsterdam, reproduced in 1966, costs $20, while the first American map of Virginia, published in 1794, is $125.

The books themselves, many of them rare, are also likely to be expensive, including a great many published in the nineteenth century. A 1764 book published in French in Berlin argues that America is not naturally inferior to the rest of the world, at $40, while five volumes of Franklin D. Roosevelt's *Public Papers* go for $35. A broad selection but no undiscovered bargains.

J. N. Bartfield Books, Inc., 45 W. 57th Street, New York, N.Y. 10019

104-page catalogue, $1; refundable.

According to Bartfield's, one of New York's finest dealers in rare books, it has "probably the most select and largest collection of fine bindings in the country, if not the world," and furthermore, its prices are "at least 15% lower" than the fine book departments of the country's leading bookstores. Bartfield's books, however, are not inexpensive and are meant for the serious collector interested either in first editions, autographs, or the like. Few are the items in their catalogue under $50, in fact books or sets over $500 are more common. Still, for collectors a three-volume set of Redouté Roses, including 183 plates partially printed in color and finished by hand, may well be a bargain at $4,750. For people with the money to spare, collecting books has become an increasingly popular pastime, and while it is obvious that catalogues from all over the world must be consulted, Bartfield's is one of the American lists that should be looked at.

Philip C. Duschnes, 699 Madison Avenue, New York, N.Y. 10021

Various catalogues, free.

Duschnes is one of the country's best-known dealers in rare books and first editions and also sells individual manuscript leaves to collectors. There is an enormous difference between the country's many antiquarian or old-book dealers who sell just about any book that has been published at prices that are often still very low and firms such as Duschnes which are both highly selective and, it must be added, very expensive. Rare-book collectors, like all collectors, will often pay extremely high prices for one-of-a-kind items, but I was surprised at some of the prices charged for modern first editions. If you are looking for a rare Forster or Orwell, then you should get some of the English lists to compare prices.

On the other hand, Duschnes offers some illuminated manuscript pages at prices that again surprised me, but this time for their reasonableness. There is a page from a French Bible (A.D. 1300) in black and red with gold initials and headings for only $20, or a lovely page from a fifteenth-century French Book of Hours with a delicate border of ivy sprays for $25. Prices go up to ten times as much for a page, and if you want an original Book of Hours, there are some for $3,000 and $3,500. The catalogue also includes some exquisite pages from Persian manuscripts for a little as $7.50.

RUSSIAN

Four Continents Book Corporation, 156 Fifth Avenue, New York, N.Y. 10010

Price lists of books in English, sociopolitical books in Russian, Soviet periodicals and reference works, slides, film strips and facsimiles, and Russian music on records, free.

For years Four Continents has been importing books, magazines and other materials from the Soviet Union, and it is the major American source of published works in Russian and the other languages used in the U.S.S.R. Its large, dark old-fashioned shop on lower Fifth Avenue has always struck me as a sample of Russia itself, an effect heightened by the samovars and other souvenirs from Russia that Four Continents also sells. Readers who have no Russian should know at the outset that there is a great deal in these catalogues in English, and in fact, Soviet translations into English have long been among the best bargains available to book buyers. Though Russian book production is still very old-fashioned and many of the books look as if they had been published years ago, the translations are for the most part excellent and the prices are unbeatable. The great works of the nineteenth century—Tolstoy, Turgenev, Dostoevsky and such less-known writers as Kuprin, Lermontov and Saltykov-Shchedrin—are available at incredibly low prices. The last-named author's most famous work, *Judas Golovlyov*, 366 pages long, costs $1.60 and other bound books cost from $1 for an illustrated edition of Pushkin's *Tales of Ivan Belkin* to $2 for a collection of Tolstoy novella, the most expensive item being $7.50 for a two-volume *The Idiot*.

The choice of contemporary authors is of course not as wide, and many of the best-known Soviet authors have not been translated by their government. But while there is no Pasternak or Sinyavsky here, there are volumes by Paustovsky and of course the most popular and officially approved authors such as Sholokhov, Bek, Fedin and a great many other authors barely known here. There is also a large choice of the excellent Soviet children's books, many in inexpensive but full-color paperbacks, from 50 cents up. Soviet science fiction is also widely available in English as well as a wide choice of books on the arts. Here are such specialized works as *Spanish Glassware in the Hermitage Collection* ($20) or a book on Uzbek miniatures, as well as more general works on the Bolshoi Ballet, the Moscow Theater and other major Soviet institutions. Over seventy guide books are available, as well as a choice of postcards, in case you simply wish to pretend you've been to Russia.

Four Continents' major business, however, is supplying books and periodicals in Russian on all subjects, and its catalogues, in Russian, list their holdings in detail. You may also subscribe to Soviet periodicals through this firm. Finally, an excellent choice of Soviet LP's averaging $4.50 each, is also available, featuring both contemporary and classical music, as well as a number of readings of plays, verse and prose.

SECONDHAND BOOKS

Strand Book Store, Inc., 828 Broadway, New York, N.Y. 10003

Price lists in most categories, free.

The Strand is probably New York's best-known used-book store—the largest, I believe, of the old Fourth Avenue stores—which stocks, as its ads proudly proclaim, over a million volumes. The Strand is best known for selling unwanted reviewer's copies, and the tables at the front are filled with brand-new books at half price, books that no one wanted to keep, even though they were free, and in some cases no one even bothered to open. Each Christmas I walk by stacks of books still in their plastic wrappings, a convincing negative version of the best-seller list. These new books are not listed in the Strand's catalogues, but their lists do cover just about every field of interest and you can write in and ask for what they have, be it literature, Americana, etc. The choice is extensive and the books are reasonably priced; no exceptional bargains but on the other hand, no feeling that one is being taken advantage of. A good place to look for the more general kind of book as well as real strength in books on American life and culture over the last fifty years.

TRANSPORTATION

Owen Davies, Bookseller, 1214 N. LaSalle Street, Chicago, Ill. 60610

Catalogue, free. Published four times a year.

Owen Davies is another of the country's specialized booksellers whose thriving business shows the extraordinary varieties of interests that exist in this world. The store stocks some seventy-five hundred items, all on the history of railroads and ships, and mails its catalogues to thirty-five hundred people here and abroad. I knew there were lots of railroad buffs, but I didn't realize that an audience existed for books such as *The Era of Streetcars in Winnipeg, 1881-1955* ($3), or *The Tramways of Portugal*, a visitor's guide ($2). Davies imports many books from England and Europe, and also publishes a number of its own monographs, such as *History of the Louisville and Nashville R.R.*, ($10.95). It also carries railroad memorabilia such as old timetables, passes, maps and brochures.

BOOKPLATES

Antioch Bookplate Company, Yellow Springs, Ohio 45387
36-page catalogue, some color, free.

This company was started forty-eight years ago by Ernest Morgan, a crusader for many social causes who made a point of hiring Jewish refugees before World War II and Japanese-Americans from California concentration camps after the war. The firm is now the world's largest producer of bookmarks and bookplates, and the catalogue shows a good selection of fairly varied standard modern designs, and a few pages of designs for "young people." Most of them cost about $10, including the name, for the first two hundred, and about $3 for each hundred after that.

Berliner and McGinnis, Nevada City, Calif. 95959
32-page color catalogue, free.

In the Sierra Nevada Mountains, Berliner and McGinnis publishes a gorgeous collection of bookplates. They have both beautifully colored modern plates designed by artists in various countries and elegant reproductions of old plates designed for or by famous people.

Samuel Pepys' bookplate is here—his diary of July 21, 1668, says: "Went to my plate maker's and there spent an hour about contriving my little plates for my books . . ." In the seventeenth and eighteenth centuries everybody who was anybody had their own personal bookplates designed, so here you'll find Paul Revere's, Captain Cook's and Earl Egerton of Tattons, as well as the first bookplate known.

Without a name, the plates cost $3 per hundred; with a name, $6.50. And at no extra charge the plates can be printed with the words "The Record Collection of" if you'd like to label your records.

See also New York Public Library in the Museums section.

7

8

9

7 • *Antioch Bookplate Company* Bookplate printed in black ink on rough-finished cream-colored Antioch Vellum paper. First two hundred, including a name, $10. Each additional hundred ordered at the same time, with the same name, $3.

8 • *Berliner and McGinnis* "Blue Owl" book or record plate in different shades of blue on white. One hundred, not imprinted, $3. First hundred, with a name, $6.50. Each additional hundred ordered at the same time with the same name, $3.75.

9 • *Berliner and McGinnis* "Sagittarius" book or record plate, one of twelve zodiac bookplates with the figure in red, the lettering, etc., in black. One hundred, not imprinted, $3. First hundred with name, $6.50. Each additional hundred ordered at the same time with the same name, $3.75.

10 • *Berliner and McGinnis* Book or record plate, a reproduction of Kate Greenaway's design for Mr. Frederick Locker-Lampson. One hundred, not imprinted, $2.50. First hundred with name, $6. Each additional hundred ordered at the same time with the same name, $3.

10

4
CHRISTMAS & OTHER CELEBRATIONS

1

2

3

4

1 • *Stell and Shevis* (see Handicrafts section) Handmade ceramic crèche in wood box. Seven pieces (the largest is about 4″ high), $45 postpaid.

2 • *Metropolitan Museum of Art* Each year the Metropolitan Museum commissions a different artist to design a sterling-silver snowflake ornament. The year is marked on the back and there is additional space for your own engraving, and there is a hole at the top for hanging. $10.
photo David Fletcher

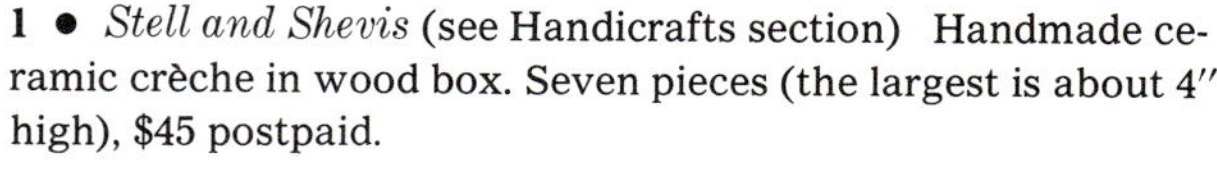

3 • *Printed Papers* A bird cut from one of six cards sold with black designs on red, intended to be cut out by the sender or the recipient and used as a mobile. Six cards, $1.50.

4 • *Printed Papers* Crèche, hand-screened in red on white, to be cut out and used as an ornament or to be sent as a card. 10½″ by 8½″ on folded white card with envelope. $2.

5

5 • *12/25 Christmas Shop* Angel candleholder in natural German spruce with blue wings. About $5.

12/25 Christmas Shop Swedish Christmas elf. Hand-painted wood and cloth cap. About $5.

12/25 Christmas Shop Russian nesting *Metryoshka.* About $4.

DECORATIONS

Abbey Press, St. Meinrad, Ind. 47577
Yearly subscription to three color Christian Family catalogues, 35 cents. January, April, September.

This press, owned by a Benedictine monastery, publishes a cheerful and colorful collection of posters, writing paper and cards. The Christmas catalogue, which is sent out in September, has nice painted wood decorations, modern Nativity sets, including a paper one for about $1.50 to color and cut out, and some brilliantly colored 10-cent Christmas cards.

Emgee Corp., 3210 Koapaka Street, Honolulu, Hawaii 98619
16-page color catalogue, $1.

Humorous Christmas ornaments made out of wood and hand-painted are sold here and are apparently popular with visitors to Hawaii. There are flat ornaments to hang on the tree, and three-dimensional scenes for the table or mantelpiece. Figures include Santa Claus engaged in various activities such as eating ice cream, examining a sick reindeer with a stethoscope, or playing a guitar; also mice and reindeer peeping out of stockings, owls wearing nightcaps, and dogs hanging up stockings. Most things cost between $3 and $6, but there are little wooden espalier trees for about $8 which you decorate by standing gifts, candles and decorations along the branches.

Paradise Products, Inc., P.O. Box 568, El Cerrito, Calif. 94530
56-page color catalogue, 50 cents.

"America's party host" sells supplies for parties, mainly to organizations–judging by the catalogue–and there is a $20 minimum. There are kits, and sometimes even food for parties with themes ranging from Easter, Halloween, Thanksgiving and Christmas, through regional American themes such as Western Chuck Wagon, Mardi Gras and Night on the Delta Queen to Hawaiian (for the Hawaiian you can have fresh flowers flown in), Mexican, German, Parisienne and Italian ones, or miscellaneous Roaring Twenties, Gay Nineties. Costumes, make-up, hats (specially printed if you like), masks, beards, mustaches, wigs, streamers, blowers, etc., are also sold, and although goods aren't exactly in the best of taste, there are oddities like gold and silver balloons ($1.80 a dozen) which would be very popular at children's parties, if you could find friends to order with to reach the $20 minimum.

Printed Papers, R.F.D. 1, New Market. N.H. 03857
Leaflet, 25 cents.

Two sisters sell printed Christmas cards, papers and ornaments by mail, one does the designing and the other handles the business part. The goods all have a pleasingly homemade look about them, such as the cards with curly childlike line drawings in black printed on thick mat colored paper. The only trouble is that the cards look so easy to make that one ends up wondering whether one couldn't do the same sort of thing at home and save money. However, if you are not afflicted by such feelings, you'll find here Christmas cards and gift tags, writing paper and gift wrap, and several kits to make paper mobiles, felt birds and Santa decorations, and, most useful, your own cookie cutters, so you are not stuck with the commercial shapes.

6 • *June Zimonick's Decoupage Studio* Christmas ornaments made in satin, braid, German gold paper and imported jewels. Kits to make each of these ornaments are sold at prices from $2.50 to $8.

7a

7b

8

7c

7a, b, c • *Metropolitan Museum of Art* (see Museums section) Each year the Metropolitan publishes new Christmas cards; these are some of the designs that will be on sale for Christmas 1973 at prices between 15 and 25 cents.

8 • *Philadelphia Museum of Art* Card with color woodcut, "December" by William P. Nicholson, sold with or without the words "Merry Christmas and Happy New Year." 20 cents.
photo A. J. Wyatt

Santons de Provence, Box 457, Damariscotta, Maine 04543
Color leaflet, 25 cents.

A gift shop—The Cricket Shop—imports from France the colorful clay figures called *santons*, which have been made in Provence for more than two hundred years. You can buy a wooden stable made of fragrant Maine pine for about $6.50, or several molded Provençal stables complete with olive and cypress trees, and then add the little clay figures as you like: just the basic crèche group of Joseph, Mary, Jesus, the kings, animals and angels, or else as many as you want of the more than sixty figures in French peasant dress or working costumes from the "Brigand" with knife to "M. le Curé" mopping his forehead with a red handkerchief. The *santons* come in three sizes and various prices.

The SERRV Self Help Handcrafts, Church World Service Center, New Windsor, Md. 21776
32-page color catalogue, free.
Color Christmas leaflet, free. Fall.

This nonprofit organization, which sells handicrafts from over thirty countries, publishes a special Christmas leaflet with cards and carved Nativity sets in wood.

Surma, 11 E. 7th Street, New York, N.Y. 10003
Leaflets for cossack shirts, ribbons and Easter-egg decorating, free.

Here you can get dyes, styluses, design cards and an instruction booklet for decorating Easter eggs in the Ukranian way—thin lines scratching patterns into brilliant colors. A complete Easter-egg decorating kit is available at $6. According to the Ukranians, the year we stop decorating Easter eggs, the world will end. So keep at it.

Toy Balloon Co., 204 E. 38th Street, New York, N.Y. 10016
Free price list and leaflet.

Although this firm is geared to selling to stores, (its prices are listed by the gross), it will fill orders from individuals. Any parent who in preparing a party or a school fair has wondered why on earth balloons should be so expensive can now order them for as little as $2 a gross. A balloon shower, released from your ceiling from a net, costs $6.50 and includes 144 balloons. Balloons shaped like birds, cats, dogs, etc., are $5 a gross, and large display balloons are available from $1 to $7 each. If you are so inclined, your name or any sentiment can be imprinted on the balloons. Blow pumps are also available, at 60 cents each.

12/25 Christmas Crafts, Edcom Systems, Inc., 145 Witherspoon Street, Princeton, N.J. 08540
22-page color catalogue, free. September.

Several people who used to be with Creative Playthings, including their president, have started this firm, which sells Christmas things from over thirty countries, small toys and stocking stuffers for all ages, and as the director says, the general character is nostalgic and folkloric with emphasis on good contemporary design. The catalogue is very appealing: Christmas stories, cookie figures and hot-pink and red backgrounds set off a witty and delightful collection of little things—for Christmas, silver balls from Germany, wooden stars from Austria, straw stars from Bavaria, embroidered felt stockings from Hungary, Santa finger puppets from Czechoslovakia and woven angels from Ecuador. And although the catalogue is called 12/25 Christmas Crafts, it is in fact available, and the contents are on sale, all year round. For children there are pick-up sticks, pop guns and ten color ballpoint pens, as well as all the tiny animals, painted houses, puppets and puzzles that are always so happily received. For adults there are Peruvian ski hats, Bedouin shoulder bags, brightly colored striped bedspreads, beads, little boxes and folk toys for decorations. Most things in this catalogue cost under $5; don't miss it.

June Zimonick's Decoupage Studio, Department C, Box 113, De Pere, Wis. 53115
26-page catalogue, some color. $2.

Here you can buy complete kits to make ornate Christmas-tree ornaments—jewels and braids over colored satin balls—for between $1.50 to $15 per kit. You can also get the satin balls and lots of gold and silver shapes, and braid, pearlized ornaments, jewels (from Austria), rondelles and pendant drops to make your own designs, and to decorate candles.

For glass ornaments, see Priscilla Manning Porter Studio in the Handicrafts section.

CARDS

Kristin Elliott, Inc., Box 23, Beverly, Mass. 01915
Leaflet, free.

This small family firm publishes Christmas cards and note cards, many of them with colored envelopes. The designs on all the cards consist mainly of animals or plants on a blank background, and the cards cost 10 to 15 cents each.

Miles Kimball, 41 W. 8th Avenue, Oshkosh, Wis. 54901
40-page Christmas card brochure, free.

The mail order firm Miles Kimball of Oshkosh puts out a brochure of tricky personalized Christmas cards—instead of just printing your name in the card, Miles Kimball incorporates you into the design. For the "Family Fun" greeting, you choose a drawing that represents your family's distinctive activity—it can be a sport or hobby or, failing all else, just eating or partying, and then the message will read: "Merry Christmas from those gardening [or "bird-watching" or "cruising" or whatever] Wheelers." For the "Family Silhouette Greeting" you choose the silhouettes (out of fifty-two) that look most like your own family, not forgetting your dog, and the silhouettes appear at various windows of a snowy house doing various Christmasy things like hanging decorations and wrapping parcels. For the "Your Own Home Greeting," you send a photograph and an artist will draw your home; with the "News Story Greeting" the names of your family are incorporated into various statements of good cheer; with the "Personal Diary Greeting," one hundred

words of your choice appear in a card like a diary; and with "Your Own Photo Greeting," when the card is opened your picture is automatically pulled from an instant print camera manned by Santa Claus. Cards cost from between $4 and $6 for twenty-five, and, of course, get cheaper the more you order.

UNICEF, 331 E. 38th Street, New York, N.Y. 10016
All-occasion cards brochure. Spring.
Holiday cards brochure. Fall.

The best-known UNICEF products are the bright Christmas cards, which UNICEF calls "holiday" cards, as they have rather general messages inside like "Peace on Earth" and "Season's Greetings" which will offend the sensibilities of only the most ardent hawks and atheists. Prices for these are $2 to $3 for twelve cards. But as well as the "holiday" cards there is a small but very pretty collection of cards for gifts, invitations, baby announcements and thank-you notes. These cost $2 for twenty-five, and a big gift pack of fifty assorted cards costs $5. There are also some books and games for children and an appointment calendar. The money earned by these cards and gifts goes to UNICEF programs: emergency relief and rehabilitation, and also long-range programs in child nutrition, disease eradication, and education in developing countries.

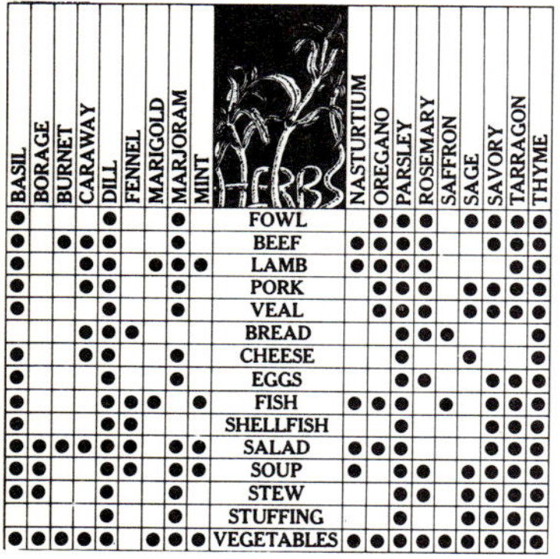

BASIL	BORAGE	BURNET	CARAWAY	DILL	FENNEL	MARIGOLD	MARJORAM	MINT	HERBS	NASTURTIUM	OREGANO	PARSLEY	ROSEMARY	SAFFRON	SAGE	SAVORY	TARRAGON	THYME
●				●			●		FOWL		●	●	●		●	●	●	●
●		●	●	●			●		BEEF	●	●	●	●			●	●	●
●			●	●		●	●	●	LAMB	●	●	●	●				●	●
●			●	●			●		PORK		●	●	●		●	●	●	●
●				●			●		VEAL		●	●	●		●	●	●	●
			●	●	●				BREAD			●	●	●				●
●			●	●			●		CHEESE			●			●			●
●				●			●		EGGS			●	●			●	●	●
●				●	●	●		●	FISH	●	●	●		●		●	●	●
●				●	●				SHELLFISH			●				●	●	●
●	●	●	●	●	●		●	●	SALAD	●	●	●				●	●	●
●	●			●	●		●	●	SOUP	●		●	●		●	●	●	●
●	●			●			●		STEW			●	●		●	●	●	●
				●			●		STUFFING			●			●	●	●	●
●	●	●	●	●		●	●	●	VEGETABLES	●	●	●	●	●	●	●	●	●

9 • *Museum of Modern Art* A typical collection of Christmas Cards.

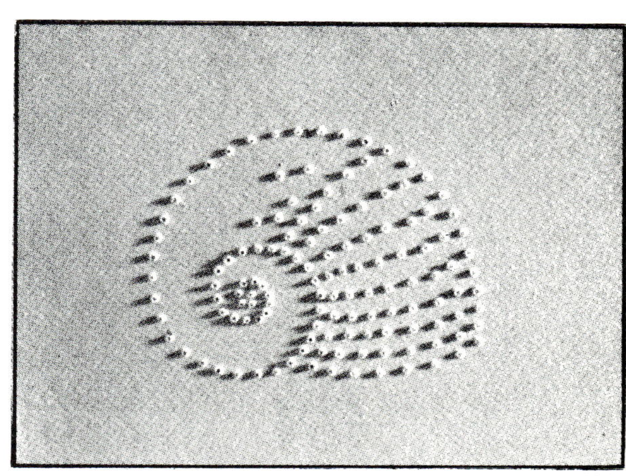

5
CIGARS & PIPES

1

2

1 • *Georgetown Tobacco and Pipe Stores* Gift collection of fourteen handmade cigars, including Royal Jamaica, Punch, Bances, Casa Buena and Suerdieck. About $10.

2 • *The Kenton Collection* (see the Household Objects and Gifts section) Cigar smoker's crystal ashtray by Dunhill. $39.50.

CIGARS AND PIPES

Wally Frank Ltd., 132 Church Street, New York, N.Y. 10007
46-page catalogue, free.

Frank's specializes in pipes, and its current catalogue lists a vast range, most of them in the $7 to $20 range. The catalogue also includes a large choice of pipe tobacco and accessories and over twelve pages of cigars, some surprisingly inexpensive, with regular cigars selling for as little as $7.99 for a hundred and small imported Danish cigars at $7.20 for a hundred, and a cigarette-sized cigar underselling any cigarette at $6.94 for four hundred.

Georgetown Tobacco and Pipe Stores, Inc., 3144 M Street, N.W., Washington, D.C. 20007
Catalogue, free.

Georgetown does an international mail-order business, supplying its exclusive pipes and tobaccos as well as stocking a large choice of other blends and various smoker's accessories. Among its specialties are its "Chewpies," a selection of six pipes for $18.95, and briars which it claims are hard to find under $10 each. Its pipe tobaccos draw heavily, as would be expected, on local Virginia product, but cigars are from Jamaica, Nicaragua, Brazil, the Philippines, etc. Georgetown also runs a rare mail-order repair service, replacing stems and bits, reaming shanks and bowls and carrying out other repairs on the old pipes you can't bring yourself to throw out.

Andrew Marks, The Pipe Shop, Stowe, Vt. 05672
12-page illustrated catalogue, 50 cents.

Andrew Marks makes pipes, either to your design or following his own, using Grecian or Corsican root briar. The pipes are expensive, ranging from $35 to $60, but offer a rare opportunity to pipe lovers to select exactly the characteristics they would like to have.

The Pipe Rack, Box 3259, Grand Central Station, New York, N.Y. 10017
Leaflet, free.

The Pipe Rack makes its own pipes and tobacco, which is marketed under the name of Duffy. Their specialty is briar pipes, made from aged Greek briar, "natural pipes . . . with no plugs, putty, paint or gadgets." The pipes are handmade, with vulcanite mouthpieces, and sell from $5 to $24. Duffy's pipe blends come in a large variety, ranging in price from $3.55 to $6 a pound but all available in 1¼ oz. packages for sampling. The Pipe Rack has the excellent idea of offering a standing order plan, so that any quantity you want of your usual tobacco will be regularly mailed to you at whatever interval you choose.

Nat Sherman, Inc., 1400 Broadway, New York, N.Y. 10018
36-page color catalogue, free.

Sherman is best known for his gimmickry in selling tobacco; cigars and cigarettes with your name imprinted on them or on their box, cigarettes that are extra long or come in fifteen different colors. But the search for something different has also led Sherman to develop cigarettes without any additives, and cigars that are particularly mild. In addition, Sherman has a wide stock of cigars, many using "pre-Castro Havana tobacco" (surely the most long-lasting natural resource since the loaves and fishes), and a broad choice of pipes and pipe tobacco.

3 • *Andrew Marks, The Pipe Shop* Pipe completely handmade from seasoned Greek or Corsican briarroot. After the pipe has been filed into shape, it is sanded by hand and rubbed with oil. $35.

4 • *Andrew Marks, The Pipe Shop* Pipe completely handmade from seasoned Greek or Corsican briarroot. $50.

6
CLOTHES & ACCESSORIES

For many people, buying clothes in person is one of the most grueling of life's occupations—I have a friend who lives in central Manhattan, yet buys all her clothes through ads in *The New Yorker*. For people like her, and people who live far away from good clothes shops, and for people who wear special sizes, there is a wide choice of ready to wear clothes available by mail. Not only shops in this section but also the department stores, mail-order houses and the general sports stores are important sources for clothes by mail, and they all include clothes in their catalogues. The only people who are out of luck are people who like clothes made to measure. Few American firms do it, although several in Europe and Hong Kong do at very reasonable prices.

FOR MEN AND WOMEN

Carol Brown, Putney, Vt. 05346
Leaflet, free.

Carol Brown mainly sells imported fabrics to home sewers, but she also has a few clothes from Ireland: heavy Aran sweaters in various rich colors, hostess skirts in lacy wool or in heavy, brilliantly colored wool lined with silk at about $40, and several capes and cloaks which have to be ordered from Ireland, so take about eight weeks to arrive; they cost about $150 each.

Budget Uniform Center, Inc., 1613 Chestnut Street, Philadelphia, Pa. 19103
60-page color general catalogue, free. January, April, September.
Restaurant Industry catalogue, free.

About sixty of the uniforms in the general catalogue are in white and for women—trim little dresses (some of them maternity dresses) and pants suits, with white or pale stockings and white shoes to match. But there are also uniforms in color, and jackets and lab coats for men. Lighter uniforms in polyester and cotton cost under $10, and heavier ones in Dacron polyester knit jersey cost about $16.

FBS, 659 Main Street, New Rochelle, N.Y. 10801
Spring/Summer clothes catalogue, free. January 15.
Fall/Winter clothes, free. July 15.
"Summer House"/catalogue, free. March 15.
"Holiday" catalogue, free. September 15.

Clothes by mail for people who are "young, savvy and lazy about shopping" says the FBS fashion co-ordinator, a fair comment. These catalogues are just the thing for people who want to look more young and savvy than lazy but hate to shop. The clothes are a fine mixture of the understated with the new, they are modeled by skinny and smashing models, and are far more fashionable than many mail-order clothes.

For men, sporty-looking trousers cost between $15 and $20, shirts between $10 and $15, and there are sweaters, cotton-cord suits and coats too. For women, at this writing, there are trousers and vests, buckskin shirts and skirts, as well as caftans, long clingy knit dresses and opulent coats. Prices run from $6 for a floor-length cotton knit T-shirt to $160 for an almost floor-length sheepskin greatcoat.

FBS has recently started producing "Summer House" and "Holiday" catalogues with fanciful gifts for the home.

Peter Glenn of Vermont, Box 837, Montpelier, Vt. 05602
Color catalogue, free. Available September through December.

The Peter Glenn ski shops published a catalogue for the first time in 1973. It has a small range of good, casual, medium-priced clothes: buckskin jackets, heathery knit shirts and corduroy trousers for men; gray flannel suits and loden coats for women; striped jeans and sweaters for children. For skiing there are beautifully colored wind shirts; imported sweaters, including traditional hand knits from Denmark at about $45; parkas, warm-up pants and gloves; skis and wax kits.

Greek Island Ltd., 215 E. 49th Street, New York, N.Y. 10017
24-page catalogue, free.

This small but compact store puts out a nice catalogue which includes the clothes that they design themselves and have made up in Greece. The clothes are sophisticated versions of traditional styles—the *evzone* work shirt with wide sleeves and a belt, for men or women, at $25; Greek sailor's shirts for $10.50; a long hooded *kelebia* caftan, for men or women, at $22. For men there are shirts of various kinds, caftans, and hand-knitted sweaters; for women there is more: long skirts, shawls and dresses designed by Mario Forte and Anthea Johns.

Outdoor World, 129–139 East Elkhorn Avenue, P.O. Box 1880, Estes Park, Colo. 80517
Catalogue, free.

This Western catalogue has no Eastern frills, and the clothes, at least, are all the better for it. There is a very good stock of hopsack trousers, denim and corduroy jeans, tab and chambray shirts and cowhide jackets for men and women (and a few for children), all by Levi. Other items in the "all-American natural look" include leather bags, quantities of boots, including hand-cut, handsewn, hand-lasted trail boots; sheepskin and leather vests; "reservation," "gamblers," safari and even derby hats; corduroy and climbing knickers; overalls; and from the mountains of Mexico: hand-embroidered shirts and blouses.

Caroll Reed (Mail Order, Inc.), North Conway, N.H. 03860
24-page color catalogue "First Call for Spring," free.
40-page color catalogue "Spring/Summer," free.
16-page color catalogue "Summertime," free.
32-page color catalogue "First Call for Fall," free.
40-page color catalogue "Winter Holiday," free.

Caroll Reed started with ski equipment in 1936 but has gradually expanded and now sells, in several shops and by mail, discreetly affluent-looking country clothes for men, women and children—with a few ski outfits in the winter catalogue. The clothes, which are mainly separates, all look well made, are in clean-cut styles and unobstrusive patterns or, more often, solid colors—dark-blue, leaf-green, bright-red and beige seem to be the favorites. Dresses for women cost mainly between $20 and $50, and pants for men from $30 to $60.

Miller Stockman, Box 5407, Denver, Colo. 80217
72-page catalogue, some color, free. Spring, fall.

Fifty years ago Miller Stockman started to sell Western clothes by mail to ranchers who were unable to get

1

2

3

4

5

1 • *FBS* Clothes change each season, but these gowns in red or royal-blue acrylic knit with ribbed white collar and cuffs are typical FBS styles. Sizes 5 to 13, $12; children's sizes 4 to 14, $9.

2 • *FBS* Djellaba in navy, pale-green and blue, or orange, black and sand acetate jersey recently for sale. Sizes small, medium, large. $15.

3 • *Greek Island* Ribbed-wool stevedore's undervest in natural beige only. With short sleeves, $13.50; with three-quarter sleeves, $14.50.

4 • *FBS* Clothes change each season, but this nightgown in yellow or turquoise nylon is typical of FBS styles. $18.

5 • *Greek Island* Fully lined skirt and long sleeveless vest made of heavy cotton tapestry table covers with beige and cream flowers on dark-green or red background. Sizes 6 to 12; skirt $65, vest $75.

6

7

8

6 • *Norm Thompson* Wool-twill "Halibut shirt," with finished tails that can be worn in or out. $19.

7 • *Norm Thompson* Machine-washable "Shikari" jacket adapted from the classic bush coat, made of dirt-resistant cotton-and-nylon fabric. Five large pockets are closed with Velco fasteners that seal simply by being pressed. Men's sizes 36 to 48, women's sizes 8 to 20. $25.

8 • *Norm Thompson* Weather-repellent wool hat made by hand in Ireland, in gray or brown tweed. $14.50.

into town, but Western movies created such a demand for cowboy clothes that the firm now sends out a million catalogues a year and sells to cowboy fans as far away as Africa, Arabia and Japan. Stockman manufactures Western and imports English apparel and saddlery, and claims both to have the country's largest selection of Western wear and to stock "everything but the horse" for ranchers, farmers and equestrians as well as dudes (and some clothes for children). In the catalogue you will find English and Western saddles, bits, bridles, reins, spurs, "fast-action" holsters and belt sets, ropes and *cinchas* (the pros are using nylon lariats these days), as well as basic and inexpensive clothes by Pendleton, Levi-Strauss, Wrangler and Lee Rider, and Resistol, Dobbs West and Stetson hats. There are also duds such as frilly and decorated shirts, dresses for square dancers and country-band groups, and decorated leather belts and boots. Books on horses and rodeos are on sale, and riding clubs and posses can have their own insignia made up as patches.

Surma, 11 E. 7th Street, New York, N.Y. 10003
Leaflets for cossack shirts, ribbons and Easter-egg decorating, free.

This shop started in 1918 as a book and record shop in the Ukranian community on New York's Lower East Side, but gradually began to sell other things from the Slavic countries. Now Surma sells over a thousand imported ribbons for decorating clothes and needlework, and will send an order form with four sample ribbons that cost between $1 and $2.50 a yard. They also make cossack shirts and dresses decorated with the ribbons, in several different fabrics and black, blue, brown or burgundy, priced at $15 to $35.

Norm Thompson, 1805 N.W. Thurman Street, Portland, Oreg. 97209
40-page catalogue, some color, free. February.
80-page catalogue, some color, free. August.

Country clothes, often exclusively imported, are sold by this twenty-year-old mail-order firm; and even though I live in a city, I am overawed by the Norm Thompson blue-denim vagabond shirt, about $12.50. "This is no city shirt—but a real, rugged, don't-give-a-damn shirt for fishing, camping, boating—just plain having fun." And the brushed blue-denim schooner-cloth shikari jacket for men, copied from the jackets that were worn by "explorers, army officers, travelers, adventurers the world around." And the pure-wool Norm Thompson in-or-out Halibut shirt at $19 "first used by the Alaskan fishermen who wear their shirts through days of fierce storms," and the Norm Thompson Versatile Cruiser jacket at $23 "like the coats worn by the timber cruisers—men who spend their lives roaming the woods to check on timber resources." But even if you are looking for something slightly less imposing, you'll find English sweaters and raincoats, Irish hats and dresses, French workmen's overalls, rugged shoes, sheepskins, luggage, and a man's double-knit blazer suit for about $95, developed by the owner of Norm Thompson, who wanted a comfortable, packable, wrinkle-free suit for traveling.

The Tog Shop, Lester Square, Americus, Ga. 31709
96-page color catalogue, free. January, August.

The Tog Shop started off, twenty-two years ago, selling only robes and beachwear made out of terry cloth, but

9 • *Antartex* Coat with hood and toggles which can be fastened up to the neck, available in several different skins and colors. In dense sheepskin with ½″ wool, just over $200.

now, although about half the catalogue is devoted to terry dresses, shorts, jackets, skirts, jumpsuits and robes (some of them quite nice), the other half of the catalogue shows regular shoes and sportswear. Crisp sleeveless dresses, pleated skirts, and blazers, usually in solid colors, make up a no-nonsense collection of clothes for people who'd rather look neat than devastating. Prices for separates are between $20 and $30. There are one or two terry robes, jumpsuits and jackets for men, but most of the clothes are for women by Vera, David Crystal, and Gordon of Philadelphia.

For more clothes, see General—Large Stores and Mail-Order Houses and also Sports Equipment and Clothes.

LEATHER AND SHEEPSKIN

Antartex, 120 Greenwich Avenue, Greenwich, Conn. 06830
Coat and sundries catalogue, $1. August. Available during the winter.

This well-known Scottish firm sends their sheepskin coats by air freight to be sold through their American stores and by mail from Greenwich. About fifty styles are shown in the catalogue (including two coats for children aged two to eleven, prices $35 to $73). Prices are roughly $70 to $150 for jackets, and $170 to $240 for coats. Sheepskin slippers, hats and rugs are available (rugs include Shetland and Icelandic and prices go from $15 to $30, depending on size). You can also buy 3″ fur squares to make into crazy-quilt pillows, bags, or even rugs and coats.

The Deerskin Trading Post, 119 Foster Street, Peabody, Mass. 01960
84-page color catalogue, free. January, September.

A few years after a failed attempt to start a horoscopes-by-mail business, Mr. Henry Englehardt started selling deerskin moccasins and built *them* into a large mail-order business. The Deerskin Trading Post (not a real trading post, despite the man in Indonesia who sent a box of tea in exchange for a hat) is one of the largest retailers in the country of suede and leather. The catalogue shows quantities of leather coats (and a few sheepskin), jackets, shoes, gloves and hats for men and women in most standard styles and colors. For women there are also skirts, capes and handbags, and for children fringed "frontier jackets." The Deerskin Trading Post says that its prices are somewhat lower than comparable items in major department stores, and according to my calculations, prices do tend to be slightly but not dramatically lower here (and you do get a wider choice).

Leathercrafter, 303 E. 51st Street, New York, N.Y. 10022
32-page leather-chair brochure and 24-page handbag and luggage brochure, 50 cents for both.

This firm, which manufactures leather chairs, also has a small collection of unassuming bags and belts. Hand-cut, stained and waxed with no artificial lacquers or finishes, the bags should stay pliable for years; prices $5 to $25. There is also a traveling bar with four metal cups, four stirrers, an opener, a strainer and space for two bottles in a leather case for $42.

10

11

12

10 • *Bloom's Shoe Gallery* Brown leather sandal in sizes 5 to 10. $18.

11 • *Bloom's Shoe Gallery* "Lady Stockholm," a perforated patent-leather top in red, blue or white with a wooden sole. Women's sizes 4 to 10, $9.95; children's sizes 3 to 10, $8.95.

12 • *Kalsø Earth Shoe* "Demi-boot," one of several shoes designed to give the wearer correct posture and, among other things, to prevent backache. This one is available in brown leather, and brown or tan suede. $37.50.

SHOES

Belgian Shoes, 60 E. 56th Street, New York, N.Y. 10022
Leaflet, free.

Entirely handmade shoes for men and women have been imported by this firm for forty years. Casual shoes for men and women are $30 to $50. Formal shoes for women—styles restrained. Prices less restrained: about $85 a pair.

Bloom's Shoe Gallery, 311 Sixth Avenue, New York, N.Y. 10014
Brochure, free.

One of the few places that sells "with-it" shoes by mail, Bloom's calls itself a Greenwich Village landmark and says that President Kennedy ordered boots for Jackie by mail from the White House and that Dick Gregory, Bob Dylan, Rod Steiger, Dustin Hoffman and Zero Mostel all have been inside the store (no news as to whether they actually bought). But at least they looked at the handsome hand-made water-buffalo leather sandals for about $12, clogs from Sweden, boots from England and Finland, and shoes from Italy, Greece, Spain and India for prices between $20 and $45.

English Boot Shop, 297 Danbury Road, Route 7, Wilton, Conn. 06897
20-page catalogue, 50 cents.

This firm specializes in selling shoes by mail and stocks both famous brands, such as Clarks desert boots and wallabees, and its own label shoes, which they state cost "considerably less than comparable shoes" in retail shops. Their Monk Strap shoe for men, for instance, sells for $32, as opposed to $40 elsewhere. Several models of men's shoes are available, as well as boots for men and women in their private label, costing as little as $28. No other shoes for women are available except for the Clarks models.

Kalsø Earth Shoe, 117 E. 17th Street, New York, N.Y. 10003.
Leaflet, free.

The clumpy-looking Kalsø earth shoe was developed by a Danish yoga teacher, Anne Kalsø, who studied the relationship between posture and respiration, and while in a Hindu monastery in Brazil noticed that in the footprint of the Indians on the earth, the heel always sank lower than the toes. Back in Denmark she experimented with this principle and after ten years developed the earth shoe, which does, indeed, leave the heel lower than the toes. The leaflet quotes raves from the press and warns that wearers will feel off balance and have stiff leg muscles for a few days while they adjust to the new way of walking. There are sandals and shoes for about $24 and $36.

Pedi-Mold of New York, 565 Fifth Avenue, New York, N.Y. 10017
Leaflet, free.

Pedi-Mold advises people with tired feet to walk barefoot. If they can't do that, the next-best thing is to wear Pedi-Mold sandals, which have a cupped platform of cork, a lining rim for secure fit, a wide, adjustable leather strap and plenty of room for the toes. The sandals come in four different colors and cost about $14 a pair. Pedi-Mold also has foam-rubber arch-supporting insoles for flat and high-heeled shoes, and pads to stop heels from slipping out of shoes.

The Slipper House, 1200 Ala Moana Center, Honolulu, Hawaii 96814
Brochure, free.

Enough sandals to shoe an army, this firm has for twenty years been selling thongs and slip-ons made by eight Hawaiian manufacturers. Most prices are from around $2 to around $10, and styles vary so much that there should be something to please everyone. The least expensive are simple fiber crisscross slippers at $1.50; the most expensive are handsome open sandals in pigskin. Sizes 4 to 12, and there are a few flip-flops for children.

Super Sandal, 9 Maine Street, Bar Harbour, Maine 04609
Brochure, free.

This small store in Maine makes sandals to your own measurements through the winter months, at prices just over $20 per pair. They also, with the help of an eighty-two-year-old shoe-boot maker, make a boot to order and a woman's low-heeled lace-up shoe. Ready-made they stock hand-stitched wallets, billfolds, checkbook covers, and rugged handbags and shoulder bags in stiff or soft cowhide at prices from $30 and up. Plain belts with brass buckles cost $8 and up.

UMBRELLAS

Stanley Novak Co., 186 Fifth Avenue, New York, N.Y. 10010
Brochure, free.

A purveyor of walking sticks and canes, whose offerings are more straightforward than those of Uncle Sam's Umbrella Shop. These canes seem, for the most part, to be aimed at those who use them for walking, though a few appear more decorative or theatrical. A plain ash cane costs only $3 and most of the others are in the $4–$8 range (with police whistles attached as optional extras, for $1). Posher silver and gold canes, for the opera, etc., are from $16 to $24.

Uncle Sam Umbrella Shop, 110 W. 45th Street, New York, N.Y. 10019
Price list, free.

"Makers and importers of walking sticks, umbrellas and parasols," says this stationery, next to a picture of Uncle Sam carrying an umbrella. Founded in 1866 by a German immigrant, and still run by a member of the Simon family, this out-of-the-ordinary store stocks over forty thousand walking sticks and an equal number of umbrellas, only a few of which are shown in the brochure. Traditional canes and walking sticks are available, but clearly, Uncle Sam is happiest carrying, if not a big stick, a Malacca cane or a shillelagh. The former, the store's most popular item, costs $15, while imported Irish Black Thorns are $8 and up. An evening cane of black ebony costs $20, and sport-seat canes run from $7.50 to $35. Umbrellas are $5 and up and come in all the traditional shapes and sizes as well as in giant sizes for doormen or in many colors for golfing.

Uncle Sam made Charlie Chaplin's cane and has specialized in theatrical items for years, so if you're planning a musical comedy you can buy the traditional parasol that's always twirled by chorus lines, at $2.25 or $24 a dozen, while the accompanying country cane, the kind that's used with a straw hat, costs a mere $9 a dozen.

For home theatricals, Uncle Sam lists "bull whips, carriage whips, cat-o-nine tails and popular riding accessories." How much of Uncle Sam's commerce is due to selling these, I don't know, but seven different whips are illustrated, not to mention the riding crops and other things which are intended for horses and described as "not meant to hurt . . . merely frighten." Working in this atmosphere seems to have its effects, since Uncle Sam's order blank is headed: "We obey your orders, quickly." This applies not just to purchases, but to a repair service (for umbrellas).

FOR MEN

Brooks Brothers, Madison Avenue at 44th Street, New York, N.Y. 10017
32- to 28-page black-and-white catalogues, free. Three times a year.

Brooks Brothers is America's oldest men's clothier, founded in 1818, and one of its best-known. What I didn't know is that Brooks does a large mail-order business. Most of Brooks' clothing, including the famous "Brooks Brothers suit," is made for it exclusively, and its catalogue gives an excellent sampling of the store's wares. Brooks' "conservative good taste" is not inexpensive, but prices vary. Cotton shirts can be bought from $8.50 or $15, and the less expensive ones seemed more attractive to me, though one of the few drawbacks of ordering by mail is that only a few shops will send sample materials, such as L. L. Bean (see Sports section). Brooks suits are in the more expensive $190–$225 range, though some of their outerwear, such as their popular (and in New York omnipresent) alpaca-lined greatcoat, is much more reasonably priced: $100 for the full-length coat, $70 for the short nylon parka. Brooks' Christmas catalogue has a large choice of gifts, such as luggage, belts, wallets, etc., as well as things like fur hats that may be hard to find outside the major cities. There is also in each catalogue a section devoted to boys' clothing and a few clothes for women.

Chipp, Custom Tailors and Furnishers, 14 E. 44th Street, New York, N.Y. 10017
20-page color catalogue, free. Twice a year.

Chipp is one of Madison Avenue's posh clothiers, smaller than Brooks Brothers and, they feel, somewhat less conservative, but in the same league. They sell by mail through a small but thorough mail-order catalogue and also send exhibits around the country of their latest styles. As would be expected, their clothes are costly, though there are more expensive stores in New York: their suits are around $150 to $170, but these are tailored in England, often using all-wool double knits. A full range of men's clothes is listed, most of it in the traditional Madison Avenue gray-flannel suit but with a number of more daring departures, the kind of sports jacket that will cause a flurry of comment at the golf club.

Eleganza, Manley Street, Brockton, Mass. 02403
96-page color brochure, free.

"They won't stop looking at you in this coat," says the Eleganza catalogue, and they won't stop looking at you whatever you choose from this collection of dramatically styled apparel and imported footwear. Shirts have whopping pleated sleeves, hats are wide-brimmed or jumbo, trousers have contrasting patch pockets, coats are made of velvet, and everything comes in purple and often bright red, green and blue. The shoes are practically all high-heeled and two-toned. Most trousers cost about $20, shirts about $18, and shoes just under $30.

The Village Squire, 49 W. 8th Street, New York, N.Y. 10011
Illustrated brochure, free.

The Village Squire specializes in the kind of men's clothing that my children would call "groovy," and someone of an earlier period, "dandyish." The store sells clothes that for the most part it designs itself and has manufactured. It has, among its specialties, thousands of swimsuits; indeed, the first six pages of its brochure feature dozens of nearly naked, uniformly dazzling young men clad either in these bikinis or in equally brief undergarments called minims, brief strings, and the like. The bathing suits have equally suggestive names and promise to do all sorts of things, e.g., "immortalizes the Tarzan image of masculine pulchritude." Well, $9.95 may seem a lot for a bit of cloth, but if it does that . . .

Outer garments, by contrast, tend toward the maxi look: a flared calfskin double-breasted coat for $140, bell bottoms galore, hour-glass jackets in velvets, and bold-checked Edwardian suits. The descriptions are as suggestive as those of Frederick's of Hollywood and may limit the audience, but the prices are not exorbitant and the fashions are certainly not those you'd be likely to find in many places.

13 • *Brooks Brothers* The two most popular things in the Brooks Brothers catalogues: oxford button-down-collar cotton shirt with single cuffs and left breast pocket—in white, $12.50, and in blue, pink, yellow, green, stone, ecru and peach, $13; and silk rep ties in various color combinations—3½″ wide, $7.50; 4″ wide, $8.50.

SPECIAL SIZES

Lewis Bryant, Inc., 2300 Southeastern Avenue, Indianapolis, Ind. 46201
48-page catalogue, free.

Clothes for the stout or tall, and the tall-and-stout man. Prices are much lower than at the Imperial Wear and slightly lower than at the King-Size Co.; shirts start at $6, trousers at $9, but there is nowhere near the same choice as at King-Size.

Hitchcock Shoes Inc., 165 Beal Street, Hingham, Mass. 02043
24-page color catalogue, free. Spring/Summer, Winter/Fall.

Hitchcock sells shoes and boots in widths from double E to six E, made for them on specially designed and proportioned lasts. These variously shaped lasts are given different names, so that once a customer has discovered which fits him best, he will always be able to choose shoes in the same last (though different styles) and know that the shoe will fit. Prices for shoes are between $20 and $30. Slippers, sports shoes, boots and ski boots are also sold.

14

15

14 • *White's Shoe Shop* No. 375. Black greased uppers, Vibram soles and heels over full oak-leather middle soles. This shoe originated in Europe for mountain climbing and has non-slip soles. Standard sizes, $67.15; made to measure, $10 extra.

15 • *White's Shoe Shop* No. 75. Uppers of best-grade black kip. Soles of heavy calking leather over half-length middle sole. The heels are high and set well under for the greater arch strength of a short arch span. Standard sizes, $67.65; made to measure, $10 extra.

Imperial Wear, 48 W. 48th Street, New York, N.Y. 10036
40-page catalogue, free.

The store for above-average men, with above-average incomes, sells clothes by well-known manufacturers in sizes 46 to 60 regular and long; portlies in regular, short and long, and extra long sizes 40 to 54. Suits from makers such as GGG, Petrocelli, Botany and John Vance cost between $110 and $220, trousers cost $16 to $40. There are shirts from Excello, John Weitz, Manhattan and Geoffrey Beene; coats (including suede and leather) by Eagle, Lakeland and Zero King; raincoats by London Fog; cashmere sweaters, mohair tuxedos and a couple of pages of boots and shoes.

The King-Size Co., 613 King-Size Building, 24 Forest Street, Brockton, Mass. 02402
120-page catalogue, free for anyone over 6'3" tall or whose shoe size is from 10AAA to 16EEE. Catalogues sent out nine times a year.

Everything except suits for the tall man, thin or fat—from watertight overalls to ruffled dress shirts, including Arrow shirts, Shetland sweaters, corduroy jackets, insulated sports clothes, work clothes, underwear, pajamas, shoes and boots, and even a shoe bag for outsize shoes and an extra large down-filled sleeping bag. Plenty of everything to choose from. Shirts start at $8, trousers at $13.

White's Shoe Shop, W. 430 Main Avenue, Spokane, Wash. 99201
20-page brochure, free.

Excellent, expensive handmade boots with extra high, strong arches, which make them comfortable for rough country and standing on hard surfaces, cost from $52 to $77. They can be made to measure for an extra $10, and people with really unusually shaped feet can have lasts made. These can be used for a lifetime, but cost $75 to $150 and you have to go to Spokane for at least one day.

FOR WOMEN

Acadian Crafts Association, Inc., 29 St. Catherine Street, Madawaska, Maine 04756
Adult clothes catalogue, free.
Baby clothes price list, free.

The Acadians came from northern France in the sixteenth and seventeenth centuries. In the eighteenth century George II decreed that they must swear allegiance to the crown, and when they refused, had them moved from their homes and scattered throughout the Colonies. Many of the original Acadians resettled in along the St. John River in Maine, and among other traditions, kept up the custom of hand-crocheting complete wardrobes for babies.

In 1970 a women's group, whose members were descendants of the original Acadians, had the idea of getting together to sell their work, and managed with a lot of hard work and the help of VISTA and the St. John Valley Action Council to start this nonprofit and marketing co-operative. At the moment, about forty-eight women are crocheting, and there is a waiting list of people who will join as soon as there is a greater demand for the work.

The co-op sells completely handmade baby clothes, crocheted in machine-washable Orlon yarn—pastel-colored blankets, sweater sets, dresses, ponchos and scarves, all for below $10. And for women, brightly colored ponchos, shawls, vests, scarves, evening skirts and beach costumes in Orlon or wool for prices mainly over $20, and up to $125 for a long skirt and matching shawl in wool. Bedspreads and afghans, or anything else, can be made in any color or pattern you want.

When I talked to the Acadian manager, Theresa Violette, she said that they are hoping to put out color leaflets but at the moment have just a descriptive price list for their baby clothes, and about three hundred copies left of a black-and-white catalogue for the women's clothes. She hopes the color leaflets will be ready by the time this book appears, but please don't be surprised if you have to wait.

Johnny Appleseed's, Beverly, Mass. 01915
Color catalogues, free. January, February, August, September.

This well-known firm sends catalogues to one million "discriminating customers" throughout America. Unfortunately the clothes are drawn, not photographed, so it's hard to see what they really look like. Prices are mainly between $10 and $45 for a good assortment of fairly classic separates, dresses, pants and suits in synthetic fabrics, lots of checks and plaids and some floral designs. The colors don't look very good, but that may well be the fault of the reproductions.

Elegance International, 152–20 Rockaway Boulevard, Baisley Park, N.Y. 11434
170-page color catalogue of patterns, $3.95.
170-page color catalogue with fabric swatches, $12.95.
84-page color "Boutique" clothes catalogue, $2.50.

Elegance International has two big catalogues of patterns and fabrics, and the "Boutique" catalogue of ready-to-wear clothes. The "Boutique" shows about a hundred crisp continental shirts, trousers and dresses well photographed in excellent color. Possibly because of the very good presentation, which makes the catalogue look like a fashion magazine, these clothes are more tempting than most (and more expensive). A skinny little bare-back dress in orange, green or purple synthetic jersey costs $35; a really lovely short-sleeved summer suit in beige silk, lined in matching taffeta, $155. A short-sleeved black polyester trouser suit is $145. The clothes come in sizes 10 to 20, and belts, bags, sweaters and jewelry are also sold.

Frederick's of Hollywood, 6608 Hollywood Boulevard, Hollywood, Calif. 90028
72-page catalogue, 50 cents. Two-year subscription, $1.50.

After years on the periphery of American life, Frederick's, like *Playboy*, has successfully moved into the mainstream of American life. What was once a small mail-order operation has expanded to sixty-three shops and an annual mailing of 7.5 million catalogues. "The Frederick's customer puts self-beautification and improvement first at any price. She dresses to please the men in her life . . . Frederick's is world-famous for offering women fashions that are ultra-feminine, glamorous and unique."

The catalogue itself is for the most part illustrated with incredibly slim and incredibly busty young women, in a style that is halfway between 1940's pinups and the

16 • *Treasures of Asia* Long cotton dress, "Denise," in color combinations of cranberry and white, or yellow and white. Sizes 5 to 15, $24. A short version of the same dress, "Frances," costs $18.

17 • *Treasures of Asia* "Ketti" multicolor-plaid crinkle-cotton safari shirt with elasticized pants, mainly in blue, yellow, red, brown, green or purple plaid. Sizes 5 to 15, $22. Shirt only, $6.

early fashion drawings of teen-age girls. The few photographs are, of necessity, anticlimactic, and Frederick's knows enough about fantasy to have as few of these as possible. Satins—or their modern equivalents, see-throughs—and push-up bras abound, all with a running commentary that is strictly pre-Women's Lib: "Every man's a voyeur at heart! So encourage his peeking in this sensational baby doll that's open all down the front," or, "Baby stars in hot pants romper! No little kiddy stuff here. Low V neck Empire bustline dramatizes the OOMPH of your cleavage." If, by some miracle, you don't have the superhuman figure required for most of these garments, Frederick's offers girdles, bras and other devices that will "shape" you properly, or if this isn't enough, either, to make those dreams come true, there are falsies "for the girl who can't make it on her own . . ." and the first false bottom that I've seen since nineteenth-century England, "slip these removable polyester hi-rise pads . . . and he'll think every curvable inch is really, truly you." One of the classic American wish books.

Honeybee, 566 Seventh Avenue, New York, N.Y. 10018
30-page brochure, free. Spring, summer, fall, winter.

Everything looks new and snazzy in the Honeybee brochure. The clothes—which are aimed at the young-in-attitude twenties-to-thirties women with "contemporary but understated" tastes—are sketchily drawn on wispy girls with billowing hair. The average customer is very active, says Honeybee proudly, career-minded, plays tennis, swims, etc., all of which keeps her fit for sizes 4 to 12, though I notice Honeybee does stock some 13's too. The winter brochures I looked at had pale woolly knits in all the latest shapes for $20 and under; wide-legged cuffed pants, $30, matching a shirt jacket for $40; floppy satin shirts, velvet blazers, shimmery long dresses and pants suits for evening wear—all to be snatched up quickly by the trimmest of customers, as stock is kept for only six to eight weeks after brochures appear.

J. Jill Ltd., Southfield, Mass. 01259
12-page brochure, free.

A small collection of unusual, deliberately old-fashioned country clothes for evening wear in cotton, denim and wool. Ten different evening skirts cost from $15 to $30 each, in fabrics printed with small patterns taken from old Meissen or Staffordshire porcelain, Victorian Calico, or in one case older farmer's-almanac prints. Another, more severe group of clothes is made from imported Swedish fabrics in traditional shapes. A shirt dress in navy, brick or spicy-brown is based on a workman's shirt in Stockholm's Nordiska Museum; a skirt in bolster stripes is based on a dressy skirt worn on Saturday evenings. There is also a long, narrow mohair coat with pewter buttons from Norway in navy, black, dark gray or red for about $85.

Lanz of California Inc., 6150 Wilshire Boulevard, Los Angeles, Calif. 90048
Color leaflet, free. Spring, fall, Christmas.

Lanz of Austria was selling so many dirndls to American tourists in Salzburg that in 1935 they opened a dirndl and peasant-blouse shop in New York, and a few years later another in Los Angeles. The clothes that they now manufacture and sell in Los Angeles still have traces, but faint ones, of the Austrian dirndl, in a tendency to puffy sleeves, gathered skirts and little-flower prints. A few dresses, skirts and blouses are illustrated on their mail-order leaflet at prices mainly between $12 and $65, and so is their popular old-fashioned flanelette nightgown, which each year is made in a new print.

Maharani Creations, 7158 Fifth Avenue, Scottsdale, Ariz. 85251
16-page color catalogue, free.

Maharani sells flowing, exotic clothes for romantic evenings at home. A typical page shows a Maharani Afro for $45, a Mylar lamé caftan for $45, a Grecian goddess hostess in which "you'll feel like Mr. O's favorite," and a chiffon djellaba "based on the Moroccan djellaba worn for centuries by Moorish Turkish princesses." Jingly jewelry and sexy sandals also on sale.

Old Pueblo Traders, 622 Country Club, Tucson, Ariz. 85716
32-page catalogue, 50 cents, refundable.

This twenty-five-year-old firm started out selling moccasins, but as Indian merchandise became harder to get, went into fashion. Most of the clothes are colorful and occasionally flowery casual clothes in synthetic fabrics. Typical titles are "casbah culottes," "Acapulco blouses" and "mucho poncho." Prices for dresses are between $20 and $40, though quite a few are cheaper.

Pinecroft, Juniper Ridge Fabrics, Dunbarton, N.H. 03301
Leaflet with color swatches, 35 cents.

Mr. and Mrs. Lord import virgin wool from Canada and weave it by hand into a very beautiful range of pale and powdery fabrics—twenty-two solid colors and twenty-two small checks and plaids. You can buy the fabrics by the yard with knitting yarn to match, or else the Lords will make them up for you. A custom skirt costs $21 and up, and a hand-knitted sweater $24 and up. Both of these normally take about three weeks to make. Jumpers, capes, vests, ponchos and afghans can also be made up from the fabric, or crocheted from the yarn. Prices on request.

Treasures of Asia Ltd., 13 E. 30th Street, New York, N.Y. 10016
24-page catalogue, 25 cents.

The name isn't auspicious, but in fact, Treasures of Asia imports very pretty and inexpensive dresses specially made for them in Afghanistan, India, Pakistan and Turkey. The catalogue that I looked at had embroidered smocks and blouses, velvet battle jackets and long cotton dresses in beautiful prints. Everything in sizes 5 to 15, and most prices below $25.

SPECIAL SIZES

Lane Bryant, Inc., 2300 Southeastern Avenue, Indianapolis, Ind. 46201
120-page catalogue, free.
80-page "Tall Girl" catalogue, free.

Lane Bryant was a dressmaker who, at a customer's request, made a maternity dress at a time when pregnant women didn't use maternity dresses because they didn't appear in public. A few years later the Lane Bryant company, which had begun to mass-produce maternity dresses, put an ad in the New York *Herald:*

"It is no longer the fashion for expectant mothers to stay in seclusion. Doctors, nurses and psychologists agree that at this time a woman should think and live as normally as possible. To do this, she must go among other people. She must look like other people.

"Lane Bryant has originated maternity apparel in which the expectant mother may feel as other women feel because she looks as other women look."

The next day the entire stock of street maternity wear was sold out.

Some years later Lane Bryant received a letter asking for "some ingenious man to take pity on stout women," and after studying the measurements of two hundred thousand women on the books of an insurance firm, and discovering that 40 percent were overweight, Lane Bryant went into the outsized women's clothes for which it is well known. Unfortunately, in spite of the pioneering start, the clothes are still only clothes to be bought for lack of a more exciting alternative. They are inexpensive (dresses are under $20) and quite a few of the styles are acceptably classic.

There are also catalogues for tall women, listing clothes, shoes and stockings.

Hayes, 2300 Southeastern Avenue, Indianapolis, Ind. 46201
80-page catalogue of half sizes.

Hayes is a division of Lane Bryant and sells clothes in half sizes. Like the Lane Bryant clothes, these are inexpensive but designs and fabrics tend to be uninspired.

Mooney and Gilbert Inc., 31 W. 57th Street, New York, N.Y. 10019
12-page catalogue, free.

Specialists in the "long and narrow aristocratic" foot, Mooney and Gilbert say they have the largest selection anywhere for the slender heel. All of their shoes and boots are available to 5A width and many to 6A. Prices are between $20 and $36.

Roaman's, Saddle Brook, N.J. 07662
80-page color catalogue, free. January.
40-page flyer, free. April 1.
80-page color catalogue, free. July.

Roaman's says that it tries to bring to the larger woman the same youthfully styled fashion that is available to the woman who wears a junior or a misses size, and their clothes in sizes 14½ to 28½ and 38 to 60 are certainly worth looking at, with quite a few dresses, trousers and tops that are in solid colors and simply cut. Dresses cost mostly between $10 and $20, and there are glamorous nightgowns, hostess outfits and shoes to size 12EEE.

Solby Bayes, 45 Winter Street, Boston, Mass. 02108
20-page catalogue, free. Spring, fall.

The "Home of Sizes 1 to 14—Widths AAAAAA to EEEEE," as the catalogue says, sells quality footwear: shoes, boots and slippers in unusual widths for women, at prices between $20 and $30. The styles look dependable rather than exciting.

18 • *Snugli Cottage Industries* Cotton infant carrier, "Snugli," can be used as a front pouch, as a nursing sling or as a back pack. It can also be expanded to fit children up to the age of two. $28.95, including postage, and unlike most other things photographed in this book, it can be ordered direct without checking the price.

CHILDREN'S CLOTHES AND MATERNITY SUPPLIES

Jean Gale, Inc., 535 Madison Avenue, New York, N.Y. 10022
Leaflet, free.

This posh little shop says that they "cater to an elegant clientele and have enjoyed a very nice reputation." They sell linen and classic clothes for little girls; the leaflet shows plaid skirts, about $12, and wool sweaters, about $9, gingham dresses with linen collars, beige wool jumpers, red coats trimmed with black velvet, about $50, and a black velvet party dress trimmed with imported lace for about $33. Many of the clothes are specially made for Jean Gale, and sizes go from baby clothes up to 14.

Maternity Products Corporation, P.O. Box 6101, Stanford, Calif. 94305
Leaflet, free.

A hollowed-out cushion, developed and sold by a medical engineer, is intended to relieve back strain and to provide a comfortable way for pregnant women to lie with their stomachs supported by the pillow. It costs $11, including postage.

Rabbit Hole Productions, 1510 Mariposa, Boulder, Colo. 80302
Brochure planned, free. March, August.

The wives of two Colorado University professors started business in what they call "the usual way" by selling things that they made to friends, then to nearby shops. At the moment they are planning a small elegant catalogue which will illustrate the children's clothes they make, as well as toys made by themselves and friends. The clothes they describe as romantic but durable, and they sent me pictures of a patchwork midi-skirt which reverses to solid-colored fabric; a yellow piqué hand-embroidered sundress with the back cut out, and a bonnet; a navy-blue dress embroidered by hand with pots of geraniums. They also make to special order Christmas dresses of velvet and antique lace, and communion dresses in styles which can be worn again later. No prices were given to me for the clothes, but I imagine that with all the hand embroidery, they are not low. Another specialty is designing complete wardrobes for "children who are going abroad for a summer or a year and are not traveling with great numbers of steamer trunks."

The toy designs often come from "delving through old magazines and maiden aunts' scrapbooks" and include enormous animal pillows, in the shapes of a walrus, a hippo, an elephant and a buffalo. Prices for stuffed toys run from $6 for a mouse with a parasol to $20 for Mary Poppins with carpetbag and removable clothes, even gloves, stockings and high-button shoes. Toys made by a friend are in wood and include a Trojan horse, complete with conquering Greeks, a Punch and Judy show, a jack-in-the-box and puzzles.

Sears, Roebuck and Co., Department 139, 2650 E. Olympic Boulevard, Los Angeles, Calif. 90051, or Sears, Roebuck and Co., Department 139, 4640 Roosevelt Boulevard, Philadelphia, Pa. 19132
General spring catalogue, free. January.
General fall catalogue, free. June.

If you haven't seen the Sears catalogue lately, you'll be surprised at the children's clothes—they have improved beyond recognition. Instead of the old all-pervasive appliqués, buttons and bows, there is a general movement toward simplicity and a new "designer-inspired" Winnie the Pooh collection, which Sears says is "made of the best-quality fabrics . . . checked and double-checked for washability, color retention and shrinkage control." They and many of the other clothes are in good colors, smart casual styles and still modestly priced.

Snugli Cottage Industries, Inc., Route 1, Box 685, Evergreen, Colo. 80439
Leaflet, free.

The Snugli baby carrier was designed by a young couple who wanted to carry their baby around like the African mothers they had seen while in the Peace Corps. The carrier is made of cloth and can be used for newborn babies as it supports the head—colicky babies can be held and carried around with less strain for the mother, and children up to the age of two can use it. Highly recommended. $28.95.

Stone Free Kids, 243 Columbus Avenue, New York, N.Y. 10023
Leaflet planned, free.

Stone Free Kids sells an informal collection of clothes for children up to the age of seven at prices mainly between $5 and $15. The owner says that the leaflet will show an enormous number of work clothes and overalls, even for babies; "Flight Suits" with plain or appliqued jackets; clothes from India, Pakistan and Mexico; and for $16, hand-knitted sweaters with any child's name knitted in.

19 • *Shaker Workshops* (see Reproduction Furniture in the House section) A copy of the classic Shaker cloak made in wool with a cape collar, lined hood, pleated back and 3″-wide sash. Deep-blue, cranberry-red or mink-brown (swatches, 25 cents). $125.

7
COLLECTING

ARTIFACTS

Aladdin House, 648 Ninth Avenue, New York, N.Y. 10036
12-page catalogue, 50 cents.

Aladdin House specializes in antiquities at low prices, selling small items from archaeological digs which even museums and large antique dealers relish and which can be of interest to people who would like to have something from the ancient world. Aladdin started by selling primarily small items, coins, arrowheads, scarabs, amulets, but has since begun to sell more expensive items as well. In fact, some of the pieces, of extremely fine quality, range in the thousands of dollars. Aladdin will send you a Certificate of Attribution upon request, and there is a two-week money-back guarantee.

Having said all of this, I should add that many of the items in the Aladdin catalogue are lovely and may well be bargains. I particularly liked a small statue of a draped lady from Turkey, dated 200 B.C., for $295, and ancient Indian statuary at roughly the same price. In addition to statues there are a great many lamps, jewels, glass pieces and examples of art from the ancient Mediterranean world as well as Asia and Latin America.

Casa de Mexico, Box 411, Donna, Tex. 78537
Price list, 50 cents; refundable.

Casa de Mexico is a one-man operation, near the Mexican border, that specializes both in Mexican and in old Western items. The Mexican are for the most part pre-Columbian artifacts, which the owner says are genuine to the best of his belief. He offers a money-back guarantee on everything and will send photos, charging a 50 cent fee for each photo of objects under $10. A heartening number are in that price range, with arrowheads costing $1.50 for four, obsidian knives going for 35 cents, axes $5 and up depending on size, and clay figures $3 and up.

In addition to these, there is a very nice selection of old ironware; stirrups, spurs, branding irons, horse bits, keys and flatirons, ranging from $2.50 to $10. Brass spittoons are now rare collector's items, but you can be put on a waiting list for "vase types" ranging from $10 to $25, depending on size. An intriguing collection at very reasonable prices.

AUTOGRAPHS

Walter A. Benjamin, Autographs, Inc., 790 Madison Avenue, New York, N.Y. 10021
"The Collector" catalogue, free after purchase of $25; or $5 subscription.

Founded in 1887, this is the oldest firm in the United States dealing with autograph letters and manuscripts. Benjamin stocks thousands, ranging in price from a dollar to several thousand. "The Collector," which has been published since the firm began, lists a small fraction of the holdings and appears four to five times a year. In addition there are supplements listing the less expensive items stocked by Benjamin.

It is difficult for a noncollector to understand the prices, which seem to follow no clear system. Bars of music signed by composers, for instance, will run from $100 for Francis Poulenc to close to $1,000 for Brahms and Tchaikovsky, and hit the jackpot of $1,500 for Verdi and Wagner.

Letters depend more on content and the sentiments being expressed, a great many of the items for sale being, understandably, formal notes of thanks, but some being of intrinsic interest. A note from President Herbert Hoover declining an invitation is $25, while one from Queen Marie of Rumania denying that she was shot in a family quarrel goes for $100. Benjamin is particularly strong in American history and has autographs from all the American Presidents and a large number of lesser figures, some of whom are ignominiously consigned to the $2 category ("no approvals, no returns"—it seems somehow the judgment of history).

BUTTERFLIES

The Butterfly Company, 51-17 Rockaway Beach Boulevard, Far Rockaway, N.Y. 11691
Color catalogue, $1.

This is the world's largest dealer in butterflies and moths, and its catalogue shows some nine hundred of them (plus beetles) in full color, a very handsome item in itself. These include insects from North America and Europe as well as such exotic places as New Guinea, Australia, Africa and Malaysia. All are listed by their name, and range in price from 35 cents to $15, but for beginners there are sets of twenty-five North American butterflies for $5 or fifty Peruvian for $10, or if you prefer, a Beetle Grabbag of a hundred beetles for $25.

The Butterfly Company also sells the requisite equipment, from nets to mounting kits, display cases and a number of books. The company is also interested in buying or trading these insects in quantity and is willing to answer any questions on entomology or lepidoptera.

DOLLS

Mark Farmer Co., 36 Washington Avenue, Pt. Richmond, Calif. 94801
48-page doll catalogue, 50 cents.
Miniature catalogue, 25 cents.

Very well known to doll collectors, Mark Farmer sells china and bisque doll parts, undressed dolls and dressed dolls, all with an old-fashioned look about them, quite unlike most dolls available. Some are sweet little creatures that are suitable for older children, others are fashion dolls to be elaborately dressed and used as decorations. There is one model which you can buy different wigs for, and different dress patterns, and make a collection of First Ladies—up to Patricia Ryan Nixon. Sizes go from 4″ to 30″, and prices from about $5 for the smallest kit to about $40 for the largest doll dressed. Patterns for dresses, shoe kits, glass domes for displaying the dolls, and collections of miniature furniture are available, and some doll repairs are made.

Standard Doll Co., 23-83 31st Street, Long Island City, N.Y. 11105
40-page catalogue, 25 cents.

Eyes, legs, arms, faces and wigs are on sale here for doll makers, and for doll dressers there is even more: modern and antique replica undressed baby, toddler, pre-teen and teen dolls—black, white and Indian for under $1 each. There is also fancy fabric, such as satin lace and tulle, and trimmings, beads and sequins, buttons and buckles and tiny zippers. Patterns to make clothes and rag dolls are available, as well as instruction books.

1 • *Casa de Mexico* An old but not antique charcoal iron, 7″ by 8″ high. $10.

FOSSILS

Malick's Fossils, Inc., 5514 Plymouth Road, Baltimore, Md. 21214
90-page catalogue, $2. Published annually.

I hesitate to list Malick's under "Collections," since its catalogue is so clearly an instrument of serious scientific work, but it does serve to show the ways in which buying by mail can place the amateur on an equal footing with the country's largest museums and research establishments. The Malick's catalogue is aimed at those who know exactly what they want and should not be sent for by the rank beginner, but for a serious collector or researcher it is a perfect tool. Its prices seem extraordinarily reasonable compared to what one sees in stores, most of the items listed being well under a dollar.

Malick's lists animal and plant fossils, classified scientifically so that under Mollusks you will find eight pages of gastropods starting with the family Acteocinidae, etc. Each item is listed according to its period, formation, locale (where it was found), number in stock and unit price. It is certainly the most thorough and carefully set out list imaginable.

As so often happens, however, there is another aspect to Malick's that may appeal to people who have no real interest in fossils as such, and that is the section devoted to artifacts of Early Man. This includes not only arrowheads, knives, and the like, all very reasonably priced, but some beautiful terra-cotta figurines from Mexico, fertility figures from Siam, pottery, and so on. These are, of course, much more expensive, but are definitely worth looking into as a unique and obviously very reliable source of primitive art.

There is also a selection of books related to Fossils and Artifacts.

For more fossils, see Dover in this section, under Shells.

2 • *Malick's Fossils* Shark tooth, **Carcharodon megalodon,** Miocene period, Calvert formation, Plum Point, Maryland. Similar pieces cost from $10 to $70.

3 • *Malick's Fossils* Trilobite, **Phacops rana milleri,** Devonian period. Silica shale formation, Silica, Ohio. Similar pieces cost from $15 to $20.

4

5

6

7

4 • *Chestnut Hill Studio* Miniature stoves in wood and metal simulating cast iron. *Left to right:* country-store stove, parlor stove (exact copy of a Victorian stove), cook stove and Shaker stove. Prices between $10 and $30.

5 • *Chestnut Hill Studio* Miniature oil paintings on fine linen, mounted and framed in gilt frames. Portraits, landscapes, seascapes and still lifes, and often reproductions of actual paintings are for sale at prices between $15 and $30.

6 • *Chestnut Hill Studio* Miniature mahogany clocks in various antique styles are available from $3 to $18.

7 • *Woody's Handcrafted Miniatures* Miniature Victorian five-piece bedroom set of mahogany with maple overlay. The complete set costs $225, but the pieces can be bought separately.

8 • *Chestnut Hill Studio* Miniature toys and decorative objects. $4 to $10.

8

MINERALS

Walker Mineral Co., 805 Lexington Avenue, New York, N.Y. 10021
Manufacturers' brochures, free.

"Distributors of mineralights, Geiger counters, geologist's hammers, books, ultraviolet supplies, lapidary equipment," says this firms letterhead, leaving me very little to add. Walker's has been in business for eighteen years, supplying hobbyists and institutions with the above, along with metal detectors, for prospecting, and some loose cut stones and semiprecious gemstones for making jewelry at home. Most of the items here are fair-traded, and therefore Walker sells at list price.

MINIATURES

Chestnut Hill Studio, Ltd., Box 38, Churchville, N.Y. 14428
44-page catalogue, $1.50.

If you are interested in authentic period pieces in 1″-1′ scale, this is an excellent catalogue for you. This family business sells mostly its own designs, and stresses authenticity and scale (even the wood grains are to scale), and everything in the large selection is handmade. Furniture, in most antique styles, is only the beginning of what they offer, but here are some prices: Empire sofa in Phyfe style is $70, piano $50, and a Queen Anne stool $16. Then there are paintings ($10-$45) and rugs (9″ by 12″ Aubusson, $270).

The room accessories abound in the most minute details: dishes, mirrors, etc. They have sterling silver miniatures for fine dining and cooking, an eggbeater costs $3.75. Chestnut Hill is, obviously, for the serious dollhouser, and if you can afford it, for older children.

The House of Miniatures, 708 Canyon Road, P.O. Box 1816, Santa Fe, N.M. 87501
24-page catalogue, 50 cents. April, October.

The House of Miniatures stocks imported and locally made 1″-1′ furniture and accessories at prices from 15 cents for little metal tools that work, such as a closing pocketknife, to $11 for a walnut dresser with six opening drawers. A small collection, but it includes Southwestern and Mexican accessories: tin dustpans, red clay bowls, woven baskets and rustic straw brooms.

Irma Park, 7541 9th Street, Buena Park, Calif. 90624
4-page list, 50 cents. (Send stamped, self-addressed envelope.)

A harassed-sounding mimeographed list gives a few details about each of the ¼″- to 2″-tall collector's dolls that Irma Park makes. Most of them are dolls' dolls, babies, boys and girls at between $5 and $18; she does not make regular 1″-1′ scale adult dollhouse dolls. There is a waiting list and no orders are sent out in December. Here is the description for one of the dolls: "*Little Kate* c. 1820s in Kate Greenaway style. Lavender dress, blk dots. Sleeveless all over cover wht apron. Brn short hair. Wht straw bonnet, red bow and strings. Carries ⅞″ doll in blue with bonnet. $15."

The Miniature Mart, 883 39th Avenue, San Francisco, Calif. 94121
56-page catalogue, $1.50

In 1962 John M. Blaur bought the Jack Norworth miniature collection (Jack Norworth wrote the lyrics for "Take Me Out to the Ball Game" and "Shine On, Harvest Moon"), which had been started by Mr. Norworth's father, consisting of over ten thousand pieces and representing over a hundred years of collecting. Since then Mr. Blaur has been copying and selling the 1″-1′ miniatures in the collection and also importing some. The catalogue, which announces "WE APPRECIATE THE LITTLE THINGS IN LIFE," has dinnerware, lamps, and chandeliers made for them exclusively by Ellen Krucker, as well as silver, glass, sewing accessories and toys (these for under $1 and good for children's dollhouses), fireplaces, antique furniture, some nice old-fashioned kitchen furniture and accessories; and a brass bed with a mattress, "patchwork" quilt and hot-water bottle for $8.50. There are also country-store accessories with wooden tubs, sacks of flour, bolts of cloth, parcels, tools and barrels, mostly for under $1 each; a school room; books, magazines and newspaper, old fashioned ones and modern ones—a set of *Time, Better Homes, Good Housekeeping,* etc., costs 50 cents. The styles here are plainer and more countrified than at Chestnut Hill, and the prices are much lower, but there is much less to choose from.

The Peddler's Shop, 883 39th Avenue, San Francisco, Calif. 94121
25-page catalogue, $1.

The catalogue arrived with a note from the owner to her valued customers announcing that on February 3 she had married John Blaur of The Miniature Mart and would consequently be moving to his address in San Francisco. It sounds like an eminently suitable match, and their catalogues, at least, complement each other very well.

The Peddler's Shop has no furniture but lots of accessories, and is the only place I have seen that stocks wallpaper for dollhouses and miniature settings. There are several exclusive reproductions of old American wallpapers on a 1″-1′ scale, and a flocked paper that is suitable for French and Victorian rooms. Besides the wallpapers, there are pages and pages of brass hardware, although not all of it is 1″-1′: kitchen accessories, frames, chandelier pieces, wall sconces, fireplace screens, weather vanes, and hinges and pulls for boxes. Also castle décor (crests, axes, swords, etc.), and cupids and animal miniatures.

The Village Smithy, 73 Kensington Road, Bronxville, N.Y. 10708
Catalogue, $1.

A jolly catalogue, illustrated by A. Atkins himself, shows the intricate iron miniatures that he makes: furniture (most of it antique, but the Barcelona ottoman is there too), kitchen implements, lights, lanterns, gates, garden railings and hardware—all on a 1″-1′ scale and with a pleasing liability to bumps and crookedness which, as Mr. Atkins says, comes under the umbrella phrase "part of the charm" of smithy work. Prices are mostly between $6 and $20, and when people express surprise that Mr. Atkins can make a living by making miniatures, he smartly replies that he makes a miniature living.

Woody's Hand-Crafted Miniatures, P.O. Box 3211, Green Bay, Wis. 54303
10-page catalogue, $1; refundable.

Woody's says: "You may or may not know that miniature collecting is now the third largest hobby in the U.S. and sources of supply are very few and scarce of U.S. made. Most are imported and, in our opinion, are of inferior construction and poor value, and do not remotely compare to ours." A small collection of Colonial period furniture in wood with metal fittings 1″-1′ is illustrated in the catalogue and usually on hand at prices between $4.50 and $15, and Woody's is prepared to reproduce special pieces of furniture at customer's requests. The specialty, which none of the other firms have, is a collection of very ornate and decorative model circus wagons and stagecoaches, and also a kit to make a circus wagon for about $40.

MODELS

America's Hobby Center, 146 W. 22nd Street, New York, N.Y. 10011
Several different catalogues for trains, boats, cars, etc.—$1.79 the complete set.

In business since 1931, this firm deals in models for vehicular hobbyists. It carries a complete line of modeling items, and although it has a retail store, its emphasis is on mail ordering. It doesn't have as convenient and easy-to-read catalogue as Polk's, but it is known for having a very large inventory. The catalogues are crammed full of listings and explanations—you have to see to believe. One can buy anything from ready-to-run sets to ready-to-build kits. There is even a selection of supplies for scratch builders—for the train modeler, for example, HO track, nails, couplers, and even stained basswood ties. Well worth battling with the ungainly catalogues if you are a modeler of trains, boats, cars, or anything else "vehicular."

James Bliss & Co., Route 128, Dedham, Mass. 02026
88-page model catalogue, 50 cents.
288-page marine catalogue, $1.

James Bliss handles both model kits and built-up models (ready to display) from all over the world. You can get, for example, the schooner *Blue Goose* as a ready-to-build kit for $33, or as a finished model for $138. A model kit of the *Santa Maria* costs $30, plus $11 for the paint kit. Also listed are cannon and gun kits. A Civil War cannon with a 4½″ brass barrel costs $17. You can even buy kits for building operating steam engines. The Stuart No. One weighs twenty-six pounds and costs $65, and "Whilst this engine is equal to any amount of hard work, it is so beautifully proportioned that many give lasting satisfaction as glass-case models."

Beyond the kits there are all the fittings, parts, tools, paints, etc., that any scratch modeler could ever hope for. The little accessories which help in achieving authenticity are fascinating—½″ by ⅞″ paper flags are 10 cents each, ¾″ dummy cannon 40 cents, 3″ brass oars 50 cents each. Bliss has been in business for 142 years, and their catalogue reflects the experience. Nautical books on both modeling and history are available too.

Polk's Model Craft, 314 Fifth Avenue, New York, N.Y. 10001
General catalogue, $3.

Polk's five-story building on lower Fifth Avenue is filled with more model ships, planes, soldiers, railroads, and related impedimenta than I thought existed, and its catalogue reflects the store's infinite variety. Here are models and kits that replicate reality in such endless detail that model railroad enthusiasts can choose between different styles of depot stations, not to mention the trains or tracks, or twelve different kinds of refrigerator cars. At times, I suspect, not just reality but fantasy is the goal, since the highly detailed listing of model soldiers includes a surprising number of naked Egyptian slave girls or equally naked "native Celtic chieftains daughters" ($3.50 each).

Whatever the intent, Polk's catalogues show a remarkable specialists' thoroughness. The imported and American soldiers range from Carlist Guipuzcoan Infantry to Vietcong. There are samurai, cannons galore, miniature vehicles of every description, and do it yourself molds and casts. The airplane listings go from the humblest plywood models to the most expensive radio-control kits with units costing hundreds of dollars. Because of the investment involved in some of these hobbies, the serious enthusiast should probably compare prices with some of the foreign catalogues before spending all of his military procurement budget.

MODEL RAILROADS

Model Railroad Equipment Corp., 23 W. 45th Street, New York, N.Y. 10036
Price list, free.

Well known to model-railroad enthusiasts, this shop stocks the world's largest selection, some sixty thousand items. As a result, this store does a large mail-order business, with customers throughout the world. Their price list is not illustrated, but based on the assumption that customers will know exactly what each description means.

Hundreds of locomotives, passenger and freight cars, track and various kits are listed, as well as a cheery selection of passengers climbing and descending from trains, women washing clothes by the wayside, and other reminders of a time when trains ran regularly outside people's homes. Model Railroad's prices are not discounted, but the shop stresses its immediate and personal attention to all orders.

MODEL SHIPS

Nautical Americana, P.O. Box 949, Plandome, N.Y. 11030
14-page catalogue, $1 (cash only).

This catalogue represents another, smaller version of Preston's (below). Among their models are several unusual ones, such as an original antique "Sovereign of the Seas" ($2,950). Among the gifts is a set of ale mugs decorated with beautiful old English fighting ships, a set of four for $5, and there is also a life-size reproduction of full Royal Guard armor for $1,950.

Preston's, At Main Street Wharf, Greenport, N.Y. 11944
144-page catalogue, plus supplemental mailings, free.

Preston's began ninety-two years ago as boating outfitters in this early whaling center of eastern Long Island. Today they handle nostalgic items and reproductions, reminiscent of this earlier era. They carry ship models, both kits and ready-made models—a handmade model of the yacht *America* costs $239. In general, the prices on the models average the same as those mentioned elsewhere in this book. The assortment of nautical decorations is intriguing—fabulous reproductions of ship figureheads run from $25 to $125. Also offered are various lamps, books and numerous other accessories. The scrimshaw jewelry is very attractive (cuff links, $16.95 a pair). You can buy whole pieces of scrimshaw, $40 a piece, and no two are alike. Preston's has a large selection of lithographs of famous oils, watercolors and prints of the sea. In addition to this they offer a custom-framing service—they indicate the recommended frame and the price for the service. The prints range from $5 to $30; framed they cost from $40 to about $55.

9 • *James Bliss* "Flying Cloud"—1851," a complete kit to make this ship in a bottle, including the bottle and step-by-step instructions. $12. (For correct identification when you order, use *"Fig. No. 100 SHIP 'N' BOTTLE."*)

The Seacrafters, P.O. Box 770, Ocean Avenue, Kennebunkport, Maine 04046
22-page catalogue, 25 cents.
Catalogue of nautical lamps from Holland, $1.

Besides ships, this eight-year-old firm sells "nautical giftwares for home and office." Its catalogue is similar to Preston's but smaller. Prices are about the same. They claim, however, to carry several things which are not available elsewhere. Among these are a German gimbal candle lamp, $27.95, and a selection of nautical lamps from Holland. The tone of the catalogue is enthusiastic—eager to give a personal service via the mails.

SHIP AND PLANE MODELS

Scientific Models, Inc., 340 Snyder Avenue, Berkeley Heights, N.J. 07922
8-page catalogue, 25 cents.

Scientific Models builds its own ship and airplane model kits. All ship models include a pre-carved wood hull, cast metal fittings, wood display stand, tapered masts and yards, and assembly plans and instructions. Most of the airplanes are flying models, and have a carvel balsa fuselage and airfoil shaped wings, for the beginner.

MUSIC BOXES

Richter's, Ghirardelli Square, San Francisco, Calif. 94109
32-page catalogue, some color, $1; refundable.

Richter's imports modern music boxes, and the catalogue shows more of them than I ever expected to see in one place, and in a greater variety of styles too. A marvelous selection for children includes tiny wooden merry-go-rounds and toy soldiers that turn as the music plays, banks that play when money is put in; and

10 • *Richter's* Bisque bird in a cage has a whistling bird call. $29.95.

clothes hangers that play Brahms' "Lullaby" when a chain is pulled are about $8.

Very popular with "pop" newlyweds, says Richter's, is a Mickey Mouse mug that plays Mickey's "Marching Song" when you lift it, $7, and also a box—on which Shroeder goes to Lucy, who is behind a stand saying "Psychiatric Help, five cents" which plays "Try to Remember" and costs about $28. For the more traditionally inclined there are inlayed boxes from Italy, hand-painted boxes from Russia, lacquered boxes from Switzerland and decorated Limoges mosques in which you can keep cigarettes, $150. And there are also luscious musical Christmas-tree ornaments, musical clocks, musical vintage cars with storage space for "men's accessories," a two-decanter set in the shape of a San Francisco cable car that plays "I Left My Heart in San Francisco," and hand-engraved Indian silver pieces. If you ever get tired of the tune you have chosen, send the box back with $1 and Richter's will change it for you.

PAPER AMERICANA

The Rebel Peddler Inc., P.O. Box 3092, Springfield, Mass. 01101

10-page price lists, 50 cents each. Issued every six months.

This new firm (started in 1972) specializes in movie items and comic books, but also sells circus and Coke items, radio premiums, World War I and II recruiting posters, gum cards, postcards, paper Americana and other nostalgia items that they happen to come across. The brochure that I was sent listed, with no descriptions at all, movie posters, mainly of the 1960's, for $3 and under, Marilyn Monroe and Humphrey Bogart materials, lobby cards, comics, Big Little Books, and a page of "old toys" which were mostly under $15 and were not described or dated.

11 • *Richter's* Barnyard owl, 12"-high music box with a cavity for candy or trinkets. $99.

PAPERWEIGHTS

L. H. Selman Antiques, 23 White Street, San Francisco, Calif. 94109

36-page catalogue, some color, $2.

L. H. Selman stocks antique and modern paperweights, as well as books about them. He sells to people who collect them for their decorative value alone, as well as those who buy to invest. A flyer arrives with the catalogue, welcoming the newcomer to the exciting world of paperweight collecting, and advises him to buy four books (about $50 worth) which make up a basic reference library, before buying seriously.

Fine crystal paperweights were first produced in France from about 1840 to 1860, the fad then spread to England, Europe and finally America. Collectors of antique paperweights try to find representative weights from the finest French factories, and sometimes from the English and American. The value of antique weights depends on the beauty of the design as well as the scarcity. Mr. Selman supplies and searches for antique paperweights by request.

Modern paperweights, at prices from $20 to $300, are illustrated and described in the small catalogue, which lists weights from firms such as Baccarat, Clichy, St. Louis and Perthshire, as well as from individual craftsmen who make signed weights.

12

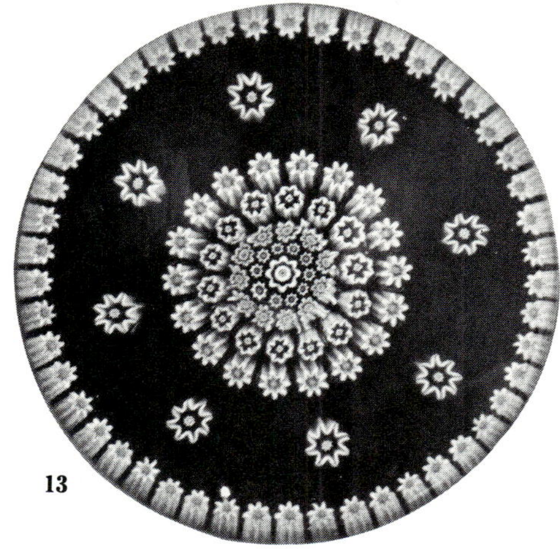

13

12 • *L. H. Selman Antiques* Millefiori paperweight with spoke design, available in small size at $7.50, medium $12.50, and large $15.

13 • *L. H. Selman Antiques* Patterned millefiori on a cobalt ground, produced by Perthshire of Scotland in a limited edition, 300 pieces. Sold with certificate. $35.
photo L. H. Selman and S. Pacholski

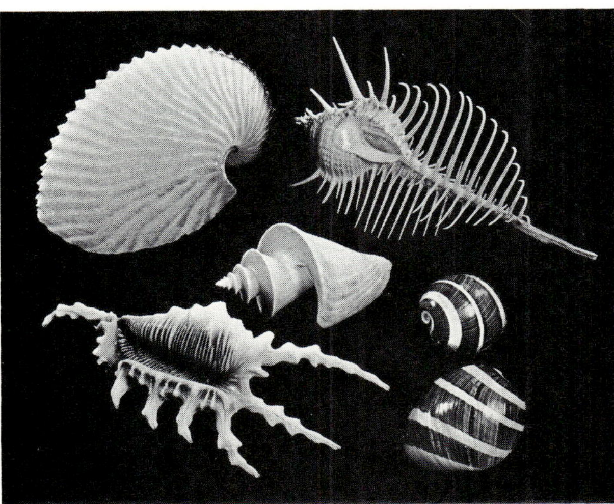

14 • *Dover Scientific Corp. Reading left to right and top to bottom:* paper nautilus, $4; Venus's-comb, $7; turrid shell, $4.50; scorpion conch, $4; banded bubbles, $1.75 each.

PLATES

Fredericks, 540 Sutter Street, San Francisco, Calif. 94102
Occasional price lists, free.

Fredericks sells fine crystal, handwrought gold and silver jewelry, and "table appointments" and "porcelain arts" for collectors. They publish lists of their collector's plates and their Cybis, Royal Worcester, Ispansky, Burgues, Bonnie, Charles Parks and Gregory Higgins figurines, which sell at prices from $35 (for non-limited editions by Cybis) but are mostly several hundred dollars.

Robert Harris, Limited Editions, 2145 Crooks Road, Suite 204, Troy, Mich. 48084
Price lists and leaflets, free.

Robert Harris has a miscellany of leaflets about Kirk Silver, Frame House Gallery prints (see Art section). For the increasingly popular limited-edition plates he has a price list of over fifty manufacturers he carries, mostly of 1970 and on. He says "plate collecting is a broad field and no one has all the answers: but we will be happy to give you any specific information on any plates, series of plates, manufacturer, or current market value."

RAILWAY RELICS

Broadway Limited Antique Company, 2768 Broadway, New York, N.Y. 10025
Want lists solicited.

The Broadway Limited (which belongs to Suzanne Samelson, who helped me with this book) offers everything in the way of railroad memorabilia for the train buff, the historian, and anyone who has any nostalgia for the glorious days of railroading. Their selection includes timetables (from pre-1900 to the present), dining-car china and silverware, maps, photographs, transportation tokens, lanterns, furnishings, etc. The firm also carries similar items from other transportation fields (steamship, bus, plane, subway, trolley, etc.), over twenty thousand old postcards, old advertising items such as posters and buttons, and a general selection of paper Americana. Want lists are solicited.

SHELLS

Dover Scientific Corp., Box 6011, Long Island City, N.Y. 11106
40-page catalogue, 25 cents. Published every September.

Dover publishes a very satisfactory businesslike catalogue offering fossils, shells, minerals, and Indian artifacts, and books relating to these. The prices on the whole seem reasonable, though you can splurge and spend as much as $100 for a large mammoth tooth from a Texas Pleistocene formation. A fossilized fish, 40 million years old, however, sells for as little as $12 and up to $40. The large choice of minerals goes from a small polished slab of Mexican agate at $1.25, to malachite at $25 and $50. There are also polished stones, and larger pieces that are described as potential ashtrays but strike me as much too beautiful to be used as anything but decorations.

The catalogue has an extensive and detailed eight-page list of shells, as well as a number of Indian artifacts such as arrowheads, small pots, etc. Dover says that all its specimens are of top quality and that any purchase can be exchanged within a week of receipt. Dover also offers books on the sciences.

K & K Nature Supply Co., 1515 Marshall Road, Kirkwood, Mo. 63122
Price list, free.

K & K is the result of many a schoolboy's dream, having been started by its owner, George Karleskint, Jr., when he was a junior in high school and being continued from his home as a sideline to teaching high school science. K & K deals primarily in specimen shells for collectors, and while his stock is not as extensive as that of some competitors, Mr. Karleskint says that his prices are generally the lowest in the field. He also deals, in a smaller way, in lapidary and gemstones and lapidary equipment.

STAMPS AND COINS

H. R. Harmer, Inc., 6 W. 48th Street, New York, N.Y. 10036
Harmer, Rooke & Co., 3 E. 57th Street, New York, N.Y. 10022
Auction catalogues at various prices.

The world of stamp and coin collecting is so complex and so well documented that I have decided not to try and list the many firms that deal with these two hobbies. Each has a vast literature, specialized magazines are available which list hundreds of dealers, and many Sunday newspapers have special pages or columns devoted to news and ads. The two firms listed above are among the most famous stamp and coin auctioneers—Harmer, Rooke dealing in both, H. R. Harmer dealing exclusively in stamps. Both seem to do a great deal of business with estates, selling collections for heirs, etc. Harmer, Rooke "normally offer about 30,000 lots during any 12-month period." Both firms offer subscribers a chance to get all their catalogues as well as lists of prices realized. Those around New York may pick up the auction catalogues free from Harmer, Rooke, which will also sell individual catalogues. All this is, of course, of primary interest to serious, and affluent, collectors.

TOY SOLDIERS

Bussler Miniatures, Inc., Box 107, Wollaston, Mass. 02170
30-page catalogue, 50 cents.

Bussler deals in military miniatures of all kinds and has been in business since 1947. The figures are either ready to display or they are "knockdowns"—unfinished castings right from the mold which must be assembled. The catalogue covers quite a span of history. U.S. Marine figures from the 1770's cost $1.95 each (knockdowns), knockdown figures from World War I, $1.25 each. For historians of the present, there is a Vietcong guerrilla for $1.95. There are full series for many wars and there are "very special miniatures" with elaborate costumes; for example, a hussar general in dress uniform (c. 1900) is $1.95. Supplies are available; files, paints, etc., as well as selected books. Interest in this hobby has grown in the past few years and this catalogue certainly offers a well-rounded selection for "war gamers and collectors of good quality figures."

WEAPONS

Golden Age Arms Co., Inc., Box 82, Worthington, Ohio 43085
124-page annual catalogue, $1; foreign, $2.25.

The firm, organized in 1962, sells reproductions of muzzle-loading rifles, and pistol parts, and books on antique firearms, Americana, and antiques in general. The concern is more with the actual making of a firearm from parts reproduced from age-old designs and plans rather than the using of the rifle. There are details of the meticulous care with which the parts and the wholes have been made.

As for actual products, this firm sells kits as well as parts, and there is generally a saving in the kit price. A Golden Age Percussion Pistol Kit costs $80. You can buy bullet molds for making your own munitions. A six-piece set of wood-carving tools costs $20. For the arms which require powder, there are horns which run from $2.50 to $16. For your wardrobe, there are many leather items: belts, around $3; a large leather hat, $6; bags of all kinds (hunting bag, $10, kit, $8.50); and a full line of moccasins. The book department has a good selection, not only on guns but also on Americana and antiques, crafts and Indians. Under "Miscellaneous" I even found *Yankee Hill Country Cook Book,* by Vaughn, for $4.50. Something for everyone.

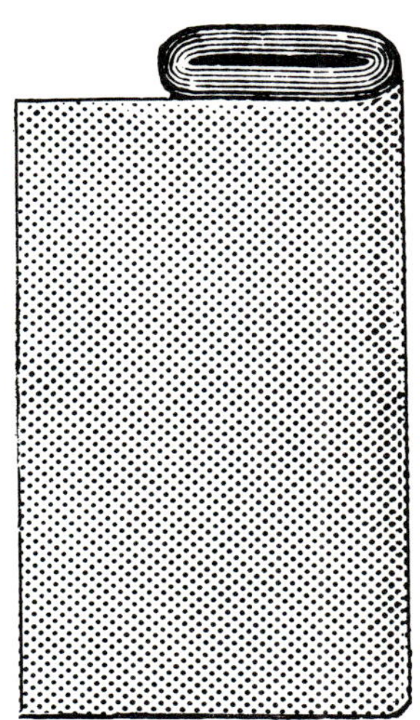

Per yard..............

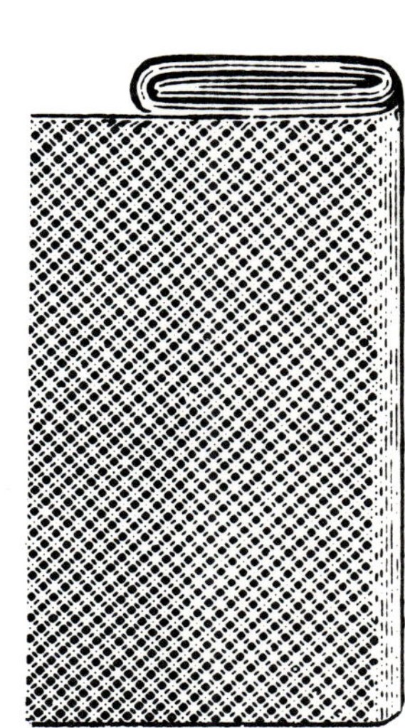

1

2

3

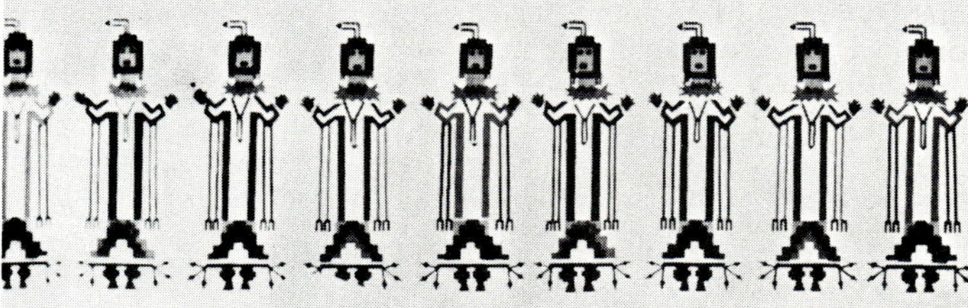
4

5

1 • *Nizhonie* *Left:* 45″-wide "Indian Symbols"—one-color design based on pictographs found in ruins and cliff dwellings. *Right:* 45″-wide "Zia Deer"—one-color design based on deer commonly painted on Zia and Zuni pottery. Both designs are available on several different fabrics at prices between $3.29 and $9.98 per yard.

2 • *Nizhonie* *Left:* 45″-wide "Indian Emblems"—one-color design showing the basic Indian symbols: night/day, thunderbird, rainclouds, etc. *Right:* 45″-wide "Storm"—one-color design based on Navajo Storm-pattern rug. Both designs are available on several different fabrics at prices between $3.29 and $9.98 per yard.

3 • *Nizhonie* 45″-wide design available in various different fabrics at prices between $3.29 and $9.98 per yard.
photo Duane's Photography

4 • *Nizhonie* Six-color design, "Yei-Bei-Chai," based on a Navajo sign-painting figure. 17″-wide linen, $3.65 per yard; 52″-wide linen, $6.98 per yard.
photo Duane's Photography

5 • *Nizhonie* Keith Austin (*on the left*) and Baha Zonie checking a silkscreen design.

FABRICS

Carol Brown, Putney, Vt. 05346
Leaflet, free.
Fabric swatches on request (to be returned), free.

Carol Brown and nephew sell imported fabrics for people who do their own sewing. They manage their shop alone and each mail order requires correspondence, so if too many people write to them service will slow down—be warned.

The fabrics sound marvelous: Irish tweeds from the Avoca handweavers in Wicklow, and the Weavers' Shed in Dublin; Irish blankets in glowing colors like stained glass to be made into hostess skirts or jackets; heavy unbleached yarn for clothes and upholstery. There are also Indian cottons, printed and plain; Finnish cottons with big bright designs; and Dutch/African cottons made in Holland for the African trade. Prices start at around $3.50 per yard for the cottons and go up to around $16 for the tweeds. Samples with prices can be sent, but you must be absolutely specific about the color and use of the fabric, and the samples *must* be returned.

Cherry Blossom, Inc., 2184 Kalakaua Avenue, Honolulu, Hawaii 96815.
Swatches, free.

Although the Cherry Blossom people have no price list, they answer letters individually and send swatches in answer to very specific requests. They sell Hawaiian prints from tapa designs to flower patterns in washable cotton or acrylic. Tell them whether you want drip-dry or not, and which colors and what kind of patterns you are interested in, and they will send cuttings of some of their stock. Price per yard for broadcloth-type cotton is about $1.50; for textured cotton bark cloth and cotton crepe, about $2.50; for acrylics, $2 to $3.50. Most fabrics are 44″ wide.

Cohasset Colonials by Hagerty, Cohasset, Mass. 02025
32-page catalogue, 50 cents.
36 fabric samples, $3; refundable.

In this catalogue of kits to make furniture, there are two pages of Colonial-style fabrics, both the lovely, natural rough cottons and sophisticated polished chintzes based on old designs. Fabrics cost between $3 and $4 per yard, and samples are 25 cents each. The $3 for a selection of thirty-six samples is refundable if you order fabrics or ready-made curtains worth more than $10.

Elegance International, 152-20 Rockaway Boulevard, Baisley Park, N.Y. 11434
170-page color catalogue of patterns, $3.95.
170-page color catalogue with fabric swatches, $12.95.
84-page "Boutique" clothes catalogue, $2.50.

I should think these huge catalogues would be invaluable to the well-heeled home dressmakers, or indeed to anyone who has ever thought of having clothes made to measure. The firm belongs to Butterick's and each issue shows well over a hundred impressively smart Vogue patterns made up and in full glorious color. The useful part is that you can order the patterns, with the illustrated fabrics and all matching necessities such as zippers and lining direct from Elegance International. You can also order the accessories. The only hitch is that the fabrics, many of which are very beautiful imports, cost mostly between $10 and $25 a yard, although I did see a Swiss acetate for $5 and an Indian shantung for $9. The idea in sending for one of these catalogues would not be to get clothes dirt-cheap, but to make, or have made, clothes that are far nicer than the usual store-bought ones.

The only difference between the two pattern catalogues is that the $12.95 one has small swatches pasted in the book opposite the modeled clothes. In many cases the photographs of the fabrics in the $3.95 catalogue are accurate, but sometimes the colors of the actual fabrics are clearer and brighter, so if you are going to buy fabrics, I think the catalogue with swatches is the one to get.

Gurian's, 276 Fifth Avenue, New York, N.Y. 10001
Color brochure, 50 cents.

Gurian's has been importing hand-embroidered crewel (wool embroidery on cotton) from India for twenty-six years. Several patterns and colors are sold by the yard; the fabric is 50″ wide and costs from $10 to $14 per yard. Crewel bedspreads, starting at $50 for twin-bed size, and namda (felt) hand-embroidered rugs are also sold and shown in color in the brochure.

Nizhonie Inc., P.O. Box 729, Cortez, Colo. 81321
Leaflet, free (send stamped, self-addressed envelope).

As the leaflet says, this is an Indian-owned enterprise producing hand-printed (silkscreened) textiles based on Indian patterns. One design is an abstract taken from Navajo storm-pattern rugs, others are based on sand-painting figures, pictographs taken from cliff dwellings, and deer painted on Zai and Zuni pueblo pottery. Prices per yard run from $3 to $10, and several kinds of fabric are available: homespun, cotton broadcloth, batiste, linen and velveteen. Towels, place mats, calendars with Indian designs, and handwoven fabric from Guatemala are also available.

Pinecroft, Juniper Ridge Fabrics, Dunbarton, N.H. 03301
Leaflet with color swatches, 35 cents.

Mr. Lord retired from machine weaving to take up handweaving, and now he and his wife make beautiful wool fabrics and sell them in a shop converted from an old barn. They import virgin wool from Canada for their weaving, and hand-spun yarn in matching colors for knitting. Their color wheel shows twenty-two solid colors, and twenty-two checks and plaids. Apart from a cherry red and a royal blue, the other colors are all subtle heathery blends. You are almost sure to find several colors you like very much. The fabric is 33″ wide and costs only $6 per yard; the knitting yarn costs $1.50 per 4-oz. skein.

Thai Silks, 393 Main Street, Los Altos, Calif. 94022
Price list, free
Swatches on specific request, 10 to 50 cents for each batch.

Here you can get brilliantly colored handwoven Thai silks at low prices. The price list indicates the different weights and kinds of fabric, and you send a deposit of from 10 cents to 50 cents according to the kind of swatch you want. Besides dress-weight Thai silks at about $7.50 per yard and coat weight for $12, there are

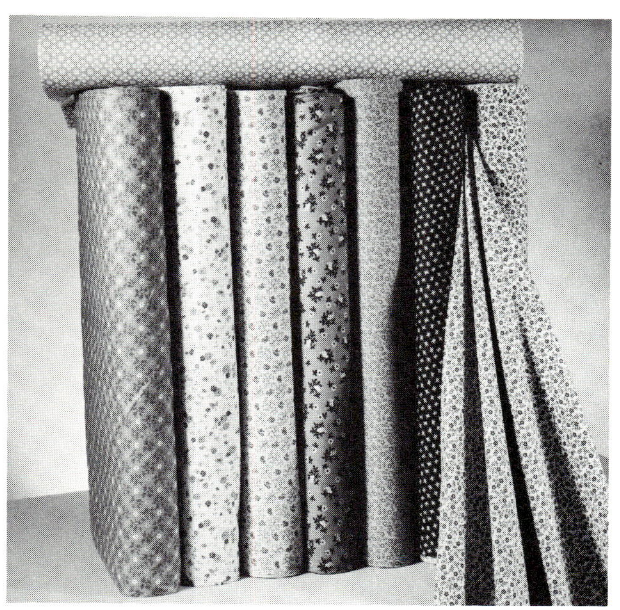

printed Thai, Hawaiian and Indonesian cottons, Indian, Chinese, Japanese and Italian silks, gold-printed Indian silk saris (about $45 each), silk scarves, silk purses and silver- and gold-plated buttons from Thailand.

The Vermont Country Store, Inc., Weston, Vt. 05161
96-page catalogue, 25 cents. Spring, fall.
Fabric swatches, 50 cents.

The Vermont Country Store sells traditional calico at about $1.10 a yard. They will only sell in quantities of half a yard and up of each pattern, but anyone interested can send 50 cents for swatches.

For higher-priced furnishing fabrics, see the Craft House, Williamsburg, in the Reproduction Furniture section.

6 • *The Vermont Country Store* Traditional calico patterns for sale at about $1.10 per yard.

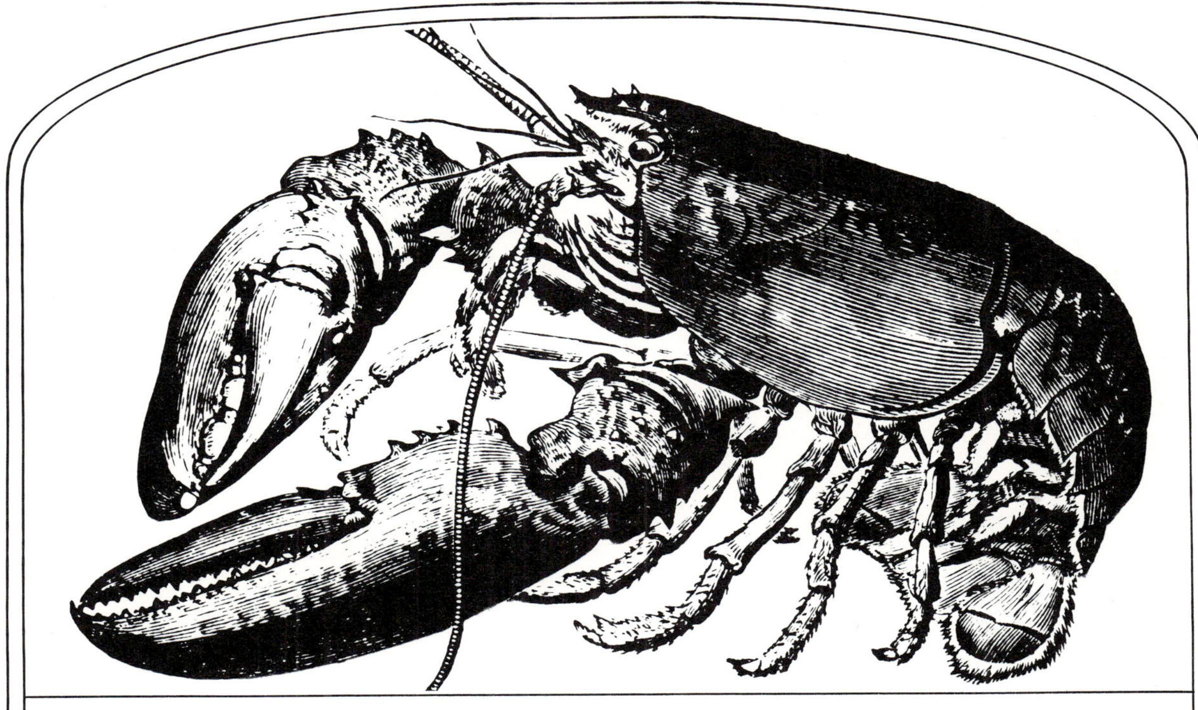

9
FOOD

Judging from stores and restaurants throughout the country, people are more interested in food than ever. It seems to be the area where all interests meet; from the counterculture's discovery of natural foods and home cooking to the increasing sophistication of a population that watches Julia Child and her fellow television cooks. Supermarkets regularly have gourmet and natural-food sections, city dwellers form food co-ops to buy better as well as cheaper produce from the wholesale markets; special-interest restaurants proliferate.

All this literally whets the appetite, but many of those who are dying to create a *charlotte malakoff au chocolat* or to make their own crunchy granola will discover that all too few of the ingredients are available locally. Buying by mail thus makes sense for most would-be gourmets living outside the largest cities, and even there a supply of catalogues is a useful adjunct to the cookbooks, both as a source of supply and of inspiration, since it's easier to plan a meal around food you know you can get than to start from the recipe in the abstract. But even big-city dwellers, or rather, anyone in all but the rarest and luckiest of towns, needs to buy by mail in order to obtain some of America's regional specialties. Curiously enough, the very fashions that have led to so many new sources of food have largely by-passed the great American cuisines, from whatever part of the country. I can think of no major city north of the Mason-Dixon line (including Washington, D.C.) where you can find a good Southern restaurant, and a good New England dish seems difficult to find south of Boston.

The foods listed below are therefore both foreign and domestic, with fewer sources for regional food than I would have liked. Perhaps by my next edition, more of these will have been established.

REGIONAL FOOD

Amana Society Meat Department, Amana, Iowa 52203
Leaflets, free.

The Amana colonies, or villages, are a settlement of German Protestants who came to America in the nineteenth century and who have retained a communal arrangement similar in some respects to the Mennonites, though the Amana people have adopted modern ways and are concerned lest their often visited area become too commercialized. While all sorts of produce are sold locally, the Amana meats are available nationally by mail, and their smoked meats and sausages come highly recommended. One of my most enthusiastically gastronomic friends is eloquent about their summer sausage, which resembles salami. Their ham comes boned or not, the latter being roughly half the price of the former, but pre-cooked in any case; $20 for a 14- or 15-lb. ham with bone. Smoked bacon is available in slabs of 7 lbs. for $12, an enormous saving over local prices of that increasingly expensive staple. Various assortments and smaller quantities are available. Prices cited include shipping.

R. H. Chamberlin, 1940 Barr Street, Merritt Island, Fla. 32952
Leaflets, free.

Chamberlin specializes in the sale of Florida citrus and frozen seafood which he ships throughout North America and even air-freights to Europe. The various assortments and gift hampers contain oranges, grapefruits, tangelos, tangerines and Temple oranges, but all these fruits are available separately at the uniform price of $13.95 a bushel.

Chamberlin's seafood looks equally tempting and includes Florida lobster, stone crab, red snapper, frog's legs and "pen-raised" quail. Various combinations are available and some "dinners" come complete with that delicious local dessert, Key Lime pie.

Prices are relatively high: four lobsters, weighing about 4½ lbs., cost $32.50; stone-crab claws are $32.50 for 6 lbs., but $41.00 for 10 lbs. Likewise, 4 lbs. of Florida rock shrimp cost $29.95, whereas 8 lbs. cost only $42.50, so clearly, if you're tempted by this kind of extravagance, you will do better to go in for it wholeheartedly, or find friends who will share your indulgence.

Colonial Garden Kitchens, 270 W. Merrick Road, Valley Stream, N.Y. 11582
80-page catalogue, free.

This catalogue includes both food and kitchen appliances and has a wide variety to choose from, but the most interesting food items are the American specialties that it is not always possible to buy directly from the source. Colonial Garden offers such New England exports as corn and clam chowder (three cans for $1.95 and $2.35, respectively) or fancy clam meats, two 10-oz. cans for $1.98.

Pennsylvania Dutch specialties include apple, peach and prune butter, scrapple and dried sweet corn, used for corn fritters, etc. Maple-sugar products, old-fashioned candies and similar country-store goodies also abound. A good selection, but one that makes me wish there were more specialized regional equivalents offering the full range of local products.

Creole Delicacies Co., 533 St. Ann Street, New Orleans, La. 70116
Illustrated brochure, free.

A New Orleans store that packs and sells its own produce by mail, Creole Delicacies supplies a nice selection of Louisiana specialties.

Louisiana strawberry preserve is offered by itself at $7.95 for 2½ lbs., or as part of a pack of 10-oz. jars, which includes Louisiana figs, watermelon rind, etc., three jars for $5.75, six for $9.95, etc. Other local specialties include Creole fruit cake at $7.75 for 2½ lbs., pecans at $4.95 and $7.95 for 3-lb. or 5-lb. bags, or $6.95 for 2½ lbs. shelled; and a 12-lb. sugar-cured ham for $23.50. There are also special sauces and syrups, a "sirop plantage" pure cane syrup and "La Cuite," an eighteenth-century syrup used with chopped nutmeats or served on biscuits. Pecan pralines, which I've always thought of as quintessentially Southern, date back to recipes from Louis XIV time and sell for $3.45 for a 1-lb. box. Finally, Creole Delicacies offers cans of local soups, the gumbo, shrimp Creole, crayfish bisque and other delicacies that make the old Louisiana cuisine practically unique for its range. These are sold at roughly $1 per 10-oz. can, slightly more for six cans, slightly less for twenty-four, and all prices are postpaid.

The Great Valley Mills, Quakertown, Bucks County, Pa. 18951
16-page catalogue and price lists, free.

Great Valley Mills sells a number of foods which it produces itself, the most important being its stone-ground flours and meals and its own smoked meats. The former all cost roughly $1 for 3 lbs., and even less in 6-lb. amounts, so that 6 lbs. of buckwheat groats (for kasha) cost only $2.20, rye flour $1.70, corn meal $1.70, and unbleached organic white flour $1.70.

Breakfast foods include honey wheat, ready to serve, at $1.50 for 3 lbs., and $1 for 3 lbs. of Irish or Scotch oatmeal. Barley, millet, hominy grits and other grains are also available at similar prices, as are sesame and sunflower seeds, wheat germ and other health foods.

Great Valley's smoked meats are very reasonably priced, and their hickory and apple-wood triple-smoked ham is only $1.75 per pound, delivered—this for a ham which has already been boned and from which excess skin and fat has been removed. The minimum weight is 10 lbs. Smoked turkey is $2.25 a pound, and smokehouse bacon is $6.60 for 4 lbs. Other meat products include beer, Lebanon and ring bologna, smoked tongue and smoked sausage.

Among other local specialties there are home-packed peaches, averaging ten whole peaches a quart, costing $3.75 for three jars; Pennsylvania Dutch apple, peach, quince and maple butter; and a nice range of preserves, relishes and honeys, all at similar, sensible prices.

Harry and David, Bear Creek Orchards, Medford, Oreg. 97501
32-page annual "color" catalogue, free.

Harry and David is one of the country's most famous vendors of fruit by mail, and there was a time when the back of every popular magazine seemed to advertise their Fruit of the Month Club. A look at the catalogue shows that their business is actually based on two fruits that they grow locally, the Royal Riviera Pear being their most popular item and selling in packages of 6¾ lbs. for $6.95, or $8.45 for 7½ or 9 lbs., depending on the size of the fruit, the smaller being the least expensive. There is a variant called the Maverick Royal Riviera, which sells for considerably less, 15 lbs. for $9.95, or 25 lbs. for $15.95, but the Harry and David catalogue copy is so cute and pseudo-rural that it is impossible to tell from it if these taste any different from the "real" Royal Riviera.

The Mavericks are described as having "shapes sorta like Queen Victoria outside, yet jest as ripe and regal inside." I'm not quite sure what Queen Victoria's insides taste like, but doubt that I'd want a pear to remind me of them. I suspect the catalogue is trying to convey that these pears don't look as much like pears as their cousins and are therefore cheaper, but you'd have to buy both to find out if there is any difference in taste; crisp Mountain Apples are also offered at roughly the same price as pears, and other packages contain combinations of these and various preserves, etc.

The Fruit of the Month choice is based on apples and pears, and adds other items from outside of Oregon. Be sure to get the catalogue in the early fall, since the local fruit is available for delivery only between November 10 and January 25.

1

2

1 • *Harry and David* 9 lbs. of Royal Riviera pears (twenty to twenty-five). $8.45, including postage.

2 • *Paprikas Weiss* Hungarian Linzer tarts. Linzer dough made with eggs and butter filled with apricot or raspberry preserve. $7.20 a dozen.

3

4

3 • *Paprikas Weiss* Beef and pork salami, cured and mildly seasoned specially for American tastes. $5.98 a pound.

4 • *Paprikas Weiss* Middle European cheeses: ham-shaped *Ostyepka*, $11 each (about 2 lbs.); ribbon cheese *Parenyica*, $6.50 (about 1 lb.); and crumbly *Bryndza*, $4.50 a pound.

Hickin's Farm and Greenhouse, R.F.D. #1, Black Mountain Road, Brattleboro, Vt. 05301
Brochures and price lists, free.

This is one of the few real produce farms that sells by mail, though unfortunately most of its fresh fruits and vegetables can be sold only to those visiting the area. Hickin's brochure temptingly lists "100 different kinds of vegetables and fruits including snow peas, radishetta, lemon cucumbers . . . as well as raspberries, young sweet carrots and tiny new potatoes only big as marbles." Some of these items are available by mail in the forms of jams, jellies and pickles. Jam and jellies are sold at prices that go from 50 cents for 2 ounces to $2.20 a pound and $14.95 a gallon. For these rather high prices you have a choice of such exotic items as lemon-mint or parsley jelly, or pear, or strawberry-rhubarb jam. Pickles and relishes are slightly less expensive, $1.69 a pound. Honey is $1.90 a pound, and various cheeses are available, most of them at $1.70 a pound.

Hickin's also sells smoked meat at very reasonable prices, whole hams at $1.59 a pound and bacon at $1.50. Maple syrup, candies and maple fruit cake are also on sale. Fudge, which is usually not that readily available by mail, is $1.90 a pound in a choice of penuche, chocolate, chocolate nut, peanut butter and chocolate peanut. Herbs, shallots and a number of other plants are also available for kitchen gardens or window boxes.

Koinonia Partners, Route 2, Americus, Ga. 31709
Brochures and leaflets, free.

Koinonia Partners is one of those remarkable utopian adventures that shine through America's past. Started as a Christian communal farm in 1942, it sought to establish a peaceful example and help its neighbors to introduce scientific farming methods. Though at first the experiment succeeded, in time their integrationist position led to hostility and then a series of violent acts from the outside. After surviving these attacks, Koinonia re-formed itself, stressing aid to those nearby and helping to start a series of local industries. These include pecan shelling, the making of fruit cakes, candy, pottery and various sewing enterprises. Among the products that can be bought by mail are fruit cakes and pecans.

La Casa Rosa, San Juan Bautista, Calif. 95045
Price list, free.

La Casa Rosa is an example of the local restaurant whose customers are so enthusiastic that a mail-order business develops. (I can't help but wonder whether Mildred Pierce might have stayed out of all that trouble if only she could have sold her pies by mail.) La Casa Rosa specializes in the kinds of relishes and jellies that are so hard to find in big cities, though still available in towns that have an ample supply of church bazaars. It offers such specialties as spiced watermelon rind and cantaloupe chunks, corn relish, peach chutney with ginger, pear chutney with almonds and other appetizing combinations, as well as various jams and preserves, including apricot mixed with pineapple, which is surely not available in most places.

Their jars are just under a pound each, and six will cost about $10.

Sugarbush Farms, Woodstock, Vt. 05091
Leaflets, free.

Sugarbush is a small business started in the way that so many city dwellers dream of—by a couple who left New York, took their savings and bought a farm. They make maple-syrup products from their own trees and have a smokehouse for their own cheeses. Their Cheddar is so famous that it has been written up glowingly in *Gourmet* magazine and the *New York Times* food section.

Maple syrup is available in quarts and half-gallon cans at $3.95 and $7.50, plus postage. Maple sugar costs $4.60 for 1 lb. 14 oz., plus postage, and candies are more expensive.

Sugarbush cheeses are sold in bars, wheels or blocks. A 2-lb. block of sharp Cheddar is $3.95, 5½ lbs. is $8.75, and the smaller, foot-long bars of Cheddar, Stilton blue, sage, and a mild cheese of their own called Green Mountain Jack, all sell at $2.45, plus postage.

The Vermont Country Store, Weston, Vt. 05161
96-page catalogue, 25 cents. Issued March and October.

A nice selection of New England foods is included at the end of this very varied catalogue. There are, of course, genuine maple sugar and genuine maple syrup sold in containers of one pint to a half gallon. Pickles, relishes and jams make use of local fruits and vegetables, not to mention other unexpected traditional ingredients, as in plum rum preserves, than which, the Vermont catalogue says, "nothing is more traditional." Cranberry conserve and rose-hip jelly are other local favorites.

The Vermont Country Store makes its own peanut butter, and they say that it tastes far better than the mass-produced kind, since it contains only peanuts rather than being 87 percent peanuts as are most commercial brands.

Vermont Cheddar can be exceptionally tasty and this catalogue offers various kinds. Their basic Cheddar comes in sizes ranging from 1 to 12 lbs., and is also available with sage or caraway. To go with the Cheddar are old fashioned "common crackers," baked crackers with neither sweet nor salty taste, available in half-peck baskets containing 1½ lbs. for $2.95, with a refill of the same for only $1.65.

The store also offers a wide choice of beans, peas and grains. New England beans, the kind that make Boston baked beans, are available in 2-lb. bags at $1.09 each. Already baked, with pork, they sell at $1.38 for two 28-oz. cans.

A comprehensive list of whole grains includes nine kinds of stone-ground grains suitable for breakfast, as well as nine kinds of flour, including yellow corn meal, oat and rye flour, and buckwheat. If you share an enthusiasm for these natural foods with a number of friends, you can buy many of these grains in quantities of 25 lbs. for $7.25 and 100 lbs. for only $23.50.

Finally, the Vermont Country Store offers a choice of canned seafood (clam and fish chowder, minced clams); corn chowder, Indian pudding and dandelion greens, and a delicate fern of which I'd never heard before, Fiddlehead fern greens, which apparently can be served hot or in salads.

IMPORTED FOOD

CHINESE

Kam Shing Co., 2246 Wentworth Avenue, Chicago, Ill. 60616
Price list, free.

While many large cities have Chinese food stores, few sell by mail, so the Kam Shing price list is a welcome one. It lists about eighty items, starting with soy sauce and ending with dried seaweed, and offers in cans, jars or packets such hard-to-find items as preserved mustard greens, quail eggs, fried fish stomach, sea cucumber, shark fins and bird's nests, dried shrimp, mushrooms, lili flower and bean curd, as well as the bamboo shoots, water chestnuts and other products that are sometimes obtainable in grocery stores. Prices seem moderate, though quantities on the whole are not specified and you have to guess at just what you're getting. Orders must total at least $10.

EAST EUROPEAN

Paprikas Weiss, 1546 Second Avenue, New York, N.Y. 10026
64-page illustrated catalogue, $1.00 annual subscription.

Paprikas Weiss, along with its competitor, H. Roth and Son, is known to many food lovers as the leading importer of food and cooking utensils from what used to be called Middle Europe. Located near Yorkville, around Eightieth Street, it is part of New York's own Austro-Hungarian Empire, the area just below the German district where Hungarians, Austrians and Czechs live close together, just as they used to in pre-World War I Europe and with, one assumes, far friendlier feelings than of old.

The founder of Paprikas Weiss, the present owner's grandfather, began his career in the classic manner, a Hungarian immigrant selling paprika to friends and neighbors. Now his grandson presides over a rich selection of over ten thousand items, many of which are in his catalogue. Just about any food that you can think of from that part of the world is amply represented: sheets of strudel dough (4 for $1), prune butter (Lekvar), Hungarian ham or salami, dried mushrooms, poppy seeds, pages of the rarest herbs and such far flung imports as fresh green pepper from Madagascar, tea from mainland China, couscous from Tunisia, herbal teas from all over and so on.

Here are merchants who know their field perfectly and have every variant you could imagine, as well as a large number you never knew existed. Their catalogue also has a vast selection of cooking, coffee-making and particularly baking utensils listed under Kitchen in the House section. For a marvelous whiff of the subtle and, for most people, still-unknown wonders of the part of Europe you are least likely to visit, Paprikas Weiss offers an admirable start.

H. Roth and Son, Lekvar by the Barrel, 1577 First Avenue, New York, N.Y. 10028
56-page catalogue, free.

Close to Paprikas Weiss in geography as well as in spirit, Roth offers an excellent catalogue, which specializes in food from abroad and spices but is particularly strong on kitchenware. This part of the catalogue is described below (under Kitchen in the House section), but is clearly a necessary complement to much of what is sold in the food department. What are snails without a proper snail dish, or more important, good coffee without a proper coffee machine?

Roth's imports are similar to other good shops in this category, but probably stronger in the sweet-tooth department.

The "Lekvar" in their name refers to a thick puree of prunes, beloved of Austro-Hungarians as a filling for strudel, Danish pastry, and the like, and other strudel ingredients are of course available as well. This is also a good place to buy such classic delicacies as Pischinger Torte, the Viennese crisp chocolate cake, as rich as the unfortunately unexportable Sachertorte. There are also anise and honey drops, Turkish delight, and other relatively unobtainable indulgences. A word should be said about the more mundane but equally rare foods available here, such as candied or dried fruit (currants, apricots, pears, candied lemon or orange peel) and other ingredients for cakes or even for lush turkey stuffings.

Roth also sells dried beans and peas of all sorts as well as various flours, and what, in a marvelous Magyarization of an old American product, their catalogue lists as Gritz.

Finally, a word should be said about the two pages of baking and cooking specialties which should encourage even the most experienced baker to try new and daring experiments. There are several dozen nonalcoholic essences for flavor, from anisette through lingonberry to walnut. There are vanilla beans, meringue powder, imported gelatin powder and, nicest of all, cake and cookie decorations such as crystallized lavender or mimosa, crystal sugar in all colors, and assorted silver and other "shots," for that final touch. An imaginative but businesslike catalogue for people who take food seriously.

GERMAN

Bremen House, 200 E. 86th Street, New York, N.Y. 10028
12-page price list. Issued free twice a year.

Bremen House has been one of the central shops of New York's German neighborhood, Yorkville, for as long as I can remember, and at Christmas time, with its piles of *Stollen* (the delicious German coffee cake), marzipan and chocolates, it is thronged by thousands who long for the traditional German *Weihnachten* goodies. The Germans don't just eat chocolate at Christmas, they decorate their Christmas trees with it, and Bremen has the requisite jelly and chocolate rings, lebkuchen (the rich chocolate-covered ginger cookies), and the like. Even if you're not familiar with the original, you can soon get into the spirit of things with "marzipan good-luck pig in wooden crate" or a chocolate-covered marzipan chimney sweep. The Bremen catalogue reflects this holiday emphasis, with a page full of German and Swiss chocolates, marzipan, Droste's delightful chocolate apples and oranges, and all sorts of other treats.

In addition to all these sweetmeats, other ingredients for German cooking are available from Bremen. Imported cheese and smoked meats, jams, even imported vegetables are listed. These include giant asparagus, celery (either in knobs or salad), and mushrooms, both Bavarian and Swiss. Reflecting Germany's new links with Eastern Europe, Bremen sells a wide choice of Polish canned game, roe deer in fillets or goulash, wild boar in juniper sauce, wild boar with mushrooms or haunch of hare, all under $3 a pound. In addition to these relatively local specialties, Bremen is a good source of other imported foods that Germans import back home: a wide variety of Scandinavian seafood—herrings, anchovies, etc.; French cheese; honey, and other delicacies. Bremen also sells its own meat products, ranging from smoked goose breast at $8 a pound to liverwurst at $1.69 a pound.

Bremen also has a second store that sells other German products, such as German colognes and cosmetics, which are included in this price list along with the German magazines, calendars, records and Christmas decorations that the store also stocks.

INDIAN

Javin Brands, Inc. (Java-India Condiment Co.), 440 Hudson Street, New York, N.Y. 10014
Price list and recipe leaflet, free.

There are so many more people from the Indian subcontinent in New York now that a genuine Indian neighborhood has sprung up, with a dozen new spice and grocery shops where once an exclusively Armenian neighborhood flourished. In time, more of these will doubtless sell by mail. The ancestor of all these is Javin's, selling wholesale and by mail since 1935. Their list includes a large selection of spices as well as the best-known Indian condiments, such as Major Grey's Chutney, which they import, and various mango, lemon and other pickles. Here too are pappadums and other relatively unobtainable ingredients such as rice and chickpea flour, crushed wheat, whole raw betel nuts and various dahls. A rare source for lovers of Indian food.

Kalustyan's, 123 Lexington Avenue, New York, N.Y. 10016
Price list on receipt of self-addressed envelope.

The price list announces "All Oriental Foods," but isn't, in fact, that comprehensive, as it concentrates on Indian specialties: curries, spices, dahls, pappadums, pickles, chutneys, and betel and other nuts.

Trinacria Importing Co., 415 Third Avenue, New York, N.Y. 10016
Price list, free.

Entering Trinacria's incredibly crowded Third Avenue store is like stumbling into a fantastic attic jammed to the rafters with every conceivable food and kitchen appliance. Unfortunately, only a few of these foods are sold by mail, and Trinacria's modest price list concentrates on Indian food and spices. This is, however, a very useful place to buy dahls, pappadums, chutneys, and various spices and condiments. Here are mango pickles, raw cashews, mustard and coconut oil, and fresh ginger root, coriander and "garlick." Trinacria also sells various flours—rice flour for only 35 cents a pound, chickpea and whole-wheat flour—as well as Basmati rice. However, if you know specifically what you need in this area, then ask Trinacria. "We probably have it," they'll say with assurance, and judging from the look of their store, they are undoubtedly right.

INDONESIAN

Mrs. De Wildt, 245-A Fox Gap Road, R.D. #3, Bangor, Pa. 18013

Price list, free.

I had known of this firm as the best place in America to get Indonesian food and spices, but I did not realize that it also has an extensive stock of Dutch food. As you would imagine, the firm was started (twenty years ago) by a couple who had been living in Indonesia and moved to America. Since then, they not only have built up a mail-order business but have begun to serve the classic Indonesian Rijsttafel dinner to a small number of people who reserve a place on weekends and holidays. If you'd like to try to make your own, their price list includes all the requisite ingredients, from *sambal* (hot pepper pastes) to *krupuk udang* (shrimp tapioca wafers that are deep-fried and then served with rice). All sorts of spices are listed, as well as Javanese fruits that are recommended with vanilla ice cream. Indonesian cooking is hardly known in America, but anything that requires wild-lime leaves or dried lily flowers seems very tempting to me.

De Wildt's Dutch list has to look stolid by comparison, but is well worth thinking about. The traditional cheeses are all here—Gouda, Edam, Leyden cumin—priced at $1.40-$1.60 a pound, and Dutch cookies, candies, honeys, herrings, as well as dried beans, peas, etc. Finally, De Wildt offers various other Asian chutneys, curry powders and gingers as well as fruit, teas and other items useful in recipes from Hawaii to India.

5 • *Maryland Gourmet Mart* Goose, either ready to cook or prepared with herbs and spices, then smoked over apple-wood fires. $25.95.

ITALIAN

Manganaro Foods, 488 Ninth Avenue, New York, N.Y. 10018

20-page catalogue, free.

While many second- or third-generation Americans have left the city, the stores they used to patronize have stayed behind, thriving on weekend visits from the suburbs, and in some cases, on mail order. Unfortunately, few Italian American stores sell by mail, but Manganaro's can probably supply everything that you would like in this area. Located since 1893 near one of New York's few remaining market districts, Manganaro's store is reassuringly bedecked with the hams and cheeses that make Italian stores such a delight to visit. Their catalogue is a thorough and businesslike listing, mostly of food from Italy but with a few interesting exceptions, such as meat-filled cannelloni from France. Salami and proscuitto start the list, with imported salami ranging from $2.80 to $3.50 a pound, domestic at $2.20 to $2.60. Imported proscuitto

6

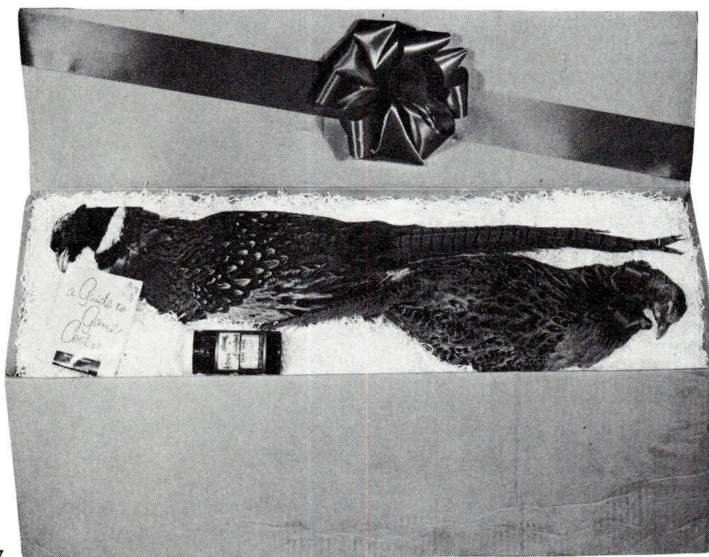

7

8

6 • *Maryland Gourmet Mart* Aged short-cut steaks are flash-frozen and mailed in dry ice. Sold in boxes of ten (16 oz. each) for $46.75; twelve (12 oz. each) for $42; or eighteen (8 oz. each) for $42.

7 • *Maryland Gourmet Mart* A brace of specially raised pheasants in full plumage, weighing not less than 5 lbs., with a jar of Maryland Game Sauce. $15.

8 • *Maryland Gourmet Mart* Half-gallon kegs (3 lbs.) of California pears in rum, $12.95.

is among the most expensive of delicacies, $4.50 a pound in bulk (5 lbs. average) and $5 sliced thin.

All the makings for antipasto are listed either in prepared packages—a 1-lb. 5-oz. jar of anchovies, peppers, mushrooms, artichokes, etc., for $7.50—or separately. There is a selection of herbs, vegetables, soups, etc., as well as such relatively unobtainable items as dry mushrooms from northern Italy ($1.20 per ounce) and white or back truffles ($4.80 or $3.50 per ounce).

Cheese is one of Manganaro's strong points and the catalogue thoughtfully describes each in case you didn't really know that parmigiano is finely textured, semihard cheese with a delicate mellow flavor ($3.40 a pound), while Gorgonzola is blue-veined, soft and slightly creamy with a spicelike flavor ($2.50 a pound). There are special imported grating cheeses—don't grind your $3.10-a-pound provolone, use a $2.60 pecorino or even an Argentine fiore sardo at a mere $1.50.

Manganaro's also has lists of such seafood as *scungili* (conch) that is hard to come by locally, as well as anchovies, *calamares* (cuttlefish) and *baccala*, the boneless dry cod that is a staple of all Latin popular cooking. Then the pasta list, which sounds like a grand Verdi aria: spaghetti, spaghettini, capellini, fini lingue di passero piccole, and so on. Prices range from 55 cents a pound for green (spinach) noodles to $1 a pound for homemade noodles, so fresh that, alas, mail orders are precluded. Altogether there are five hundred varieties of pasta, shapes and kinds, to choose from.

Finally, desserts: *panettone*, the traditional holiday cake; *torrone*, the dark Italian nougat; *colomba*, the dove-shaped Easter cake; *amaretti*, the marvelous hard Italian macaroons that come wrapped in a tissue so delicately printed that they look like banknotes; the Viennese *panforte* (a slim, round flat cake thick with candied citrus, sugar and almonds), and assorted fruits, chestnuts and other sweets in brandy or outrageously thick syrup. Most of these are made by the traditional Italian firms, Motta, Alemagna, and the like, which all charge roughly the same, $2.40 a pound for *panettone* and roughly the same for other pastries. *Torrone* is close to 50 cents a pound, but the famous Perugina chocolates are much more expensive. These include the delicious *baci*, hazelnut-filled chocolate kisses, at $1.90 for twenty. At Eastertime, chocolate eggs are a specialty, including some with a white candy coating, which look just like the real thing and are perfect for those who wish to combine the spirit of April Fool's Day with their Easter-egg hunt.

Manganaro's also sells the special kitchen implements needed to make your own noodles, ravioli, etc., and these are listed in detail in the House section.

JAPANESE

Katagiri and Co., Inc., 224 E. 59th Street, New York, N.Y. 10022
Price list, free.

For over sixty years Katagiri has been importing Japanese food and utensils, and some Chinese food, in this store in the midst of what is now New York's newest shopping area. Ironic that some of the hardest-to-find foods should be available so centrally. Katagiri stocks many of the basics for Japanese cooking: bean paste, various noodles and cereals, seaweed, sauces and condiments, and canned vegetables, fruits and pickles. A few fish such as broiled eel, octopus and squid are also available. Teas, and confections such as seaweed candy and rice cakes, are also listed. Prices are reasonable and the firm seems quite accustomed to mail order.

MIDDLE-EASTERN

Sahadi Importing Co., Inc., 187 Atlantic Avenue, Brooklyn, N.Y. 11201
20-page catalogue, free.

The Sahadi family has been importing food from the Middle East since 1895 and used to be located at the southern tip of Manhattan, which once contained a marvelous mixture of Arabic and Armenian shops and restaurants. Urban renewal destroyed that neighborhood, but many of the Middle-Eastern shops regrouped in Brooklyn's Atlantic Avenue, forming a new and unexpected center in the midst of a traditional Jewish neighborhood. For those who are not able to visit that delightful row of shops, the Sahadi catalogue offers a very tempting sampler, though unfortunately that is not enough to give you a taste of the extraordinarily rich Arabic ice creams, whose flavors of honey, pistachio and apricots are undreamt of even by Baskin and Robbins.

As is the case with so many of these ethnic catalogues, you find not only the ingredients for Middle-Eastern (and to some degree Greek and Indian) cuisine but a range of foods of special interest to natural-food enthusiasts. Sahadi sells a wide range of cereals and beans: bulgur wheat for pilaffs at 22 cents a pound; chickpeas, to be eaten as is or turned into *hummos;* and fava beans for *falafel* (or, if you are less sure of yourself or if you don't want to bother, dry mixes for these delicious appetizers). Nuts of all sorts are available at very reasonable prices; pumpkin and melon seeds, all at prices that are much lower than those charged in local stores; for instance, $8.75 for a 5-lb. bag of jumbo pistachios. Spices, dried vegetables, canned goods, even seeds from Syria are all listed, fulfilling the requirements of the most ambitious recipe.

But the most elaborate offerings are the sweets. I suppose it is the Moslem prohibition against alcohol that makes this alternate form of indulgence so popular, but here are desserts that may change your own tastes. Turkish Delight in all sorts of varieties, costing surprisingly little: 75 cents a pound for plain, $1.40 for pistachio fillings, $3 for the special; apricot candy (halawa), again remarkably cheap: one kilo (2.2 lbs.) imported from Lebanon for $2.50; preserved fruits, fig or rose-petal jam, tamarind syrup or dark honey—Scheherazade's spirit clearly moves through these enchanting listings. Sahadi even offers the traditional honey-and-nut pastries, which I didn't think could be mailed, but which are sold in cans at $2.25 a pound.

Sahadi also sells a number of kitchen appliances, such as the lovely small copper pots used to make Turkish coffee, couscous pots and special wooden cookie stamps, garlic pounders, and the like.

MISCELLANEOUS

Les Echalottes, Ramsey, N.J. 07446
20-page catalogue, 25 cents.

This good-humored catalogue has gained an excellent reputation both for the variety of imported foods it contains and for its low prices. But its most original contribution may be the fresh shallots grown by the owner and available at $1 a pound, plus postage, or, for $13.50, 12 ounces sent you each month of the year.

The catalogue lists the most popular of French gourmet foods—pâté de foie gras, caviar, snails, truffles, all at very reasonable prices. But they also stock some out-of-the-way specialties such as the Indonesian curry powders, chili pastes and other condiments necessary for so many Southeast Asian recipes, a nice selection of chutneys, and a number of Mexican foods which apparently survive the canning process and are suitably inexpensive: 2 lbs. of tortillas for $1.40; 15 oz. of enchilada sauce for 65 cents; beans at 45 cents for 15 oz.

Among the other hard-to-find foods in this catalogue are French quenelles, the delicious pike dumplings that are so hard to make yourself; French and German soups; and French chestnuts, either as marrons glacés, in vanilla syrup, or puréed (marvelous for desserts, or as a vegetable with venison). A pleasant and unpretentious catalogue with, as you can see, a catholic selection.

Pepperidge Farm Mail Order Co., Inc., P.O. Box 7000, Norwalk, Conn. 06856
8-page color brochure, free.

Pepperidge Farm, one of the big quality bakers in the East, has set up a mail-order company that sells speciality foods, most of which appear to come from other firms. Vermont maple syrup, ham, bacon, meats are among the goods offered, but I'm not too sure why these items should be bought from Pepperidge rather than smaller, local firms. On the other hand, this catalogue is a source for Godiva chocolates, those highly priced, originally Belgian chocolates that are now sold in America. Pepperidge also offers their own fruit cake, which they say is made entirely without artificial preservatives.

MEAT

Maryland Gourmet Mart, 414 Amsterdam Avenue, New York, N.Y. 10024
Catalogue, free. Available November and December. Special leaflets on wild game, game birds and poultry specialties.

I first discovered this store before it had a thriving mail-order business. Located in the heart of New York's upper West Side (appropriately enough, right behind the Museum of Natural History), it was one of the few places in New York offering venison, pheasant and the like for sale to our more prosperous neighbors. The store has kept much of the feel of a neighborhood family enterprise and stresses that no order goes out without the personal supervision of a member of the family. But now only 2 percent of its customers buy

9

10

9 • *Byrd Mill* Todd's old Virginia slab bacon, cloth-wrapped and sold in weights from 4 to 10 lbs. $1.79 per pound.

10 • *Byrd Mill* Todd's old Virginia ham, sold uncooked, $1.99 per pound; cooked—bone in, $2.59, boneless, $3.79.

direct; the rest order their filet mignon or suckling pig by mail. Meat is quick-frozen, packed in dry ice and then air-expressed throughout the country. A box of twelve prime cut filet mignons, weighing 8 oz. each, costs $40.95. Venison steaks are $3.25 a pound and buffalo steak $3.90, and wild boar is only $1.75 per pound if you buy a whole one (from 30 to 60 lbs.).

The special game leaflet lists such exotica as elk, elephant, whale and turtle ($2.25 a pound), as well as every imaginable game bird, from oven-ready pheasant averaging a pound each for $2.65 to Scotch grouse, wild turkey, partridge, peacock and ptarmigan (only penguins and puffins seem to be missing).

In addition to offering these rare birds, Maryland Gourmet does some astonishing and very appetizing things to the humble chicken. There is a mouth-watering list of stuffed chicken breasts prepared in ways that only the most daring cooks would try: Alfredo—stuffed with noodles, sour-cream sauce and nutmeg, and topped with French-bread crumbs and parmesan cheese; apple-and-almond-filled (Dutch style, i.e., filled with tart green apples braised in butter with white raisins, toasted almonds, bread crumbs and a dash of cinnamon). Both Alfredo and Dutch style are $1.40 for each 6-oz. portion, or $15.95 a dozen.

There is the classic chicken Kiev and a stuffing of wild rice at a price of $1.60 per 7-oz. serving. Boneless stuffed legs are available for considerably less (90 cents for apple and $1 for wild rice), as well as squab, rock cornish hen, etc.

The rest of Maryland Gourmet's delicacies are listed in their annual illustrated catalogue, which includes a good selection of cheeses, jams, Smithfield ham, etc.

New Yorkers can order by phone. Those living outside the city should add $2 for dry ice and be prepared to pay extra for air freight and order certain minimum quantities. Free mailing pieces are sent to customers throughout the year and sound as if they should permanently subvert your domestic economy.

McArthur's Smokehouse, Millerton, N.Y. 12546
Price list and descriptive brochure, free.

While a number of stores offer some smoked meat (usually ham and bacon) by mail, it is rare to find someone offering the full range of smokehouse foods. McArthur's offers the widest range that I've seen, from game hens ($2.50 for each 1-lb. bird) to smoked trout ($2 per ½-lb. fish). Their baked ham (bathed in molasses for seven weeks) is only $2.55 per pound, available in 4-lb. or 9-lb. weights. McArthur's also sells some smoked meats I've never tried: smoked leg of mutton at $2.75 a pound; crown roast of pork, (quite enough for ten) at $2.70; and smoked capon and turkey. Then there is the usual Canadian bacon at $3.20 and hickory-smoked bacon at $1.80, again a price that compares well with local grocery stores.

Schaller & Weber, 22-35 46th Street, Long Island City, N.Y. 11105
Catalogue, free.

To those who know New York's German section, Yorkville, the Schaller & Weber window, decorated with yards if not kilometers of hanging sausages of all sorts, is one of the gastronomic and indeed esthetic landmarks.

The owners proudly claim on the cover of the price list that theirs is the only American-made products ever to win the highest prizes at the Utrecht International Exposition, and even without that endorsement, I would agree that theirs are among the best wursts available in America. Their catalogue lists some eighty varieties of the most popular of all German foods, from the various sausages (knockbauern, bock and weiss-wursts) to liverwurst and bolognas (which bear no relation at all to what is sold in supermarkets under that name), as well as Westphalian smoked hams and other delicacies. Even if you have no fond gastronomic memories of Germany, it is worth trying some of these surprisingly delicate foods, and the Schaller & Weber catalogue may be habit-forming.

FISH

Briggs Way Company, Ugashik, Alaska 99683
Price list and information sheet, free.

Those of us who live in zip code 100 rarely communicate with those in 99 and it's nice to hear of this unique, family-owned firm specializing in fresh Alaska seafoods packed in glass. The packed-in-glass is apparently a major point, since the fish goes from sea to glass in twelve hours, avoiding the many impurities that can be picked up on the way to the cannery, as well as the resins that are part of the canning process itself and to which some people are allergic. Briggs Way ships by parcel post throughout the country and offers packages of 12, 24 or 48 jars of natural Alaskan salmon at roughly $1 a jar, plus postage and insurance. An interesting addition to the growing list of pure and naturally grown foods.

Embassy Seafoods, Inc., P.O. Box 165, Gloucester, Mass. 01930
Leaflet, free.

This firm presents an interesting change from the usual fish that can be ordered by mail. The specialties are salt cod and mackerel, cured in the traditional way of fishermen before freezing, using salt and brine. A wooden bucket of one-pound mackerel costs $9.50 for 5 lbs., $16.50 for 10 lbs.; cod being more expensive at $11.15 for 5 lbs. In addition to this, Embassy offers its own brands of canned seafood and soups: lobster, codfish cakes, clams, and lobster soups and various chowders. The lobster is the most expensive, costing $11.55 for just under a pound, but minced clams cost $1.75 for three 7-oz. cans. Dips and spreads made from these fish are also available in cans, as is shad roe, steamed clams in their shells and other delicacies.

Hegg and Hegg Smoked Salmon, Inc., 801 Marine Drive, Port Angeles, Wash. 98362
Price lists and brochures, free.

Hegg and Hegg have been selling smoked salmon and canned fish through the mails for twenty-one years, the smoked salmon being available direct only from them. The salmon, from Puget Sound, comes vacuum-sealed in a plastic container, and a whole fish, weighing approximately 4 lbs., costs an incredibly low $11 ($11.75 east of the Rockies), with a half salmon costing $6.25 ($7). This is much cheaper than Nova Scotia or Scottish salmon—the least expensive of the former costs around $6-$8 a pound in New York, though the taste may be very different. The salmon, smoked or not, is

11 • *McArthur's Smokehouse* Smoked trout, about 8 oz. each. $2 each. *photo Martha Porter*

available in 6½-oz. cans, at roughly $1 a can for the regular and $1.50 for the smoked. Smoked sturgeon is about the same price. Tuna and shrimp cost about the same as the salmon, $6.25 for six cans ($6.75 east of the Rockies). Various gift assortments mixing these are available, and various other delicacies, such as smoked Pacific oysters, or smoked butter clams are included in these.

Saltwater Farm, York Harbor, Maine 03911
22-page catalogue, free.

Saltwater Farm is the country's leading purveyor of live lobsters, a complicated business that concentrates on shipping from eight to twenty lobsters (with or without clams) by air freight to lobster lovers throughout the country. Once the ready-to-cook container reaches you, you are instructed simply to punch a few holes in the metal lid and pour in salt water and cook, to spare you from having to watch them being boiled alive. If your scruples extend to not wishing to boil lobsters personally, even when shielded from view, you can buy lobster tails from Saltwater Farm, or limit yourself to clams. Lobsters average 1⅛ lbs., and cost roughly $5 each (plus shipping). Clams are $19.95 for two pecks, $25.75 for three, but somewhat less, around $6 a peck, if bought in conjunction with the lobsters.

When Saltwater Farm started, over twenty years ago, lobsters were shipped by rail, and railway employees would ice down lobster barrels every few hundred miles (far better service than I can remember ever getting on the Boston & Maine), but now the jet age allows the firm to send its lobsters all over the world, and also to import smoked salmon from Ireland, which it sells along with a number of other delicacies not native to Maine, such as stuffed red snapper, crab, and various smoked and fresh meats. Of the latter, the most interesting is a package of eight 12-oz. sirloins for $39 from the renowned Boston butcher Dole & Bailey. The catalogue also lists various lobster-eating accessories and a number of related items.

CHEESE

Cheese of All Nations, 153 Chambers Street, New York, N.Y. 10003
68-page catalogue, free if you mention this book.

Cheese of All Nations is the best source that I have found for buying imported cheese by mail, and their catalogue will be a relief to beleagured cheese lovers who have opened packets and cans of foreign cheese only to be disappointed by the results. Very few stores have an adequate supply of good imported cheeses, and none, I should think, can match this one.

Prices are reasonable and compare favorably with other New York stores, and the catalogue lists meticulously whether the cheese is prepackaged or not, in what months certain cheeses are available, etc. The list of nations involved in this enterprise is vast. While you may not find yourself tempted by cheeses from Alaska or Albania, the descriptions from Argentina and Armenia may whet your appetite, and by the time you reach Austria the twenty-eight varieties, all under $2, may seem irrestible. Recent prices for a 3-lb. Stilton or Brie were $7.50 and $7.95 respectively; $10.95 for a 5-lb. Port-Salut; and $8.50 for 6 lbs. of Danish Tybo.

In addition to all this, the store offers various assortments, a Cheese of the Month Club, and even a Big Cheese Club which offers various discounts, a newsletter, and if you live near New York, invitations to tastings, lectures, etc.

Cheese Unlimited, 1263 Lexington Avenue, New York, N.Y. 10028
Leaflet, free.

Cheese Unlimited mails cheese throughout the world, but it has no catalogue or price list as such. It will send you a leaflet listing their French cheeses, but the simplest thing to do is write and ask for the price of the cheese you want or order blind (minimum order accepted, $10). Cheese prices vary constantly but the fluctuations are not enormous, so if you want some Brie, for instance, the price will probably be between $3 and $4, per pound whatever happens. Among the imported cheeses listed are Cantal, chèvre chabichou, Alsatian Münster and Roblechon, as well as the better-known favorites.

Crowley Cheese, Healdville, Vt. 05147

The Crowley family has been making cheese for sale since 1824, and have occupied their current factory since 1882. Their cheese is still made according to the old Vermont process, cutting and raking the curds by hand and using old-fashioned crank presses. The result is that Crowley Cheddar bears little resemblance to store-bought cheese. It comes in 3-lb. and 5-lb. wheels, mild, medium or sharp, and costs from $6.50 to $7.25 and $9 to $10, respectively, depending on postage. The cheese factory is open to visitors, and the Crowley shop nearby also sells a variety of local foods and handicrafts.

Wisconsin Cheese Makers Guild, 6048 W. Beloit Road, Milwaukee, Wis. 53219
Large color catalogue once a year, free.

Figi's, Inc., Marshfield, Wis. 54449
60-page annual illustrated catalogue in color, free.

The Swiss Cheese Shop and Factory, Highway 69, Monroe, Wis. 53566
Leaflet, free.

The Swiss Colony, 1112 7th Avenue, Monroe, Wis. 53566
84-page color catalogue.

Buying Wisconsin cheese by mail is apparently one of America's favorite indoor sports, judging from these catalogues and from the many ads that appear for these and similar companies. The Wisconsin Guild mails out over seven million catalogues a year, Figi's nine million. Both firms appear to have started with food and then gone "upmarket," offering more expensive but less interesting items, such as cooking appliances, trays and the like, packaged with the food. These are reminiscent of the holiday suggestion corner in shopping-center drugstores, and seem geared to people who want to give a present worth about ten or twenty or whatever dollars. Assuming that you are genuinely interested in Wisconsin cheese, there are a few items that seem worthwhile. Wisconsin offers a 2-lb. crock of Cheddar at $3.95, and an 8-lb. mixed-cheese assortment at $11.95.

Disregarding the cellophane wrappers and plastic boxes, Wisconsin's best offer is their custom cuts, 5 lbs. of sharp Cheddar for $8.95, etc., modestly listed on the catalogue's back cover. Swiss Colony's Cheddar is $1.75 a pound, as is their Swiss and Port-Salut. Figi's offers a similar choice, as well as some wheels of aged Cheddar at $6.50 for 3 lbs. The catalogues offer a large variety of meats, desserts, etc., but few of these seem to be locally made.

Their smoked hams and turkeys seem to be about the same price as other suppliers', but again, I have no indication of origin.

The Swiss Cheese Shop publishes a more modest leaflet, but with an equally good listing of bulk cheeses, at similar prices.

For more cheese, see Regional and Imported Food shops in this section.

NATURAL FOOD

Byrd Mill, P.O. Box 5167, Richmond, Va. 23220
Price list, free.

Byrd Mill is an actual mill specializing in stone-ground whole grains. Its price list should warm the heart of any expatriate Southerner and whet the appetite of any natural-food buff. Its products are such organic stand-bys as unbleached flour and wheat germ, various pancake mixes (buckwheat, whole wheat, and even wild rice), such regional specialties as white or yellow grits, pioneer's porridge (a high-protein cereal made of wheat, corn, rye, oats and rice) and rice flour.

Greenberg's Natural Foods, Inc., 125 First Avenue, New York, N.Y. 10003
44-page price list, 50 cents.

While most natural-food stores have started in the last few years, Greenberg's is now in its fiftieth year and fourth generation. The store's catalogue is one of the most comprehensive, and the store itself also sells organic vegetables and frozen foods. The catalogue lists the standard health foods as well as having an extensive macrobiotic section and a choice of Japanese products, such as seaweed, dried fish, dried radishes and seaweed-gelatin bars. Grains, beans, nuts and flour are available in bulk, all being available in quantities of up to 100 lbs. except for the nuts, where the largest amount is a 30-lb. box.

Greenberg has a selection of baked goods, including "Lima" rice cakes from Belgium, which includes all sorts of cakes and cookies. Candies, fruit concentrates, nut butters and oils are among the other foods listed. Vitamins and food supplements, from Hoffman and Nature Plus, are also available. Finally, the store is the East Coast distributor of L & A Juices and carries the full range of the juices and fruits sold under the label.

Paul C. Laing Apiaries, 8448 Chestnut Ridge Road, N.Y. Route 77, Gasport, N.Y. 14067
Price list, free.

Paul Laing has no catalogue, but simply produces organic honey for sale by the pail. An impassioned believer in the importance of bees, he stresses that his honey is from areas of little or no sprays or herbicides.

12 • *Paprikas Weiss* Liptauer cheese ball, adapted from an old European recipe. Well-aged Cheddar is mixed with Hungarian paprika and Dutch caraway seeds, and shaped into a ball. 12-oz. ball in a gift box, $3.98.

13 • *Byrd Mill* 9-lb. "country breakfast" package, which includes three 1-lb. packages of mixes, a pint of maple syrup, and 4 lbs. of dry-cured, hickory-smoked Todd slab bacon. $11, including postage.

14 • *Paprikas Weiss* Ten different shapes of pasta, 98 cents a pound.

His honey is neither heated nor filtered and clearly will primarily interest natural-food enthusiasts. The cost of a 5-lb. pail, postpaid and insured, is $4. Three cost $11, and six, $20.

Nichols Garden Nursery, 1190 North Pacific Highway, Albany, Oreg. 97321
Catalogue, free.

In addition to selling a very wide choice of herbs and spices, Nichols has a number of gastronomic aids. Here, for instance, is one of the few catalogues to offer yoghurt cultures. These sell for $1.75 or $2.25, but once you start making yoghurt you can go on forever, using part of each new batch to make the next. Nichols also has a wide range of materials needed for home beer and wine making—from the wine yeasts to corking machines.

There is a page of herbal teas and various other health foods such as carob drink, natural chicken broth, etc. In addition to this, Nichols sells a number of macrobiotic foods, various sea vegetables and dried Japanese vegetables, as well as related Japanese seasonings from "pure soy sauce" to seasonings that I've not heard of, including one made from black sesame seeds. Finally, Nichols offers a special range of southern Oregon cheeses. A goat Cheddar cheese costs close to $5 for 2 lbs. and their raw-milk Cheddar is nearly as expensive. A wheel of blue cheese is slightly less, $8.50 for 5 lbs. ($9.50 east of the Rockies). Nichols' catalogue also lists several pages of books about herbs, herb growing and natural foods in general.

Walnut Acres, Inc., Penns Creek, Pa. 17862
Catalogue, brochures and price lists, free.

The Walnut Acres catalogue is the most complete of any of the natural-food suppliers that I have seen. The name refers to an actual farm, 360 acres of it, which has been growing and shipping whole foods since 1945. It started in a practically classic fashion with a couple, the Keenes, inspired by Gandhi and others who urged a back-to-the-soil movement, left college teaching to farm, at first for themselves and gradually for others. Success came after some time and a stone mill, a cannery and other facilities were added. The farm is open to visitors, and very good brochures describing Walnut Acres (and how to get there) are free for the asking.

The actual catalogue is just about comprehensive, listing not only the usual grains, fruits and nuts, but meat, fish, eggs, vegetables, even bottled water. Walnut Acres also sells a large selection of vitamins and natural cosmetics, and even laundry detergents and cleaners free of phosphates and NTA.

If you're a serious user of natural foods, or have friends who are, then it makes sense to buy in bulk. These prices offer considerable savings; wheat germ toasted, for instance, costs 53 cents per pound, but $17.76 for 50 lbs. (curiously, the 100-lb. price offers no further saving). Spanish peanuts are 68 cents a pound and $12.22 for 25 lbs., though there, too, the savings stop.

Walnut Acres is one of the few firms selling homemade bread, which is shipped the day it is baked and can be frozen once you get it. Whole wheat and rye cost roughly 50 cents for a 1¼-lb. loaf. Various cookies and special breads, such as blueberry and cranberry date-nut are also available. Walnut Acres also makes its own fruit and vegetable juices—apple, cranberry, pear, tomato and vegetable—and its canned produce can supply you with most foods you'd want. What it does not grow itself Walnut Acres obtains from others, and the catalogue lists just about everything except fresh fruit or anything frozen.

There is also a large choice of books and various household appliances, from yoghurt makers to baby-food grinders.

DEHYDRATED FOOD

Chuck Wagon Foods, Micro Drive, Woburn, Mass. 01801
List, free.

Like Perma Pak, these are specialists in food for camping and hiking, selling easy-to-pack units that should feed a camper on less than twenty ounces a day. Chuck Wagon also estimates that about $2 a day will feed each of six campers. Their catalogue is very efficiently organized to give you the cost of feeding two, four and six persons, and the cooking time needed, so that you can splurge on Beef Stroganoff at $3.58 for six with twelve minutes' cooking time, or have a hurried meal of Spanish Rice which takes five minutes to cook and costs $1.70 for six. Full repasts, from breakfast to dinner, are available, as well as special emergency kits to store in boats, etc. Chuck Wagon also sells a range of High Energy fruit-and-nut bars, made of such appetizing combinations as fig, orange and walnut, which you may want to have around for everyday use.

Perma Pak, 40 E. 2430 South, Salt Lake City, Utah 84115 *Brochures, free.*

Perma Pak specializes in dehydrated foods suitable for home storage—"tangible insurance," to quote its brochure, against "food shortages, unemployment, civil unrest," and though they are too delicate to mention it, I suppose, atomic attack and enemies from outer space. For people in areas that are likely to be flooded, these practical and easily stored packets may be the ideal way to fill an attic; for those of us in areas where civil unrest is more likely, food may not be the insurance we need. But for campers, there is no doubt that Perma Pak is really useful. A complete catalogue of foods for backpacking, trailering and camping is available, offering a vast array of economically packed essential foods that can be prepared with ease.

HERBS

Aphrodisia, 28 Carmine Street, New York, N.Y. 10014
64-page price list, 35 cents. Fall.

Aphrodisia deals in "everything in herbs and spices" but hastens to add that its name is not intended to convey any aphrodisiac qualities. The store does have by far the most complete list that I've seen and says that they are "growing at a dizzying speed." The catalogue includes not only thirty-five pages of spices known to the West but a selection of Indian, Indonesian and Chinese items. Oils, herbal teas, organic cosmetics and flower waxes, which can be used as perfume, are also available. There are also five pages of books on herbs, spices, etc.

Aphrodisia includes a useful and fascinating description of most herbs listed sometimes offering cooking advice or supplying a recipe. I learned that periwinkle was an herbal tea, and that nettle, which Shakespeare used to describe Ophelia, could be used in soup or teas or for the hair and skin. Mugwort takes you on a tour through history, being used in medieval times to make beer (hence mug), for Christmas-goose stuffing and now, appropriately enough, for macrobiotic teas.

Shuttle Hill Herbs, 256B Delaware Avenue, Delmar, N.Y. 12054
Price list, 25 cents.

Shuttle Hill Herbs is a small shop that specializes in dried herbs but also sells a number of other foods which they make themselves. The selection of herbs is limited to the more common cooking varieties, basil, sage, rosemary, etc., but there is a nice choice of herb teas. There are herb plants and a very full range of seeds.

Shuttle Hill Herbs stocks a large variety of pure jams and jellies made without preservatives and including such rare flavors as elderberry, ginger-rhubarb, quince, etc. It also makes its own mustard and mustard sauce and vinegar, though warns against shipping this last item because of possible breakage. Potpourri and pomanders fill out the list, along with an old herbal specialty I'd never seen before, a mint pillow, which used to be recommended for insomnia and headaches.

For more herbs, see the Gardening, and Perfume and Cosmetics sections.

NUTS

California Almond Growers Exchange, P.O. Box 1768, Sacramento, Calif. 95808
16-page color catalogue, free. Published every September.

The California Almond growers have done an excellent job of publicizing their smoked almonds; you may have seen their ads or tasted their product on airplane rides. But they don't seem to have gotten them into the stores as effectively, and buying from their tempting catalogue may be the only way for you to get these "Blue Diamond" almonds. Various gift assortments are available, averaging $5.25 for six 6-oz. tins, or $8.50 for twelve. Larger tins, 4 lbs., or $7, offer considerable savings. In addition to these appetizer nuts, there are other varieties: cooking almonds, slivered, diced, etc., at roughly $2 a pound, and for marzipan makers, a real bargain of 7 lbs. of almond paste for $8.45. Prices include shipping and end up being much cheaper than those little plastic bags that you usually buy at the last minute at exorbitant prices.

The Packing Shed, P.O. Box 11, Weyers Cave, Va. 24486
Leaflet, free.

This small firm specializes in a traditional Tidewater delicacy, peanuts cooked in coconut oil. These nuts are free from the preservatives and additives usually involved in commercial processing. The nuts are also on sale at Colonial Williamsburg. The Packing Shed sells a 4-lb. tin for $5.

Priester's Pecans, Fort Deposit, Ala. 36032
32-page color catalogue, free.

Another purveyor of pecans, this firm specializes in handsome gift packaging and assortments. For plain pecans, their 2¼-lb. box costs $6.35; in gift tins the price goes up somewhat. Pecan brittle, a nice idea, costs $3.25 a pound and pecan pralines are only slightly more. Other variants include pecan glacé, at $5.85 for 20 ounces, smoked pecans, chocolate and pecans, and pecan crunch. Pecan fruit cake, pecan fruit assortments and pecan-stuffed dates are yet other possibilities. All the confections are handmade and look very tempting indeed.

Sternberg Pecan Co., P.O. Box 193, Jackson, Miss. 39205
Price lists and brochures, free.

Sternberg's is a family estblishment that sells shelled pecans, and only this, by mail. It was one of the first firms to make these nuts available outside of the region that grows, I learned to my surprise, the world's total output. As a result, they know a great deal about pecans and enclose with their mailings a tempting little list of recipes. Their prices range from $6.75 for 2 lbs. to $27 for 10 lbs. Their season runs only from November 1, when the new crop is ready, to February or March.

Young Pecan Sales Corp., P.O. Box 632, Florence, S.C. 29501
Annual brochure, free.

For some reason, pecans are among the easiest of Southern agricultural products to buy by mail, and though I have unfortunately yet to find someone to send me a good pecan pie, the ingredients are readily available. Young's sells pecan halves at $2 a pound, plus postage, as well as pecan logs and pecan fruit cakes.

HONEY

Thousand Island Apiaries, Clayton, 1000 Islands, N.Y. 13624
Price list, free.

This family business is now in its second generation of beekeeping. One of the owners says that he was practically born with a bee smoker in his hand, and the elves that decorate the Elfin Gold Honey price list are the work of a fourteen-year-old granddaughter. The honey is unsprayed and comes liquid, creamed (finely granulated honey) or in combs. These last are the most expensive, costing $2 for a 12-oz. comb, or $4.50 for three. Liquid honey is $4 for 3 lbs., and somewhat less in larger quantities, and creamed costs $5.55 for 4½ lbs.

For more honey, see Natural Food (above).

MAPLE SYRUP

Henry and Cordelia Swayze, Brookside Farm, Turnbridge, Vt. 05077
Price list, free.

Organic maple syrup, straight from the farm, made by very serious producers who liken the work to wine making. As a result, they specially blend complementary flavors, since each batch of syrup differs in taste. The syrup that doesn't live up to their high standards is sold to commercial packers, and your satisfaction is guaranteed. With all this, Brookside Farm's prices are competitive with those of far larger commercial outfits, 1 quart of syrup costing $3.75, and 10 quarts to the same address, $32.50, plus postage, which can be very high on small quantities if you live far away. Cooking syrup costs only $4.75 per half-gallon, and comes with a recipe booklet.

CAKE

Butterfield Farms, Inc., 919 Third Avenue, New York, N.Y. 10022
Leaflet and sample.

Despite their inauspicious address, Butterfield Farms makes a very tasty fruit cake and has the excellent idea of sending you a free and persuasive sample. The cakes are not inexpensive—2 lbs. for $5.95 up to 5 lbs. for $11.95—but the makers claim it is the world's most expensively made fruit cake. Perhaps their lushly written leaflet will persuade you that what you've just eaten is as special as they say it is.

CHOCOLATE

Bailey's, 26 Temple Place, Boston, Mass. 02111
Price list, free.

Any visitor to Boston is bound, sooner or later, to pass one of Bailey's enticing, old-fashioned candy stores and it is good to know that they are among the few shops that specialize in mailing chocolates all over the world.

Bailey's lists a number of mail-order selections, such as the Caramel Nut Chew Assortment ($2.90 per pound) or the Jelly Selection ($1.95), but you can choose from a full range of hand-dipped chocolates, caramels, nuts, hard candies, etc. Prices are reasonable, $2.85 a pound for most chocolates, $1.65 for fudge, etc. Chocolates and candies are made each day, so even with the delay of mailing, your order should be considerably fresher than the similarly priced packaged candies sold nationally.

Bissinger's, 205 W. Fourth Street, Cincinnati, Ohio 45202
Annual catalogue, free.

Bissinger's catalogue describes its wares as "the world's most elegant chocolates" and describes their first offering as "Mrs. Santa's Hot Pants, plush, red and lacy and packed with a pound tube of hard candies and a box of French mints" ($7.50). But beneath the outer "elegance" are some more serious chocolates, which sound both tempting and, by New York standards, reasonably priced. Bissinger's specialty are Nut Balls—freshly ground almond paste backed between pecans and walnuts, then dipped in chocolate—and a 2-lb. box costs $4.40. The catalogue has several pages of similarly rich goodies, as well as various gift boxes and assortments.

Perugina of Italy, 636 Lexington Avenue, New York, N.Y. 10022
Color leaflet, free.

Perugina's New York store has some of the most attractively packaged chocolates and candies available in New York, and its leaflet gives an idea of their special appeal. Various Italian ceramics, glass and crystal plates, boxes and ornaments hold some of the more lavish gifts, but even the regular boxes are handsomely designed. It's curious, as one looks at these toys and sweets, to think that the Perugina's New York store was closed during World War II and the company's Perugia factory totally destroyed by bombs.

Perugina now distributes a number of its more famous chocolates nationally, such as their *baci* kisses, and some may be available locally or from other stores in this book, such as Manganaro. However, the full selection is available only from the New York store. Since shipping costs are high for chocolate, you may want to think twice before ordering these not-inexpensive treats, but this may well be your only way to buy chocolate-covered marrons glacés (*castagne di bosco*), which I've never seen anywhere else, or other Perugina specials.

The Perugina touch is at its most ingenious at holiday time, particularly at Easter, and Perugina's chocolate eggs, covered with a white candy shell which is utterly convincing, come in small wooden crates that duplicate the Old World container. In addition to various boxes of assorted chocolates, nougat, marzipan and other equally sweet alternatives are available.

Plumridge, 33 E. 61st Street, New York, N.Y. 10021
Brochures, free. Issued three times a year.

"Confections for the Carriage Trade—Est. 1883" states the cerise leaflet listing these extremely expensive sweets for the rich. Plumridge started out supplying gift baskets of fruit to passengers on steamships, "as gifts from some of New York society's leading families." The seasonal nature of the fruits led the firm to develop substitutes such as candied fruits and spiced nuts, for which the firm is best known. The nuts sell from $5 a pound for ordinary pistachios in their shell (close to three times what others charge) to $5.75 for spiced cinnamon and sugar walnuts and pecans. Comparatively speaking, the price is not really an issue to Plumridge customers, and for most of the items the brochure doesn't even bother to list weight. A Golden Cabinet—a little gold-and-white paisley chest with five to nine trays—costs from $20 to $30. Plumridge makes its own jams and jellies, and sells an appealing mixture of dessert fruits, apricots, dates, prunes and figs. Baskets and other gift assortments are also available.

Schwartz Candies, Inc., 131 W. 72nd Street, New York, N.Y. 10023
Leaflet, free.

Schwartz is one of New York's few remaining confectioners' stores that make their own chocolates and candies rather than buy from some anonymous supplier. Most of these stores are very small, so it's good to have one that is used to selling by mail. The choice is classic, but the chocolates are excellent: assortments of creams, crisp-and-chewy nuts, and fruit covered in dark or milk chocolate, mints, caramel-nut patties, gift assortments, and dietetic chocolates made without salt or sugar. Chocolate-covered marshmallows in various flavors are also available. Nearly all the above cost $3 a pound, though postage is high and supports an argument for buying in quantity if you plan to buy at all.

COFFEE AND TEA

McNulty's Tea and Coffee Co., Inc., 109 Christopher Street, New York, N.Y. 10014
Price list, free.

Founded in 1895, McNulty's is probably New York's most famous purveyor of tea, coffee and spices, and over the years its mail-order sales have brought it a national reputation. The Village store retains much of its 1890's atmosphere and the price list bears a charming Art Nouveau poster design. But behind all this flourishes the city's largest tea and coffee business, and as a result, a number of exclusives, such as a vintage Darjeeling. Tea from mainland China is now also available and the McNulty list contains all the major black and green teas, ranging in price from $10 a pound for that Darjeeling to $2.50 a pound for orange pekoe, most teas being in the $3.50–$4 range. Blended teas, tea bags and herb teas are also available.

Coffee is available "straight" or blended, ranging in price from $1.85 to $2.05 for most kinds—Jamaican Blue

15 • *Butterfield Farms* 2-lb. fruit cake, $5.95. Larger cakes are sold at $7.95 for 3 lbs. and $11.95 for 5 lbs.

16 • *Paprikas Weiss* Teas of all sorts including herb teas are for sale, and coffee is roasted and ground daily. Prices from $2.98 a pound.

Mountain, of course, being the expensive exception at $2.75. The blends include some interesting combinations, such as the Viennese made of equal parts Colombia, Java, mocha and French-roasted Colombia. But the store will mix your own blend of tea or coffee if you prefer.

Northwestern Coffee Mills Store, 217 N. Broadway, Milwaukee, Wis. 53202
Price list, free.

The Northwestern Coffee Mills Store was helped enormously by a mention in the *Whole Earth Catalog*, which brought so many orders that they had to retool in order to handle a large mail-order flow.

Northwestern offers a wider choice, often at better prices, than many of their competitors. Coffee, in beans or ground, ranges from $1.30 for "Stapleton Restaurant" (a Milwaukee firm) to $1.70 for Mocha. French Roast is $1.40, and Brazilian Santos, Italian Espresso and Venezuelan E Tachiras, $1.45—coffees for which Bloomingdale's in New York charges $2 a pound and other New York stores $1.50-$1.80. Northwestern further points out that better coffee will give you up to 25 percent more cups per pound than the ordinary and that their beans should be stored in the refrigerator.

Northwestern offers much more than coffee (and coffee makers and grinders): spices, teas, botanicals (miscellaneous herbs), nuts, flavors are all listed. The teas range from $2.05 a pound for Russian Pamir Tura to $3.92 for lemon-spiced with assam, Darjeeling at $3.20 and English Breakfast at $2.28. Yerba Maté, the Latin-American beverage, costs $1.17.

Northwestern lists a wide choice of aromatic seeds (cardamom, coriander, cumin, mustard, etc.), snack seeds (pumpkin, soybean, sunflower), seasonings (garlic powder, orange peel, dried mushrooms, mandrake, etc.), herbs and spices of all kinds, and botanicals. In addition to those listed, Northwestern will quote you prices on some two thousand botanicals. Finally, Northwestern stocks palm, coconut and other oils, various nut butters and plain nuts, these again at prices much lower than those prevailing in New York. With its excellent choice of high-quality foods, Northwestern states that if they cannot send you material of the highest standard, they will return your check.

Schapira Coffee Company, 117 W. 10th Street, New York, N.Y. 10001
Price list, free.

Freshly roasted coffee beans are hard to find outside the largest cities, and besides, stores that sell by mail are extremely rare, so those who like a really good cup of coffee can be grateful for the Schapira Coffee Company. It has been roasting coffee or blending tea since 1903, now occupying a charming store in Greenwich Village, but a third of its business is by mail, to such remote places as Alaska.

Schapira's own blends are a combination of Colombian, Arabian and Brazilian beans sold in a light breakfast blend called American Roast, and in darker French and Italian versions, suitable for demitasse or simply for stronger palates. In addition, you can order Java, Maracaibo or Guatemalan coffee. Three pounds of the American costs $4.65, the French or Italian $4.95, and the others, $5.40. The coffee can be ground to your specifications or shipped as beans. Schapira now sells a decaffeinated coffee, ground or in the bean.

Tea costs from $2.55 a pound for Ceylonese to $4.85 for Imperial Mandarin, with most other kinds costing either $3.35 (China, Keemun) or $3.85 (Darjeeling, Jasmine, Assam, etc.). One hundred tea bags are roughly $1 less. Various samplers and assortments are also available.

VITAMINS

Johnston's Vitamin Products, 2640 E. 37th Street, Los Angeles, Calif. 90058
46-page catalogue, free.

The Johnston's catalogue is a well-written and useful brochure, containing a good deal of information, from descriptions of each vitamin to Ralph Nader's address. The firm sells only by mail and is owned by Plus Products, whose vitamins are sold directly through stores. The Johnston list, to quote them, sells "products similar to Plus, and of comparable quality, at prices that are approximately 40% less" (than Plus). Johnston shares the same production facilities, and it seems reasonable to infer by reading between the lines that the two are pretty much identical.

In addition to all the vitamins, Johnston sells minerals, various multiple formulas, including some for children and older people ("mature adults" . . . but their ratings seem to differ from those of the motion picture industry), various supplements such as yeast, liver, protein, cosmetics, and even pet vitamins. Though this is clearly a field where you should compare prices and consult several catalogues, Johnston is an interesting example of a manufacturer who does sell directly by mail at a discount.

10 GARDENING

1

2

1 • *Wayside Gardens Sorbus aucuparia* (mountain ash).

2 • *Wayside Gardens Corylus avellana contorta* (hazel).

GENERAL

Mellinger's Inc., North Lima, Ohio 44452
72-page catalogue, free. Fall.

No color pictures here. "Don't be misled by breathtaking pictures and names," says Mellinger's. "A catalogue in color costs five times as much as this one. You, the customer, would pay our extra cost either in higher prices or inferior quality." An interesting catalogue lists a little of a very wide variety of plants, shrubs, and trees, and specializes in unusual and hard-to-find plants in small sizes, often at low prices. It also includes a businesslike book list and large, workmanlike collection of tools and garden equipment.

R. H. Shumway, Seedsman, Rockford, Ill. 61101
92-page color catalogue, free.

The large and crowded catalogue of Shumway Seedsman represents a good, large selection of a general nursery—seeds, plants, bulbs, shrubs and fruits.

Stern's Nurseries, Geneva, N.Y. 14456
68-page color catalogue, 50 cents.

Another large listing of general nursery stock. The catalogue is well illustrated and full of information. In addition to the explanations which accompany the plants, there are scattered reports on things of interest—ways to test soil, plants for problem areas, and special write-ups on specific plants. There is basic culture code as well as a bird-attraction code—plants which attract birds (nature's best insecticide) are marked. Stern's has some exclusive items, such as Sub-Zero Roses, exhibition type Chrysanthemums, and it is the originator of the now-famous liquid plant foods—Miracle-Gro and Miracid.

Wayside Gardens Co., Mentor, Ohio 44060
216-page color catalogue, $2; refundable.
80-page autumn planting catalogue, $1; refundable.

Wayside Gardens sells a wider variety of plants by mail than any of the other nurseries. They publish enormous, fully illustrated, detailed and fairly instructive catalogues, which are well worth the outlay of $1 or $2. They are good for beginners, as there are cultural instructions, and good for advanced gardeners, as there are unusual selections. For organic gardeners they supply praying mantises, ladybugs and pure cow manure.

The major catalogue has hardy perennials and ground covers, shrubs, hedges, trees, vines, roses, fruit, nuts and herbs, bulbs, annuals and a new section of plants that prefer shade. The autumn planting catalogue, which is available from May, lists varieties that should be planted in the late summer or autumn, such as Dutch bulbs, lilies, poppies, peonies and *Hemerocallis*, and certain trees and shrubs.

White Flower Farm, Litchfield, Conn. 06759
Annual subscription to 100-page catalogue, January; 50-page catalogue, June; and three small notes throughout the year. $3.

White Flower Farm was started twenty-three years ago by W. B. Harris, a senior editor of *Fortune*, and his wife, Jane Grant, co-founder of *The New Yorker*, and it has all the appeal of an enterprise that is taken on for love, not money. Mr. Harris says that instead of trying

3

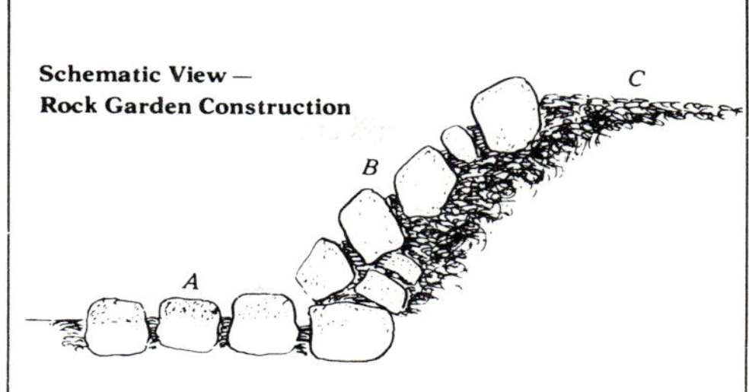

The principal error most gardeners make in rock-garden construction is in using rocks that are too small and placing them on top of the ground. Use only native rocks that are large and bury three fourths of each rock to form proper planting pockets. Section A (above) shows rock placement on level ground. B indicates building on a sharp slope. C is a plateau area atop the slope, and rocks there should be placed as in A. Note that rocks on the slope are positioned to channel water inward. Ideally major rocks in the design should be so large a contractor is needed to place them (see Rock Gardens) 4

PREPARING AND PLANTING WIRE BASKETS

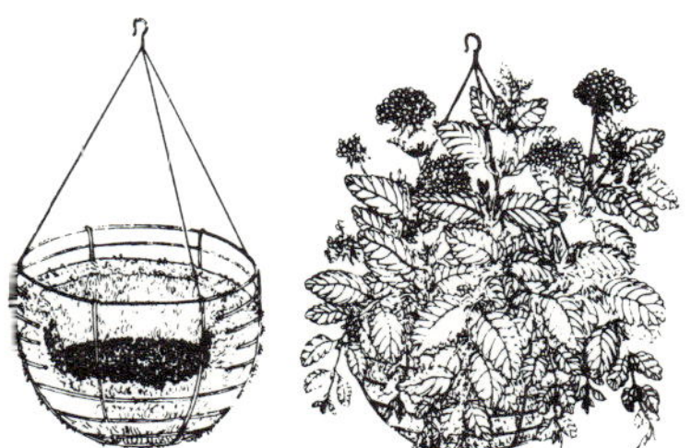

Soak sphagnum overnight; squeeze out handfuls and mat it (left), as thin as possible, to the wires, so it will hold the soil, which is added as mat is rounded over top wire. Put in plants, finish filling with soil, leaving 1½-inch dish at top. When irrigating, flood.

5

SEPARATING FRAISES DES BOIS, CHARLES V OR CATHERINE THE GREAT

cut

cut

After a full season of growth, dig the plants in earliest spring, just as they begin to show green shoots. Shake off the earth; then, either pull apart with care, or cut the crown, into two to four divisions, being sure that each has a good root system. Replant immediately. Do not dig and separate all plants at one time, for the roots dry quickly and losses result. 6

THE FUNDAMENTALS OF PRUNING

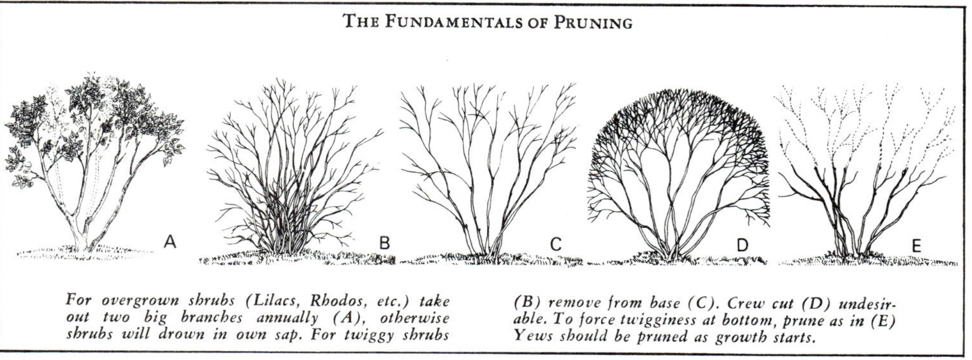

For overgrown shrubs (Lilacs, Rhodos, etc.) take out two big branches annually (A), otherwise shrubs will drown in own sap. For twiggy shrubs (B) remove from base (C). Crew cut (D) undesirable. To force twigginess at bottom, prune as in (E) Yews should be pruned as growth starts. 7

3 • *Wayside Gardens* *Dicentra valentine*, introduced in 1973.

4 • *White Flower Farm* A diagram from the catalogue of instructions for building a rock garden: "The principal error most gardeners make in rock garden construction is in using rocks that are too small and placing them on top of the ground. Use only native rocks that are large and bury three fourths of each rock to form proper planting pockets. Section A (above) shows rock placement on level ground, B indicates building on sharp slope. C is a plateau area atop the slope, and the rocks there should be placed as in A. Note that the rocks are positioned to channel water inward. Ideally major rocks in the design should be so large that a contractor is needed to place them."

5 • *White Flower Farm* A diagram from the catalogue of instructions for planting hanging wire baskets: "Soak sphagnum overnight; squeeze out handfuls and mat it (left) as thin as possible, to the wires, so it will hold the soil, which is added as mat is rounded over top wire. Put in plants, finish filling with soil, leaving 1½ inch dish at top. When irrigating, flood."

6 • *White Flower Farm* A diagram from the catalogue of instructions for separating Fraises des Bois, Charles V or Catherine the Great: "After a full season of growth, dig the plants in earliest spring, just as they begin to show green shoots. Shake off the earth; then, either pull apart with care, or cut the crown into two to four divisions, being sure that each has a good root system. Replant immediately. Do not dig and separate all plants at one time, for the roots dry out quickly and losses result."

7 • *White Flower Farm* A diagram from the catalogue of instructions for pruning: "For overgrown shrubs (Lilacs, Rhodos, etc.) take out two big branches annually (A) otherwise shrubs will drown in own sap. For twiggy shrubs (B) remove from base (C). Crew cut (D) undesirable. To force twigginess at bottom, prune as in (E). Yews should be pruned as growth starts."

to find out what gardeners want, he decides what *he* wants and then hopes that other gardeners will too.

Someone from the nurseries goes to England every year and to Japan every two years to buy new material. New plants are all tested (there are now eighty-six new plants) for performance and hardiness, and about 20 percent make it. They were the first nurseries to bring Symons-Jeuen phlox varieties from England; they tied up with a small Oregon nursery in importing the first Exbury azaleas; they were the first to offer dwarf needle evergreens; and are the only nurseries to bring in and grow, from cuttings, the Blackmore and Langdon strain of tuberous begonias.

The catalogue is a marvel. Instead of being illustrated with the often crudely colored close-up photographs, it has delicate line drawings and detailed, very enjoyable, descriptions of the plants as well as cultural instructions; in fact, as Mr. Harris says, the catalogue has more words about how-to-garden than about what-to-buy. It's arranged alphabetically, has phonetic spelling of horticultural names and terms, rates the hardiness of each plant, and is a terrifically good read. The owners also offer $100 worth of plants as a prize for the best editorial "scrubbing" of the catalogue and last year got about a hundred entries, of which two were so good that they each got the full prize (nice of White Flower Farm not to split it).

AFRICAN VIOLETS

Fischer Greenhouse, Linwood, N.J. 08221

The House Plant Corner, P.O. Box 810, Oxford, Md. 21654
24-page catalogue, 25 cents.

Both these firms send out the same catalogue, which lists around seventy African violets at prices between about 50 cents and $2. There are also some orchids and twelve foliage plants, especially chosen because they are easy to grow indoors. A tremendous amount of equipment for the indoor gardener takes up most of the catalogue: earth pots and hanging baskets, trays and trolleys, tools, timers, sprayers, plant lights, and so on.

See also Bernard D. Greeson under Supplies and Equipment, in this section.

BEGONIAS AND DELPHINIUM

Vetterle Bros., P.O. Box 1246, Watsonville, Calif. 95010
20-page catalogue, free.

Specialists in the Pacific strains of tuberous begonias, delphinium and polyanthus primroses, the Vetterle brothers have a long history of awards and citations, and a list of famous customers, including the English royal family. Their catalogue features many beautiful and exclusive selections, such as a rose-form type begonia, available in many colors (medium size—65 cents each) and a double hanging-basket type begonia (large size—$1 each).

Detailed culture information is included in the catalogue, and you are urged to write with any questions not answered in their "Hazards and Remedies" section. Also available are artichoke plants (three for $3.50) and strawberry plants (twelve for $12.75). Vetterle's carries some supplies and offers a basic fertilizer collection.

BONSAI

Girard Nurseries, P.O. Box 428, Geneva, Ohio 44041
35-page color catalogue, free. Spring.
Price list, free. Fall.

Girard sells over a hundred kinds of bonsai plants, ranging from two to eight years old. Prices for plants between two and three years old run about $1 to $2.50. The firm also carries ornamental and shade trees, and a good selection of Christmas trees (an unusual cork bark pine, imported from northwest China, costs $4.25). Girard has many of its own varieties and several money-saving collections.

Heirob Bonsai Nursery, Willowemoc Road, Livingston Manor, N.Y. 12758
15-page catalogue, free.

The catalogue explains that a bonsai is a miniature living tree or shrub and that there is a whole art in the dwarfing of trees in small containers, which is done by the restriction of root growth and by proper pruning. The aim is to create an aged-looking tree in miniature, hopefully in a natural-looking "landscape." You can choose a Japanese holly (fifteen years old) for $25 or a *Pinus Fenzeliana* (ninety years old) for $200. The popular Japanese maple costs $30 for a fifteen-year-old tree. For furthering the hobby, the catalogue lists containers (4″ to 16″ at $1.25 to $10.), and tools (six-piece gardening set for $31.95). For the proper viewing of a well-developed bonsai, the advanced hobbyist can invest in a special turntable display ($49.94). Included in the selection are various other books, supplies and accessories. The ornamental items complete the landscape—a frog for 75 cents and a pagoda for $1.50. A bonsai kit which contains, for the new tree, all necessities, including a container and a year's supply of nutrients, costs $11.50.

Western Arboretum, 435 N. Lake Avenue, Pasadena, Calif. 91101
15-page catalogue, 25 cents.

Exotic trees and shrubs, imported containers, supplies and Orientalia. There is an emphasis on bonsai plants, or rather small-tree and shrub specimens which are suitable for bonsai gardening. This is a good place for the beginner who wants to experiment in bonsai, because the plants are not very old and thus inexpensive. The selection of plants runs from about $1 to $3.50. There are about three hundred to choose from.

Among the Oriental selections are traditional clay bonsai containers in many different sizes and shapes (set of three bell-shaped bowls—about $6). There is a general selection of books, tools, supplies, etc., and a section on tea and tea sets, with a beautiful Imari teapot and four cups for about $32. Western Arboretum also carries dwarf citrus trees, which grow to a maximum of eight feet; a lemon tree costs about $13.

BULBS

P. DeJager & Sons, Inc., South Hamilton, Mass. 01982
64-page color catalogue, free. June.

This is the place for a good selection of imported Dutch bulbs. The firm has its own nurseries and offices in Holland. There are large sections in the catalogue of daffodils, narcissi and tulips, and also some hyacinths, snowdrops and other lovely small flowers.

Culture information is given in the catalogue and some gardening supplies are also listed. Soil-test kits run from $6.50 to $14.95. For the very active gardener who plants a great deal, there is a bulb planter—it does an efficient job of cutting holes for you. $12.50.

CACTI AND SUCCULENTS

Beahm Gardens, 2686 Paloma Street, Pasadena, Calif. 91007
Mimeographed list, free.

Beahm Gardens specializes in Epiphyllum, sometimes known as orchid cactus, which is misleading because there is no relationship to orchids beyond the fact that both have extraordinary flowers. These very decorative and unusual plants are simple to grow, Beahm Gardens says, but must be treated quite differently from desert cacti. Seeds are for sale for the very patient (grown from seed, Epiphyllum takes three to six years to bloom), and plants for the less patient at 75 cents to $2 each.

Desert Plant Company, P.O. Box 880, Marfa, Tex. 79843
40-page catalogue, 50 cents.

About thirty cacti of the Southwest are photographed and described in this catalogue. Cacti are picked in the field and cost around $1 each. 3″ to 4″ handmade, hand-painted bowls and planting pots made in Mexico for the cacti are sold for 50 cents each.

Henrietta's Nursery, 1345 N. Brawley, Fresno, Calif. 93705
50-page catalogue, 20 cents.

Henrietta's has specialized in cacti and succulents for fifteen years. The yearly catalogue is chatty, full of pictures (including of staff members), and fairly descriptive. Over two thousand species are listed, and books on cacti and succulents are for sale.

CAMELLIAS AND RHODODENDRONS

Orinda Nursery, Bridgeville, Del. 19933
24-page brochure, some color, 35 cents.

A neat and clear brochure lists the container-grown camellia and rhododendron plants that Orinda Nursery ships all year round. Directions as to where and when

8

9

10

8 • *Heirob Bonsai Nursery* 125-year-old *Pinus kwantungensis,* imported from Japan. $300.

9 • *Henrietta's Nursery Mammillaria bombycina,* a cactus with long brown hooked spines which form masses of cottony wool and small pink flowers in circles on the top. With age, smaller plants are grown (the one in this picture is fifteen years old). 2″ to 3″ flowering-size plants, five years old and grown from seed, cost $1 each.

10 • *Henrietta's Nursery Echinocereus knippelianus,* a cactus from central Mexico with very few spines, except some running along the ribs, which are relatively harmless. It blooms with large open pink flowers in the spring. Plants 2″ to 3″ sell for $1.50.

11

12

11 • *Rocky River Dahlia Gardens Asama yama,* a new variety of dahlia from Japan. 12″ light-salmon flowers.

12 • *Rocky River Dahlia Gardens Hakurei,* a new dahlia variety from Japan. 11″ white flowers.

the plants can be grown outside, and when the camellias should be grown inside, are given in the brochure, and cultural instructions come with the plants. Camellias cost $4.50 to $9 according to age; rhododendrons, $5 to $8.50 according to height.

CHRYSANTHEMUMS

Thon's Garden Mums, 4815 S. Oak Street, Crystal Lake, Ill. 60014
20-page color catalogue, free. January.
15-page pamphlet on "Growing Garden Mums," free.

Thon's specializes in garden (outdoor) chrysanthemums and produces exclusive offerings through their plant-breeding program. "Snowflake," pure white of course, costs $1 per plant.

The firm also puts together selected bargain collections, and for the football fans there is the University of Nebraska Football Series: Cheerleader, Homecoming, Quarterback and Stadium Queen (75 cents each).

Thon's also publishes a gardening manual, "Growing Garden Mums." Very good for the beginner—it takes you from soil requirements to winter care. The section on diseases and insects is very explicit in its suggested controls.

DAHLIAS

Rocky River Dahlia Gardens, 13089 E. River Road, Columbia Station, Ohio 44028
60-page catalogue, 25 cents.

This firm specializes in dahlias and has been producing new varieties since 1930. The catalogue, "The Dahlia Blue Book," lists many different kinds and has a large section on its culture and planting hints. You can buy the dahlias either as roots, plants or pot roots—these terms are explained, of course.

A few accessories are available, such as sprays, labels and special pruning shears.

HERBS [BULBS]

Le Jardin du Gourmet, Ramsey, N.J. 07466
Catalogue, 25 cents.

This catalogue brings to you culinary wonders from the plant world. First of all, there are shallots, very important in French cuisine (¾ lb. for $2). Next, if you want to grow your own herbs, both seeds and plants are available.

Beginning gardeners with advanced culinary skills might be interested in the Gourmet Herb Garden Kit (eight herb varieties plus soil, plus equipment, plus a guide book for $3.95).

The firm also offers other exotic and imported plants, seeds and bulbs. For example, sequoia seeds run $1 each. Imported (French) Chinese cabbage seeds cost 75 cents a packet. A selection of imported Holland bulbs includes bleeding hearts (85 cents each) and peonies ($1.10 each). Brief planting instructions are included in the listings.

Merry Gardens, Camden, Maine 04843
20-page catalogue ($1 puts you on the mailing list for extra listings, special announcements, etc.).

This family-run business is just entering its twenty-seventh year as growers of herbs and unusual indoor plants. Their concise catalogue reflects the change in emphasis which is going on right now. In the past the Rosses have specialized in the Star of Bethlehem, fuscia and some other tropical house plants. Right now, however, they are concentrating on herbs from *Alchemilla Alpina* to Roman wormwood, and in the future will have even more, with smaller listings for the general house plants. You can buy books on plants, as well as a pictorial handbook of plants put out by the firm, and a handbook of herbs ($1 each). The Rosses are also working on a "plant sanctuary" as another part of their contribution to horticulture.

HOUSE PLANTS

Logee's Greenhouses, Danielson, Conn. 06239
82-page catalogue, $1.

Logee's, started in 1892 by the father of the present owners, specializes in indoor plants. The catalogue gives brief descriptions of most plants and has photographs of just a few. Begonias, geraniums and herbs are grown and sold in profusion, and there are also cacti and succulents, vines, oxalis and a section listing "choice plants for the home and conservatory." A great deal to choose from.

McComb Greenhouses, Route One, New Straitsville, Ohio 43766
32-page catalogue, 35 cents.

This firm specializes in exotic house plants and plants from all over the world, many of which are available only from their greenhouses. Selections include such oddities as "Moses in the Boat," on which boatlike buds form at base and white flowers bloom in boat (50 cents) and "Old Man Cactus," a shaft covered with long, white hairs ($1.50). Complete culture information is provided.

IRISES [PEONIES, DAY LILIES]

Gilbert H. Wild and Son, Inc., Sarcoxie, Mo. 64862
90-page catalogue, 50 cents, also half-price "Day Lily" brochure.

This is the place for peonies, irises and day lilies. This old, established family-run business is a major source for a wide variety of these plants. There are collections listed, as well as culture information.

ORCHIDS

Acres of Orchids, Rod McLellan Co., 1450 El Camino Real, South San Francisco, Calif. 94080
32-page color catalogue, $1.

Acres of Orchids represents the third generation of a family business specializing in the orchid. Listings include many species, both common and rare, food products and accessories, books, and even hand-painted orchid china (set of four pieces, $47). There are also exotic foliage plants in hanging baskets to supplement orchid collections.

Alberts & Merkel Bros., Inc., Boynton Beach, Fla. 33435
Orchid catalogue and tropical foliage plants catalogue, $1 each.

A large selection of orchids and tropical foliage plants can be found here. The catalogue is not all that helpful, but this firm has both age and trophies from the American Orchid Society to recommend it. Revised, expanded editions of the catalogue are planned for the near future.

Shaffer's Tropical Gardens, Inc., 1220 41st Avenue, Santa Cruz, Calif. 95060
10-page catalogue, 50 cents. March.

Shaffer's specializes in orchids and carries many different varieties, including some of its own. For the beginner they recommend a starter kit which contains a *Phalaenopsis* plant (easy to grow and bloom in the house), complete with pot, fertilizer and instructions ($15).

ORGANIC

Nichols Garden Nursery, 1190 N. Pacific Hwy., Albany, Oreg. 97321
60-page price list, free.

The very cozy and readable mimeographed catalogue not only lists rare seeds, herb seeds and plants but also gives cooking suggestions, sells natural foods (and cheese rennet tablets to make cheese), wine-making supplies and books on cooking, gardening—especially organic—and topics like *How to Live on Nothing* and *Arthritis and Folk Medicine.* Their rare seeds include elephant garlic (eight times bigger than the usual), and things like a black Aztec sweet corn; Chinese leek; cucumber and winter squash; edible burdock from Japan. Sedums, sempervivums, everlasting flowers, and gadgets for food preparation are also listed. A really enjoyable catalogue for anyone who is put off by the big, professional ones.

ROCK PLANTS

Rakestraw's Perennial Gardens and Nursery, G-3094 S. Term Street, Flint, Mich. 48507
30-page price list, 25 cents.

A tidy brochure describes rare rock-garden plants and perennials. Just over fifty sedums at prices between 65 cents and $1 are listed, and a few suggestions on starting a rock garden are given. Other hard-to-find yet easy-to-grow perennials are listed and Rakestraw's says that if you are looking for anything unusual that isn't on their list, they may be able to find it for you.

ROSES

Armstrong Nurseries, P.O. Box 473, Ontario, Calif. 91764
40-page color catalogue, free.

Roses: bush, climbing and tree; exclusive varieties such as dark-red Kentucky Derby ($4.95 per plant); and bright-yellow King's Ransom ($4.45 per plant). Orders are accompanied by a planting guide with complete culture instructions. You can also get six varieties of the giant hibiscus—a good fence plant with huge flowers (one each of all six—$10.95) and dwarf fruit trees.

Jackson and Perkins, Medford, Oreg. 97501
40-page color catalogue, free.

One-hundred-year-old Jackson and Perkins is the world's largest grower of roses, and the best-known. Their catalogue has roses of every sort, as well as a few berries, vegetables and flowering trees.

Moore Miniature Roses, Sequoia Nursery, 2519 E. Noble Avenue, Visalia, Calif. 93277
Color brochure plus supplements, free.

According to the people at Sequoia Nursery, miniature roses are a rather recent arrival on the nursery scene—they were introduced about twenty-five years ago. This firm specializes in the breeding of and research on miniature roses. They are continually coming up with new offerings. Nineteen seventy-two, for example, was the year of an unusual moss rose. They feature many of their own varieties and include plenty of culture information—very useful to the beginning gardener.

Tillotson's Roses, Brown Valley Road, Watsonville, Calif. 95076
78-page catalogue, $1; refundable.

This nursery, which is owned by Dorothy C. Stemler and run by her and her daughter Patricia Wiley, grows and sells "old, rare and unusual roses." A well-produced and extremely readable catalogue has black-and-white photographs of roses, enthusiastic descriptions, plenty of advice and instruction, and quotations from customers as well as literature about the beauty of the roses. Irresistible.

Melvin E. Wyant, Johnny Cake Ridge, Mentor, Ohio 44060
Color brochure, free. Spring.

This small firm has specialized in roses in the rugged climate of northern Ohio for over fifty years. They graft their plants onto Multiflora Japonica Rose roots, which makes them hardier, they say, than those grown elsewhere, and they also produce roses with three-year roots, in contrast to the two-year plants generally sold. Tree roses, miniature roses, old-fashioned roses, shrub, floribunda, hybrid tea and climbing roses are all for sale.

STRAWBERRIES

Rayner Brothers, Inc., Salisbury, Md. 21801
35-page catalogue, plus bulletin, free.

Rayner's specializes in strawberry plants and the catalogue tells you what you need to know about choosing and growing your plants. There are selections for all climates. You can also buy other garden plants, such as asparagus, dwarf fruit trees, grape vines, and several others. Rayner's issues periodic bulletins with articles of special interest to berry gardeners.

WATER GARDENS

Three Springs Fisheries, Lilypons, Md. 21717
48-page color catalogue, 50 cents.

Take one look at either of these catalogues and you'll immediately want to set up a water garden in your bathtub or backyard, depending on your situation. This gorgeous, clear catalogue shows an extraordinary variety of lilies, old and new varieties of lotus, green plants for the pool and some magnificently exotic fish. Equipment to make a simple polyethalene lined pool, waterfall and fountain, a pool filter, and scavengers such as bullfrogs, tadpoles and snails to keep ponds and lakes clean are all for sale, and so are supplies for indoor aquariums. The catalogue is very informative, and gives suggestions as to various combinations of plant and fish that work well together, but there is a how-to-do-it book on sale called *Goldfish Pools, Water-lilies and Tropical Fishes* for anyone who wants to know more.

Van Ness Water Gardens, 2460 N. Euclid Avenue, Upland, Calif. 91786
28-page color catalogue, 25 cents.

An equally appealing but smaller catalogue has no fish (because of high transport costs) but lots of plants of all sorts, some unusual scavengers, fountains and waterfalls, eighteen books for sale and complete instructions on how to build a cement pool.

13

14

15

16

17

13 • *Shaffer's Tropical Gardens* Cabrillo Star Perfection. *Phalaenopsis* orchids start at about $6.75 for plants with a 4″ to 6″ overall leaf spread.
photo Gordon Bruce Lyon Fotografie

14 • *Shaffer's Tropical Gardens* Standard *Cymbidium* orchids. Shaffer's sells its own *Cymbidiums* as well as some grown from stock imported from McBeans in England.

15 • *Jackson and Perkins* Old-timer rose. The plants are usually about 3½′ tall with 7″ apricot-gold flowers borne singly on long stems and surrounded by leathery pointed leaves. The flowers are long-lasting and have a light, fruity smell. $4.75 each.

16 • *Gardens of the Blue Ridge* *Trillium grandiflorum* (snow trillium), a spring bloomer for woodland borders or rock gardens. 9″ to 12″ high with flowers 3″ to 4″ across. White turning to rose color in early spring. 40 cents each.
photo Artcrafts Engraving Co.

17 • *Van Ness Water Gardens* Tropical water lilies. *Reading from top to bottom:* Ted Uber, a medium-to-large white flower with yellow center, fragrant; a compact plant that is suitable for small pools. Jamie Lu Skare, large deep yellow flower, fragrant. William C. Uber, a deep rose-colored flower with large green leaves, fragrant. Each plant is $3.
photo Clint Bryan

WILD AND NATIVE PLANTS

Gardens of the Blue Ridge, Ashford, McDowell County, N.C. 28603
42-page catalogue, $1.

Wild flowers and native plants of the southern Appalachians, and hardy native orchids run from 48 cents to $3.25 each, while evergreen trees and shrubs cost from $1.50 to $12 each.

Midwest Wildflowers, Box 64, Rockton, Ill. 61072
26-page catalogue, 25 cents.

Seeds of plants native to the Midwest are hand-collected and packaged, and the packages are sold for 50 cents each. The catalogue is more like a storybook—each seed listing includes all known facts and folklore for that plant, detailed culture instructions and a full-page illustration of the plant. For example, the wild ginger, a low, twining plant, is believed to be pollinated by slugs—the first good words for slugs I've ever heard. Many ancient medicinal uses are discussed; Solomon's Seal, a lily, is said to be healer for bruises, cuts and other skin problems. The catalogue conveys the natural beauty of wild flowers and urges the reader to lend a helping hand to the many diminishing species.

Mincemoyer Nursery, County Line Road (Route 526), Jackson, N.J. 08527
22-page list, 25 cents.

This nursery lists wild flowers, ferns, herbs, perennials, trees and shrubs in its catalogue, with a separate listing of organic aids to gardening such as praying-mantis egg cases (three for $2) and ladybird beetles (half a pint for $3.25). The listings are not very well explained for the beginner.

The Theodore Payne Foundation for Wild Flowers and Native Plants, Inc., 10459 Tuxford Street, Sun Valley, Calif. 91352
Price list, free.

This nonprofit organization is run by a group of people who are interested in preserving California wild flowers. They sell seeds by mail and have a special list of "Most Popular and Showy Species of Easy Culture" which are sold in packets, by the ounce or by the pound. They also have a general list, and at the nursery (though not by mail) they sell plants.

Putney Nursery, Inc., Putney, Vt. 05346
32-page catalogue (some color) and special "Christmas Greens" brochure, free.

Putney's has a general line of nursery stock, but it is also an excellent source for New England wild flowers and ferns, as well as herbs and shrubs. Ferns are recommended as a hardy decoration for just about any place, especially where nothing else will grow. An interesting one is the walking fern, originally growing on limestone cliffs—it has an unusual appearance because the fronds root from the tips ($1 each). The wild flowers are hard to resist—Putney's offers a collection which includes such favorites as bloodroot, jack-in-the pulpit and Virginia bluebells, thirty-three plants for $28.95. There is also a large selection of hardy shrubs, as well as a variety of evergreens, shade and flowering trees, fruit trees and perennials. A separate brochure lists balsam Christmas greens such as wreaths, centerpieces and sprays.

Clyde Robin, P.O. Box 2091, Castro Valley, Calif. 94546
104-page catalogue (some color), $1.

This firm specializes in wild-flower and wild-tree seeds and plants. The listings are concise; culture information is included, as well as many words of encouragement and adages interspersed throughout. The firm handles books on the subject and some supplies, such as earthworms (the natural means for a fertile end, 1-lb. container with instructions, $3.75). They list special-interest selections, such as gardens for children, and urge the reader to purchase the Survival Garden, because of the peril of the times—enough to feed a small colony.

MISCELLANEOUS SPECIALTIES

Armstrong Associates, Inc., P.O. Box 127, Basking Ridge, N.J. 07920
Brochure, 25 cents. Spring, fall.

Armstrong specializes in carnivorous plants, and has a brochure with photographs and descriptions of them, each of which has its own method of attracting and capturing insects. Prices are generally lower than at Peter Paul's Nurseries (below), and as plants are well described, and arrive with full planting and care instructions, this is a good shop for anyone who doesn't know much about these plants. Miniature greenhouses, Gro-Dome planters and a beginner's collection for $4.

Dutch Mountain Nursery—"Berries for the Birds," 798 N. 48th Street, Route 1, Augusta, Mich. 49012
Price list, 25 cents.

For twenty years this firm has been professionally handling plants which attract birds. Their list is informative—it tells you what tree or shrub you can plant where to attract which kinds of birds. They feature a "Card File of 500 Ornamental Plants" ($8) which contains much useful information for the gardener and the landscaper. If you become seriously involved in this as an environmental movement, you can join the F.B.I.—Fruit for Birds International.

Game Food Nurseries, P.O. Box 371-K, Oshkosh, Wis. 54901
26-page catalogue, $1.

The catalogue of plants which provide food for wildlife begins with statements of concern for conservation in this country, but it continues with an emphasis on hunting and fishing. There seems to be a contradiction. Plants include such things as duckwheat, bur reed and watercress. The catalogue is well organized and very descriptive.

Peter Paul's Nurseries, Dept. A91, Route 4, Canandaigua, N.Y. 14424
4-page catalogue, 25 cents.

For the more advanced gardener of carnivorous or insectivorous plants, there is Peter Paul's, which in sixteen years has built up a good reputation. The concise, businesslike catalogue contains the standard selection of these plant oddities, as well as some rare ones. The scariest is an atomic mutation of a Venus's-flytrap, with traps from one to three feet long (three for $4.50).

Wildlife Nurseries, P.O. Box 399, Oshkosh, Wis. 54901
30-page catalogue, free.

Another outfit for natural food products for wildlife from Oshkosh, Wisconsin. In business since 1896, this firm carries a full line of natural attractions for ducks, geese, fish and many other forms of wildlife. They also feature wild rice for human consumption—$4.95 per pound.

18

SEEDS

W. Atlee Burpee Co., Box 6929, Philadelphia, Pa. 19132
164-page color catalogue, "Burpee Annual," free. January.
40-page color catalogue, free. Summer.

W. Atlee Burpee gave up medicine because, he said, he couldn't stand seeing people suffer, and took up the more peaceful profession of gardening with $1,000 borrowed from his mother. That was in 1876, a time when most seeds were imported from Europe. He started experimental farms before the government did, and his firm has ever since done a great deal of experimental work, developing new hybrid varieties in California and testing them under Eastern conditions on his Pennsylvania farm.

The catalogues of the largest mail-order seed company in the world are still, I'm glad to say, compact and easy to handle, and list about a thousand different flower-seed varieties, half that amount of vegetables and spring bulbs, and also grasses, shrubs, trees, berries, house plants, a pageful of very imaginative plants for children, and tools and garden supplies.

19

Farmer Seed and Nursery Co., Faribault, Minn. 55021
80-page color catalogue, free.

In business since 1888, this firm carries a general line of garden and agricultural seeds. They also feature midget vegetables for the home gardener, and seed stock specifically adapted for Northern climates.

Henry Field Seed and Nursery Co., 407 Sycamore Street, Shenandoah, Iowa 51601
128-page color catalogue, free. Spring.
40-page catalogue, free. Fall.

Field's deals in a general line of garden seed, field seed and nursery stock. They have a most useful and comprehensive planting guide—it tells you what to plant where, how to plan special types of gardens, and gives planting and culture tips.

18 • *Armstrong Associates* Carnivorous sundews, with sticky tendrils at the end of each arm, attract gnats, flies and other insects which stick to the plant when they touch it; then, as they struggle, other tentacles bend to trap it completely. Tiny violet flowers are borne on stalks each spring. Six plants, brandy-snifter container, culture directions and planting material are $4. Three sundews alone, $2.

19 • *Armstrong Associates* Carnivorous Venus's-flytraps have fingerlike cilia around the edges of their leaves. When flies, moths or bugs are attracted to the plant, tiny trigger hairs on the surface of the leaf sense it and the leaf snaps shut. Six bulbs with culture directions and planting material, $3.

20 • *Bountiful Ridge Nurseries* Oriental persimmons have ornamental waxy-green foliage which turns to yellow streaked with red in the fall. The trees grow slowly, so they are good for small gardens. They start bearing fruit when young, are adapted to most regions in the South and can be grown as far north as Pennsylvania. 3′ to 4′ plants, $5.25 each.

Harris Seeds, Joseph Harris Company, Inc., Moreton Far, Rochester, N.Y. 14624
86-page catalogue with some color, free.

A broad selection of vegetable and flower seeds, with many of their own varieties. Their exclusive offerings include Market Prize cabbage, recommended for its uniformity (packet, 55 cents) and Black Magic Hybrid Eggplant, a husky and vigorous variety (packet, 50 cents). In the flower department, Harris notes some of its own new offerings: Gypsy Sunshine Marigolds (packet, 40 cents); and not-so-new Kandy Kane Petunias—variegated salmon and white (packet, 60 cents). They have starter kits for the beginner and collection for those who want everything; also a full line of gardening supplies, fertilizers, plant food and books.

L. L. Olds Seed Company, Madison, Wis. 53701
82-page color catalogue, 15 cents.

Olds began in 1888 as a potato mail-order firm and has since expanded to a general line of vegetable, flower, lawn and farm seeds, as well as horticultural supplies.

Geo. W. Park Seed Co., Inc., Greenwood, S.C. 29646
Five separate 30- to 100-page color catalogues, free.

Park's claims to offer the largest selection of flower seeds in this country and publishes five different catalogues to prove it. All of them are bright, colorful and chock-full of information. At New Year's one can get the "Flower Book," a huge listing of flower seeds, some vegetable seeds and some garden supplies, with a combined index, germination and culture guide, including a key for good plants for beginners. Mid-February brings the "Springtime" book with its seasonal offerings.

Thoughtful gifts for the gardener is available in late summer and features many starter kits and lots of tools and accessories. An outdoor emphasis is found in "Good Gardening," available in the spring. Finally, there is a "Flower Book Autumn" which comes out in early August.

F. W. Schumacher Co., Horticulturists, Sandwich, Mass. 02563
26-page catalogue, free.

"Seeds for Nurserymen and Foresters" is the title of this firm's catalogue, and it is obviously professionally oriented. The listings are nondescriptive and mostly in Latin only. Schumacher carries a general line of tree, shrub, azalea, rhododendron and fruit seeds, and several specialties are listed, such as its own hybrid azalea and rhododendron varieties. There is some culture information in the back, as well as books for the "beginner."

TREES

Bountiful Ridge Nurseries, Inc., Princess Anne, Md. 21853
50-page catalogue, free.

This firm specializes in fruit trees, nut trees, ornamental trees and berry plants. As a family business they are proud of their selection and they promise quality stock. Enormous number of varieties to choose from—thirty-five types of peach trees, for instance. You might investigate the possibility of a nut tree—they claim that Chinese chestnuts are easy to grow almost anywhere ($3.75 for a five to six foot seedling tree). There are also grape vines, and all kinds of tempting berries as well as some basic gardening supplies. The catalogue has some culture information, and several helpful planting charts and guides.

Brimfield Gardens Nursery, 245 Brimfield Road, Wethersfield, Conn. 06109
29-page catalogue, $1.

This firm specializes in rare trees, shrubs and evergreens. The catalogue is basically a nondescriptive listing of unusual varieties of shade trees, flowering shade and ornamental trees, flowering shrubs, broad-leaved evergreens, ferns, climbers, ground covers, bamboo and evergreens. Many of the selections are bonsai or bonsai subjects. Prices range from 11 cents for *Pacysandra terminalis*, a ground cover, to $180 for a Ginkgo Biloba Pendula, a maidenhair tree.

Gossler Farms Nursery, 1200 Weaver Road, Springfield, Oreg. 97477
8-page catalogue, 25 cents.

This firm specializes in magnolias and "companion" plants. The small personal catalogue contains many varieties exclusive to Gossler. Magnolias run from $3 to about $25, depending on the variety and the size. Gossler lists many other plants and trees which go well as "companion plants" to the magnolias, such as a Pacific dogwood, native to the Pacific Coast woodlands, for $10 (four feet tall) or perhaps a Snow Gum eucalyptus for $10 (six feet tall).

Henry Leuthardt Nurseries, Inc., Montauk Highway, East Moriches, Long Island, N.Y. 11940
52-page brochure, 25 cents.

The art of training fruit trees into flat, symmetrical shapes was developed in Europe for decorative purposes and to take advantage of small spaces. Henry Leuthardt says that his firm produces especially large and excellent fruit because of the extra exposure to the sun and because the trees are grafted onto the proper understock.

An excellent brochure-cum-handbook gives instructions on the care of espaliers; lists dwarf fruit trees, including the delicious varieties of apples which are hard to find because they aren't commercial (don't pack and ship well or don't look red and shiny enough); berry plants; and also hybrid grapes. Mr. Leuthardt says: "It is astonishing how the public together with the majority of nurserymen are unaware of the tremendous progress that has been made during the last few decades in improving the various strains of grape vines that will grow in the rougher and colder climates of this country."

Musser Forest, Inc., Indiana, Pa. 15701
40-page color catalogue, free.

This family-operated business stocks trees of all kinds—evergreens, hardwoods, shrubs, etc. Included is a small listing of perennials (primroses $1.15 each, lily of the valley $3.95 for twelve). The prices are generally low. The serious outdoor gardener can also find his ground covers, hedges, windbreaks and screens here. The catalogue does not offer much in the way of culture explanations.

21

22

21 • *Havahart* One of the galvanized-steel traps manufactured by Allcock Manufacturing Company that capture animals alive, it can be left open at both ends; when the animal enters to get the bait the ends close. This model is sold in various sizes for different animals at prices between $5 and $20.

22 • *Struck Corporation* A 12-HP bulldozer with a 400-lb. capacity front-end loader attachment that measures 30″ across. Over twenty attachments can be used with this mini-dozer, which works in dirt, sand or snow. Available in kit form at just over $700. Plans for constructing the same model with materials bought locally, $5.

Stark Bros., Louisiana, Mo. 63353
Color catalogues, free. Spring, fall.

The largest and best-known fruit specialists publish full-color catalogues with small selections of their standard size and dwarf fruit trees.

Western Maine Forest Nursery Co., Fryeburg, Maine 04037
Color pamphlet issued twice a year, free.

This firm has just celebrated its fiftieth anniversary as growers of evergreens. They have an unusual guarantee—if the tree doesn't last for one full year, the customer can either get a replacement or his money refunded.

If you are in the market for firs, pines, spruces or hemlocks, this is the place to check. They send only freshly dug trees, usually from three to five years old. Here are a few prices: Douglas Fir—five for $5; White Pine—five for $5; and Colorado Blue—five for $6. A handy evergreen selection guide with descriptions and culture information makes it easy to choose the trees that are best for you.

SUPPLIES AND EQUIPMENT

Bio-Control Co., 10180 Ladybird Drive, Auburn, Calif. 95603
Price list and information, free.

Natural methods for the control of insects harmful to food supply of man, Bio-Control sells praying-mantis egg cases (three for $2) and ladybugs (half a pint for $2.75). Included are directions and recommendations for specific types of plants, crops and gardens. There are lower rates for larger orders.

Garden Way Research, Charlotte, Vt. 05445
Fireplace-equipment leaflets, free.
Cart leaflets, free.

Garden Way makes three garden carts and puts out a convincing brochure illustrating all their advantages and all the disadvantages of regular wheelbarrows and other people's carts. These carts, on big semi-pneumatic wheels, have a large capacity, are more easy to take up steps, aren't tippy like wheelbarrows and don't make *you* carry the weight of the load. Prices start at $32 for a complete kit to make the smallest size cart, and $47.50 for the finished model.

Gothard, Inc., P.O. Box 370, Canutillo, Tex. 79835
Brochure, free.

Gothard presents its own answer to crop pest control. Since 1959 it has been selling *Trichogramma*, little wasplike insects which become parasites to the eggs of insects that destroy crops. Gothard claims that *Trichogramma* will not feed on vegetation or destroy other beneficial insects.

Included are instructions on how to disperse the insects and how much to use. One vial, which will treat one half acre of garden, costs $2.50. Bulk orders are cheaper.

Bernard D. Greeson, Horticultural Supplies, 3548 N. Cramer Street, Milwaukee, Wis. 53211
Price list, 25 cents.

This firm has been supplying growing aids for African violets for fifteen years: from special-formula potting soil to insecticides and fungicides. Plastic plant labels come in a variety of shapes and sizes and are sold in quantity from "100 to 250,000." You can also order African violet leaves (five for $2) and rooted cuttings (four for $4.95).

Havahart, Box 551, Ossining, N.Y. 10562
36-page brochure, free.

Havahart traps catch pests and future pets alive and unhurt with the use of bait. A readable little brochure gives advice on the use of the traps and the various ways you can dispose of the animals you don't want afterward. Much of the advice comes in letters from customers who have successfully used the traps, from the twelve-year-old who caught a bear instead of a coyote, to a dog warden ordering another trap for the mayor. There are traps for everything from minnows, pigeons and the neighbor's dog to rattlesnakes. Prices are from $4 to $65 for a telescoping trap for dogs and coyotes. Bait and lures are also sold.

Hydroponic Chemical Company, Inc., Copley, Ohio 44321
8-page catalogue, free.

This company has its own line of plant foods and garden products. The plant foods are for liquid feeding and involve the purchase of mixers, sprayers ($2.29-$29.90). Other products listed include tools, pots and a few outdoor pet supplies.

Struck Corporation, Cedarburg, Wis. 53012
26-page catalogue, "School Shop Projects," 50 cents.
48-page catalogue of outdoor power equipment kits, $1.

Struck makes outdoor power equipment in kit form to be assembled without welding or drilling, as the pieces come ready to fit and bolt together.

You can get the turf rider, a miniature tractor for garden use for $700 (with attachments it will mow, plow, doze snow and dirt), or a lighter version for $400, which can also mow, plow and doze with attachments. A riding mower costs $275, a folding ¾-horsepower mini-bike $160, and a miniature dune buggy $300.

Lawn edgers, chain saws, lawnmowers are also available and there is a special catalogue for kits to make shop tools, from screwdrivers to bench drills.

Sudbury Laboratory, Inc., Sudbury, Mass. 01776
Leaflet, free.

The world's largest manufacturer of soil-test kits, Sudbury has kits of various sizes and complexity, from one for $1.75 that you can use to find out whether your soil needs lime, and comes with a chart to show how much lime more than a hundred plants need, to the professional deluxe kit for $43 that makes about two hundred individual tests for nitrogen, phosphorus, potash and acidity. Dog and cat repellent is also sold for indoors to protect furniture, dog, cat, squirrel, rabbit and deer repellent for outside to protect plants.

... wrist joint at 5, giving full length of arm.....................

Inseam—From close up in crotch at 7 to heel seam of shoe at 8..............

8

NECESSARY INFORMATION FOR BOYS' CLOTHING.

For all garments for boys up to sixteen years of age—Simply state age and say whether the boy is large, small or of average size for his age.

6¼ ....

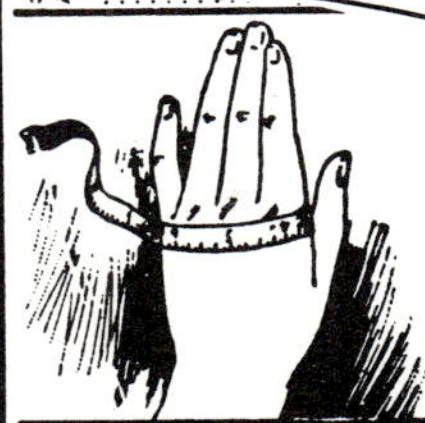

HOLD ... THUMB RAI... illustration (do n... your hand measures your gloves. ALWAYS...

Sizes ...

Women's Sizes in Fab... Gloves: 6, 6½, 7, 7½, 8...

Women's Sizes in Silk... 6¼, 6½, 6¾, 7, 7¼, 7...
Men's Sizes: 7, 7½, 7...

Measurement Form for Women's and Misses' Tailored Suits, Coats, Skirts, Dresses and Waists

First, tie a tape or cord around your waist in order that you may properly locate the natural waist line. This is important.
Second, be sure that your tape line is accurate. Then measure over a tight fitting waist or blouse, making no allowance for seams, according to the following directions:

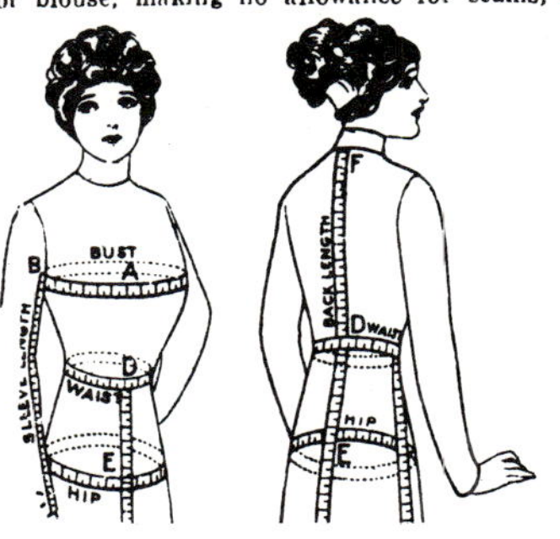

Height	Weight	Age

Measurements for Coat, Waist, Dressing Sacque, Etc.	Inches	Measurements for Skirt.	Inches
BUST MEASURE — Measure all around body		WAIST MEASURE—Remove outside belt and measure around body at natural waist line D either for regular waist or high waist line skirts. Do not	

MEASUREMENTS FOR WOMEN'S

SUITS.
State all the measurements in the form shown to the left.

COATS OR JACKETS. (Cloth or Fur.)
State bust and waist measurements, sleeve length and length in back.

TOP SKIRTS.
State waist and hip measurements and length of skirt in front and back. Women's skirts should be about 2 or 3 inches from ground; misses' skirts usually 8 or 10 inches from ground.

WAISTS.
State bust measure...

STREET DRES...
State bust measur... measure and front l... skirt.

MATERNITY DR...
State bust measure...

WRAPPERS, H... DRESSES AND ... DRESSES.
State bust measure...

NIGHTGOWN...
State bust measur...

MATERNITY CO...
Read carefully ins... on maternity corset ... order size according...

WOMEN'S RIBBED UNDERWEAR—
Size 4 for bust 32 inches. Size 5 for bust 34 and 36 inches. Size 6 for bust 38 and ... Size 7 for bust 42 inch...

WOMEN'S STOCKINGS—St...
Size of shoe..............................1 and 2
Size of stockings..........................8½

11 GENERAL

Large Stores & Mail-Order Houses

The catalogues of the large mail-order houses are invaluable as reference books, for comparing prices and simply finding out what is available in almost any field. (The firms know it, and consequently are stingy with new customers; after several attempts I got my first Sears, Roebuck catalogue by listing all the things I would buy if I could only get hold of a catalogue.) I have found them really useful for all the household things such as buckets, mops and window shades that I hate to go out and buy, but almost all their functional equipment and appliances are worth considering. They are usually tested by *Consumer Reports* and often do well (and you won't have trouble in finding the tested models, which is sometimes a difficulty with *Consumer Reports* surveys). However, I don't recommend the wares of the large mail-order houses where taste or style is involved, as things like furniture and furnishings are still astonishingly ugly and fussy, in tired old designs and nasty colors.

Department stores also have a general, though smaller and more expensive selection of goods, but although most of them have small mail-order departments to deal with individual inquiries, they do not all publish catalogues. I have listed below department stores that produce catalogues and are willing to send them to people who are not regular customers.

Alden's, Chicago, Ill. 60607
Color catalogue, free. Spring/Summer, Fall/Winter.

Not as large as the biggest mail-order firms, Sears and Montgomery Ward, Alden's sells mainly clothes, with a certain amount for the house in the way of furniture, kitchenware and brand-name appliances. Amid the more standard goods there are surprises such as chrome and glass or brilliantly colored plastic furniture, and a page of "Lights That Turn On Your Party: Mini Strobe—maxi fun for freak-out parties! Creates wild stop-action chopping light movement—just like the old-time movies" ($20) or "Rainbow Swirlee Fun Lamp—ever-turning, ever-changing. Sets a great mood for parties—smashing in a teen's room—neat touch for college dorm!" ($10).

B. Altman & Co., Fifth Avenue at 34th Street, New York, N.Y. 10016
January: White Sale. February: Sales booklet. March: Houseware booklet. April: Fashion booklet. May: Housewares booklet. June: Sales booklet. July: July/August White Sales. August: Children's booklet—back to school. September: Housewares booklet. October: Sales booklet. November: Housewares booklet. December: Christmas Magazine. All free.

Altman's department store produces a barrage of catalogues which is sent to customers throughout the year, and will happily send to anyone else who asks for specific volumes. Each catalogue is only valid for one month, so you have to be quick about both asking for the catalogue and ordering from it. The fashion catalogues show mostly casual clothes and separates for women with almost everything costing less than $50. The Christmas catalogue has an all-round selection of clothes for men, women and children; games for adults and children; luggage; household things suitable for gifts; and limited-edition collector's plates. Both the fashion and Christmas catalogues are illustrated throughout with color photographs.

Bergdorf Goodman Co., 754 Fifth Avenue at 58th Street, New York, N.Y. 10019
96-page catalogue, $1.

The reason that Bergdorf Goodman, the poshest of the New York department stores, has an air of such luxurious intimacy is that when it was built, next to the Plaza Hotel, the site was considered so far uptown as to be a mad gamble, and was accordingly designed so that it could be divided and leased off as small boutiques in case of disaster. The location turned out to be an excellent one, and the small rooms have continued to give a feeling of genteel privacy, quite unlike that of the other large clothing stores. Bergdorf claims to have been the first store to introduce really high-quality ready-to-wear women's clothes and to coax their customers out of the fitting rooms, and has just introduced a men's ready-to-wear department.

There are four catalogues a year for regular customers, which can be bought by nonregulars. Line drawings illustrate women's clothes in sizes 8 to 14 from most of the Bergdorf departments—tailored ivory pants suits, navy-and-white Italian shirt dresses, frilly flowered voile robes—almost everything at prices between $50 and $100, in the spring catalogue (winter clothes go up to $150). Linens, a few men's and children's clothes, handbags, shoes, costume jewelry and cosmetics are also illustrated.

Bloomingdale's Advertising Department, 1000 Third Avenue, New York, N.Y. 10022
Catalogues: White Sale/Home Furnishings, January, July. White Sale/Housewares, April. Children's Clothes, August. Housewares, October. Christmas catalogue, November. All free; valid for about a month each.

Bloomingdale's, which started off in 1872 announcing itself as the Great East Side Bazaar selling Clothes and Corsets, has become the liveliest and the most design-conscious of the large New York stores, and the one with the most ardently articulate customers—well-known writers drool in print over the delights of Saturday afternoons spent browsing in Bloomie's.

The catalogues, illustrated with color photos and unlike most of the other catalogues from department stores, do not concentrate on clothes but have a wide variety of medium prices and often brightly colored things for the house. The two White Sale/Home Furnishings catalogues have colorful linens, modern lamps, and some furniture and accessories; "housewares" means mainly appliances and rather good-looking things for cooking and eating; the Christmas catalogue has clothes for men, women and children (for the men and women mostly sweaters, shirts, nightwear and slippers which must be what everyone gives each other for Christmas). Also glamorous "adult games" for the coffee table, posh chocolates (Corné de la Toison d'Or flown in weekly from Belgium), plum puddings and imported cookies; lucite and crystal for the kitchen and dining room; mirrors, wine racks and sleekly modern, useful yet decorative objects for the rest of the house.

Gump's, 250 Post Street, San Francisco, Calif. 94108
80-page color catalogue, $1; refundable. October.

"A Legend in a Legendary City" says the Gump brochure "This is Gump's." Whether it's a legend or not, the store is certainly famous. It was started by Solomon Gump in the gold-rush days, when it sold gilded mirrors for the saloons, and picture frames and gilded cornices and later pictures for the newly rich.

All the merchandise was destroyed in the 1906 earthquake, and afterward Solomon's son, A. Livingston Gump, enlarged the stock and brought in more and more of the Asian art which has remained typical of the store to this day.

Now Gump's specializes in jade, Oriental antiques, gifts and modern, mostly European gifts. They also carry jewelry, art, clothes, modern and antique silver, reproduction and antique European furniture, and the largest selection of famous-name glass and china in the West.

The catalogue shows things from almost all the departments, with a distinct leaning toward the traditional rather than the modern. There are exceptions, but prices start mostly at around $15 and go up into hundreds and thousands of dollars.

Miles Kimball Company, 41 W. Eighth Avenue, Oshkosh, Wis. 54901

Sunset House, 12800 Culver Boulevard, Los Angeles, Calif. 90066

The Game Room, P.O. Box 1816, Washington, D.C. 20013

Free catalogues.

For most people, mail-order catalogues bring to mind the *TV Guide*-size catalogues that are mailed out by the millions, containing a miscellany of items that seems specially geared to be in these postal grab bags. It's a far bigger business than I had realized. Sunset, for instance, sends out some 20 million catalogues a year to some 6.5 million names and is owned by the same firm that owns Neiman-Marcus, Bergdorf Goodman and other famous stores. This, I suppose, is called diversification, since none of the items in the mail-order catalogues look as if they would be acceptable to the bigger stores. The material in these general catalogues is harmless enough, its main characteristic being that it is inexpensive and is practically never something that you would go out and look for yourself. However, if you like to receive catalogues and have an insatiable curiosity about what they'll think of next and might consider buying "Medieval clock [that] really works, authentic reproduction of a 13th-century clock for $6.99" or a pack of 100 spools of cotton thread in 50 colors for $3.49, to quote but one page of the Sunset catalogue, then you should add your name to the millions on their lists.

Mother's Truck Store Catalogue, Box 75, Unionville, Ohio 44088

100-page catalogue, 25 cents.

All the profits that Mother's Truck Store makes go to a research center that will be established to "wrestle with the problems of ecological living and alternative life styles." The store says that it is obviously easier to live a simple alternative to the consumer life if the necessary tools for such living are readily at hand. Accordingly, it sells old-time implements that are hard to find, and froes, cruppers, straight razors, bottle cappers, windmills, broadaxes, cream separators, butter churns and wood cookstoves are the examples given in the introduction. The store also wants to create a market for cottage-industry goods and invites people who make ruanas, butter molds, wooden toys, handmade tools or

1

2

1 • *B. Altman* A typical selection of goods from the Etienne Aigner boutique. *Clockwise from the top:* shoulder bag, double-zipper boot, French purse, change purse, gloves, folding wallet, dress moccasin, 2″-wide belt, ½″-wide belt, shoulder bag. Similar pieces are usually available for between $10 and $35.

2 • *B. Altman* A typical collection of jewelry.

3 

4 

3 • *B. Altman* Waterford crystal, typical of stock. *Clockwise from the top:* candlesticks, ship's decanter, cookie jar, sugar and cream jug set, 9″ bowl, cordial decanter. Similar pieces are usually available at prices between $30 and $60.

4 • *Neiman-Marcus* The Red Dragon Court robe from the Mandarin Court of the Hsien Fêng era (1851-1861). The robe is embroidered with symbols—"Five Color Clouds," omens of peace; "Mountains of Longevity"; "Sea of Happiness." For sale during 1972 for $1,500.

"just-for-fun fancies" to send in details for consideration.

At the moment the catalogue includes cast-iron stoves and cookware, kitchen utensils and stoneware, a few organic foods (they hope to add more), garden and livestock supplies, basic tools, some outdoor equipment such as snowshoes, back packs, etc., craft supplies, wooden toys and books. They also sell back numbers of *Mother Earth News* and *Lifestyle* magazines for people who have "decided to kick over the traces, grab life in both hands and begin spending their best years living exactly as they please."

National Bellas Hess, Inc., 715 Armour Road, Kansas City, Mo. 64116
Color catalogue, free. January, October.

This eighty-year-old mail-order firm says that it concentrates on "soft line" goods, although "hard line" also appeal to its type of buyers. It is too well known to leave out of this list of mail-order firms, but it reduced operations in 1970. I was sent just two small catalogues of clothes and a few appliances, nothing of special interest.

Neiman-Marcus Co., Dallas, Texas 75201
Fashion mailings throughout the year, free.
100-page Christmas catalogue, $1; refundable. October.

Neiman-Marcus was started in 1907 as a luxury clothing store. Over the years the Marcus family, which has stayed very much in charge, has added more and more goods and departments until it has the widest range of any American department store—in the luxury brackets, that is. Although slightly more moderately priced goods have been added over the years, the store still revels in its reputation for scandalous extravagance, flaunts its nouveau oil-rich customers, and manages to attract attention itself each year for gift suggestions on the "bare line of credulity," as the president says, such as his and her camels, submarines, and aquariums with real pearls instead of sand (when I asked for photographs, they didn't send a thing priced at less than $1,000). Like Walter Hoving of Tiffany's, President Stanley Marcus refuses to pander to bad public taste and will only sell things that he thinks are good for his customers. Although his idea of what's good for us is debatable, it must be admitted that Mr. Marcus pursues his mission to elevate taste with zeal; he travels the world for us, swoops into China for us and was the first U.S. merchant to enter the Forbidden City since the Revolution.

All this commitment leads to a very seductive catalogue, for unlike many of the catalogues for the ultra-rich, which show expensive *and* hideous products, this one is cleverly done with simple graphics and lovely color photographs, and listing goods which, antique Indian carousel horses and Japanese aviaries notwithstanding, are often simple. In the catalogue I looked at, clothes, jewelry, household goods, food and toys were covered, and there were beautifully designed colored suede clothes, a natural-canvas bicycle bag, an Italian stereo-component house, a baseball shirt, a glistening espresso machine, a wooden Appalachian-made toy, and some scrumptiously photographed food. I painstakingly counted and found fifty items for $10 or under.

J. C. Penney Co., Inc., 1301 Avenue of the Americas, New York, N.Y. 10019
Large catalogue—spring, fall. Supplements—summer, Christmas. All free, but to receive them regularly you must buy from them regularly.

J. C. Penney doesn't manufacture but has about 85 percent of its products made to the company's own specifications and sold under its own brand name. The goods are often tested by *Consumer Reports* and do creditably—in one test of sleeping bags for flammability, the Penney sleeping bag was the only one that was acceptably nonflammable (obviously my remark is too general and you should look up specific items before buying). Although Penney's doesn't have quite as broad a range of equipment as its competitors Sears, Roebuck and Montgomery Ward (it doesn't sell large household appliances such as dishwashers and ovens), in certain areas it does have some better-looking things than the other two. Among the usual drab, mock-traditional styles of household furnishings, you suddenly come upon a few more modern pieces in the Penney catalogue—a track lighting system, a page full of director's and bentwood chairs, a nice simple Yugoslavian folding chair in pine, unfinished furniture for children that is square and simple, vinyl floor tiles in good clear solid colors instead of the usual mottled patterns. Penney's also has, unlike the other two, a lovely kitchen section with cookbooks, copper cookware, glass preserve jars, earthenware "bean-pot" style jugs and crocks, and imported cooking implements such as a couscous cooker, a paella pan, a "Melior" coffeepot from France, clay roasters, and a whole lot of Chinese and Japanese cooking pots and accessories.

Saks Fifth Avenue, Folio Collections, Inc., P.O. Box 5138, F.D.R. Station, New York, N.Y. 10022
Catalogues: Special Events, January, Spring/Summer, April. White Sale, July. Fall Fashion with children's section, August. Christmas catalogue, October. $1 will put you on the mailing list to receive all the above catalogues.

Saks Fifth Avenue, perhaps the most famous of the New York department stores, sells mainly clothes and linen through their catalogues. The January "special events" catalogue is, in fact, a white-sale catalogue (although white sales are rarely white these days) and the one I looked at had ladylike, often flowery sheets, towels, placemats and tablecloths. Richly colored wool blankets from England, and a few bath accessories such as tissue holders and a tub tray.

Last year, for the first time and at the request, they say, of their customers, Saks published a Christmas gift catalogue—chastely elegant, with excellent color photographs and gifts that rarely cost less than $25: Louis Vuitton luggage, Baccarat crystal, velvet Pucci pants and a mink motorcycling jacket. A few clothes for men are also shown, and a few things for the house such as a large silver-plated swan for flowers ($135) or a small gold electroplated corkscrew in the shape of an owl ($10).

5

6

5 • *Neiman-Marcus* Antique carousel horses from India in carved wood with brass ornaments (c. 1850). Each horse is 2′ long, 18″ high to the saddle. The pair was for sale during 1972 for $2,500.

6 • *Neiman-Marcus* Life-size models, "reasonable facsimilies" of you or anyone else (with their permission), programmed to laugh at your jokes and say yes in any language at the touch of a remote-control button. Sold during 1972 for $3,000 each, not including the clothes and the sculptor's air fare.

Sears, Roebuck and Co., Department 139, 2650 E. Olympic Boulevard, Los Angeles, Calif. 90051, or Sears, Roebuck and Co., Department 139, 4640 Roosevelt Boulevard, Philadelphia, Pa. 19132

General spring catalogue, January. General fall catalogue, June.

Sears says that you can order its general catalogue from either of the above addresses free of charge, but that to stay on the lists you have to buy about $50 worth every three months. Sears also publishes a large number of specialized catalogues which are probably easier to get hold of: Business Equipment and Supply catalogue; Men's Apparel Catalogue of Big and Tall sizes; catalogue of Career Apparel for Women and Men (uniforms); Western catalogue; Carpet; Wonderful World of Wall Coverings; Home Improvement catalogue (awnings, doors, ironwork, tiles, etc.); Accessories and Supplies for Automobiles and Trucks; Craft Center; Accessories for Mobile Homes and Recreation Vehicles catalogue; Fishing and Supplies; Replacement Parts for Jeep Utility Vehicles, Jeepsters; Naturama (natural and organic health foods, natural vitamins, cosmetics); Home Care and Convalescent Needs catalogue; Power and Hand-Tool catalogue; Suburban, Farm and Ranch catalogue; Apparel Catalogue of Tall Misses, Women and Half Sizes.

Montgomery Ward, Chicago, Ill. 60607

General catalogues—Spring/Summer, Fall/Winter. Lawn and Garden catalogue, Fashion supplement, Sale catalogues throughout the year.

Montgomery Ward says that the only way to get one of the catalogues is to place an order first, which may sound impossible. Another suggestion is that you go into one of the Ward stores or borrow a catalogue from a friend and get yourself on the list that way. To stay on the lists you have to make at least two purchases every six months.

A true reader's guide to the Sears and Montgomery Ward catalogues would end up being a book about America as it is today, for there are few documents as basic and indicative of our consumer society as these vast telephone-directory type books. The U.S. Information Agency used to feature the catalogues at its exhibits in Eastern Europe, and one wonders what kind of a picture they gave of America. The clothes are much more up-to-date than a few years ago, but the catalogues still give a surprisingly old-fashioned image of national taste, even though, ironically enough, I didn't see one model who looked over thirty-five in their pages (and only two blacks—one male, one female).

Given the literally thousands of items sold, the question is what to choose when one has access to competing department and other stores. The answer for me has been to read the catalogues with the *Consumer Report's Buying Guide* next to me and to see which of the specially made appliances rate best. In the case of most large appliances, such as clothes dryers, the Sears and Montgomery Ward makes will be among those listed as acceptable and should be considered along with competitors'. In certain varied and at times unexpected categories, such as pruning shears, Sears is listed as a best buy, along with the famous English firm of Wilkinson, or check-rated, as is the Sears circular saw. So it makes sense to use these catalogues when comparison-shopping for articles in any of a number of categories, though in certain areas, such as furniture, these firms manufacture only the most traditional items, and in others, such as general books and records, they are out of the running altogether. In many ways these major mail-order catalogues can be used in conjunction with a book such as this, although very few of the special items listed here are to be found in their pages, but their offerings should be compared with those of the big downtown department stores.

Whole Earth Truck Store, 558 Santa Cruz Avenue, Menlo Park, Calif. 94025

The Last Whole Earth Catalog, $5.

Even though the last *Whole Earth Catalog* has been published, the Whole Earth Truck Store is alive and kicking and selling many of the things mentioned in it, mainly, they say, how-to-do-it books, but also camping equipment and merchandise with back-to-the-land leanings, so this is a good place for finding things that are usually hard to get hold of. For the people who haven't yet looked at the *Whole Earth Catalog,* not only is it engrossing reading but it is also an excellent place to find out about usual and unusual interests, hobbies, activities, books, etc., as the write-ups are frequently by readers who have been involved in them for many years and have become very knowledgeable.

* * *

Incidentally, among the many books in the style of the *Whole Earth Catalog* that have appeared are two which are scheduled to appear regularly and which, besides having the same "back-to-the-land leanings," give information about local craftsmen, small businesses and things of local interests. Both of them are essential reading for anyone interested in the district and rewarding reading for anyone else, and will, hopefully, inspire people in other areas to follow suit: *The First New England Catalogue* is distributed by Random House ($4.95) and on sale in bookstores; *The Maine Catalogue* ($2.30, including postage) is more local and amateurish but very likable and especially devoted to crafts; it is on sale at the Eosphonic Institute, P.O. Box 1770, Portland, Maine 04104.

12
HANDICRAFTS

Apart from Indian arts and crafts and quilting, most American crafts now being made are not held strictly to traditional forms but are produced by individualists who aren't interested in supplying a large number of identical pieces and who are not often willing to take the time needed to sell their works by mail. Nor are many shops in big cities, or anywhere else, able or inclined to take on the selling of such items, given the low profits involved. Luckily for the growing number of people who are interested in crafts, there are exceptions—both craftsmen and shops that manage to find enough similar pieces to make a catalogue worthwhile. However, like the antique shops, these tend to be small operations which slow down when overworked, so extra patience is required when buying handicrafts by mail.

GENERAL

Publications Department, American Crafts Council, 44 W. 53rd Street, New York, N.Y. 10019
List of craft galleries and shops, $3.50 including postage.

The American Crafts Council publishes a booklet listing galleries all over the country which sell American, and sometimes imported, crafts. It's useful if you want to know where to buy and/or sell crafts, as it tells which galleries accept work for sale.

ANAC, Box 953, Anchorage, Alaska 99501
22-page catalogue, $1.

The ANAC catalogue will delight anyone who is interested in native American crafts; it illustrates the work of Aleuts, Eskimos and Indians who belong to the Alaska Native Arts and Crafts Association, the largest marketing co-op in Alaska. The crafts, which are listed and photographed, include a good collection of baskets at prices from just a few dollars to well over a hundred for spruce-root baskets by Tlingit Indians; ivory carvings of all sorts from paper knives to elaborate cribbage boards, including little Eskimo scenes and local animals such as seal and polar bear, and cutlery with carved handles; primitive dolls in furry costumes, and Eskimo ceremonial masks at prices between $90 and $150. The co-op also stocks rabbit-skin mittens, parkas and vests, and you can put yourself on the long waiting list for Eskimo footwear—fur-lined slippers and mukluks with ankle thongs and fancy work, unlined or lined with fur. Slippers cost from $14 to $24, and mukluks from $34 to $60.

Anderson Design, Inc., Anderson Road, East Boothbay, Maine 04544
Leaflet, free.

In 1953 Weston and Brenda Anderson left jobs in teaching and designing to move to Maine, where they set up their own pottery studio, and now, with seven employees, make spare and graceful stoneware animals and bowls. Colors are mainly brown, gray and white, and the animals, although not boringly realistic, give a real sense of the bird or animal they are modeled after; they vary between 3″ and 13″ in size and cost between $6 and $35. Bowls and plates usually have a heavy white matte glaze with tree branches or animals painted in free strokes. An extra large 16″-long serving platter has a very scaly and finny fish in glossy blue and green on white for $25, but prices for these bowls, plates, vases and candlesticks are usually between $7 and $20.

Appalachiana, Inc., 4818 St. Elmo Avenue, Bethesda, Md. 20014
Catalogue, 50 cents.

This is what the owners of Appalachiana say: "Our shop was founded to help stimulate interest in the traditional crafts of the Appalachian region. Many articles, such as split oak baskets and slat bonnets, represent revivals of almost forgotten skills (the makers of these bonnets remembered hearing grandmothers speak of them and started delving back for old patterns . . .). Other articles, such as hooked rugs and apple dolls [with heads made of dried apples], carry on an unbroken tradition. Still others reflect the creativity of Appalachian craftsmen who take familiar materials and turn them into works of art—shaved wood flowers are a fine example of this."

A neat brochure illustrates, besides the crafts mentioned above, corn-shuck dolls, straw hot mats, reed and straw brooms, a few plain pieces of wood furniture including a solid cherry cradle, pottery for the kitchen, soup bowls, spice jars, herb planters, a decorated stoneware mirror and a clock, and a "doughnut"-design wine decanter in an early Colonial shape. Among the less earthy crafts are carved and pottery animals, notepaper with reproductions of wild-flower paintings, porcelain bells, sterling-silver Christmas-tree ornaments, and a collection of copper- and silver-washed copper flowers rooted in rock crystal.

Appalachian Spring, 1655 Wisconsin Avenue, N.W., Washington, D.C. 20007
22-page catalogue, $1.

This Washington store has a carefully chosen collection of mainly modern crafts made in Appalachia: handwoven pillows, place mats and rugs; lovely carved wooden spoons for the kitchen and a handsome wooden dough bowl to be used for salad or fruit by people who don't make bread; rough aluminium casseroles—one for a fish has carved designs and looks specially appetizing; handmade glass pitchers and decanters; and some pottery and modern hammered pewter. Besides a good selection of traditional patchwork quilts, patchwork pillows and patchwork toys, there is jewelry, made by various people, and also several crafts I haven't seen in other catalogues—long-lasting wild flowers made from dyed cornhusks; forged-iron wind chimes; mirrors framed in cast aluminium; pottery lamps in the shape of a cozy fat woman clutching a bunch of flowers; vases with families modeled on them (you can order one with numbers matching your own family, $8 for mother and father with one child, $1 for each additional child). There is also an extraordinary group of miniature wagons in natural wood made by a man who used to work on the originals; these cost between $38 and $125 each.

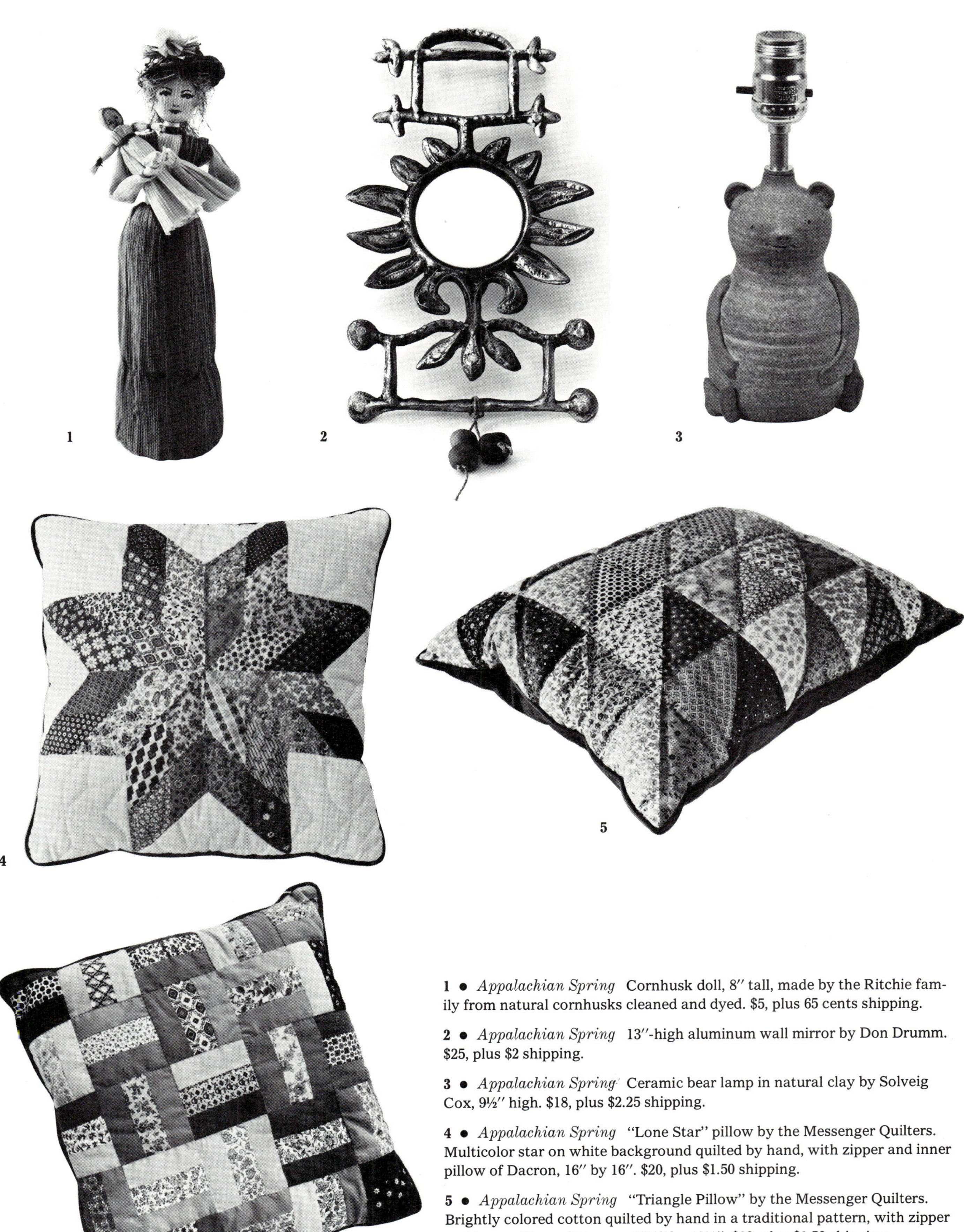

1 • *Appalachian Spring* Cornhusk doll, 8″ tall, made by the Ritchie family from natural cornhusks cleaned and dyed. $5, plus 65 cents shipping.

2 • *Appalachian Spring* 13″-high aluminum wall mirror by Don Drumm. $25, plus $2 shipping.

3 • *Appalachian Spring* Ceramic bear lamp in natural clay by Solveig Cox, 9½″ high. $18, plus $2.25 shipping.

4 • *Appalachian Spring* "Lone Star" pillow by the Messenger Quilters. Multicolor star on white background quilted by hand, with zipper and inner pillow of Dacron, 16″ by 16″. $20, plus $1.50 shipping.

5 • *Appalachian Spring* "Triangle Pillow" by the Messenger Quilters. Brightly colored cotton quilted by hand in a traditional pattern, with zipper and inner pillow of Dacron, 15½″ by 19½″. $20, plus $1.50 shipping.

6 • *Appalachian Spring* "Roman Stripe" pillow by the Messenger Quilters. Brightly colored cotton quilted by hand in a traditional pattern, with zipper and inner pillow of Dacron, 14″ by 14″. $24, plus $1.50 shipping.

7

8

7 • *Appalachian Spring* The name of this quilt varies according to region. It is often called "Dutch Children" or "Sunbonnet Sue and Calico Bill." On each quilt, boys and girls in a variety of colors are appliquéd on a white background, and borders are pink, blue, green or yellow. Washable, 44″ by 55″. $50, plus $1.50 shipping.
photo Adams Studio, Inc.

8 • *Appalachian Spring* "Double Wedding Ring" crib quilt. Perhaps the best-known of all the traditional quilt patterns, it consists of interlocking rings of multicolored cotton on a white background. Dacron-filled and hand-quilted. Washable, 40″ by 53″. $35, plus $1.50 shipping.

Artisan Gallery, 30 Witherspoon Street, Princeton, N.J. 08540
16-page brochure, free.

The Artisan Gallery was opened in 1970 by Shirle Claman, who wanted to sell well-designed art forms from the functional to the purely decorative—from pictures to frying pans. Her brochure illustrates the work of about fourteen craftsmen—the most striking pieces are the People Pots by David Davis, which have been shown twice in the Museum of Contemporary Crafts in New York and received quite a bit of publicity: mugs, mustache cups, teapots, casseroles and planters are made of brown stoneware clay with a blue glaze and shaped into the face of a mustachioed man. Prices for People Pots are between $4 and $30. Other pottery includes stoneware hanging planters and hanging bird feeders and a birdhouse by Nonnie Barnes; candlesticks, vases, bells, hanging lights and small garden statues in the shape of people and animals—but coyer ones than the People Pots—by Rosemary Taylor; and butter warmers, casseroles and skillets by the Libow family.

There is also silver and gold jewelry—quite a few silver rings and earrings for under $10, some cuff links and tiepins for under $20, bracelets made of copper and silver circles for the upper arm for $25.

Other works include small bronze sculpture, lithographs, colographs, woodcuts and woven containers for dried flowers. More weavings are displayed at the gallery but are not shown in the brochure, and you can write to the gallery about any special orders you'd like to make for weaving, rya rugs or any other craft.

Ayottes' Designery, Center Sandwich, N.H. 03227
Brochure with yarn samples planned, $1.

Robert and Roberta Ayotte design and weave by hand on six large floor looms in their studio in a New England village. They make drapery and upholstery fabrics, wall hangings, rugs, pillows and place mats, and their brochure will show some of their brightly colored clothes. Styles are loose-fitting, so it should be possible to buy by mail successfully. Hostess skirts cost from $45 to $100 depending on whether the weave is plain or patterned, bell-sleeved tunic dresses are $65, a bulky fringed coat $200, and capes, which should be easiest of all to buy by mail, are also made.

Berea College Student Craft Industries, Box 2347, Berea, Ky. 40403
28-page furniture catalogue, $1.
48-page handicraft brochure, 25 cents.

Berea students work their way through college by participating in extensive work programs, some of which involve making handicrafts. The objects are sold in a store on the campus and through their mail-order brochure. There are wooden pieces, big handsome games such as skittles, of small tops and blocks, and also egg cups, bun warmers, candlesticks and chopping blocks. Toys made of cloth, and quite a big collection of rag animals—lobsters, snakes, hippopotamuses and a kangaroo with a baby—cost from $2 to $7.50. A lot of the gifts are woven: shoulder bags, scarves, pillows, ponchos and baby blankets. And handwoven skirts are made to the customer's measurements—a hostess in a black, red, forest green or royal blue, can have one of several patterns around the border interwoven with metallic gold or silver for $36.

Bernier Studio, Route 25, Wentworth, N.H. 03282
16-page color brochure, 25 cents. May.

A mixed collection of crafts, decorative objects and things for children made by the Berniers and friends: flecked gray or beige pottery mugs for about $3 each, vases in the shape of little people to stick dried flowers in for about $7 each, hand-turned wooden salad bowls, shrimp dishes and relish trays, handwoven place mats, brass mobiles. Also stained glass, enamelware, jewelry, flower plaques, artificial flowers. For children: rag dolls, painted wooden trucks, animal book ends, homemade wall hangings, bibs, calico pinafores, and kits to make different old-fashioned buggies out of balsa wood, about $5 each, and a horse that fits, about $4. Most things cost under $10 and prices are generally low.

9

Camphill Village Gift Shop, Chrysler Pond Road, Copake, N.Y. 12516
Price list, free.

This community for mentally retarded young adults has a gift shop in which they sell weavings, toys and enamelwork made in their own workshops. They also make the "Lattoflex" bed, developed in Switzerland to help poor sleepers and people with back disorders. Instead of the usual metal springs, this bed has slightly curved wooden slats supported by rubber moldings. Anyone who is interested is invited to come by and lock at the bed.

By mail the gift shop sells a few wooden toys, woven mats and popular enameled plates and bowls with a realistic leaf shape in one color on a different-colored background; prices for ashtrays and bowls are $3 to $18. Proceeds from the shop go toward maintaining the community.

10

Circle of Arts/Objects, Inc., c/o Lee Nordness Galleries, Inc., 236 E. 75th Street, New York, N.Y. 10021
80-page color brochure, $1.

"About the new artist-craftsman—or when is a teapot sculpture?" reads the heading on the explanatory leaflet. And it goes on to say: "University-trained artists who found it inconceivable that people could hang beautiful paintings on their walls while simultaneously surrounding themselves with banal mass-produced objects, from the coffee cup to the sofa to the planter. Why couldn't a front door be a work of art? And further, how could objects be personal when handmade?" Here are ceramics, glassware, enamelware, woven hangings and jewelry chosen by Lee Nordness, director

11

9 • *Circle of Arts/Objects* "Twice Told" by Ellamarie Wolley, a wall panel constructed of enamel-on-copper units, 17″ by 16¼″. Edition of 10. $235.

10 • *Circle of Arts/Objects* "Reclining Nude" plate in an edition of 35. Hand-built stoneware with luster and low-fire glazes, prepared for hanging or table display. Widest diameter, 14½″, is $150. "Smoo" pendant in an edition of 100; hand-formed pendant with luster and low-fire glazes, approximately 4½″ in diameter, $20. Three "Current Event" cups, hand-built porcelain with luster and low-fire glazes, 6″ high with 2¼″ diameter, $40 each. Plate, pendant and cups all by Eric Gronborg.

11 • *Circle of Arts/Objects* "Cityscape" by Kurt Fishback. Chess set hand-built of clay in an edition of 5. Acrylic-painted. Highest chessman, 4½″. $200, board not included.

12

13

14

15

16

17

12 • *The Craftman's Gallery* Collar by Edwina Drobny of waxed linen macramé, pewter and colored onyx. $100.

13 • *The Craftman's Gallery* Neck sculpture by Edwina Drobny of brass and waxed linen macramé. $100.

14 • *Craft House Downtown* "Weed Person" stoneware vase for decorative grasses, etc. Similar pieces with birds in hair and/or hand, 4½″ high, $7.50.

15 • *Circle of Arts/Objects* *Top left:* "Searching Forms," paperweight in an edition of 250 by Kent Ipsen, $65. *Bottom left:* "Implosions," paperweight in an edition of 250 by Kent Ipsen, 3¾″ wide by 3¾″ high, $65. *Top right:* "Veils," paperweight/vase in an edition of 50 by Gilbert Johnson, 3″ high with a 3½″ diameter, $70. *Bottom right:* "Fan," paperweight in an edition of 75 by Gilbert Johnson, 3½″ by 3¼″ side by 2″ deep, $55.

16 • *Craft House Downtown* Stoneware hanging planter in oatmeal, rust or dark brown. 6″ in diameter, $7.50; 8″ in diameter, $10.

17 • *The Craftman's Gallery* Ceramic salt and pepper shakers by Brian Persha, 5″ long. $25 the set.

of the leading New York crafts gallery and author of a new book, *Objects: USA*. Art objects for sale by mail is a new departure, and someone from the American Crafts Council told me that the crafts world is looking on with bated breath to see whether people will buy expensive decorative, rather than functional, crafts by mail.

What the objects have in common is that they all look very individual and fantastic. Here you won't find discreet modern designs; instead there are sterling-silver key rings cast from sections of plastic toys, wavily carved wooden jewelry chests, a wall hanging with a poem by e. e. cummings silkscreened onto linen, a "Cityscape" chess set where the men are houses and trees painted in bright colors, and a Burping Bowl ($450) from which at regular intervals a monster rises, spouts water and burps (edition of twenty-five).

Craft House Downtown, 17 Exchange Street, Portland, Maine 04111
Brochure planned, 25 cents.

An ex-craftswoman opened a shop in Maine in 1967 for crafts and well-designed household objects which has proved so popular that she is now producing a brochure for the growing number of customers (tourists and "summer people") who live outside of Maine. I have seen photographs of the stock and I think the brochure will be well worth sending for. She plans to include stoneware by Maine potters—baking dishes, decanter sets, wind chimes, bells and hanging planters; kerosene lanterns made in New Hampshire with old fashioned chimney and works, and modern stoneware bases; cylindrical handwoven hanging lampshades in glowing colors and nubby textures ($25 to $45), and small balsam pillows in the same colors, $1.50; silver and gold jewelry made by a local silversmith—chain-link silver necklaces up to $15, heavy chain belt, $25. She also carries the lovable Possum Trot cloth toys fashioned by professional designers to be made by people in the Kentucky mountains as the result of a "community development of self-help initiative," and she can take orders for patchwork quilts made by a Maine antipoverty group: pillows $15, single bed quilts $75.

The Craftsman's Gallery, Box 645, Rockville, Md. 20851
24-page magazine; annual subscription $6.

This thin magazine with short book reviews and one or two articles of interest has large clear pictures of objects for sale made by craftsmen from all over the country. The issue I looked at had some classic, rather restrained stoneware pots at prices from $20 to $150; some very dramatic and African-influenced macramé for around $100 each; a ceramic base for a small table to be topped by glass, $125; a free-form walnut table for $1,500; a set of pottery salt and pepper shakers with animal faces for $25; two teapots and framed batik pictures on silk. Well worth looking at for anyone seriously interested in crafts.

Fat City Enterprises, Box 142, Spencer, W. Va. 25276
Leaflets for candlesticks, cradles and toys planned, all for 25 cents.

A husband and wife moved to a hill farm in West Virginia in the summer of 1972 determined to go back to the land, grow their own food and make a living by selling crafts. They make various things and take them around to craft fairs, besides selling them by mail. Spiked candlesticks, candelabras and chandeliers, breadboards and cutting boards from local woods are hand-finished in a linseed-oil recipe from Colonial times; candleholders cost from $1.50 to $6. Leaflets are planned for painted wooden toys, and for simple white pine or cedar cradles in several designs fashioned from pictures of Colonial cradles. The Bergs also make little animals from acorns, pine needles, feathers, nuts and seed found on the land; they make quilts too, and can supply them in the same size as the cradles. However, as there are just the two of them, I don't think they will be able to do everything at once, so I suggest that just the most patient and phlegmatic should write.

Glass Masters, Inc., 110 W. 17th Street, New York, N.Y. 10011
Leaflet of reproductions, 50 cents; refundable. Stained-glass supplies list, 25 cents.

This stained-glass studio thinks it is the only place in the world making reproductions of medieval stained glass. About forty very pretty pieces are made in the same way that the originals were made and are sold with stands or loops so that they can be hung in front of a window for the sun to shine through. Subjects include a fifteenth-century Noah's Ark, a fourteenth-century dancing bear, animals, flowers, medieval herbs and cooking scenes (which would look most apt in a kitchen window), and nineteenth-century *Alice in Wonderland* illustrations. Each piece is quite small, up to about 9″ in diameter, and prices are between $8 and $40. The studio also has a small list of supplies for making stained glass, and sells books, though these aren't listed.

Home Co-op, Route 1, Orland, Maine 04472
Catalogue, free. Fall.

In June 1970, with a grant of $7,500, Home Co-op began generating work for low-income and unemployed people in Maine who could make handcrafted products. Within six months, $16,000 worth of gross sales had been made and $12,000 returned to the craftsmen, and in 1972, $50,000 worth of gross sales, wholesale and retail, returned $32,750 to seven hundred craftsmen. The informal newsprint catalogue shows homemade things of all sorts—hand-knit baby clothes, bright-red hand-knit Christmas stockings decorated with snowmen or Santa Claus, Christmas wreaths, smocks and kimonos for women and little girls, woven aprons and place mats, stained-glass ornaments, wooden birdhouses and wooden candlesticks. The catalogue also shows two quilt patterns that I haven't seen elsewhere, "Duck's Foot in the Mud" and "Hole in the Barn Door," both dramatic designs of white on a solid color (bright red, blue or brown) or a patterned color (you can send a swatch to be matched) on white. Prices go from $102 for twin-bed size to $162 for king size.

The Co-op has started building, with the help of city folk, a Rural Life Center in Orland which by the time this book is published will have pottery studios, a leathercraft shop, a silversmith shop and an education building for classes in literary skills and craft techniques. Eventually it will also have space for metal-working, glass blowing and a local farm market.

International Craft Designs, 8 W. 19th Street, New York, N.Y. 10011
Leaflet, 10 cents.

International Craft Designs was started by New York and Maine wood craftsmen, but now, besides obtaining wooden objects from New York, New Jersey, Vermont, Maine and Pennsylvania, they import from abroad. They say that of special interest are their birdhouses made of hollowed-out logs, their Vermont cutting boards and turtle stools, their spice racks and wooden wine goblets. Pottery and kitchen utensils are also sold, but not many of them are shown in the leaflet.

Jugtown Pottery, Route Two, Seagrove, N.C. 27341
16-page catalogue, $1.

During the post-Civil War depression, farmers who couldn't sell their corn turned it into whiskey, and at the end of the nineteenth century there were nearly fifty potteries in the twenty-square-mile area which came to be known as Jugtown because so many of the potteries were making jugs for the liquor. As the depression ended, the farmers went back to farming and with prohibition in 1908 the whiskey jugs were no longer needed; then, as white china and glass became readily available, not many people wanted the potters' "dirt dishes." In 1915 a North Carolinian couple, Jacques and Juliana Busbee, found an orange pottery pie plate which they liked so much that they traced it to its source and located a few potteries still producing. The Busbees took on the task of keeping the workshops alive, by selling the pottery in New York and finally building the Jugtown Pottery. In 1968 the enterprise was bought by County Roads, Inc., a nonprofit corporation devoted to preserving and developing American handicrafts.

The pottery is all made from local clay in the very plain and pleasant forms that developed over the years. Some of the pieces are available in the traditional orange, others come in blue, brown and gray, and it really looks very different from pottery made by individual craftsmen to their own designs. Almost everything you need for cooking and eating is made—cups and mugs, plates and platters, bowls, casseroles, jugs and jars. A plate costs $4, a coffeepot $8.50, and casseroles and bean pots are from $3.75 to $8.50.

The Kennebunk Railroad Station Craft Workshop, 12 Depot Street, Kennebunk, Maine 04043
18-page handicraft catalogue, free. Bead supplement, free. October. January.

This is what Carol Standish says about her shop: "The Railroad Station was established in 1969 by John and Carol Standish as a retail shop offering only handmade articles of high quality. In the course of the first year of business it became evident that, due to the small population of the town and the short tourist season, other means of presenting the wares of our shop would have to be devised. The mail-order business was the answer and it has been growing since 1970 . . . We have a distinctly 'Yankee' attitude of self-sufficiency in that we not only produce all the handcrafted items in the handcrafts catalogue ourselves but also produce all our own catalogues from concept to printing."

The handicraft catalogue, illustrated with line drawings on orange and mustard paper, shows stained-glass animals and Christmas decorations to hang in front of windows, at prices from $4 to $24; hand-blown glass paperweights at prices from $6 to $16; sterling-silver wire jewelry at prices from $2 to $10.50 ("Bob Grant suggests that if you don't know your size, enclose a piece of string the circumference of that part of your anatomy you wish to decorate with his wares"); lovely-looking handwoven pillows ($10.50 each) and place mats ($15.50 for four). "Ann is a very mellow person and an accomplished weaver using only unscoured wool from Canada, Denmark and Iceland." Macramé belts and dog leashes and pottery jars, vases and goblets are also available.

The bead supplement has line drawings of Italian mosaic, beggar agate, Persian blue crow, porcelain, Mexican onyx, Hebron glass and other beads that can be used for either macramé or jewelry making.

Koinonia Handcrafts, Route 2, Americus, Ga. 31709
Clothes and Crafts leaflet, free.
Cake and Nut catalogue, free.

Koinonia Farm was established in the 1940's by a group of people who wanted to live out Christian ideals of sharing and brotherhood. But two aspects of their plan—the creation of a racially integrated community and the teaching of scientific farming methods to local farmers—proved to be mutually exclusive. After a short period of success, the neighbors became increasingly hostile and the community was subjected to shootings, beatings, bombings, burnings and economic boycott. Koinonia survived, but by the late sixties the remaining members began to feel that simply existing as an integrated Christian community was not enough. After much discussion it was decided, among other things, to form a "Fund for Humanity" with which farm land would be bought and given back to the people to work rent-free, and industries would be started in which people could work "in partnership" as equals.

The goods listed on the Clothes and Crafts leaflet are an outcome of the new policy, and consist mostly of inexpensive loose-flowing clothes for men and women in African prints, tie-dye cotton and unbleached embroidered muslin (fabrics are also sold by the yard). Men's shirts and smocks, long and short dresses for women, blouses made from Mexican scarves all cost under or around $10, and there are also cloth toys and very inexpensive patchwork quilts in traditional patterns—$75 to $100 for double-bed size.

Liberty House, P.O. Box 3468, Jackson, Miss. 39207
Occasional brochures, free.

In 1965 the Poor People's Corporation was formed with the idea of starting different kinds of co-operatives to help unemployed and underemployed people in Mississippi. By chance most of the groups that came to early meetings were interested in crafts, so the organizers of the Corporation found themselves totally involved in the production of crafts. Then, because the different co-ops were in rural areas and needed more efficient communication between them, it was decided to form a central organization, Liberty House, which was owned by the twelve co-ops. Now Liberty House provides full and part-time work for about three hundred people, not only the Mississippi members but also other groups—such as the Koasati Indians in Louisiana, the Seminole Indians in Florida and a large new co-operative in Brazil—which do not own Liberty House but use it to sell their products.

Many of the co-op members start with no skills at all

but are taught through an education and training program, so the crafts, except for baskets from the Koasati, are not the complicated traditional crafts but fairly easily made, imaginatively designed things: plenty of shoulder bags, cloth toys, oven gloves and a gorgeously decorative collection of felt animals from the Brazilian co-op. Prices are very low (most things are under $5), and when they wrote to me, Liberty House had just *lowered* prices, which must make them the only organization in the country to have done such a thing.

Priscilla Manning Porter Studio, Plumb Hill Road, Washington, Conn. 06793
Leaflet, free.

Priscilla Porter started as a potter, but while teaching a course in mosaics at the Museum of Modern Art in New York, developed a technique for fusing glass of different colors by firing it in a kiln, and gradually got interested in glass blowing.

In a studio workshop in Connecticut, Priscilla Porter designs and makes a variety of decorative objects in glass, animals, mushroom groups, flowers, paperweights and ashtrays. Unfortunately, there are just small line drawings of the animals in the leaflet, so it is hard to tell exactly what you are getting if you buy by mail. But there is a list of Christmas glass ornaments, including snowflakes and several kinds of stars, which sound pretty enough to buy sight unseen. Prices of many pieces are under $6, but there are very "large and showy" Christmas balls and wreaths, about 20″ in diameter, which cost about $15.

The Railroad Shop, 25 Railroad Avenue, Warwick, N.Y. 10990
Catalogue, free.

Housed in what was once the Lehigh & Hudson River Railway depot in Warwick, the Railroad Shop sells the work of a group called the Chardavogne craftsmen. A few things, such as American handmade tiles, and decorative leatherwork bowls, boxes and frames, I haven't seen anywhere else, at all. Other things, such as rug weaving to order, are quite hard to come by, so people who would like rugs of very special colors will be pleased to find that they can order rugs and tapestries for $5 to $8 per square foot for plain weave, and $10 to $15 per square foot for designs. Quilts are also made in traditional and modern patterns, old quilts are repaired (send photograph and description of damage for estimate), and evening skirts in either cotton or velvet patchwork can be made to order in all sorts of patterns. Cotton skirts cost $85 each, and velvet $125. There is a nice collection of heavy pottery with matte glazes: mugs, jugs, casseroles, a teapot, wall planters and hanging planters with leather thongs, and an unusual one with swirly lines etched into it. Wooden toys, silver earrings and rings, and some pleasantly lumpy animal candles are also sold.

SERRV Self Help Handicrafts, Church World Service Center, New Windsor, Md. 21776
32-page color catalogue, free.
Christmas color leaflet, free. Fall.

A man by the very appropriate name of William P. Nyce is the director of this nonprofit organization (affiliated with the Church World Service Center), which sells handicrafts made by the "disadvantaged"

18 • *Jugtown Pottery* Large earthenware pitcher, $6.50. Fluted pie dish, $3.75. Large noggin with handle, $2.50. Small straight jug, $5.

19 • *Stell and Shevis* "Whaling Days," a silkscreen print in blues and gold on white, 24″ by 36″. $22.50 postpaid.

in other lands in an attempt to raise their income. SERRV helps them not only by finding raw materials for them, setting up workshops, and exporting and selling their products, but also by making serious efforts to deal with noncommercial suppliers to avoid possibly exploitative middlemen. These craftsmen, who don't produce enough to sell through normal commercial channels, are paid what is considered a fair wage in each country, yet SERRV keeps selling prices low.

The goods are not always authentic handicrafts and are not as exciting a collection as they could be (too many wood carvings for my liking), but there is certainly something here to please everyone who likes crafts: a cloth-and-yarn doll Nativity set from Jordan costs about $19, handloomed change purses from Guatemala cost $1.25 each, handwoven pictures and baby toys from Peru cost under $2, a lovely alpaca-wool shoulder bag with designs in natural colors costs $7, and wood and natural-fiber doll chairs cost $2.25 each.

Willard Shepard, Jordan Cove, Waterford, Connecticut 06385
Leaflet, free.

Carving wasn't the Shepard family's traditional occupation. Willard Shepard's grandfather was a bishop and his father a professor, but after being a carpenter and a boat builder, Willard Shepard became a full-time wood carver and the resident ship carver at Seaport Marine Museum, Mystic, Connecticut. He has an illustrated price list of the standard-name boards, eagles and figureheads that he carves to order from laminated pine and finishes in brass leaf or gold leaf. Prices start at about $30 for 8″ eagles with brass leaf (which isn't weatherproof) and go up to about $470 for 72″ eagles in gold leaf. Small figureheads cost between $58 and $232. All of these take at least a month to make. Mr. Shepard will also carve to order other painted and gilded decorative objects, such as cigar-store Indians, carousel animals, circus-wagon ornaments, church angels, rudderheads, shop signs and figures, at prices according to work involved.

Stell and Shevis Handprints, 82 Elm Street, Camden, Maine 04843
Leaflets, 25 cents.

A husband and wife run a shop full of local and imported crafts. By mail they sell their own hand-printed things: handkerchiefs and guest towels at $1.75 each, imprinted with blueberries, violets, cats, owls or any of a number of similar subjects. They also have postcards and thick white notepaper with animal and plant and "coastal" designs. And for nostalgic city dwellers there are silkscreened prints, to hang on the wall, of country and sea scapes in deep blues and greens with touches of red and orange. The prints cost about $12 each, and some come matted, ready for framing.

West Rindge Baskets, Inc., Box 24, Rindge, N.H. 03461
Leaflet, free.

The Taylor family has been weaving baskets in the New England way for three generations. If the handle breaks or the bottom splits on a West Rindge basket, the Taylors will fix it for free. Baskets are woven from wide flat strips of ash in several shapes and sizes, wide square ones are called pie and cake baskets, wide flat ones are called garden baskets, tall thin ones are called bottle baskets, and in between there are shoppers, knitters, laundry, porch mail, lunch and picnic and, of course, waste. Prices run from $4 to $8.

Patricia Wing, Birdwood, Mathews, Va. 23109
Color leaflet planned, $1; refundable.

Patricia Wing designs pillows which are made locally by women in their own homes and whom, she says, she pays top salaries. The pillows all have *hand*-quilted fronts (not machines, guided by hand) and are framed with velvet. At prices from $25 to $35 there are 18″ by 18″ pillows with patchwork fronts; and Dresden plates with log cabin or eight-pointed star or pictures—botanicals, birds, dressage (horse and rider). And for $150 there is a 26″ by 32″ floor cushion of a hand-quilted red and royal-blue three-masted schooner backed in royal-blue suede cloth (or gray-and-gold schooner, backed with gold suede).

20

21

20 • *Chapulin* "La Carreta de la Muerte." This carving appears to the left of the altar in Penitente Moradas in New Mexico. The Death Cart is thought to be a relic of the time of the plagues. Carved to order by the Lopez family of Cordova, about 16″ high. $100.

21 • *Chapulin* San Juan ceremonial dolls made by a San Juan Pueblo family. *Left to right:* two 9″ drummers, $25 each; two 11″ deer dancers, $25 each; a 12″ clown, $30.

INDIAN CRAFTS

Unlike the Canadian government, our government has never managed to effectually protect and preserve native arts and crafts. Now when Indian crafts are suddenly becoming fashionable in this country and in Europe, the new demand finds the crafts, by and large, disorganized and dying, and comes too late to be of much help to the craftsmen and those who really love the crafts. In fact, it's main beneficiaries are the investors who know that as long as they buy the authentic crafts, their value will rapidly increase.

As you will see, many of the following places are extremely difficult to buy from by mail, and the reservations, which are the most sympathetic, are usually ill equipped to handle floods of inquiries or even orders. I have included some of the following sources hoping that only people with gambler's instincts and the patience of Job will write. And although some organizations say that their price lists are free, it seems to me that a stamped self-addressed envelope or 25 cents would do no harm.

DESCRIPTIVE PRICE LISTS

Bowsers' Indian Arts and Crafts, 1015 E. Florence Boulevard, Casa Grande, Ariz. 85222
Price list, 50 cents; each photograph, 50 cents' deposit.

Joanna Bowser, who owns this firm with her husband, became interested in American Indian crafts while studying Southwest Indian arts and crafts in an anthropology course at the University of Arizona, and she is Arts and Crafts chairman of the O'Odham Tash Indian Pow Wow. The Bowsers have shown Indian crafts in museums and exhibitions, and they appraise for insurance agencies and individuals. She says: "I would like to stress here, that what we have is *authentic*, no reproductions. Many people are in this business who have no training in craft-arts and are selling imitation jewelry made in Germany or the Far East, treated turquoise, Heishi (wampum shell beads) made in Japan. We can furnish personal references from authorities upon request. All our stock is Indian made."

22

23

24

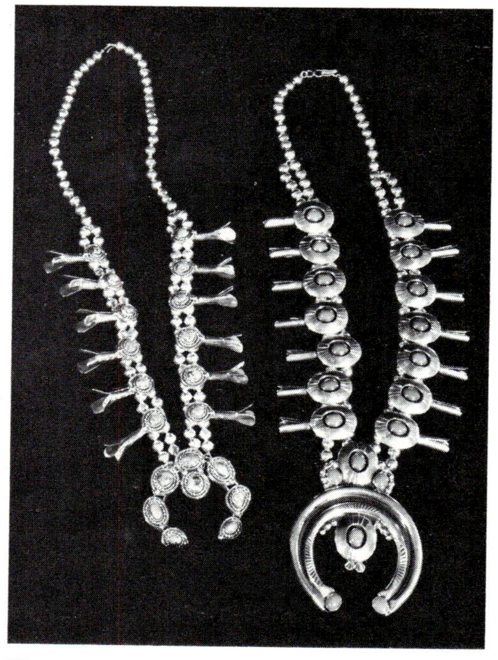

25

26

22 • *Chapulin* 6″ bowl decorated with lizard from Cochiti Pueblo, $65. Duck pitcher, 8″ high, $50.

23 • *Chapulin* Two 7″-high stuffed rag dolls made by an Indian woman at Jemez Pueblo, $5 each; clay owl from Cochiti in black, beige, terra cotta, $25.

24 • *Chapulin* "Story Teller" from Cochiti Pueblo, made of clay found near the pueblo. The 9″-high figure is painted in mineral and vegetable slips and fired twice in an open-air kiln. $245.

25 • *Chapulin* Typical handmade Navajo Indian squash-blossom necklaces. *Left:* sterling-silver set with turquoise, $375. *Right:* silver set with coral, $710.

26 • *Chapulin* Tapestry-weave hanging from Two Grey Hills area. 24″ by 42″. $700.

The price list consists of two pages, listing and briefly describing different types of jewelry available and their prices. After looking at it, you can ask for photographs and details of the jewelry and also all other crafts, including unusual things such as thimbles, old coin buttons and baby spoons. The Bowsers say they will also trade or swap anything so long as it is authentic.

Chapulin, Route 1, Box 187, Santa Fe, N. Mex. 87501
Rug catalogue, 50 cents.
Jewelry leaflet, $1.

Chapulin was recently established in response to the "growing interest in American Indian Arts and Crafts." It is the mail-order division associated with the San Juan Pueblo Trading Post in Santa Fe, New Mexico, U.S.A. (the manager of Chapulin says that many Americans are hazy as to the whereabouts of Santa Fe and often think it is part of old Mexico), established in 1863 and one of the oldest trading posts.

This is clearly by far the best organized place to deal with. They publish an excellent catalogue with pictures of objects typical of the styles in certain crafts (though here, as everywhere, the individual items are slightly different because they are all handmade) and information about all types of crafts that are available. There is pottery made by Indians, inspired by Indian designs but not strictly traditional, at prices from $50 to $250 (though one or two small figures cost only about $12 each). If you are looking for the work of a certain potter, Chapulin may be able to help you, because, although the more famous potters have two- or three-year waiting lists, they sometimes sell a few pieces at local shows.

Some very simple stylized wood carvings in pale woods of saints or birds in patterns are sold mostly at prices from $3 to $50. These are made by a family in a remote village in the Sangre de Cristo mountains of New Mexico whose members have been carving for six generations and whose work was originally inspired by ancient Spanish art. There are San Juan ceremonial dolls (no kachina, which are too expensive), which cost just over $20 each. I haven't seen the jewelry leaflet yet, but it will include handmade jewelry from the Navajo, Zuni and Hopi reservations: silver, turquoise, coral, mother of pearl and jet in both traditional Indian and modern designs.

The main part of the catalogue I have just described consists of photographs of Navajo rugs, at prices between $150 and $400. This is what Bonnie M. Drake of Chapulin says about them: "I believe our catalogue of Indian rugs is the only catalogue in print now illustrating the various types of rugs and the different designs which are available for sale. No two rugs are alike, but many of the designs from certain areas of the Navajo Reservation are similar. The designs take their names from the areas in which they were woven—Two Grey Hills, Wide Ruins, Teec Nos Pos, Ganado. We give individual attention to mail orders and are happy to search for rugs to our customers' individual specification concerning size, design, quality of weave, color and other preferences. We try to buy rugs woven in the old style—hand spun, hand woven, and with either no dyes or natural vegetable dyes only. These rugs are becoming scarce; they will undoubtedly appreciate in value. Some weavers no longer spin or dye their own yarn, but are buying commercial yarn for hand weaving. We try to select only the best quality rugs."

Treasure-house of Worldly Wares, 1880 Lincoln Avenue, Calistoga, Calif. 94515
Price list, free. Brochure planned, 25 cents.
Photographs, 50 cents' deposit each.

In spite of the unpromising name, this firm puts out a good descriptive price list, and looks well set up for mail order. The owner, Stevie S. Whitefeather, says she is a Ponca Indian who was in import, export, wholesaling and jobbing before moving to Calistoga because of the beauty of Napa Valley. She says: "I have an excellent selection of one-of-a-kind handcrafted items which include American Indian and Native folk art from all over the world. I do my own buying and travel to reservation areas for the Indian items, have buyers who purchase for me in several other countries, have especially good contacts in Java and Indonesia and Malaysia as well as Central and South America."

The price list I looked at described single-figure sand paintings at up to $100, San Juan Pueblo, Santa Clara Pueblo and Acoma Pueblo pottery at prices between $4 and $35 (though with some at over $100), Navajo rugs and wall hangings at about $75 to $450, and beadwork, mainly Sioux, at prices between $25 and $275. This is a good place for baskets, which are the only things on the price list that are illustrated (with small line drawings). They cost between $15 and $225, and the price list says: "We keep our eyes open for special requests such as feathered Pomo, beaded or 'freak' designs. Let us know your needs. First requests are first served on feather, bottle, or beaded baskets."

Unlike the Chapulin catalogue, which photographs different types of crafts that are always available, the Treasure-house lists specific objects that are for sale, so you have to be ready to snap up whatever you want or write in with specific requests.

BRIEF PRICE LISTS

American Indian Marketing Manufacturing, P.O. Box 229, Indian Hills Reservation, Petoskey, Mich. 49770
Leaflet, free.

This new firm, run by an Ottawa Indian in northern Michigan, the traditional home of the Ottawa and Chippewa Indians, sells several inexpensive crafts. The leaflet has four small pictures, and gives exact prices and estimated mailing costs, so although it isn't very descriptive, it looks quite adequate for ordering from. Small boxes of birch bark decorated with porcupine quills cost from $4 to $30, beadwork and corn-and-seed necklaces from $2 to $13, barkwork model canoes, tepees, totem poles and tomahawks from 50 cents to $3, and buckskin baby moccasins $5. There are also several black-ash baskets which are not the delicate baskets that collectors chase, but sturdier models to be used for marketing or as sewing baskets; these cost from $5 to $20.

Awaxawi Arts and Crafts, 912 N. 17th Street, Bismarck, N. Dak. 58501
Price list, free.

Indian craft items produced by local guilds in the Dakotas are sold by two non-Indians who took over the inventory of an Indian co-operative about to be dissolved, because they wanted to make authentic items

27

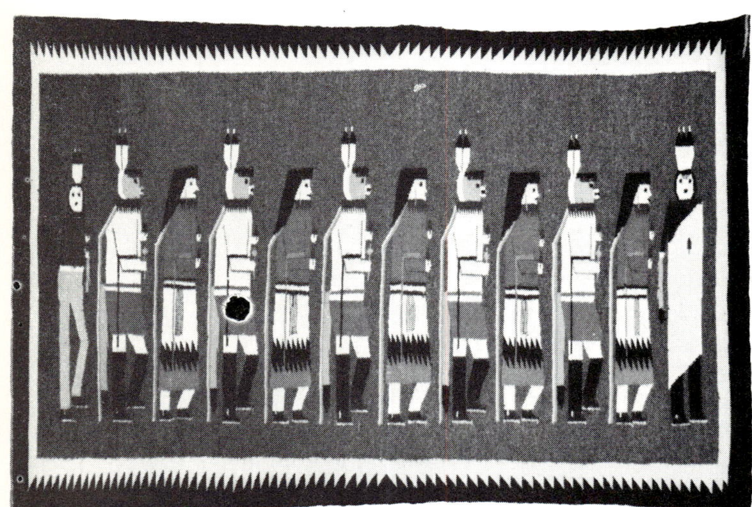

28

27 • *Treasure-house of Worldly Wares* "Storm" pattern rug, Ganado area. Black, gray and white design on white background. It is woven for hard wear, so it works well as a floor rug. Approximate size, 37″ by 60″. $400.

28 • *Treasure-house of Worldly Wares* Yeibetchai ceremonial-design wall hanging, made by Mary Nukui (Navajo), showing the masked dancers in one of their ceremonies. The design is woven horizontally even though the dancers must be hung vertically, which takes an expert weaver with a clear memory of the finished design. Size, 34″ by 51″. $780.
photos J. Bruce Wilson

available to people in the Bismarck area and visitors to the state capital and to provide an outlet for individual Indian producers.

They sell in a state office at the moment, and provide an approximate price list of articles which might be on sale, though they ask you to check before ordering. Stock consists of inexpensive beadwork to be worn rather than collected, mostly under $10, and glazed ceramics and stoneware (unlike most Indian pottery, which is unglazed and cannot hold water).

Sara Ayres, 1182 Brookwood Circle, W. Columbia, S.C. 29169
Leaflet, free.

Sara Ayers is one of the few Indians left making the traditional pottery of the Catawba Indians. The very distinctive black pottery is made from clay found near the Catawba reservation, it is shaped by hand, left to dry and then polished with stones before being dried again and then baked in a live fire. The heavy, rather awkwardly shaped pieces, will hold water and hot food, though they can't be used for cooking. Ashtrays, vases, candlesticks, cream pitchers and round jars shaped like old cooking pots all cost under $10, and new designs can be made to order.

Chippewa Cree Crafts, Rocky Boy's Reservation, Box B, Havre, Mont. 59501
Price list, free.

The smallest reservation in Montana and home of the smallest tribe was established in 1916. The name comes from the leader of the wandering band of Chippewa, Stone Child, since changed, the brochure says, by some white man to Rocky Boy. The nonprofit arts and crafts shop was formed when the successful leather-decorating school had to close because of a lack of buckskin and women to tan.

As Rocky Boy women have always been outstanding beadworkers, the craft shop started a school with two instructors to teach merchandising, "improve their ideas of color, and encourage them to branch out in their skills." Since then their products have entered national competitions and always been among the top winners.

The price list carefully describes the manufacture of the beadwork ("all beadwork is done with nylon thread or sinew"; "only the finest Czechoslovakian beads are used") and tells you exactly how to order necklaces, coin purses, pins, key rings, earrings, neckties, barrettes and moccasins, at prices from $2 to $20. Fully beaded moccasins can be made to special order, and so can high-top ceremonial moccasins which cost $50 to $75. Three intriguing Indian games for children are also sold at about $3 each.

Four Winds Trading Post, St. Ignatius, Mont. 59865
Occasional 8-page catalogue, 25 cents.

Preston E. Miller, the proprietor of Four Winds, says he has a large collection of Indian crafts, including work of the Blackfoot, Cheyenne, Cree, Sioux, Assiniboin, Kootenai, Salish, Nez Percé and Yakima.

Catalogues (which are mimeographed lists with photographs) are not produced during the summer, when there is a rapid turnover in the shop. If there is no catalogue available when you write, your name is kept and you will be sent the next catalogue that is ready. The catalogue I looked at listed five Indian suitcases at $75 each; seed necklaces; beadwork at about $20 and up, including two children's dresses at $75 and $95; an old beaded skirt for $225; moccasins; cornhusk and beaded bags; and various modern things such as brass-tack belts, tomahawks and throwing knives, tobacco-cutting boards, and little logs of balsam, fir and cedar needles to make city rooms smell like the Rocky Mountains.

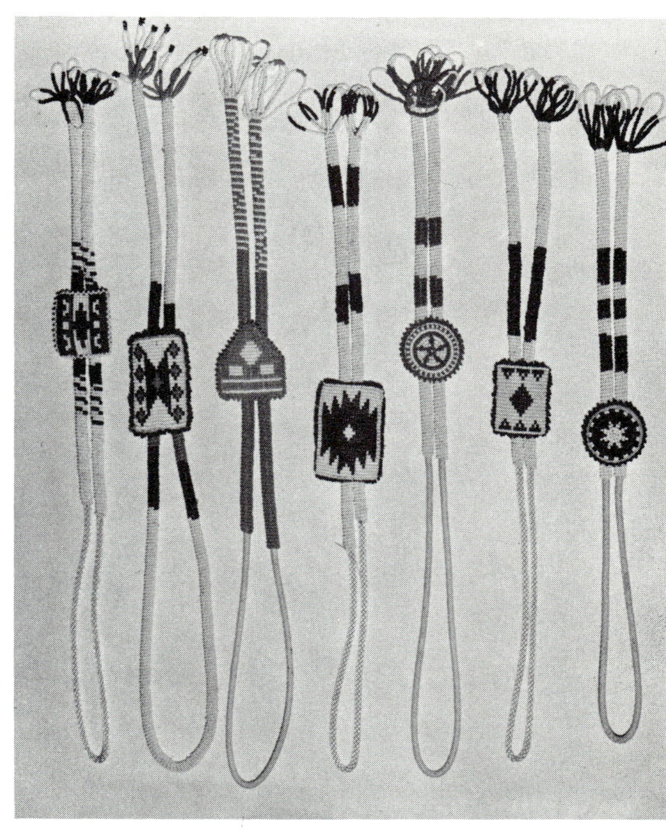

29

Pipestone Indian Shrine Association, Pipestone National Monument, Pipestone, Minn. 56164
Brochure, free.

The Pipestone Indian Shrine Association is a nonprofit co-operating agency of the National Park Service and provides an outlet for pipestone ceremonial pipes and other pipestone crafts made by local Indian craftsmen. A free illustrated brochure with photographs of representative pipes and other small crafts is available upon request. All items are moderately priced, with small craft items costing under $5, and most pipes under $20.

30

Sicangu Arts and Crafts Co-operative, Box 68, Rosebud, S. Dak. 57570
Very brief price list, free.

In spite of (and because of) a long handwritten letter, Sicangu doesn't look at all as though they can manage a large mail-order business at the moment, but I can't resist including them for the more intrepid of my readers who don't mind waiting, perhaps indefinitely, while other people's letters are answered at length by hand. As Mr. Howatt says, their prices for star quilts are *very* low, $18 to $25 for baby size and $38 and up for full size, at the moment. Here is part of the letter Mr. Howatt wrote me:

"We are a privately owned co-operative, owned by its (at present 115) members. Requirements for membership include enrollment in the Rosebud Sioux tribe. Hence the co-op is an all Indian owned and profited organization, one of the few on the reservation.

"Why was the co-op formed? The co-op was organized by Mrs. Dorothy Crane (Sioux) and Mr. Stanley Red Bird, about two years ago to provide for some of the needs of the people and to stop a few malpractices by white traders in their relationship with Indian people. Indian people are just barely etching out a living here, an economic base was needed and it had to be Indian controlled and profited. Previously Dakota Sioux art and craft work was available to the general public only through white traders who would come to the reservation and buy beadwork, quillwork, etc., at ridiculously low prices, take it outside, and sell it at a fantastic mark-up, i.e. 500% leaving the artist with a maximum of 25%, usually 10% of the selling price. This practice had to stop. We also wanted to provide an earned source of income. A centrally located shop would have the potential to provide tourist information and a general educational facility to inform incorrect ideas about Indian ways, culture, and identity, that Hollywood has labelled as Indian.

"An initial grant was received from the Catholic Committee for human development, which enabled us to channel funds to the most needy and skilled and at the same time build up an inventory, so things were looking good. A business was owned by the people, the

29 • *Awaxawi Arts and Crafts* Bolo ties, typical of beadwork from the Fort Berthold, Fort Totten and Standing Rock reservations in North Dakota. Similar pieces are available at prices between $8.75 and $15.

30 • *Pipestone Indian Shrine Association* Beaded pipe bags, $35 each.

goods were bought for cash at 90% of selling price and a 10% dividend was paid annually.

"However, since the summer sales have fallen to practically nothing, and the co-op can't sell enough, a rapid turn over of low priced items is mandatory for its success, the co-op is having difficulty paying a salary to the person running it. To solve this we have begun to search for sources for the funding of a vehicle to take the beadwork, etc. out to large conventions, pow-wows, and fairs, so we can compete with the larger organizations that do this. We feel this will help substantially as the quality of the work is very good, it is genuine and prices are quite lower than city prices. (Check prices in New York City for a star quilt and compare with our list).

"Our goods are for sale to anyone, our members could make anything, we recently had a fully porcupine quilled dress, leggings and moccasins made for a woman in Boulder, Colo. Such an item was thought to be impossible to get. The shop is attempting to encourage its members to keep the artistic traditions and continue practicing them. For example, quillwork is getting rare and very high priced, we can now supply quilled items (Sioux) desired at reasonable prices. We have six families now bringing in this type of work."

The price list has no descriptions and only approximate prices for small pieces of quillwork and beadwork (belts $20 to $50) and the star quilts.

Tipi Shop, Halley Park, P.O. Box 1270, Rapid City, S. Dak. 57701
Price list, free.

Another price list with no descriptions at all, just a list of the beadwork, quillwork, pipestone, stationery and books for sale. Some of the prices given are exact, others are too vague to be useful. And customers are simply told to "include parcel post and insurance."

13
HOBBY & PROFESSIONAL EQUIPMENT

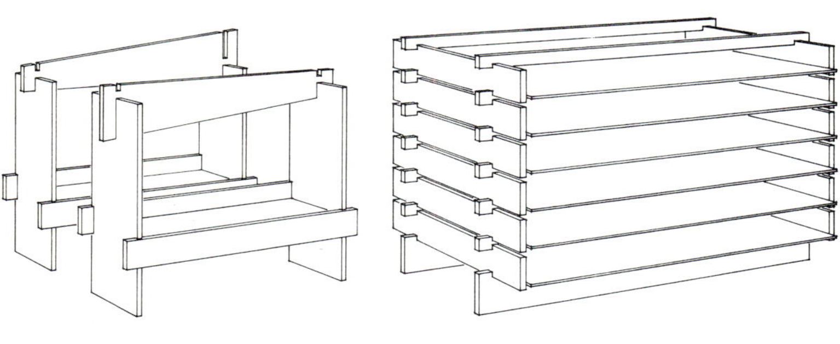

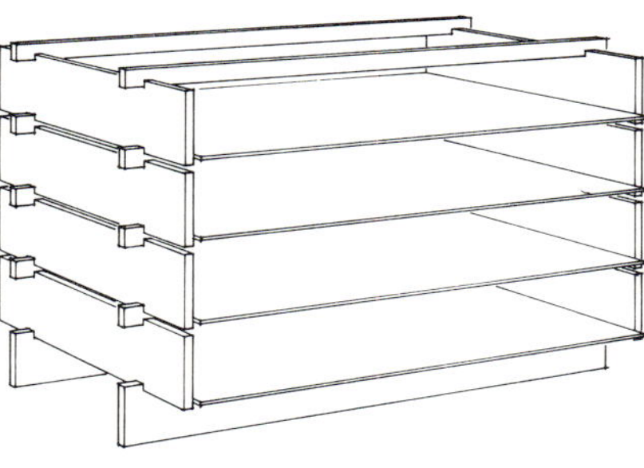

1 • *Charrette Corporation* Stacloc storage system, designed by an architect for Charrette and manufactured under his supervision. The flat storage units are made of birch plywood with a clear lacquer finish and can be moved around, added to and stacked to 6′ high with no fasteners. This desk consists of several elements available separately, but costing, in this combination, $169.50.
photo Lois M. Bowen

The catalogues in this section are among the most useful of all. Having had some nasty experiences when walking into crafts supply shops without knowing exactly what I wanted, I particularly like the way that mail-order firms, out of self-interest or enthusiasm (many of the shops are started by people who first of all used the tools), keep their customers well informed. Although most of the following firms supply professionals, the catalogues are written as carefully and as clearly as though all the customers were complete beginners. If you have ever been curious about any of the following occupations, send for a catalogue. Besides information about prices and necessary supplies, you'll get a very good idea of what is involved in the practice, and almost always an excellent book list to help you go further.

ARCHITECTURE

Charrette Corporation, 2000 Massachusetts Avenue, Cambridge, Mass. 02140
170-page catalogue, free.

Started nine years ago by two recently graduated architects, Charrette is the only business in the world to specialize in supplies for architects. Here you can find everything necessary for design, presentation and model making, as well as lots of other supplies of interest to designers, artists and anyone who regularly draws or drafts. The catalogue is very pleasantly laid out and easy to look through. Goods go from desks, chairs, storage systems and lights through instruments, paints and papers to twenty-seven different erasers, and include hundreds of special products, too many to list. The owners say that their basswood for model making, "Corbu" stencils for lettering, Caran D'Ache lead holders and Charprint tracing paper are of special interest.

ART

New York Central Supply Company, 62 Third Avenue, New York, N.Y. 10003

Grand Central Artists Materials, 3 E. 40th Street, New York, N.Y. 10016
224-page black-and-white catalogue, $1; refundable with purchase.

Both of these firms send out the same large catalogue, which is particularly strong in the fields of commercial and graphic art. In addition to a very full range of first-rate imported paints, papers and brushes, they also carry such specialized items as retouch colors, hyplar mediums, drafting and drawing tables, templates, perspective aids and other tools of this kind. Amateur painters or students, however, will also find much here for their needs, including Belgian canvas and rice papers, of which special sample books can be requested.

Grand Central has a large custom framing department and will either do framing there or give advice to home framers. For these there are metal-section and wooded frames as well as plexiglass box and slip frames.

Utrecht Linens, Inc., 33 Thirty-fifth Street, Brooklyn, N.Y. 11232
28-page catalogue, free.

Utrecht Linens manufactures its own acrylics, oils, tempera, watercolors, canvas and stretchers, so their prices are low. The firm was originally well known for its canvases; its paints came later and are good buys for students or beginners who want to save money. The well-illustrated catalogue shows paints, canvases, brushes and palettes and has an article on how to stretch and prepare canvas.

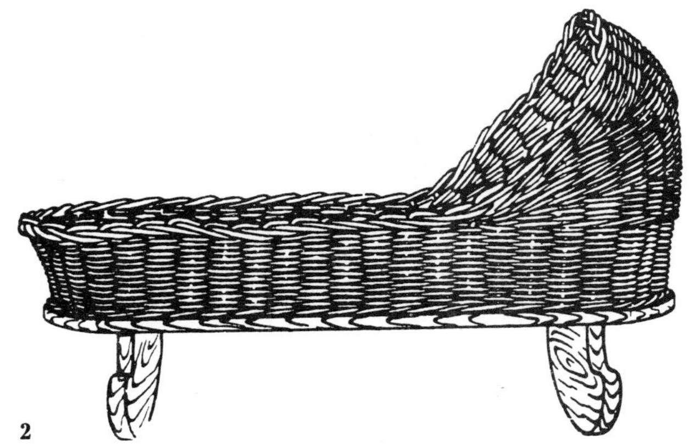
2

BASKETRY

H. H. Perkins Company, 10 South Bradley Road, Woodbridge, Conn. 06525
Perkins Reed Crafts, free.
Seat Weaving for Pleasure and Profit, free.
Instructions in Methods of Seat Weaving, 25 cents.

When I was in the hospital I turned out masses of reed wastepaper baskets, trays and lamp bases. It's a messier business than you might think, because you have to keep the reeds damp in the bath before working with them. However, this can be avoided by using plastic cane, which these brochures say has proved "more satisfactory than natural cane in many ways." If the idea of plastic cane makes your flesh crawl, you'll find natural cane, reed, rush and grass at this supplier, together with kits to make doll cradles, sewing baskets and mail baskets. Good, informative leaflets give instructions on seat weaving and illustrate some reasonably priced kits to make rustic Early American chairs with rush seats. Children's chairs and stools cost under $10, and a cathedral ladder-back rocker, adult size, costs about $14 for a partly assembled, smoothly finished ash frame, fiber rush, glue and instructions. Books and bulletins on raffia work, weaving with cane and reed, and wood finishing are listed and described.

3

2 • *H. H. Perkins* A kit to make a 7″ by 15″ basket-work cradle, including all materials needed and directions. $2.75, plus postage.

3 • *Walter T. Kelley* Beginner's beekeeping outfit with a hive, book of instructions and everything you need, including bees. $38.

BATIK

Glen Black/Local Color, 1414 Grant Avenue, San Francisco, Calif. 94133
Price list, free.

Glen Black, a weaver, sells by mail supplies for batik workers and textile craftsmen. Procion and acid dyes, wax, untreated white cotton and batik tools are listed, and instructions on using the dyes (but none on how to do batik) are given.

BEEKEEPING

The Walter T. Kelley Co., Inc., Clarkson, Ky. 42726
66-page catalogue, free.

Walter T. Kelley got his first beekeeping book in 1908 when he was eleven, and by 1924 he was a full-time beekeeper, manufacturer and seller of beekeeping equipment. Now he has a large beehive factory, sends goods all over the world, and puts out a catalogue that can provide everything you need to follow in his footsteps (in a more modest way, of course). His list of recommendations to beginners starts with "1. Buy our book *How to Keep Bees and Sell Honey*"—and if you buy *Kelley's Complete Beginner's Outfit* (about $38) the book is included. First comes the book with a knockdown hive, bee gloves, bee veil, etc., then, when you are ready, let Walter T. Kelley know and a three-pound swarm of Italian bees ("average temperament") with a select young queen will arrive on your doorstep via parcel post. Mr. Kelley says that after working with the beginner's equipment for a short time, you will be able to order intelligently your future requirements.

BIRD WATCHING

Bird Photographs, Inc., 254 Sapsucker Woods Road, Ithaca, N.Y. 14850
Price list, free.

Over thirty years ago Professor Arthur Allen, the author of such books as *Stalking Birds with Color Camera*, began to sell duplicates of his color slides of birds. His collection has now grown to include over six hundred species of North American and Mexican birds which are of use to amateur and professional ornithologists. The slides are 85 cents each or may be bought in sets, such as $64 for the warblers of North America or a three-part series on the breeding cycle of birds. Sets are accompanied by a script. Twenty-nine slides are also available on the frogs and toads of North America. All in all, over fifteen hundred color photographs are available.

BOOKBINDING

Basic Crafts Co., 312 E. 23rd Street, New York, N.Y. 10010
12-page catalogue, free.

Basic Crafts provides bookbinding tools and supplies for individual craftsmen, schools and libraries. Their catalogue is very good for beginners; it not only shows three kits, and instruction books and pamphlets, but also has two pages of clear directions on how to repair hard covers, and one page of illustrations showing basic tools and bookbinding methods. The cheapest of the three kits costs $14 and contains enough material to rebind twelve books, especially suitable for turning paperbacks into hardbacks. Apart from the beginner's kits there are presses, cutting boards, handmade papers from England and France, several cloths and leathers for covers, and gold-tooling supplies for the really ambitious.

BRASS AND STONE RUBBING

Oldstone Enterprises, 77 Summer Street, Boston, Mass. 02110
Leaflet, free.

Rubbing is the cheapest and healthiest (it takes place out of doors) of hobbies. Genevieve Jacobs, the manager of Oldstone Enterprises, describes it as "the art of transferring any textured surface to a piece of paper or fabric." You do it by taping paper over the surface to be rubbed and then rubbing the paper with special wax in whatever color you like until the imprint appears. The most elegant things to rub are gravestones in New England (or further afield, there are marvelous carved stones and church brasses to be rubbed on vacations in Latin America and Europe), but manhole covers, company plaques, grillwork and all sorts of other things are popular too and, cleverly mounted, can make beautiful decorations. You can buy supplies individually from Oldstone, or for $6.50 a beginner's kit which consists of an instruction booklet, five sheets of the right kind of paper, two cakes of wax, masking tape and a brush to clean the surface of the gravestone, or whatever, you are going to work on.

BUTTONS

The House of Burlap, West Chatham, Cape Cod, Mass. 02669
Leaflet, free.

The House of Burlap, a Cape Cod gift shop, doesn't sell burlap by mail, but it does sell Norwegian hand-molded pewter buttons in designs that go back to the eleventh century. Over thirty variations are shown in the leaflet, including reindeer and Viking-ship patterns for sports jackets. The buttons cost between $1.75 and $2.25 for eight. Brightly colored handwoven stoles, ponchos and throws are also for sale.

The House of York, 63 Oakleaf Lane, Doylestown, Pa. 18901
Leaflet, 15 cents.

The House of York sells *only* unusual modern buttons. It was started by the Yorks three years ago because Sue York had such trouble finding out-of-the-ordinary buttons for her sewing projects. Some buttons, such as "Dresden Flowers," are American, in this case made specially for the House of York by L. Hager of Bucks County; others are imported from several different countries. For children's clothes there are mushrooms, mice, teddy bears, elephants, etc. For adults there are designs for people with special interests, such as card players, knitters, horse lovers, sailors, golfers, skiers, and also zodiac buttons, reproductions of old American army buttons, and monogramed buttons, nearly a hundred different kinds—all for casual clothes rather than high fashion.

CANDLEMAKING

Celebration, Box 28, Pentwater, Mich. 49449
8-page list, 25 cents.

A handwritten catalogue lists basic candlemaking supplies: wax, stearic acid, dyes, scents and a few simple molds in star and pillar shapes. The catalogue is extremely helpful, with advise and explanations throughout, and the owners of the firm, who are basically candlemakers, say that their next catalogue will include their own ready-made candles. I haven't seen the candles, but judging by the appealing way that the price list has been decorated with wood-block prints, the candles should be nice.

Pourette Mfg. Co., 6818 Roosevelt Way N.E., Seattle, Wash. 98115
68-page catalogue, 35 cents.

The largest and oldest supplier of candlemaking equipment has a huge selection of molds, both plain and fancy, as well as equipment to decorate the candles with, holders of various kinds, and books and pamphlets on the subject—and, of course, basic waxes, wicks, dyes and perfumes. To decorate the candles there are small molds for modeling designs to stick on the side, tools for carving, gold seals and decals of all sorts, including some for special occasions such as birthdays and anniversaries. You can buy decals to make candles that last for several years,—the ones you take out each year for a birthday or anniversary and burn down to the next mark.

4

CANING

Newell Workshop, 19 Blaine Avenue, Hinsdale, Ill. 60521
Brochure, free.

If the seat on your antique bentwood rocker needs recaning and you just heard an estimate of $30, then Newell Workshop may be your salvation. This firm deals in everything you need to do it yourself or, as their brochure puts it, "antique restoration materials." The shop's main product is a caning kit, especially designed for the beginner. It consists of enough cane to cover one average chair, a 6″ awl, a moistening sponge, four pointed wooden pegs, and an illustrated instruction book, all for $3. Cane is also available by the hank. Other seat materials listed are cane webbing (prewoven cane for seats with grooves around the seat rather than holes), rushing materials and several other flat weaving materials. The Newell Workshop owners say they are happy to answer questions and resolve problems.

5

4 • *Oldstone Enterprises* Supplies for making brass and stone rubbings are available in kits or individually.

5 • *Newell Workshop* Caning kits designed for beginners contain tools, caning material and instructions to cane one average chair. $3.

7

CERAMICS

A. D. Alpine, Inc., 353 Coral Circle, El Segundo, Calif. 90245
26-page catalogue, free.

This famous old firm manufactures mainly gas and electric kilns but also wheels and larger equipment such as wedging tables, drying cabinets and ware trucks, many of which are sold to institutions and industrial plants. Kiln prices start at $780 for electric - front-loading kiln with a 2-cubic-foot capacity; kick-wheels start at $230 and power wheels at $275. There is a kit to make a kickwheel for $60, but you provide the wooden frame yourself.

Pacifica Crafts, P.O. Box 1407, Ferndale, Wash. 98248
Leaflet, free.

Bob Luitweiler, a teacher who, like Gandhi, believes that everyone should work with his hands, has an organization which makes and promotes handcrafts and also makes knockdown wheel kits. He hopes to make the industry the basis of a high school where students would have a well-rounded education that would include vocational training gained by actually working in the different sections of the firm.

The wheel kits are more flexible than most: the kick-wheel can be raised and lowered, and the weight of the wheel can be adjusted from 24 to 160 lbs. Prices for kits without wood frames start at about $50. Pacifica is planning to introduce an especially light and inexpensive kiln, and a light-weight electric wheel which, they say, their dealers are convinced will "shake up the market." This wheel will weigh less than 30 lbs., yet will be able to handle more than 30 lbs. of clay, and it will be so compact that it can be stored in a broom closet.

Oscar Paul Corporation, 522 W. 182nd Street, Gardena, Calif. 90247
8-page catalogue, free.

Two electric wheels are manufactured by this firm; the single-speed wheel costs $275, and the two-speed $350.

Rovin Ceramics, 6912 Schaefer Road, Dearborn, Mich. 48126
26-page catalogue, 50 cents; refundable.

Rovin Ceramics was started by a potter fifteen years ago and is now a four-man operation with a homey recycled-paper catalogue. The firm sells supplies for potters and sculptors, manufacture their own clay bodies and glazes, sells tools, balances, kiln furniture, Shimpo electric wheels and Crusader electric kilns.

Soldner Pottery Equipment, P.O. Box 90, Aspen, Colo. 81611
Leaflet, free.

Paul Soldner, a potter and trustee of the American Crafts Council, has designed four wheels and a clay mixer. Wheels start at about $140 for a knockdown kit for a kickwheel, and go up to about $430 for the "professional model" electric wheel. The clay mixer costs about $945.

6 • *Oscar Paul* Electric wheel available in a single-speed model for $275, and a two-speed model for $350.

7 • *Soldner Pottery Equipment* Kickwheels designed by Paul Soldner. Prices start at $140 for a knockdown kit. Electric wheels start at $330.

Stewart Clay Co., Inc., 133 Mulberry Street, New York, N.Y. 10013
60-page catalogue, free.

This well-known store has a catalogue which they say "represents the most complete collection of materials and supplies for the plastic arts available today." They sell a few wheels, a kickwheel kit without lumber for $55, and some kilns, but the main emphasis is on smaller supplies. There are thirteen ceramic clays and eight kinds of neatly packaged modeling materials that don't need firing or that can be fired in any kitchen oven, and several clay kits for children. There are supplies for plaster casting, modeling, sculpting and enameling, tools, lots of glazes, and a list of books on ceramics, sculpting and enameling.

Westwood Ceramic Supply Co., 14400 Lomitas Avenue, City of Industry, Calif. 91744
40-page pottery-supplies catalogue, free.
Kiln and gas firing manual, $1.
Glass-supplies catalogue, free.

This large firm sells Nordstrom gas kilns, J. J. Cress electric kilns, Walker and Wegner pug mills, and Shimpo wheels, and has a large supply of clays, glazes, tools and books.

CHINA PAINTING

Rynne China Company, 222 W. 8 Mile Road, Hazel Park, Mich. 48030
108-page catalogue, 50 cents.

Agnes Rynne started this firm when she took up china painting and had a hard time finding supplies. A large catalogue illustrates white china plates, cups, teapots, etc., mainly copies of antiques, and also china "novelties" such as jam jars, mustard pots, cigarette boxes, vases and soap dishes. Dinner plates cost from $3 to $4.50, and a child's set from Japan, which consists of a plate, a bowl and a mug, costs $2. Patterns, brushes, magnifying glasses and instruction books are also on sale, and so are kilns to fire the china once you have painted it.

CLOCKMAKING

Craft Products Co., Route 64 at Route 83, Elmhurst, Ill. 60126
Home Ideas Book, 60 cents.
Clocks and clockworks catalogue, 25 cents.

Craft Products sells plans and kits to make about twenty-five clocks: grandfather, grandmother, school, steeple, and various wall clocks including "planter clocks" which have shelves for hanging plants beside or below the clocks. The plans cost under $1, and there is a wide choice in the parts: imported and American movements from $10 to over $100, faces and hands from $6 to $64, all illustrated and well described. You can also get the wooden molding for the cases, and for a few clocks, all the lumber you'll need, cut to size or not, as you like, in cherry, mahogany or walnut. Ba-

8

9

8 • *Mason and Sullivan* A reproduction of an octagonal school clock, the kind that was used in schools and railroad stations, 21¾″ high by 15″ wide by 4½″ deep. Plans, instructions and all parts to build this clock, including solid cherry or walnut wood for the case, are $52.75 and $55, respectively.

9 • *Mason and Sullivan* A reproduction of the pillar-and-scroll clock designed by Eli Terry of Plymouth, Conn., in 1808, one of the most popular nineteenth-century clocks. Plans, instructions and all parts including cherry wood or Honduras mahogany to build this clock, $86 using T61 movement; $99 using T126 movement.

10

11 12

10 • *Heath Company* Color TV kit with VHF/UHF detent tuning. A 25″ diagonal-measure unit that lets you "click in" to UHF channels with the same dial action as conventional VHF tuners. After you pre-set the selector for up to twelve UHF channels, automatic tuning scans both VHF and UHF stations in either direction at a touch of the finger. $599.95.

11 • *Heath Company* A new fish spotter with a dual-range depth-sounding capability. A push-pull knob sets the audible alarm, which beeps when anything passes above any selected depth between 5 feet and the 240-foot bottom, and an exclusive Heath noise-rejection circuit eliminates engine ignition interference for stable readings while under way. Kit, $99.95.

12 • *Heath Company* A spinet-organ kit which is almost identical to the Thomas spinet organ. It includes two 44-note keyboards with Color-Glo keys, which light up to show notes and chords that correspond with the "Quick Play" organ course, and sheet music. Eleven instrument voices can be combined to provide hundreds of orchestral combinations. There are front-panel jacks for headphones or cassette deck. Kit price, $549.95.

rometer plans and parts as well as music-box movements are for sale, and the catalogue includes a short history of clockmaking.

Mason and Sullivan Co., 39 Blossom Avenue, Osterville, Mass. 02655
24-page brochure, 25 cents.

Here you can get the complete kits or assorted parts and plans to make about twenty reproduction clocks. The catalogue is well laid out, with a bit of information about the original of each model and a list of prices for the parts or the whole kit for each clock. Prices run from about $28 for a crewel-embroidery clock kit to about $290 for all the parts needed to make an 89″-high Aaron Willard grandfather clock in black walnut. One of three books for beginners explains how clocks and watches work and how to repair them; the other two deal with woodwork and staining and finishing wood.

DECOUPAGE

The O-P Craft Co., Inc., 425 Warren Street, Sandusky, Ohio 44870
16-page catalogue, $1.

Sixteen pages of plain wooden boxes, trays, candleholders, napkin rings, picture frames and about fifty other things to decorate either by painting or by decoupage, which is the art of decorating by covering a surface with cutouts. Varnish, applicator and instruction books are for sale.

ELECTRONICS

Allied Electronics Corp., 2400 Washington Boulevard, Chicago, Ill. 60612
420-page black-and-white catalogue, $5.

Allied is the Sears of the electronics world and its catalogue is a professional reference tool which any amateur can use. Here are both the leading brand names and a large choice of Allied's own products. The catalogue starts with semiconductors and integrated circuits and goes on to list tens of thousands of items from banana jacks to walkie-talkies.

Allied stocks both the parts and the tools to put them together, from knobs, fuses and switches to far more expensive panel meters, digital test equipment, VOM's and oscilloscopes. Prices are given for single items and for larger orders, but Allied will fill any order above $5.

Of more general interest to craftsmen in a number of fields is the vast choice of tools sold by Allied. The largest listing is of precision soldering equipment, but there are also pliers, screwdrivers and tool sets, particularly suited to electronics work, as well as rivet guns, drills, knives and lathes.

For the less technically minded, there is a large selection of excellent, adjustable low-priced lamps, cassette tape recorders, audio and video tape players and various utility cabinets that can be used by any collector. There is also a selection of electronic handbooks.

Heath Company, Benton Harbor, Mich. 49022
80-page catalogue, free.

The Heath Company was started in 1918 by Edward Bayard Heath, a flying enthusiast who sold a single-seater plane "ready-to-fly" (for $999) or in various stages of completion. The plane has long since been dropped from the books of this now enormous firm, which specializes in ready-to-assemble kits of electronic equipment. There are kits for beginners who can change a light bulb but don't know a volt from an ohm or a transistor from a capacitor, says Heath. But if you still want to start small, there is a "first kit" for $5: a photoelectric lamp switch to turn lights on automatically at night and scare burglars. New kits are developed all the time and sold by mail (catalogues come out five times a year) or at slightly higher prices in Heathkit shops. At the moment, kits include stereo components, color television sets, intercoms, cassette recorders, an electronic oven, and much more. You should be able to save up to 40 percent of the price of equivalent ready-made equipment by doing the assembling yourself. There are also a few electronic "workshops" to teach children basic electronic circuitry.

Sonic Devices, Inc., 69-29 Queens Boulevard, Woodside, N.Y. 11377
32-page semiannual catalogue, 35 cents.

This intriguing catalogue (the ideal list for the paranoid or the person who wishes to be sure that he isn't) is filled with Dick Tracy devices for everyman—machines that are supposed to tell you whether your phone is tapped or your room bugged ("If you feel there is *EVEN A POSSIBILITY* of a hidden transmitter in your HOME, OFFICE or AUTO . . . this unit is for you"), assuming of course that your enemy is using machines that can be found out by the Sonics $59.50 room bugging detector. If, the catalogue suggests, you've ever lost an argument, then the attaché-case recorder is for you ($69.50), and if you are losing your spouse then you may want Auto Tail for those "times when it may become necessary to follow a car without being observed" ($249.50), or at a more reasonable price, a lie detector for $29.95.

Sonic also sells more mundane devices, such as a telephone answering machine that will record up to seventy-five incoming messages ($59.50), or one that will relay calls from one number to another, though the accompanying illustration of a man in a night club assuring his wife that he is still at the office suggests that spouses may need special devices to detect the arrival of this catalogue into home or office.

FLOWER ARRANGING

Dorothy Biddle Service, DBS Building, Hawthorne, N.Y. 10532
12-page brochure, 10 cents.

Rodney Biddle, son of Dorothy Biddle, has been running this firm of supplies for flower arrangers since 1936 and has built up a good stock of basic equipment: several kinds of holders, of course, including some that are specially suitable for artificial flowers, as well as pebbles and moss to hide the holders, a gadget to fix and clean the holders, sticky tape, clay and ties for the plants, clippers, gloves, sprayers, tool kits and containers for tiered, hanging and floating arrangements and arrangements around candles. Also mixtures to preserve flowers, and clean artificial flowers, and books and calendars with illustrations of arrangements and instructions.

GENERAL CRAFTS

Artisan Crafts, Star Route No. 4, Box No. 179-F, Reeds Spring, Mo. 65737
Sample magazine issue, $1.25. Annual subscription (four issues), $5.

This friendly and informal new magazine is largely devoted to passing around useful information among professional craftsmen, but will also be of interest to amateurs. Most crafts and some hobbies are touched upon (in the issue I looked at there were articles on macramé, egg decorating, candle dipping, wrought-iron work and photography), and there were several pieces on how and where to sell, descriptions of new crafts shops, and notices about directories, catalogues, brochures and magazines that might be useful but would otherwise remain unknown. Artisan Crafts also publishes separately a directory of information on sources of craft supplies, craftsmen interested in selling or consigning their work, galleries and stores that want to be contacted, craftsmen who like being visited. Here, instead of attractive widows in search of interesting gentlemen with a view to matrimony, you find hairpin lacers looking for woodworkers with clog soles for sale.

Bergen Arts and Crafts, P.O. Box 689, Salem, Mass. 01970
190-page catalogue, $1; refundable.

A big catalogue with supplies for many crafts and pastimes that can fairly easily be indulged in at home, also a list of how-to books, most of which cost $1 and some of which are rated as to popularity. This is what is covered: metal enameling, ceramics, with several kinds of clay, some especially for modeling, plaster to make molds, and porcelain flowers to decorate the ceramic boxes (or make jewelry out of); music boxes to decorate; lamp parts; colored glass for mosaics; stained glass (kits start at $14); jewelry-making supplies, including settings; pipe-cleaner art; plastic mosaic tiles; silkscreening; acrylic painting; candlemaking (a kit costs $5); plastic casting; printmaking; lettering; colored foil; decoupage; beaded-flower making; and macramé.

Dick Blick Co., P.O. Box 1267, Galesburg, Ill. 61401
40-page catalogue, $1.

"Dick Blick ships quick" is the slogan of this firm located far from any major city but whose crowded catalogue of art and craft supplies shows that theirs is a very successful mail-order business. Blick specializes in materials needed for the graphic arts but stocks a wide variety of other supplies and a great deal that would be useful for home craftsmen or for children. Blick has a large line of paints, crayons, paper, brushes, frames, etc., but also silkscreens and small presses, suitable for printing signs, as well as etchings, woodcuts and lithographs. The Blick #1 etching press, made of steel and weighing 100 lbs., costs $198.80, with a smaller model at half the price. Small block printing presses are available for $12.40 and $29.90. Blick also sells the plates, inks and etching tools needed for these processes.

The catalogue lists a wide range of sculptor's tools and carving materials, as well as the requisites for pottery, from wheels to kilns. Another section is devoted to all the crafts now so popular, and Blick has both kits and specific materials needed for batik, raffia work, stitching and embroidery, weaving, beadwork, canework and photography. There is also a choice of the kind of furniture needed for all these activities, from easels to filing cabinets and a large selection of books. Whether you are an amateur, professional or schoolteacher, this is a basic list to consult.

Craftool Company, Inc., 1421 W. 240th Street, Harbor City, Calif. 90710
150-page Craftool color catalogue, $1.
Dryad Instruction book list, free.
Star Diamond catalogue for lapidary work, free.

An ideal catalogue for beginners, beautifully laid out, gorgeously illustrated, it lists supplies, kits and books for most crafts. In looking through the catalogues of more specialized firms, you may find supplies at lower prices, but the clarity and simplicity of the Craftool catalogue, together with the quality of the books listed at the end, makes it unbeatable for the serious beginner who isn't quite sure what he needs, but it is also widely used by professionals.

There are small but complete collections of tools and supplies for ceramics, lapidary, gem cutting, sculpture, art metal jewelry, bookbinding, papermaking, batik, weaving, and graphics, which includes all the different kinds of printing. There are complete beginner's kits wherever beginner's kits are useful. An eight-piece wood-carving set costs $22.50, a graphic-arts etching and block printing set costs $60, a bookbinding repair kit costs $13, a stone-tumbling and jewelry-making kit costs $25, a small loom $40, and a small electric wheel for potters $80. Each kit comes with an instruction booklet, but you will also have the well-chosen list of titles at the back of the catalogue which includes practical books of advice on the crafts covered by Craftool and other crafts such as basket work, paper sculpture, metal foil, toy making, etc., and also books of interest and inspiration such as *English Smocks* and *Navajo and Pueblo Silversmiths.* Many of the books are photographed in the catalogue so that you can see their style, and they are all described in detail.

Besides the books listed in the general catalogue, there is a separate list of excellent how-to books published by the English firm Dryad.

Gemex Company, 900 W. Los Vallecitos Boulevard, San Marcos, Calif. 92069
48-page illustrated beginner's jewelry catalogue, free.

A colorful and thorough catalogue of supplies for costume jewelry, beaded flowers, candles, metalwork, stained glass, decoupage (with several pages of prints for framing or decoupage), flower preserving, feather birds, jeweled ornaments, Christmas ornaments. There are also loose materials such as tulle, felt, gold paper, tissue paper and belt buckles. The emphasis is on kits where there is nothing for you to do except put the various parts together.

The Handcrafters, One West Brown Street, Waupun, Wis. 53963
84-page catalogue, 50 cents.

Unusual craft supplies for rehabilitation, therapeutic and educational purposes, proclaims the letterhead, and the president says that he is specially interested in selling to nursing homes. Besides equipment for plenty of fairly standard crafts such as raffia work, decoupage and candlemaking, there are supplies for Norwegian *rosemaling* (an intricate kind of painting on wood), wire-jewelry making, cork craft, fur craft and jigsaw making, as well as supplies such as scissors, crayons, crepe and tissue paper, etc.

GLASS BLOWING

Westwood Ceramic Supply Co., 14400 Lomitas Avenue, City of Industry, Calif. 91744
26-page glass-supplies catalogue, free.
Pottery-supplies catalogue, free.
Kiln and gas firing manual, $1.

Best known for its large stock of equipment for making pottery, Westwood also sells supplies for glass blowing. The catalogue lists hand tools, blowpipes and all the equipment needed to use them, as well as raw materials. General information, such as estimating data and compositions, is given in the catalogue, but it all looks fairly technical and I don't recommend glass blowing to the casual hobbyist.

GOVERNMENT SURPLUS

Palley Supply Company, Inc., 2263 E. Vernon Avenue, Dept. M-70, Los Angeles, Calif. 90058
256-page catalogue, $1.

The largest "surplus" store in America has 7½ acres of government and industrial "excess inventory" goods, of which a portion is listed and illustrated in their big catalogue. Hydraulic equipment is, they say, their biggest business, and they have a complete line of hydraulic pumps, motors, cylinders, valves, hose, accumulators, filters and test stands; they do overhaul/repair work as well. Field telephones and telephone wire are also popular with forestry services and on farms. Palley says that universities and governments buy from them, and many small businesses have been launched by incorporating Palley stock into their finished products, but they also have less specialized stuff: shop equipment, microscopes, camping equipment.

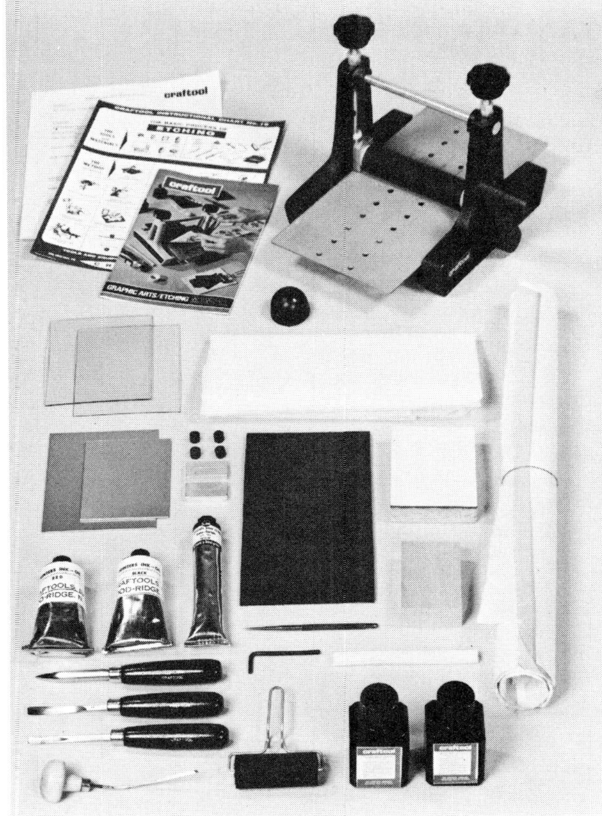

13

14

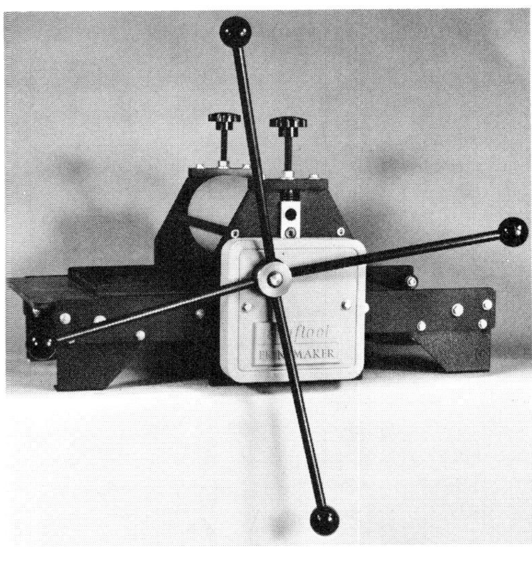

15

16

17

13 • *Craftool* Graphic arts etching and block printing set for printing etchings, wood cuts and lithoprints. The kit comprises the Micro press and everything needed to start printing greeting cards and small pictures, including handmade Japanese paper and instruction manual. $59.95. Press alone, $40.

14 • *Craftool* Workbench with a tool recess, left wood vise and right wood vise, easily assembled and knocked down for storage. 55″ long, 30″ wide, 29″ tall. $129.50. Similar bench with drawers and storage underneath, $189.50.

15 • *Craftool* Printmaker graphic arts press for etchings, drypoint, linoleum cuts, wood blocks, wood engravings, lithographs, type, photoengravings. The press can be used for all three printing processes: relief (raised surface), intaglio (recessed surface) and lithography (flat surface). $625.

16 • *Grey Owl Indian Craft* Costume in the style of the North Eastern Woodland Indians with typical floral beadwork on velvet. The cape is available unfinished, two panels for $28.75 or finished for $33.35. The apron is available finished for $31. The arm band is 5″ wide and 20″ long and can be mounted on trousers or shirt, $14.90 per pair.

17 • *Grey Owl Indian Craft* Kaibab Ute boots, with soles of white bleached rawhide, uppers of buckskin in rust, natural tan, white or black, cost $42.50.

18 • *Del Trading Post* Mosaic beads for Indian jewelry in various sizes and prices from 10 cents to $5 each.

HOOKING AND BRAIDING

The Dorr Mill Store, Dorr Woolen Company, Guild, N.H. 03754
26-page brochure, 50 cents.
60-color wool sample card, $1.

The Dorr Mill Store sells the fabrics they weave only through their retail shop, but by mail they sell supplies for hooking and braiding. Lots of kits for hooking are available, at prices between $5 and $17, and there are some kits for braiding. There are also instruction books for both crafts and all the necessary supplies, such as scissors, hooks and stands. People who want to dye their own wool can buy white yarn and Cushing dyes, after selecting the color from the wool sample card.

INDIAN SUPPLIES

Grey Owl Indian Craft Mfg. Co., 150-02 Beaver Road, Jamaica, N.Y. 11433
102-page catalogue, 25 cents.

Here are kits and supplies to make American Indian costumes of all kinds. Prices are low, but the goods are not especially authentic—plastic imitation beadwork and plastic Iroquois face-mask kits can be found. There is a lot of everything, however, including tools and accessories such as Plasticine to change the shape of a nose, and make-up and body paint.

Plume Trading and Sales Co., Inc., P.O. Box 585, Monroe, N.Y. 10950
36-page catalogue, 25 cents; refundable.

James Luongo, the owner, who is also the founder of an Indian museum near Monroe, got interested in Indian culture almost by chance in 1926. He was in the declining feathers-for-hats business and discovered that the Boy Scouts were having trouble finding feathers for their Indian-craft projects. He arranged to make Indian kits for the scouts, and then found that other youth groups, children and hobbyists, and even Indians, liked them too.

The kits to make headdresses, jewelry and clothing are "as authentic as possible." For small children there are simple sets for under and around $2 to make headbands, little totems and kachinas and moccasins; for teen-agers and adults there are elaborate projects such as the dramatic Eagle Dance costume for about $19. "Authoritative" books about Indians and Indian records are also for sale.

Supernaw's Oklahoma Indian Supply, 301 East WC Rogers Boulevard, Skiatook, Okla. 74070
Price list, 25 cents.

This Indian-owned supply house was started at a time when most Indian supply houses were owned by non-Indians, and the owners say they helped lower prices in Oklahoma for supplies and raise the prices paid to Indian craftsmen. The firm sells all supplies to make Oklahoma Indian-type crafts, and is particularly strong on modern fancy-dress costumes. However, the price list is not illustrated or very descriptive, and mentions no kits, so it is obviously for people who know what they need.

Feather, skins, fringes, gun-rod sections, hackles, bustle-maker's supplies, German silver, beads, bells, needles and ribbons are listed, and so is broadcloth, which they say is the best of its kind. Supernaw's also has finished goods such as moccasins, leggings, fans, silverwork, shawls, paintings, bustles, roaches and all types of beadwork—*all* made by Indians. However, these must be inquired about individually. As there are no listings, you must state exactly what you are looking for and enclose a stamped, self-addressed envelope whenever you ask about something not listed.

JEWELRY MAKING AND LAPIDARY EQUIPMENT

Allcraft Tool and Supply Company, Inc., 215 Park Avenue, Hicksville, N.Y. 11801
98-page catalogue, $1; refundable.

A good and thorough catalogue of supplies for jewelry making, silversmithing, metalsmithing, casting or enameling. Everything is listed, from metal tool cabinets, chairs and protective clothing to the smallest tweezer. In addition to an extraordinarily complete range of tools, you can get metals: silver, pewter, copper and brass in sheets, sterling-silver and 14-carat gold chain, and gold-filled and silver findings—but just the basic shapes, none of the pseudo-antique findings that Gemex, Geode and Grieger's (below) sell.

Bead Game, 505 N. Fairfax Avenue, Los Angeles, Calif. 90036
56-page catalogue, free.

A fascinating catalogue of unusual beads, many of them imported: baby bracelet supplies, including alphabet beads and instructions, evil-eye beads, earthenware beads, zodiac beads, organic beads made of nuts, bones and seeds. The catalogue also lists tools and findings, and the owners say they are always adding to the collection.

California Crafts Supply, 1096 Main Street, Orange, Calif. 92667
Catalogue, $1.50.

A brief but clear and very appealing catalogue lists basic supplies for silversmithing, lost-wax casting, forged brass jewelry, plastic projects and contemporary leathercraft. Although the catalogue doesn't contain as much as some of the others, it does have the simple necessities, including books, and is well organized and agreeable to look through. This firm also publishes an instruction booklet on lost-wax casting (a method of making jewelry which started with the ancient Egyptians). *Lost Wax Steam Casting* costs $1.50 and describes a new method of working that can be used at home without expensive equipment. Another booklet, *Five Projects in Leather*, for $2, has instructions and full-scale patterns for making first a barrette and then a watchband, belt, visor and handbag.

Craftool Company, Inc., 1421 W. 240th Street, Harbor City, Calif. 90710
Star Diamond catalogue for lapidary work, free.
150-page Craftool color catalogue, $1.
Dryad Instruction book list, free.

Craftool, whose big catalogue includes tools for all crafts, publishes a smaller catalogue listing just the supplies for lapidary work mentioned in the large Craftool catalogue. Like the big catalogue, this is a good one for beginners, with an introduction that describes what gem making as a hobby consists of, and an article on the various steps in gem making, and other useful information. Machines and tools for sanding, polishing, lapping, tumbling and carving are sold, and there are tumbling and jewelry-making kits that start at $25, as well as instructional and background books.

Del Trading Post, Mission, S. Dak. 57555
18-page catalogue, 50 cents.

This firm sells supplies for American Indian beadwork and has a beautiful collection, one of the best they say, of fancy "trade beads." Patterned beads in glass and metal are photographed close up and well described, and the firm has recently started manufacturing reproductions of old-style trade goods that are hard to find: brass beads, brass "hawk bells," brass shoe buttons, genuine bone beads and "hair pipes."

Otto Frei–Jules Borel, P.O. Box 796, Oakland, Calif. 94604
162-page catalogue, $1.50.

This catalogue lists tools, supplies and equipment for jewelers, watchmakers, engravers, opticians. It is really geared for professionals, but advanced amateurs will find it useful, as it has everything from benches and anvils down to packaging supplies, envelopes, labels and price tickets. Books are also sold.

Gemex Company, 900 W. Los Vallecitos Boulevard, San Marcos, Calif. 92069
180-page jewelry-making color catalogue, $1.
144-page crafts color catalogue, free.
48-page jewelry catalogue for beginners, free.

For anyone who would like to save a lot of money by assembling their own jewelry, Gemex has a big assortment of elaborate mountings and findings in gold and silver color, sterling silver and 14-carat gold. (And in the case of the rings, you can even choose a mounting and stone and pay Gemex $3.50 to put them together.) For mounting yourself, which is *very* easy, you can choose from coral, jade, opal and turquoise cabochons, tumbled stones, drilled semiprecious stones, imitation and genuine scarabs, imitation and genuine shell cameos, and painted porcelain ovals. For people who would rather do it all themselves, silver sheets, and wire and tools for working them, are for sale, as well as machines for finishing stones, and plenty of books.

Geode Industries, Inc., 106 W. Maine Street, New London, Iowa 52645
200-page catalogue, some color, $1.
16-page brochure, free.

Grieger's Inc., 900 S. Arroyo Parkway, Pasadena, Calif. 91109
240-page catalogue, some color, free.

Two more large catalogues with metal mountings and stones for assembling to make jewelry, and extensive lists of supplies for lapidary work. Both have enormous numbers of grinding machines, tumbling machines and saws, etc., as well as good supplies of tumbled and untumbled stones.

International Import Company, P.O. Box 747, Stone Mountain, Ga 30083
56-page price list, free. October.

Besides writing monthly articles for *Modern Jeweler*, George A. Bruce, the owner of International Import Company, is a picturesquely named Ordinary Fellow of the Geomological Association of Great Britain. A list of about 3,000 of the 100,000 precious and semiprecious stones in stock is published each October and gives customers an idea of which stones are available in what sizes, weights, shapes and prices. As the specific stones listed are sold, close substitutes are sent. The list is matter-of-fact and the descriptions abbreviated. Prices run from under $2 for amazonites to over $2,000 for star sapphires.

KNITTING

Elizabeth Zimmerman, Meg Swansen, Box 57, Trumansburg, N.Y. 14886
Price list and sample card, 50 cents.

Two designers sell subtly colored imported yarns: Canadian fisherman and "homespun," Scottish Shetland, Finnish Suomi, and unspun, undyed wool from Iceland. They send a biannual newsletter with an original knitting pattern in each issue to customers who have bought over $5 worth of yarn.

LEATHER

Leathercrafters Supply Company, 25 Great Jones (E. 3rd) Street, New York, N.Y. 10012
Catalogue planned, $1; refundable.

In 1971 Leathercrafters was created by the owner of Charles Horowitz, Inc., an excellent leather wholesaler firm, and a catalogue is planned for the spring of 1973. I haven't seen the catalogue, but as the shop carries just about everything that anyone working with leather needs, it should be good. They stock the famous Osborne tools as well as Craftool and Rampart, and also cleaners, preservatives, cements, Fiebling dyes, findings, threads, and cobbler sandal supplies. They claim to have the largest buckle selection in the country, and it does sound like it—twelve different lines in solid brass, bronze, pewter, glass gems, Brittanian, also cast-metal buckles in the above finishes, many designed specially for Leathercrafters. As for leather, they have cowhide bag and belt leather, Western and Canadian latigo, English kip and hide skins, and leathers for clothes such as suede, chamois, deerskin, antelope and elk. Books about working with leather are for sale, too.

National Handicraft Co., Inc., 337 Lincoln Road, Miami Beach, Fla. 33139
Brochure, free.

This firm specializes in belt-making tools and supplies. The selection is small and geared to the essentials. A simple, one-piece size 00 punch costs 90 cents. A pair of 8″ heavy-duty leather shears lists for $4.50. As for the leather, they list one type, top-grain 8/9-oz. cowhide in natural only. The belts are all over 44″ in length and come in widths from 1″ to 2″ (90 cents to $1.80). There is a surprising variety of "buckles, belt buckles, and fancy belt buckles." These range from an antiqued butterfly style for 90 cents to an attractive floral design, 4½″ by 2½″ for $1.80. This catalogue might be good for the beginner—the small selection won't present too many difficult choices.

MACRAMÉ

Macramé and Weaving Supply Co., 63 E. Adam Street, Chicago, Ill, 60603
Brochure, free. Samples $1; 50 cents refundable.

This is how the rather specialized Macramé and Weaving Supply Co. came into being: "During the early summer of 1970, I accompanied my daughter, Jan Arnow, to her weaving class at the Art Institute of Chicago. I did this because she had boasted that her dad knew how to do macramé and would be very happy to teach some of the kids in her class a unique method of tying knots. At the class I presented a little dissertation of what I thought was the history, or at least my history, of knot tying. On the way back Jan and I agreed that since the supply for the knot tier was so poor in the city of Chicago, she and I would open a small shop to the students of the Art Institute with material with which they could tie knots and at the same time take in some items for their weaving classes as well. There was just no other place in downtown Chicago where they could obtain such items." The shop opened on 100 square feet of a sixth-floor lunchroom, but it wasn't long before it got publicity in the Chicago papers and people dropped in from all over town and then from all over the country—all complaining that there was no other place with such a selection, so the shop went into mail order.

Devotees of macramé, the art of decorative knot tying, will find here, besides twines, yarns, cords and rope of all kinds, very nice belt buckles both plain and ornate in brass, pewter and bronze-plated zinc, bells in various sizes, shells, beads made of clay, or nuts, or imported from India, and sixteen inexpensive books on macramé.

Reeves Knotique, Box 5011, Riverside, Calif. 92507
16-page brochure, 75 cents. Bead sample card, $2.50.

This neat brochure illustrates with line drawings stoneware and porcelain beads, buckles and pendants for macramé work. Stoneware planters are sold with holes so that you can thread and hang them with your own macramé creations. Cords are listed, and so are about five inexpensive how-to books, a couple for a $1 each.

MAGIC

D. Robbins and Co., Inc., 127 W. 17th Street, New York, N.Y. 10011
74-page catalogue, 50 cents.

"E-Z magic" is the D. Robbins trademark, and there are plenty of simple stunts for under $1 in this catalogue of "practical tricks for stage-club-parlor." All the favorites that delight children are listed and illustrated in the oddly old-fashioned style that magic catalogues seem to keep to. About forty books are sold on all aspects of magic and tricks, among them *Spook Show in Your Parlour* ($1), which describes ten black-out stunts that you can perform in your own home, and *64 Ways to Make Magic Pay,* which tells you how to make magic pay off in popularity and money, and claims to answer such questions as, How can you stay in the same town and make your entire living from magic? How can you make magic increase your regular business? How can you get dates when none are to be had?

MOVIES

Audio Brandon, 334 MacQuesten Parkway So., Mount Vernon, N.Y. 10550
International catalogue, 532 pages, American 298 pages, free to groups.

Brandon is one of the country's largest renters of films and its huge catalogues are available on request to any group wanting to show movies, whether free or for admission. The fee depends on the type of movie you have in mind and the size of your audience, and there is a sliding scale but not to exceed 50 percent of your take. Prices range from $30 for the least expensive film before a small, nonpaying audience to $250 for the largest, paying. Those in the latter category are major films that have had full distribution, such as Antonioni's *Red Desert,* while such classics as *Triumph of the Will* or the German version of *The Threepenny Opera* fall into the less expensive category.

The Brandon International catalogue is a veritable cinemathèque, listing almost 900 feature films and 600 shorts, from every film-producing country and including many of the world's great films. Among the directors are Eisenstein, Pabst, D. W. Griffith, Fellini, Renoir, Welles, Hitchcock—in other words, just about everyone. This illustrated catalogue is a fascinating reference work in itself and obviously a gold mine to anyone running a film series. Having read through it, I wondered why every group in the country isn't tempted to go into the film business, since there are so many communities where these films are completely unavailable and only a very few are ever shown on television. The Brandon catalogue also lists the great American silent movies, plus a broad choice of short films, some experimental, others educational, or on art, music and the dance, as well as a number suited to classroom discussion.

19 • *Leathercrafters* Cast-brass reproductions of antique Tiffany Express and commemorative plates, at $7.60 each, are Leathercrafters' most expensive buckles.

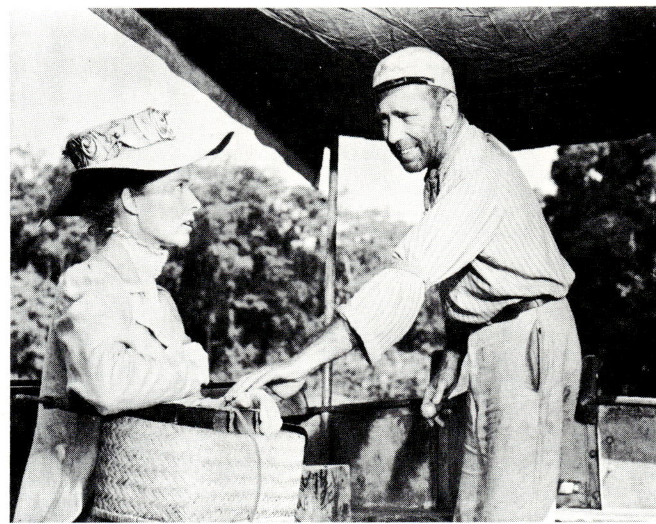

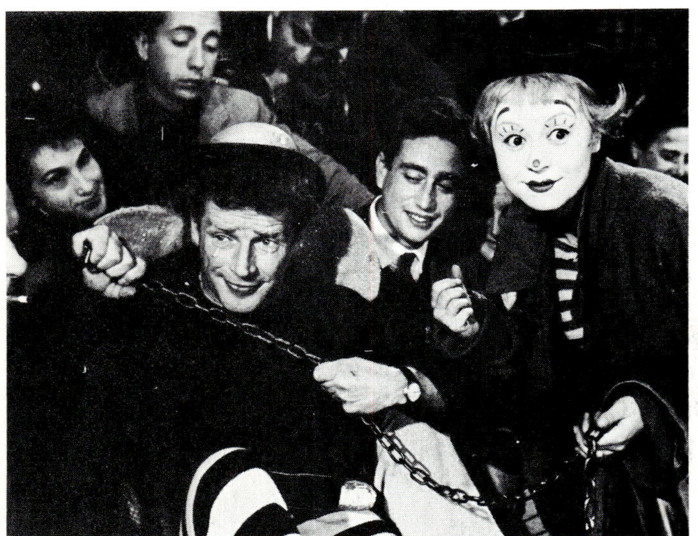

20 • *Audio Brandon Battle of Algiers, The African Queen, La Strada, Bonnie and Clyde, The Graduate*—some of the most popular of the many films available for rent.

Blackhawk Films, The Eastin-Phelan Corporation, 1235 W. 5th Street, Davenport, Iowa 52808
64-page catalogue, free.
Occasional sales catalogues, free.

Blackhawk specializes in selling, not renting, old Hollywood films, mostly shorts. It seems to have many of the famous shorts, from Laurel & Hardy to *The Perils of Pauline*, but also sells such full-length classics as *Intolerance, The Phantom of the Opera, Orphans of the Storm* and other feature films starring Mary Pickford, Douglas Fairbanks, Lon Chaney, Will Rogers and others. Prices vary widely, and most films are available in standard 8mm, super 8 or 16mm, this last costing so much more that *The Phantom of the Opera* is $56 for 8mm but $240 for 16mm. The shorter films, such as the Chaplins, cost as little as $13 for 8mm, while the full *Hunchback of Notre Dame* costs $70.

In addition to these better-known films, Blackhawk offers a wide choice of cartoons and newsreels, and a surprising number of films of railroads, which apparently have a strong hold on people's memories. These include historical films of early trains, but also such items as "On the Norfolk and Western" or "Steam Trains out of Dearborn." Various movie and slide accessory items are also available, as well as records of music to accompany silent films, etc. A fascinating catalogue not only for home entertainment but for students of American popular culture and film history.

Canyon Cinema Cooperative, Catalogue Department, Room 200, Industrial Center Building, Sausalito, Calif. 94965
230-page catalogue, $2.

Started six years ago by a small group of avant-garde film makers, Canyon Cinema has grown to a large, cooperative group, handling about a thousand films. The group's aim is to "minimalize the censoring, exploiting and judgmental procedures commercial distribution seems to fall prey to—or find necessary for survival. Our first concern is really the film maker who receives ⅔ of the gross profit from the rental." The Coop is nonprofit and rents films to groups at prices that can be as low as $5, but in this case "the film was made by me (age 12) with some help from my brother (age 6) and our friends." On the other hand, films by directors as famous as Stan Brakhage, made when they were already grown-up, also rent for $10 to $30, though many of these are not full length. Such famous feature films as *The Brig*, by Jonas Mekas, rent for $80.

The catalogue is fascinating as an introduction to contemporary American film making. Not only does one get an idea of what is being filmed but the descriptions by the film makers themselves are also revealing and often amusing, with a number of entries that may or may not be put-ons: "*The Naked Zodiac*, astrological figure and character studies in the nudie genre . . . None are hardcore porno and no overlit clinical photography is used. These films are most suitable for a college-age audience, perhaps used as a serial . . ."

NEEDLEWORK

Although European canvases often come unpainted, with charts to be followed, or else *trammé* (under-stitched) in the correct colors, American canvases almost always come painted in colors to match the yarn that should be used for each section. Many shops have their own designers, yet as I looked through these catalogues, it was hard to see really dramatic differences. Obviously there *are* differences between the designs at the different stores, but almost all of them have mainly designs based on animals and flowers, from naturalistic ones to more stylized, modern ones, and there are usually a few abstracts to be found. There are two kinds of stores in this section, small stores with their own designer that sell kits with Persian yarn, and larger stores that buy kits from several manufacturers and have some kits with synthetic yarns at much lower prices.

Anyone who would like to vary their diet should look at the museum catalogues which have some outstanding designs from objects in their own collections, and the English and Scandinavian catalogues (listed in my previous book, *The Catalogue of Catalogues*), where kits are unusual and much less expensive.

The Artisans Guild, Inc., 10 "B" Street, Burlington, Mass. 01803
24-page color catalogue of Danish cross-stitch kits, $2.
56-page catalogue of hot-iron transfers, $1.

The needlework supplies sold here are quite different from those of the other stores listed. A catalogue in color shows charts of typically Danish light and flowery cross-stitch designs which you transfer to the unmarked fabric by counting threads as you sew. The kits (which are mostly for pillows, place mats and hangings, and include a section of Christmassy designs) come with chart, fabric, yarn and instructions.

Another catalogue illustrates an impressive collection of transfers which you press with a hot iron onto whatever you want to embroider; yarns, in whatever colors you like, must be bought from other sources. Obviously the transfers are a great opportunity not only to decorate things for the house but also to embroider in glowing colors and gold and silver thread things to wear such as belts, cloth boots, trousers, cloaks and anything else you can think of.

Gemex Company, 900 W. Los Vallecitos Boulevard, San Marcos, Calif. 92069
180-page jewelry-making color catalogue, $1.
48-page needlework color catalogue, free.

A fairly varied lot of inexpensive needlework kits are shown in this catalogue: crewel-embroidery pictures of German towns; cotton-embroidery pictures of dolls and flowers; rya rugs and pillows; hook rugs made with acrylic yarn; rather old-fashioned needlepoint pictures with country scenes of deer at woodland streams or snowy cottages next to windmills; needlepoint belts and plenty of pillows—all at prices between $4 and $16.

Suzy Girard, 1042 Lexington Avenue, New York, N.Y. 10021
Leaflets, some color, $1.

The husband of Susan Goodnow, who runs this shop, is an established commercial artist and he designs many of the kits. Most of the designs are of animals, funny or serious; some are of great big flowers, and a few are geometric abstracts. About fifty kits are shown in the two leaflets, of which almost all are for pillows costing $25 to $65, but there are also kits to make 4″ by 4″ coasters with funny animals on them, $5 each. Suzy

Girard will design to order for customers, and will mount finished work.

Home Sew, Inc., Bethlehem, Pa. 18018
20-page catalogue, some color, free.

This firm sells mainly trimmings and says that as far as they know they are the only firm in America that mails out trimming samples. Prices are very low, starting at five yards for 90 cents. Threads, zippers, elastic, pins, needles are also sold.

In Stitches, 356 E. 19th Street, New York, N.Y. 10003
24-page catalogue, $1.

Muriel Crowell says that her shop is usually described as folksy or neighborhoody, which is fine because it is, but she is also interested in spreading her wings to other localities through her catalogue.

About sixty original designs are shown in the catalogue: stylized plants and animals or geometric abstracts, and all to be made into pillows or pictures. Kits cost between $12 and $60, and they come with 3-ply Persian yarn. French silk thread is available but costs extra.

Mary Maxim, 2001 Holland Avenue, Port Huron, Mich. 48060
Color catalogues, free. January, March, July, October. Each catalogue is valid for about three months.

Mary Maxim sends out about four million of its large colorful catalogues each year. Each one contains a very large, inexpensive assortment of embroidery, crewel, needlepoint kits, quilts and hook rugs to make, and toys, sweaters and baby clothes to knit. They say that the firm's specialty, when it began in the Depression years, was motif sweaters, and these are still very popular: the catalogues have several pages of heavy knitted jackets for men, women and children decorated with fish, deer, wild ducks or football, golf and bowling scenes at prices around $20 for adult sizes; kits available in orlon or wool. Only kits are on sale; no patterns without yarns.

Mazaltov's, 758 Madison Avenue, New York, N.Y. 10021
40-page color brochure, $3.

The firm was started forty-two years ago by Robert Mazaltov, a weaver and tapestry restorer. It is now one of the biggest and best-known of the needlepoint shops and has the most professional of the catalogues. Prices start at $20 for kits of 12″ by 12″ squares of animals, designs for children, and go up to $2,350 for a 7′ by 9′ carpet with an elegant design of curling flowers and plants on a white background. 131 kits are shown in all, and they include "wild and woolly" animal pillows, "floral and faunal pillows" (all 16″ by 16″) and zodiac pillows. Incidentally, rugs can be made by joining the pillow squares. There are also rugs of all sizes, tennis racquet covers, telephone-book and address-book covers, cummerbunds and picture frames. The designs vary from stylized modern to delicate old-fashioned floral, though none are the strictly traditional designs that you get in European shops. About eight of the kits are based on popular paintings by Van Gogh, Gauguin, Matisse, Mondrian, Picasso and Grandma Moses.

Merribee Needlecraft Company, 2904 West Lancaster, P.O. Box 9680, Fort Worth, Tex. 76107
80-page catalogue, some color, free.

You'll find here a bigger variety of needlework projects than at any of the other needlework shops, except Mary Maxim. There are a great many crewel pillows and pictures at prices below $10; a few antique-style needlepoint designs; but also permanent-press tablecloths, cotton pillowcases, and Belgian linen bedroom sets stamped for embroidery; afghans and clothes to knit or crochet (in synthetic yarn); knotted rugs and pillows; and quilts for beds. Prices are very low, and although many of the designs are run-of-the-mill, it should be possible to find one or two you like.

The Nimble Thimble, P.O. Box 713, Aptos, Calif. 95003
36-page catalogue, $1.

Five designers design canvases for this firm, which started out trying to cut costs by selling only by mail, but because of a recent California law that mail-order firms must have a retail outlet, has opened a small shop at La Selva Beach, Monterey Bay. About eighty kits are shown in the brochure: pillows at around $30 each; belts, including co-ordinated buckles, $20 each; racquet covers, luggage straps, brick covers for doorstops or book ends, and eyeglass cases. On the whole, the designs are fairly naturalistic pictures of birds and flowers, and both imported tapestry yarn and Paternayan yarn are stocked, so customers can choose whichever kind they prefer.

Papillon, Cates Plaza, 375 Pharr Road NE, Atlanta, Ga. 30305
Annual subscription to three brochures, $2. February, June, October.

Each brochure has about forty line drawings of needlepoint kits that come with handpainted canvas, Persian yarn and printed instructions. The kits tend to be expensive—eyeglass cases are about $17, and a Louis Quatorze chair seat, back and arms are $235—but the design are often unusual. Besides more common animals and flowers, there are designs made up of intricate shell patterns, an Audubon series, a wreath of holly and glazed fruit based on a fifteenth-century Florentine original, and a rug made of Art Nouveau flowers. Designs can be painted in customer's colors on receipt of swatches and an extra $10. The October brochure has several kits with Christmas themes.

Peacock Alley, 650 Croswell Street, S.W., Grand Rapids, Mich. 49506
24-page catalogue, $1.

Peacock Alley was opened seven years ago by four needlepointing friends who couldn't find Persian yarn locally. Since the opening coincided with the growing popularity of needlepoint, the shop was a great success, and now has bevies of housewives painting canvases and gaggles of students packing kits. Pillows cost around $20 each and there are coasters, (favorites with beginners), belts and luggage-rack straps, (favorites with teen-agers, who use them as guitar straps), children's picture frames, eyeglass cases, brick covers for doorstops or book ends, pincushions and several rugs, and about eleven handbag and purse kits—more handbags than any other catalogue.

21

22

23

24

21 • *Philadelphia Museum of Art* (see the Museums section) Bargello and needlepoint kits: small purses and glass cases about $10 each, belt (without buckle), 30″, $10; 38″, $12. Cupid pillow or brick cover with a dark-blue or olive-green background, adapted from Coptic textile, $25. *photo Patrick Radebaugh*

22 • *Museum of Fine Arts* (see the Museums section) Needlepoint kit: a golden peacock on a brown background with touches of turquoise adapted from a tenth-century Persian bowl from Nishapur. Design size—12¾″ circle on 14″ square canvas. Fine-grade canvas, needle and wool to make a round or square pillow. $38.
photo Frederick G. S. Clow

23 • *The Nimble Thimble* Needlepoint kit "Giant Anemone" pillow, 16″ by 16″. Available in black, white and brown on white or beige background (specify which background you want) or mustard, black, taupe and white on white background, $37.50.

24 • *Peacock Alley* "Star" pillow chart. The design is not painted on the canvas; you get plain 14-mesh canvas and a diagram. $7.25 if you want to use up your own yarn left over; $15.75 with brightly colored yarns to make a 10″ by 11″ pillow.

25

26

25 • *Jane Snead Samplers* Sampler kit: "Rejoice," Psalm 118:24. Finished, size 12" by 16". About $3.

26 • *Jane Snead Samplers* Sampler kit: "God Bless Our Home," copied from an old New England cookbook. Colors—royal blue, red, green and black. Framed, size 11" by 13". About $2.

Jane Snead Samplers, Box 4909, Philadelphia, Pa. 19119
36-page brochure, 20 cents.

This firm designs and makes only kits for "keepsake needlework"—samplers—and have a temptingly wide range from old-fashioned prayers, tender sentiments, and virtuous thoughts such as "When others hate, oppose, ignore, Help me, dear God, to love them more" through quips such as "A happy couple, the husband deaf, the wife blind" and "Work is the curse of the drinking class" to useful admonitions about leaving the bathroom tidy. Plenty of beautiful thoughts about love and friendship to give away to lovers and friends. Most of the kits cost between $2 and $3, and frames of several kinds are on sale.

The Stitchery, Wellesley Hills, Mass. 02181
48-page color catalogue, subscription for three, 25 cents.

Unlike many of the other firms in this section, The Stitchery does not design and manufacture its own needlepoint kits; instead they stock inexpensive kits of all sorts from American and foreign manufacturers: needlepoint, crewel embroidery and creative stitchery. A full-color catalogue shows pillow kits for between $10 and $20, pictures, and one or two coaster sets, desk sets, clothes hangers, and appliquéd and embroidered quilts for beds. And for about $16 each, there is a collection of Career and Sports plaques, "handsome, personalized gifts for the very special people in your life." The homemaker gets a picture of washing hanging up to dry, a vacuum cleaner, a carrot, a tomato and herself in curlers, while the dentist gets toothbrush and paste, a syringe and a large molar. There are plaques for doctors, teachers, lawyers, stockbrokers, athletes, golfers, accountants and pharmacists, all of a bright and colorful bent.

The Yellow Binding, 4701 Sangamore Road, Washington, D.C. 20016
Leaflet, $1.

Twenty kits are shown on this leaflet, mostly animals and flowers for pictures or pillows; some small ones for beginners start at $7. There are also eyeglass and scissor cases for about $9, and ten Christmas-tree ornaments—angels, bells, snowmen, etc., which cost just under $5 each.

For more needlework kits, see the Museums section and the listings for Craft House, Williamsburg, and Guild of Shaker Crafts (in the House section).

NORWEGIAN ROSEMALING

Traditional Norwegian Rosemaling, 1506 Lynn Avenue, Marquette, Mich. 49855
12-page catalogue, free.

Rose painting was a Norwegian folk art of the eighteenth and nineteenth centuries. Stylized roses with acanthus leaves and scrolls were painted on walls, ceilings, bedsteads, doors, ale bowls and dowry chests to decorate the house. At the end of the nineteenth century *rosemaling* more or less died out in Norway, but is now becoming popular again in the United States.

Pat Virch teaches it in Michigan, mainly to women of Norwegian descent (although it was the men that used to do it in Norway), and she also sells paints, patterns and books, and wooden objects to paint on—absolutely everything you need—through her catalogue. The nicest of them are rough bowls, butter tubs, serving trays and framed mirrors imported from Norway.

OCCULT

New York Astrology Center, 127 Madison Avenue, New York, N.Y. 10016
32-page catalogue, free.

This center is run by the National Astrological Society, carries the largest selection of books on astrology in the country and is the publisher of two astrological journals as well. A school has also been started, which is applying for New York State certification and where, the Society tells me, students are already receiving college transfer credit.

As you can see from all this, the Center represents astrology at its most serious, and its catalogue is a fascinating introduction to the subject. Not only does it list a large number of books but it also offers the tables, wall charts and even chart paper that are necessary tools of the trade. Finally, its back pages contain some of the arguments for astrology, drawing on recent research in astronomy and the new study of body rhythms and biological clocks to show some of the scientific bases for astrological beliefs and practices.

The books listed start with the basic texts, from *Teach Yourself Astrology* to a list of longitudes and latitudes in the United States; the complete beginner's kit of seven items is only $20. Specific titles cover Indian and German astrology, body time, sun-sign studies and a large number of recommended textbooks. If you are interested in decoding Stonehenge or seeing what light astrology has to shed on murder, there are books here to help you.

The Society states that it is its policy to sell books for as little as possible and that its prices are therefore lower than those of others in the field.

Templestar Co., Times Plaza Station, Box 224, Brooklyn, N.Y. 11217
Catalogue, free.

Just to receive the Templestar catalogue is to enter another world: "Describing a Most Remarkable World Wide Collection of High Grade Personal Curios, Psychic Aids, Unusual Jewelry and Sacred Articles." From the first page, featuring the famous secret hidden-number curio candle or the symbolic bearded-prophet ring, there opens a world of mystery, belief and search for the unknown that is both suggestive and fascinating. The Templestar catalogue is one of the few in this book that should be studied by future scholars with a view to understanding the complexity of what we blithely think of as a modern and industrialized society. Here, for the delectation of anthropologists and others, is a mixture of magic wands, exotically named sachet-incense powders, holy religious statues of the various saints, *The Book of the Dead* and "How to Get a Civil Service Job."

Here are dream books, books of numbers, books exposing the terrors of the evil eye, many priced at only

27 • *U.S. Games Systems* Deck of seventy-eight tarot cards with classic designs in full color. English titles on the cards and instruction booklet that gives the meaning of each card, $5. The book, *Tarot Classic* by Stuart R. Kaplan, is a complete history of tarot, illustrated with photographs and line drawings of rare decks and books, with an annotated bibliography. $5.95.

28 • *U.S. Games Systems* Jesus deck, sold with a pamphlet of explanations and instructions. $5.

$1 each. I am sure that within a few years these will be reprinted at great expense while the originals will still be available at these modest prices from Templestar. And will these new publishers be as scrupulous as Templestar, which, after each description, notes, "We make no supernatural claims for the information in this curious book," and offers a money-back guarantee.

A fascinating catalogue as well as an all-too-rare glimpse into the many alternatives to the formal psychiatric counseling and religious establishments that have flourished in our unpredictable society.

U.S. Games Systems, Inc., 468 Park Avenue South, New York, N.Y. 10016
Color leaflet, 15 cents.

Tarot cards, which are used for fortunetelling, are believed to have originated in Italy in the fourteenth century. The deck consists of 78 cards in two groups: the 22 symbolic Major Arcana cards, and the 56 Lesser Arcana cards which are divided into four suits numbered from 10 to 1, with a king, queen, cavalier and page in each suit. The modern 52-card deck comes from the tarot, with the Major Arcana cards dropped and the cavalier and page combined as the jack.

U.S. Games Systems sells by mail fascinating reproductions of several of the most famous tarot decks, posters and napkins decorated with the cards, books about them and also fortunetelling cards and instructions, including a reproduction of the nineteenth-century deck of Marianne A. Lenormand, the famous diviner to Napoleon. Packs cost from $3 to $5 and are all shown in full color.

World-Wide Curio House, Box 17095, Minneapolis, Minn. 55417
64-page catalogue, 25 cents.

World-Wide specializes in curios, which is actually a pretty good word to describe the extraordinary variety of objects they sell, from incense to Polynesian ritual weapons (carved handle and gleaming blade, $12.95). With its subsidiaries, Tyrad and Marlar, World-Wide offers everything from the more traditional magic tricks to perfumed oils, occult seals and pendants, and a vast assortment of herb and root candles which "can be used in rituals, with prayers and for other purposes, especially where the burning of herbs and roots is suggested." Their most impressive offerings are the herbs, roots, barks and berries useful for teas, culinary delights and many other uses, though "since we are a supply house only, we can offer no advice as to their use," which left me somewhat stranded. But if you do know what can be done with these, there is an amazing list of cat's-wort, broom tops, lupulin and many others, available by the pound or in smaller quantities.

The Marlar list is a comprehensive book service covering books on the occult, magic, the tarot, fortunetelling, even the mysterious science of electronics. There are a number of dream books as well as a large selection of self-help titles.

PHOTOGRAPHY

There are no stores in America that have as consistently low prices as the Hong Kong photographic stores. If you want to save money on the top brands of camera equipment, the thing to do is go to a local discount store (and try bargaining, this seems to be one of the areas where you can still do it in this country), find out where good secondhand cameras are sold and traded locally, or watch advertisement in newspapers and the photography magazines. But always compare prices with the Hong Kong firms; although prices differ and in some cases are hardly worthwhile, spectacular savings can be made by buying from Hong Kong.

Camera Haven, P.O. Box 125, St. Ann, Mo. 63074
16-page catalogue, free.

Although Camera Haven has a complete photo catalogue, its best selling goods are accessory lenses and electronic flash units for Kodak Instamatic cameras and accessory lenses for Polaroids, which, they say, are not easily found in photo stores. The electronic flash unit costs about $15, and sounds very useful indeed: you don't have to change flash bulbs all the time, and hopefully, unlike bulbs, it always works.

Miko Photo and Sound Co., 1257 Santa Monica Mall, Santa Monica, Calif. 90401
74-page catalogue, $1.

Miko sends out by far the largest of the photographic catalogues, subtitled "A Complete Listing of the Photographic Products Available." It looks like some sort of trade publication, lists and describes an enormous amount of equipment, gives list prices, carries short articles of explanation for people who don't know much about photographic equipment, and generally appears to be a useful reference work.

Modernage Photographic Services, Inc., 319 E. 44th Street, New York, N.Y. 10017
Price list, free.

An excellent but expensive film-developing service for professionals, and for amateurs who want their photographs to look more professional (as I write, photographic exhibitions printed by Modernage are showing at the Metropolitan Museum and the Museum of Modern Art in New York, as well as six other museums throughout the country). Besides routine developing and printing (a roll of 120mm or 135mm film costs $2.60 to develop with contact sheet, a 5″ by 3″ enlargement costs $1.65). Almost anything can be done to special order. When you get your contact sheet, you can decide which photographs you would like enlarged, and then, by marking the contact with symbols, show where you would like the print to be darkened or lightened and where you would like it cut.

Modernage can also file negatives for out-of-town customers and then send them out when wanted for publicity or publishing.

National Camera, 2000 W. Union Avenue, Englewood, Colo. 80110
Catalogue, free.

National Camera has a home study course for camera repairmen, manufactures photo test equipment and also small tools for repairing cameras and for use by other technicians. The catalogue lists basic precision tools, hard-to-find tools and then "Useful and efficient items to make the job easier," including such things as small portable work stations which open out so that all the tools are easily accessible around you in their trays.

Spiratone, Inc., 135-06 Northern Boulevard, Flushing, N.Y. 11354
Brochures, free.

Spiratone says it is the only camera store in the world that sells no cameras. In the forties they started selling Japanese lenses and accessories before anyone else in America, and before Nikon, Canon, etc., were known here. Since then they have specialized in lenses for single-lens reflex cameras, front-lense attachments and dark-room equipment. They design their own goods, which are made in their own factories in America, Europe and Japan, and their prices are *much* lower than those of the famous brands. Warmly recommended in the *Whole Earth Catalog* by a man who has been using their products for three years.

Superior Bulk Film Co., 442-450 N. Wells Street, Chicago, Ill. 60610
74-page catalogue, free.

Superior Bulk film has designed and developed home-processing equipment and provides chemicals to go with it, for the movie fan who wants to process his own film. They say they are the only company in the country that specializes in such equipment and that, furthermore, they have more kinds of film in super 8, 8mm and 16mm than any other firm. They also process cine film themselves and have other services for the amateur film maker; for example, they make film duplicates and do sound stripping.

PRINTING

The Kelsey Company, Box 941, Meriden, Conn. 06450
Do Your Own Printing brochure, 25 cents.
Printer's Supply book, 50 cents; refundable.

The Kelsey Company, the last of the hand-press manufacturers, says that they sell their presses almost at "break even" in order to entice people into taking up printing and thus becoming regular customers of their printer's supplies. Their specialty is a complete line of supplies that is used with letterpress equipment, and they concentrate on the "small" printer to whom they sell cards, paper, envelopes, type, etc., with a minimum order of $2.50. Kelsey says that most paper-supply houses have minimum-order requirements of $25 or more.

The *Do Your Own Printing* brochure for beginners shows a representative selection of equipment and several complete printing outfits: one for children at about $32, another for adults at about $80, and these can be added to, of course. The brochure also pushes printing as a hobby (print your own poems, cards, family history, town history, etc.) and as a spare-time business—"Never has the opportunity for the small printer been so great. Large printers' prices are so high that anyone with a small press can get all the work he can handle," says the brochure.

29 • *Colonial Textiles* Spinning wheel, similar to Colonial wheels, unfinished—you apply the stain and oil, $95. Finished, about $120.

SCIENCE

Edmund Scientific Company, 555 Edscorp Building, Barrington, N.J. 08007
164-page catalogue, free.

Edmund's catalogue is a sheer delight, not only because it lists some 4,500 items in all sorts of areas but because it suggests a whole world of home experimenters working in every field of science—amateur astronomers or biologists, chemists and entomologists leading double lives. I've been set off on this reverie in part because the Edmund catalogue is so genuine; it offers real scientific tools without the gimmickry and plastic wrapping of so many of the products usually sold to American children. The catalogue is straightforward and honest, no unnecessary adjectives, just simple facts that tell you, for example, that 25 amoeba proteus will cost you $4.50, while 100 are $8, and that they will be sent to you fresh by air mail or air special delivery.

Edmund's started in a very small way thirty years ago selling lenses by mail and has grown to a large business but one that still delights in bargains, unique surplus items, etc. One of the nicest things about Edmund's is that they encourage you to try and make your own equivalents of the products they sell. While they offer a wide choice of telescopes, for instance, ranging from a $32.95 "first telescope" to a $512 instrument for the "serious amateur," they also show how, for $20, you can buy the optical parts that will allow you to build the equivalent of a $250 telescope. The astronomy section alone is twenty pages, and the catalogue includes major sections on most of the sciences. For rock collectors there are rock tumblers from $11.25 to $39.95. Botany, biology, chemistry, entomology all have detailed sections, going from the rank beginner to the specialist. A basic butterfly and insect collecting kit is $4.95, a crystal growing kit is $11, and a stereoscopic microscope sells for $104.25.

There are laser kits, holograms, an enormous selection of lenses and a vast lighting section, offering strobes, black lights and a lumia light box marked down from $29.95 to $11.95. Obviously I could go on forever, but it must be clear that this is the catalogue for anyone with any scientific bent, and I should think for any child, not just the classic budding scientist but any youngster whose natural curiosity cannot but be helped by this kind of equipment.

In addition to all this, there are a surprising number of fascinating items that one would never think of going out to buy, but when described sound irresistible. Giant weather balloons that inflate to 8′ or 16′ cost only $2.50 and $8.75, respectively, can be used by amateur meterologists or simply inflated in a backyard or a small ship's cabin for instant effect. Here is a geodesic dome kit for $9.75, a pollution testing kit for $10.95, an underwater camera case for $21, or a see-through model of the new Wankel rotary engine for $6.75.

Edmund's obviously does a great deal of its business with schools, but clearly, science learning can go on even in the least scientific of homes—the Edmund catalogue thrilled even my children, who are relatively jaded as far as catalogues go. It's great fun to look at, and a genuinely helpful tool.

SCULPTURE

Sculpture House, 38 E. 30th Street, New York, N.Y. 10016
48-page catalogue $1.

As the catalogue announces, here you can get tools, materials and accessories for casting, wax modeling, wood carving, stone carving, plastic sculpturing and ceramic sculpturing. This fifty-year-old firm says it produces the world's most complete line of products for sculptors and also does custom casting, restoring, etc. Books on sculpturing and potting are also sold.

SPINNING

Colonial Textiles, 82 Plants Dam Road, East Lyme, Conn. 06333
Price list, free.

Colonial carries spinning and weaving things, and they feature one style of spinning wheel, the saxony, for about $120 (or $95 without stain and oil). They carry a variety of accessories and spinning fibers, as well as hand-spun yarn. You can also buy looms from them. Their price list includes a large selection of books on weaving, spinning and dyeing. They carry dyes (both organic and inorganic) with exotic-sounding names such as Cape York Orchil, Fustic Chips and Ladies Bedstraw.

Tromp and Treadle, 41901 Woodbrook Drive, Wayne, Mich. 48184
Price list, free.

This small firm produces and sells its own spinning wheels. They make four models—walking wheel, saxony 22″; saxony 30″ and castle wheel with distaff—priced from about $130 to $200. They also handle some accessories—bobbins, niddy noddys, and fibers for hand spinning.

STAINED GLASS

Whittemore-Durgin Glass Company, Box 2065 DF, Hanover, Mass. 02339
Complete literature package, 50 cents.

A truly amazing catalogue or, as it puts it: "New Improved, Non-Salacious price list of merchandise calculated to appeal to the non-prurient interest." This firm claims to be the only source of supply in the world for all materials, patterns, tools, etc., for the production of stained-glass windows, lampshades and ornaments. There are many sources of supply, they say, but nowhere else are they all available under one roof. The amazing part is that the stained-glass supplies are there, all right, but so are lots of other things, such as 1894 parasol ornaments, stocks for defunct railroad companies, pre-1912 doll's eyes, reproductions of nineteenth-century medicine bottles, Victorian button starter collections, unused school inkwells, and a collection of posters chosen by the Whittemore-Durgin selection committee of prominent housewives—and all this written up with inordinate good cheer. Whittemore-Durgin is terrified of a flood of catalogue requests on postcards (the nightmare of mail-order firms; they think if you don't care enough to lick an envelope, you won't care enough to sign a check). However, the catalogue is well worth while for anyone who is not too proud to pay 50 cents for a spot of good humor and a joke or two.

TOOLS

Brookstone Company, Peterborough, N.H. 03458
Six catalogues a year, 50 cents.

"Hard to Find Tools" announces the mock old-fashioned cover of the Brookstone Company. In fact, the tools are often the usual ones, but the catalogue, which is persuasively written, does give the impression that a great deal of effort has been spent in finding the very best. For instance, they say of their stainless-steel sponge: "Cleans many times better than steel wool. Won't rust, rot, or leave splinters in hands . . . Made of one strand of 18-8 stainless steel. Slit from a roll, thus has four sharp cutting corners (ordinary sponges are merely round-edged flattened wire)." And this about "the File Cleaner That Works": "Most file cleaners can't work—the bristles are too short, too stiff to get down between the file teeth. This one works on *any* file—fine, coarse or raspe. Also cleans saw teeth clogged with sawdust, metal chips or dirt. Cleans soldering tips"—and the text goes on to describe why it works and several features to the file's credit. Tools for home repairs, woodworking and precision work are here; some of them are professional tools used by jewelers or developed for use on business machines. There are impressive garden tools including a stainless-steel set that has been chosen for display by the English Council of Industrial Design, and is sold only by Brookstone here.

Goldblatt Tool Co., 511 Osage, Kansas City, Kans. 66110
71-page catalogue, free.

Goldblatt's started as a small general store eighty-seven years ago and is now the world's biggest producer of quality "trowel trade tools." In spite of the firm's sounding so specialized, I should think that any handy person would find several useful tools to make any repairs easier that they do undertake. Besides an impressive array of machines, there are brushes and hammers, tools to lay tiles and plastic flooring, terrific-looking tape measures, knee pads, stilts to use instead of ladders or scaffolding, gadgets to prevent sticky tape from wrinkling, and some very handsome canvas tool bags and heavy leather tool pouches for between $5 and $10.

TYPEWRITERS

Tytell Typewriter Company, 116 Fulton Street, New York, N.Y. 10038

Tytell has typewriters that write in 145 languages; they have keyboards for doctors, dentists, botanists who need special symbols; they have keyboards for the disabled; and they have type styles of all kinds and sizes, and carriage widths to 30″. They have no catalogue, but can adapt typewriters to suit almost any need, so write with your request—over half of the Tytell orders come by mail from abroad.

WEAVING

Here are some of the good basic sources for both inexpensive yarn and more costly but exceptionally beautiful yarn. However, if you have the patience to wait, yarn is worth buying from abroad because you can save about a clear dollar a pound on the very good yarns, either undyed (natural) or in excellent colors.

LOOMS

Harrisville Designs, Harrisville, N.H. 03450
Brochure and swatches, 50 cents.

This is what John Colony says about his firm: "I established Harrisville Designs in 1971 as an attempt to sustain the textile heritage of a small mill town which was on the verge of collapse at the end of 1970. We operate in close conjunction with a larger effort by local people to revitalize the village of Harrisville without altering its essential character as a nineteenth century mill town . . . Our objective in Harrisville Designs is to make the highest quality yarns and supplies available to handweavers at reasonable prices."

According to a weaver and teacher I talked to, they succeed remarkably well. She says that the loom is very nice and excellent value for the money (it is a four-harness loom with a weaving width of 22″, and costs $114 as a kit and $151 assembled). She recommends the natural yarns, which are reasonably priced, and the dyed wool yarns, which are in good and vivid colors.

Robert C. Nelson, Rural Route 2, Box 540, Rands Pond Road, Newport, N.H. 03773
Leaflet, free.

Over the last five years Robert Nelson has developed three wooden waist looms, which he makes himself. They are small and cheap (between $6 and $12) and handy. You tie one end of the yarn to a table or chair, the other around your waist, and according to the width of the loom you have, you can weave cloth from 12″ to 24″ wide. Even on the 12″ loom you can weave scarves, bags, belts, ties, place mats, etc. When you finish, the whole thing is easy to fold up and put away. The loom can also be carried around, as it weighs just a few ounces.

Norwood Loom Company, Box 272, Baldwin, Mich. 49304
Leaflet, free.

Norwood looms are reputable and have been around for a while. They are made of Northern cherry, to order, and there is a waiting list of about nine months at the moment. Prices are from about $222 for a 24″ reed, four-harness loom.

The Pendleton Shop, Box 233, Sedona, Ariz. 86336
Leaflet, free.

Mary Pendleton runs the Pendleton Fabric Craft School in "the heart of the red rock country," where you can take courses for from one to six weeks in handweaving and non-loom weaving, creative stitchery, Navajo weaving and macramé. There is a bimonthly newsletter, which contains instructions and advice and also actual weaving samples (small regular designs in the issue I looked at). Weaving supplies are sold: a Navajo loom (about $23, including postage), hand-spun Navajo yarn, and folding looms made of birch hardwood that start at just over $200.

Schacht Spindle Company, 1708 Walnut Street, Boulder, Colo. 80302
Leaflet, free.

Looms and accessories: an inkle loom for about $17, a tapestry loom for about $28, and a good four-harness table loom for about $70.

School Products Co., Inc., 312 E. 23rd Street, New York, N.Y. 10010
14-page catalogue, free.

One of the largest suppliers of weaving equipment in the country, School Products sells Artcraft and Leclerc looms. Leclerc is one of the three most famous and long-established looms, but with the boom in weaving there is some question as to whether Leclerc will manage to keep up standards while producing in such increased quantities. (The other two firms have long waiting lists.)

YARN

Contessa Yarns, P.O. Box 37, Lebanon, Conn. 06249
Price list and samples, 25 cents.

Very inexpensive odd-lot yarns of all sorts are sold here. The price list and samples I saw included colored worsted, single-ply jute, 2-ply spun nylon, white or natural snowflake novelty cotton, natural silk noil yarn, white rayon novelty with nontarnishable gold metallic, and Irish imported sisal for macramé. Mailings of new stock are sent throughout the year, and customers are asked to write in with special needs.

Craft Yarns of Rhode Island, Inc., 603 Mineral Springs Avenue, Pawtucket, R.I. 02862
Price list and master style chart, $1.

A beautiful selection of higher-priced exotic yarns for weaving, macramé and needlepoint. The master style chart has samples of about twenty-five styles of yarn, and after looking at it, you can ask for charts showing the complete color range of each style at about 25 cents each. Rug-making supplies are also sold here.

The Mannings, R.D. 2, East Berlin, Pa. 17316
Price list and samples, 50 cents.

A very well-known studio that gives weaving courses, offers a consultation service to weavers, sells looms (Gallinger, Leclerc and Structo, among others) and very inexpensive yarns (about $3 per pound at this writing). They also sell spinning wheels and supplies, including wool.

Mexiskeins, P.O. Box 1624, Missoula, Mont. 59801
Price list and samples, $1.

Mexiskeins belongs to a Cornell-trained architect who designed and built a factory in Mexico that produces rugs and hand-spun Mexican wool in three fairly heavy weights, all of a special dense and felted character. The heaviest weight consists of a single strand about the thickness of a little finger. There are eighty vivid colors, hand-washed and dyed with European dyes. Prices about $5 to $6.50 a pound.

Paula Simmons, Box 12, Suquamish, Wash. 98392
Price list sent on receipt of stamped, self-addressed envelope.
Small sample cards of hand-spun yarn in solid colors, 25 cents.
Longer card of tweeds, irregulars with variegated shading, 50 cents.

Paula Simmons and her husband spin yarn to order. The customer chooses the yarn size, the texture and the color shade (though all the yarns are natural colors) in solid shades, heathers or tweeds. The yarn costs 92 cents an ounce. The Simmons' do all their own wool processing—sheep raising, shearing, wool washing and carding, spinning and weaving, and hire no help, so they say they are sometimes slow on sending out sample cards. They also weave blankets to order in all sizes.

Tahki Imports, 336 West End Avenue, New York, N.Y. 10023
Sample card, 75 cents.

Very beautiful imported yarns to weave, knot, knit or hook. Donegal tweeds from Ireland, hand-spun sheep's wool and goat's hair from Greece.

WINE MAKING

Presque Isle Wine Making Cellars, 9440 Buffalo Road, Northeast, Pa. 16428
40-page catalogue, free.

Making wine at home is easier than you may think. You don't have to wait for a grape harvest, and you don't even need fresh fruit, as firms that sell wine-making supplies all sell canned fruit concentrates instead. And they all sell plenty of instruction books.

I checked the prices at several places and found that they are roughly the same—most firms charge a little more than the average on some things and a little less on others.

Presque Isle Wine Making Cellars has a good reputation and puts out a small, businesslike catalogue, but is the only firm that does not sell kits for beginners. They think that part of the pleasure of wine making is in using your wits to determine what is and is not needed. Instead of kits they offer the beginners advice and information.

Semplex of U.S.A., Box 12276, Minneapolis, Minn. 55412
22-page catalogue, free.

Semplex of U.S.A. is the agent for a very reputable English firm, and the catalogue is a good basic listing of

30 • *Wine Art* "Connoisseurs Choice"—everything you need to make seventy-five bottles (15 gallons) of either Zinfandel, Ruby Cabernet or French Red Beaujolais. Kits are available at prices from $8.95 to $250. For permission to make up to 200 gallons a year, write to your regional office of U.S. Bureau of Alcohol, Tobacco and Firearms, for Form 1541.

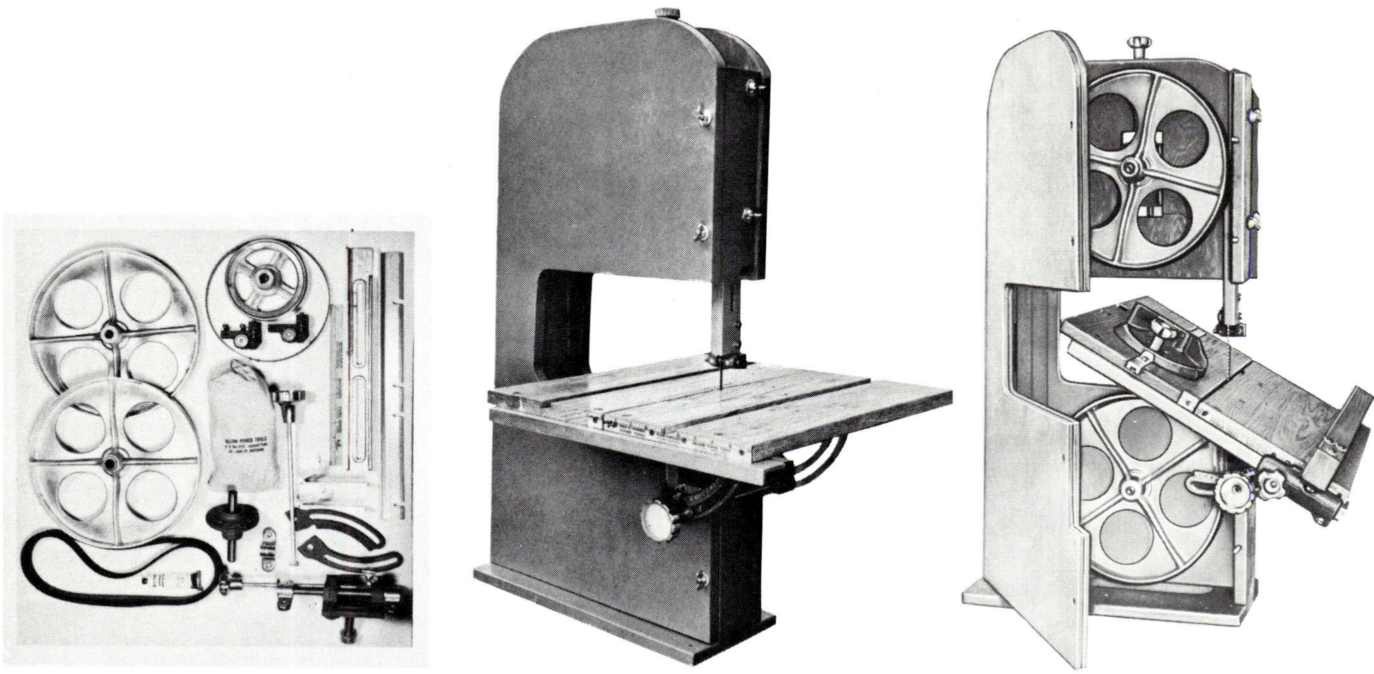

31 • *Gilliom* 12″ band saw can cut wood up to 6″ deep, has a table that can tilt up to 45 degrees. Plans only for making the saw, $2. All metal parts and plans (but not the materials needed for the wood frame) are for sale at $28.99.

32 • *Gilliom* 6″ belt sander with 108″ of flat sanding area. Plans only for making the sander, $2. All metal parts and plans (but not the materials needed for the wood frame) are for sale at $24.99.

wine-making supplies, American and English books about wine making, and a few promising recipes.

Vino Corp., Box 7498, Rochester, N.Y. 14615
64-page catalogue, $1; refundable.

The "Encyclopedia of Wine Making Equipment," Vino's catalogue, is the best-organized of the catalogues and has a good selection, but prices are slightly higher.

Wine Art, Inc., 4324 Geary Boulevard, San Francisco, Calif. 94118
26-page color catalogue, free.

A big, glossy and easy-to-read catalogue filled with beautiful color photographs and descriptions and explanations of the equipment. The listings are numerous, from necessities to accessories, so this is probably the best firm for beginners. For the advanced amateur there are even temperature-controlled wine vaults ranging from $995 to $2,995.

WOODWORKING

American Machine Tool Co., Inc., Fourth and Spring Street, Royersford, Pa. 19468
Leaflet, free.

The American Machine Tool Company manufactures bench power tools for home workshop enthusiasts who want something more than the portable power tools that people use for "fix-up" jobs around the house, yet not as expensive as the bigger, fancier more nearly automatic tools that some home workshop enthusiasts buy. There is a small market for simpler, less expensive tools, and A.M.T. reaches it by mail order and says that by eliminating "expensive gingerbread," they keep most of their prices low. Fully assembled power saws cost $20 and $30, a belt sander $20, and a 22″ joiner-planer $30, all without motors. A 1-horsepower motor costs $20, and a 1½-horsepower $30.

Albert Constantine and Son, Inc., 2050 Eastchester Road, Bronx, N.Y. 10461
96-page catalogue, some color, 50 cents. December.

Constantine's was founded in 1812 by a neighbor of Duncan Phyfe's, Thomas Constantine, an authority on mahogany who was engaged by the Vice-President to make mahogany desks and chairs for the Senate. They now sell lumber, fine woods and veneers, mainly by mail, and have an astonishing range of woods, many that I had never even heard of. Twenty-six veneers are illustrated in color, and more veneers and 240 sizes and kinds of cabinet lumber are listed. If you want to look at new woods, for about $5 you can get a pack of fifty wood samples. Then, besides wood, they have other things that are needed for specific projects: moldings for framing pictures, hardware such as handles and hinges for furniture, lamp parts, shelf brackets, plenty of different wood finishes and tools. The book ends with 101 suggestions for "things to do in shop and home," and tells you where in the catalogue you'll find the appropriate supplies.

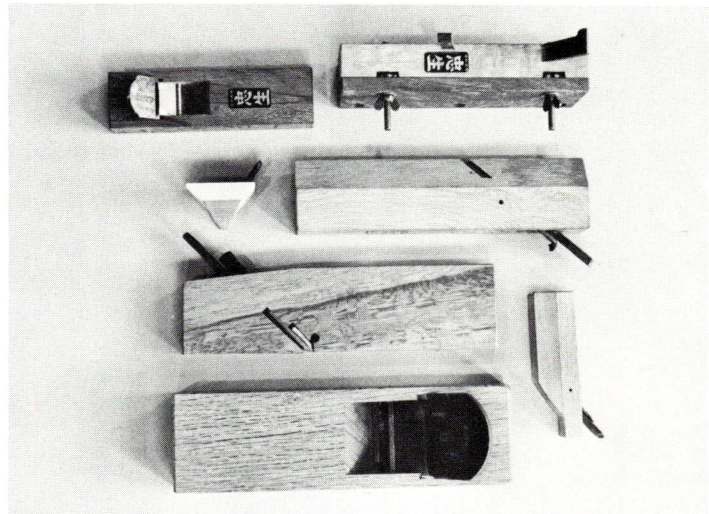

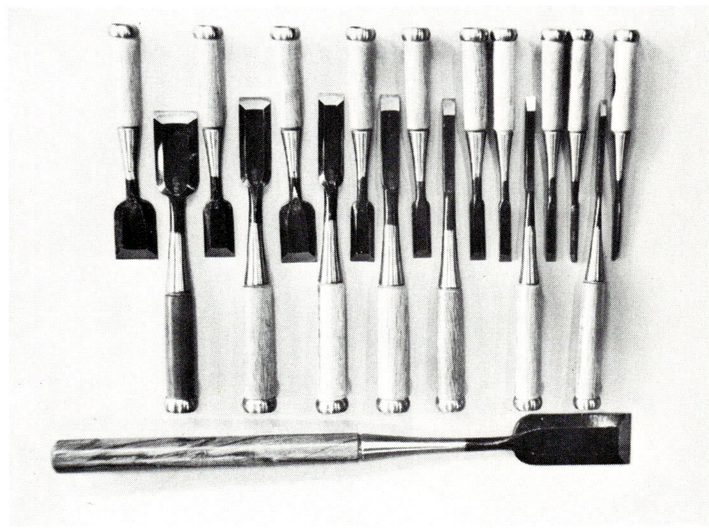

33 • *The Japan Woodworker* Chisels, files, saws and planes on sale for between $4 and $14.

Craftplans, 8011 Lewis Road, Minneapolis, Minn. 55427
23-page brochure, 25 cents.

Things to make and do for—yes, fun and profit. Here you can get the plans to make 3 different kinds of spinning wheels, 6 desks, 13 workbenches, 16 pieces of lawn furniture, 27 birdhouses, 32 home bars or 129 jigsaw puzzles. Plans cost under $2 each, and some look very useful.

Craft Products Co., Route 64 at Route 83, Elmhurst, Ill. 60126
Home Ideas book, 50 cents.
Clocks and clockwork, 25 cents.

Craft patterns were first published in the Chicago *Sunday Tribune* in 1940 and are now widely syndicated in America and several other countries. This 100-page catalogue shows an extraordinary variety of patterns for making things in wood-"helpful guides for the amateur and time-savers for the experienced woodworker," as the catalogue says and all the patterns are 65 cents each, whether they are for a birdhouse or a garage. The furniture patterns are mostly for rather dull, although functional furniture, but some of the plans for home improvements look very worthwhile: kitchen cabinets with excellent storage arrangements, built-in beds and desks for children's rooms, tool cabinets and benches for the workshop, lots of outdoor furniture, barbecues, planters, birdhouses and tempting play equipment and playhouses for children. There are also really mammoth projects like trailers and home extensions.

Craftsman Wood Service Co., 2729 S. Mary Street, Chicago, Ill. 60608
144-page brochure, some color, 50 cents.

A handy and clear brochure is published by this firm, which stocks woodworking tools and supplies and hard-to-find lumber. Thirty-two of the best-known rare and fancy woods are shown in color, as well as inlays, overlays and picture-frame moldings and inlaid picture kits. In black-and-white there are all sorts of metal accessories: Dremel and other tools, guitar and dulcimer kits for about $35. A book list with full descriptions of the volumes includes subjects like upholstery, refinishing furniture, house wiring, built-in furniture and how to build cabinets for the modern kitchen.

Gilliom Manufacturing Co., 1109 N. Second Street, St. Charles, Mo. 63301
Brochure, 25 cents.

Started in a spare bedroom, and still a small business, says the owner, Gilliom's makes and sells good kits for amateur woodworkers with plans to build woodworking machines. The firm supplies the metal parts and plans, the customer uses his own wood. A 12″ band saw costs about $31, and 8″ tilt table bench saw about $21, a belt sander about $27. Other kits for woodworking machines are available too, and if you like, you can get the metal parts and the plans separately. A kit for a children's motor wagon, and a mini-bike made from an old 26″ bicycle frame are also on sale.

The Japan Woodworker, 1701 Grove Street, Berkeley, Calif. 94709
8-page catalogue, 25 cents.

Ron Herman was in Japan buying woodworking tools for his partner when he decided to start importing tools from Kansai in central Japan, where woodworking tools have been made for over five hundred years. The highest-grade steel is used in these tools, and it has an extremely hard edge that stays sharp longer, although it is brittle and needs more care than the lower-quality steel usually used in woodworking tools. Saws cost about $7 to $10, planes about $7 to $14, chisels about $4 to $10.

Minnesota Woodworkers Supply Company, 925 Winnetka Avenue No., Minneapolis, Minn. 55427
104-page catalogue, 50 cents.

This firm carries "creative materials for the imaginative craftsman"—everything you need for making or repairing furniture, cabinets, lamps and picture frames. There is an excellent hardware section, which includes such things as bedrail fasteners, a variety of hinges, catches and handles. They also have a good selection of veneers and inlays, and a full line of finishing materials: stains, varnishes, lacquers and a gold-leafing kit. For people who want to know more about a variety of these crafts and skills, there is a large selection of "how to" books.

14
HOUSE

BEDSPREADS

Cabin Creek Quilts, P.O. Box 295, Eskdale, W. Va. 25075
Leaflet, some color, 50 cents.

This organization was started in 1970 by a VISTA volunteer with five women in Cabin Creek, a thirty-mile hollow in the mountains of West Virginia, and now has over a hundred quilters all over the state. Eight different-patterned quilts in four sizes each are made at prices from $50 to $145 for single size, and from $125 to $265 for king size. Baby quilts start at $20, pillows at $8, and there are also children's vests, place mats, tablecloths, aprons, shoulder bags, and wall hangings for children's rooms, all in patchwork and just a few cloth dolls and puppets.

Laura Copenhaver Industries, Inc., Box 149, Rosemont, Va. 24354
24-page brochure, 35 cents.

Laura Copenhaver, a teacher and writer, started this enterprise during the Depression to help mountain families. Her daughter is now the president, and the firm specializes in reproducing old American quilts, coverlets, canopies and curtains. Three flowered quilt patterns start at $130 for twin-bed size and go up to $250 for king-size. The coverlets, which are based on the old handwoven coverlets but are not woven on handlooms, have the intricate, regular designs in two colors, and start at $37 for twin size in cotton and $49 for twin size in wool. The curtains are made in several styles with hand-tied fringes, but always in natural or white cotton. Four samples of curtain fabric are sent with the brochure.

The Freedom Quilting Bee, Route 1, Box 72, Alberta, Ala. 36720
Color leaflet, free.

This is what the manager, Estelle Witherspoon, says about this co-operative composed of black women: "The Quilting Bee started in 1965, immediately after the Selma Freedom marches. A civil rights worker saw beautiful quilts on the lines in rural areas and suggested that the people sew quilts for marketing. A small business was started, it grew, a larger sewing center was built. Presently we have about twenty women working daily. We do a mail-order business and also sell quilts through a representative in New York. Our sewing ladies have used their salary (small) to improve their homes and improve the family's standard of living . . . the Bee has been the means of much improvement in this poverty area of Alabama. We are still poor people."

The quilts are made in five designs that come from a 140-year tradition in Alabama's Black Belt area. They are made in all basic colors and you can choose the main color you'd like. Prices are on the low side, starting at $65 for a single, $80 for double and $110 for king-size. Unfortunately, the color photographs on the leaflet are a bit drab and don't quite do justice to the colors, I am told by someone who has seen the quilts.

Virginia Goodwin, P.O. Box 3603, Charlotte, N.C. 28203
Leaflet, 25 cents.

Virginia Goodwin says that the Goodwin family have been weavers since 1812, first in England and then in America. On antique looms they make what they think are the only handloomed patterns in coverlets woven without a seam. The creamy white "Honeycomb" spread design is taken from an 1849 book of weaving instructions, costs $55 for twin-bed size, and is available in several solid colors. Other designs, "Morning Star" and "The Whig Rose" (first woven in Tennessee to comemmorate the formation of the Whig party under Andrew Jackson), are woven in color on white, and start at $58 for twin-bed size. A tablecloth, an afghan, and hand-knotted fishnet canopies are made.

Greek Island Ltd., 215 E. 49th Street, New York, N.Y. 10017
24-page catalogue, free.

This shop, which imports clothes and things for the house, shows a few Greek-made bedspreads in the catalogue: a restful beige-and-white seersuckery striped peasant coverlet costs $24.50 in twin-bed size, and two heavy, reversible wool and cotton spreads elaborately patterned in a deep color on white cost $50 each in twin-size.

The Rainbow, 9640 Santa Monica Boulevard, Beverly Hills, Calif. 90210
68-page catalogue, free, but a 50-cent contribution would be welcome.

Everyone who works for the Rainbow is a volunteer, and all profits from this shop go toward treatment of children with cancer (see main listing under Toys). Here you can buy batik crib coverlets for $30 and pillows for $8, patchwork baby quilts in Early American folk-art designs, handmade pillows for between $6 and $16, and beautiful quilts handmade by Amish women in Pennsylvania or by Sarah Powell (fifty times a Blue Ribbon winner at the State Fair in California). Quilts can be made in any style, traditional or contemporary, in any size and any color. Prices start at about $75 for a simple twin-size and go up to about $350 for the most complicated king-size.

EIDERDOWNS

Bedding Down Supply, P.O. Box 29, Cambridgeport, Vt. 05141
Leaflet, 25 cents.

Several people have mentioned how glad they were to discover the European eiderdowns listed in *The Catalogue of Catalogues;* here is a small and very appealing firm that makes similar eiderdowns in America. Richard Lesnick made the first "warmer," as he calls them, for a wedding present; as usual with these eiderdowns, everyone who saw it wanted one too and a business was started. The warmers, which are full of down, can be used on top of sheets, or if you make a washable cover for them out of sheets, or seersucker, they can be used instead of sheets and blankets so you don't have to make the bed. They are especially useful with beds that are hard to make, such as bunks.

Richard Lesnick writes: "The appeal of our warmers (both to us and our customers) is that they are quality products (heirlooms). Each warmer is individually made by one person from start to finish. Our fabrics are the finest quality natural fibers available and we use nothing but prime down and lots of it. Every seam is double-stitched and hemmed with a French seam. Above all, we are making products for other people as if we were making them for ourselves—with joy!"

The warmers can be made with no stitching in the center or with lengthwise seams to divide the down into sections (European eiderdowns are divided in this way and I believe it prevents the down from bunching up on one side). They cost from $50 for single-bed size to $100 for king-size, and the covers, in handsome, strongly colored fabrics, cost from $20 up.

Scanda Duo, Inc., 3131 Western Avenue, Seattle, Wash. 98121
Leaflets, free.

Scanda Duo is a larger firm which sells more professionally made eiderdown/comforters, made in Seattle and their leaflets not only have grateful quotes from satisfied customers ("I never realized how I *hated* bedmaking until you came along") who use them at home to eliminate bedmaking, but also recommend them for icy trailers. The comforters come in five sizes including bunk-size, and prices vary between about $90 and $200 for down (rather more than comforters bought direct from Europe) and between $60 and $120 for comforters filled with Fortrel Poly. Scanda Duo makes covers from various brightly colored famous-brand sheets, and also sells bottom sheets, pillowcases and often towels to match (though they do not, unfortunately, sell fitted bunk-size sheets). Best of all, they allow you to try a comforter for thirty days. Since sleeping under one, especially if you use it instead of blankets and regular sheets, may not appeal to people who like to be tightly tucked in or who kick and turn a lot in their sleep, the try-out is especially useful and something you can't do if you buy from Europe.

For kits to make your own comforters, see Frostline in the Sports Equipment and Clothes section.

FLATWARE

Julius Goodman and Son, 113 Madison Avenue, Memphis, Tenn. 38101
Price lists, free.

This unusual firm has been in the same family since it was established in 1862. They stock antique and odd holloware, antique jewelry and sterling-silver flatware. The unusual part is that they carry over a thousand flat-silver patterns, including many obsolete and inactive designs which can't be found anywhere else, and which they have gathered over the past thirty years from estates, individuals and other jewelers. People from all over the country write in with rubbings or drawings of silver that they are trying to match, or else, with oddities they are looking for. (Have you ever wanted a silver-lined ostrich-egg tobacco jar, or silver ear trumpet?)

Taylor and Ng, 651 Howard Street, San Francisco, Calif. 94105
22-page brochure, 25 cents.

This shop sells kitchen utensils and decorative objects for the house, and shows, in the brochure, three very simple, graceful flatware sets with wooden handles.

1

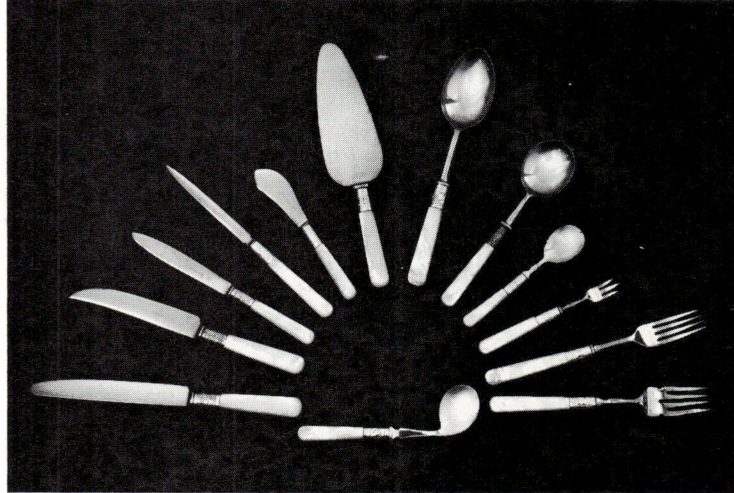

2

1 • *Taylor and Ng* Hand-turned teak plates, stain-resistant and washable. 11½" dinner plate, $4.50; 8" salad plate, $3.50. "Habitat" flatware inspired by traditional Japanese cutlery; the handles are made of palownia wood bonded to forged stainless steel and finished with a brass bolster. Can be washed in a dishwasher. Five-piece place setting, $6.25.

2 • *Carl Forslund* (see Reproduction Furniture in this section) Pearl-handled serving pieces at prices between $8 and $24. Matching pearl-handled flatware is also sold.
photo Woods Advertising Photography

3

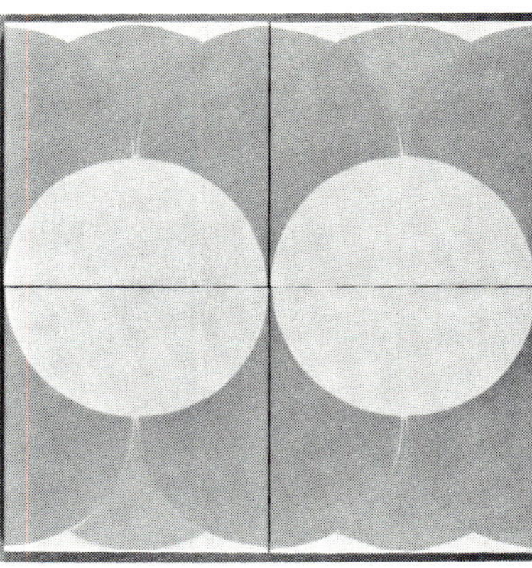
4

5

6

3 • *Agency Tile* 8″ square tile in blue and white, $6.80 per square foot.

4 • *Agency Tile* 8″ square tile in yellow and white, $5.15 per square foot.

5 • *Country Floors* "Lattice and Star" relief wall tile in gold, green and white, $7.23 per square foot; in gold, blue and white, $6.07.

6 • *Country Floors* "Igreija" wall tile in pink and yellow, $6.38 per square foot; in green and yellow, $6.38 per square foot; in blue and yellow, $5.19 per square foot.

Prices are $6.25 to $8.75 per five-piece place setting. Wooden, stoneware and china plates are also shown.

For more flatware, see Reproduction Furniture (below) and the General section.

FLOORS

TILE

Agency Tile, Inc., 979 Third Avenue, New York, N.Y. 10022
Color brochure, 50 cents.

This firm, which imports ceramic tiles from Italy, Brazil, Spain and Japan, has traditional tiles, nondescript tiles with speckles or flowers, and modern tiles with strong geometric designs based on circles, squares.

Country Floors, Inc., 300 E. 61st Street, New York, N.Y. 10021
20-page color catalogue, 50 cents.

A brilliantly colored catalogue shows a gorgeous and varied collection of American and imported tiles. As the owner says, tiles don't represent the most ideal mail-order business but in most parts of the United States there is no other way. Customers who can't get to the shop buy a catalogue, then a sample or two, and finally send in a complete order.

There are highly patterned traditional tiles from Holland, Italy, Spain and Portugal, gorgeous orangy terra cotta and rich solid colors from France, but my own favorites are "rugged glazed brick" floor tiles from Ohio, in various shades of blue, brown and white. Prices run from $2 to $17 per square foot, but most of the tiles cost around $4 or $5 per square foot. You can also get hand-painted tile name plates made to order, for $50, and buy large sculptured terra-cotta pots embellished with Greek figures for from $20 to $190.

Elon Inc., 964 Third Avenue, New York, N.Y. 10022
Color brochure, free.

A beautifully designed leaflet displays the handmade Mexican tiles in modern and traditional designs that Elon has been importing for ten years. The tiles are uneven and look much more handmade than any of the other tiles in this section. There are simple designs, patterns with flowers or fruit, and some really good solid colors. Two of my friends have Elon's very large unglazed terra-cotta tiles in their kitchens, varnished—Elon has worked out how to do this, and it brings out the color magnificently.

Tiles cost about $3.25 to $10 per square foot, and can be used for tables, benches and planters as well as for floors. Samples cost $1 for the first and 50 cents for subsequent specimens. Basins, bath accessories, switch plates and knobs are also sold.

WOOD

Designed Wood Flooring Center, Inc., 137 E. 57th Street, New York, N.Y. 10022
Leaflet, 50 cents.

This firm makes and fits wood flooring in teak and other woods in a variety of designs, but they also sell prefinished parquet floors which they claim any handy person can install in a day and walk on within twenty-four hours. Karpawood, oak, teak and acrylic impregnated teak for "heavy-traffic areas" are sold at around 65 cents to $1.50 a square foot. Matching miscellaneous wood such as baseboard molding and threshold strip is sold, and so is double-faced tape for temporary installation, mastic for permanent installation and wax. Complete installation instructions come with each order.

7

FURNITURE

I am disappointed at the modern furniture to be found in stores and catalogues in America. The most interesting furniture is terribly expensive and often only available through decorators, or is imported. Apart from H.U.D.D.L.E., I couldn't find a single small firm producing flexible, inexpensive, attractive furniture, although that kind of firm is all over the place in Europe. Much of the furniture is this section is imported.

8

MODERN AND MISCELLANEOUS FURNITURE

J. & D. Brauner, Inc., 298 Bowery, New York, N.Y. 10012 and 1331 S. Michigan Avenue. Chicago, Ill. 60605
50-page brochure, $1.

Butcher block in all shapes and sizes is listed, as well as cutting boards and lazy Susans, shelves, storage cabinets, wheeled serving work carts and about thirty tables that nod at different styles. There is a French baker's table with a fantasy of wrought iron for the legs, about $225; a Provincial dining table with turned legs, about $144 and up; heavy medieval trestle tables at about $224 and up; and workmanlike tops on sawhorses for about $170 and up. Expanding tables, small nesting tables and coffee tables are also for sale, and there are a few newly added plain oak tables. Butcherblock tops for kitchen counters can be made to order with cutouts for sink and cooking top; minimum length, 3 feet.

Butcher Block and More, 1600 So. Clinton Street, Chicago, Ill. 60616
44-page catalogue, 50 cents.

Butcher Block and More sells lots of tables and side chairs. Many of the tables are made of butcher block (and they have trolleys, and chopping boards of butcher block, too). And glass, oak, slate laminate tops can be cut to any size, and you can choose out of a range of legs and pedestals. The side chairs are modern—bentwood, the Bauhaus, and various folding chairs—and shelves of oak or walnut veneer are also available.

7 • *J. & D. Brauner* Maple butcherblock sofa with loose back and seat pillows stuffed with polyurethane foam and covered in blue denim. 76″ long. $590.

8 • *J. & D. Brauner* French baker's cart, 30″ high, with Shepherd casters that lock. Top is 42″ by 24″. $225. A table is available (at the same price) that is exactly the same but without casters.

The Cabinet Shop, 1583 First Avenue, New York, N.Y. 10028
Leaflet, free.

This firm manufactures and sells unpainted furniture, and their leaflet shows just three perfectly simple and rather attractive beds at low prices: a platform bed in four widths up to 39″, with three drawers underneath, costs $85; a trundle bed costs $95; and a bunk bed with three drawers under the bottom bed comes in three widths, can be converted to two single beds and costs $120. All of them are assembled and ready to paint or varnish.

Children's Workbench, 470 Park Avenue South, New York, N.Y. 10016
40-page catalogue, $1.

Smart furniture for children or anyone with a taste for light wood and bright colors. Most of the furniture is imported and expensive, but at least it won't have to be changed when the children get too old to like babyish things. Most things are made to be used in several ways: bunks can be pulled apart and used as two single beds; other beds have trundle beds underneath them; most of the desks are made from sets of drawers with boards across them; and wall systems are made up from shelves that can be arranged in all sorts of ways.

Exclusively for children are a couple of cribs, one of which handily converts to a settee between or after babies; rollaway play carts; little tables and chairs; a birch and white-painted Finnish highchair for about $50; and very, very useful for anyone who hopes to persuade her children to hang up their coats—a small orange-painted coat tree, about $22.

Country Workshop, 95 Rome Street, Newark, N.J. 07105
16-page catalogue, 25 cents.

Country Workshop has been making modern ready-to-paint furniture and selling it by mail since 1950. The designs, although more graceful than much unfinished furniture, are unadventurous. You can get most basic pieces to furnish an apartment in either white poplar or black walnut. Each piece comes in an enormous number of sizes, which can be combined in various ways. There are twenty sizes in the bookcase, fifty sizes in the chests, some with various combinations of shallow drawers. There are also cabinets which can be fitted with sliding or hinged doors in poplar, walnut, masonite or glass; desks, vanity units, corner desks, file cabinets, hanging desks and bookcase shelves made from standards and planks to cover a wall (and with neat book ends, too); dining tables (any size made on request); parson's tables; beds and headboards. A 36″-wide three-drawer chest of drawers costs $54 in poplar and $103 in walnut. A 30″-wide storage bed with three drawers underneath costs $140 without the mattress.

Deutsch, Inc., 196 Lexington Avenue, New York, N.Y. 10016
64-page catalogue, $2.

This firm imports a big selection of sophisticated but expensive rattan furniture. There are beds, sofas, chests of drawers, tables, swings, bar carts and mirror frames in enough different styles to please people who want sparse, modern shapes, as well as those who want curly Victorian ones. This is the place for a canopy bed, a rickshaw or a gazebo.

Door Store of Washington, D.C., 3140 M Street, N.W., Washington, D.C. 20007
56-page catalogue, $1.

A big catalogue of imported furniture that is mainly modern but starts with twenty chairs made in Italy and Spain in the styles of Louis XV, Louis XVI, Chippendale, Chinese Chippendale, "Regence," "Bamboo Ballroom" (with gold finish), French Country and assorted styles such as "Country Café" and "Circa 1800"; the chairs are beech or walnut finish and cost between $35 and $100. After the traditional reproductions come about thirty bentwood pieces, very elaborate rockers, an "Edwardian Arm Chair" and the simple Bauhaus chairs. Most prices are between $20 and $40, but the rockers are around $100. After the bentwood come painted and teak dining chairs, formica parson's tables, a few folding tables, and table tops in butcher block or heavy plate glass, and an inordinate amount of pedestals and bases in chrome, plexiglass, brightly colored steel tubes or wrought iron; table legs in wood or chrome; standard shelf systems; walnut desks, trundle beds; some inexpensive white or red painted chests of drawers from Poland; four bunk beds; and tables and chairs and rollaway playcarts for children.

Fran's Basket House, 89 W. Main Street, Rockaway, N.J. 07866
32-page catalogue, 25 cents.

A large collection of inexpensive rattan and willow furniture, and objects for the house from simple wicker planters, lampshades and magazine racks to Victorian settees and headboards. Umbrella stands, small tables, bookshelves, laundry hampers, towel holders, chests, mirrors, children's chairs and rocking chairs—practically everything seems to be available in rattan or wicker.

Hammock Master, 325 Seventh Avenue, New York, N.Y. 10001
Color leaflet, free.

Sandford Cohen decided to import hammocks while living in Yucatán, where children are put in hammocks to keep them out of the way, adults sleep in hammocks and women give birth in hammocks. He is very keen about them and recommends them as sofas and extra beds. The hammocks are woven by hand of fine cotton and come multicolored or in solid colors. Prices run from $15 for a small hammock to $60 for a double hammock, and you can get mosquito netting for them too.

House of Hammocks, Box 263, Cotuit, Mass. 02635
Leaflet, free.

Here you can buy lovely Brazilian hammocks, 5′ wide and 8′ long. In Brazil they are used to sleep in, and a Brazilian friend of mine has some instead of chairs. They come in solid colors, in white or in plaids, with white fringes. Prices run from $10 for a small fringeless one to $37 for one with almost 1,400 bobbles tied into the fringes.

H.U.D.D.L.E., Inc., 10918 Kincross Avenue, Los Angeles, Calif. 90024
Leaflet, $1.

By far the most interesting of the modern furniture shops, H.U.D.D.L.E. was started by an urban designer and teacher who wanted to re-think furniture for city living. Jim and Penny Hull were anxious to avoid waste

9 10 11 12 13 14

9 • *The Country Workshop* Campaign chests are available in many different sizes at prices from $49 for poplar and $93 for walnut, plus $8 extra per drawer.

10 • *Door Store of Washington, D.C.* "Youth" chair for a child to sit at table with everyone else. Red, yellow, blue or white. $27.

11 • *Door Store of Washington, D.C.* Hand-caned bentwood swivel chair in walnut, natural or black. $79.

12 • *Door Store of Washington, D.C.* "Amerika" table folds up to 6″ and extends to 110″ to seat twelve. Walnut $99, teak $119, rosewood $129.

13 • *Door Store of Washington, D.C.* "The Candy Apple" chair with cane seat and a glossy finish over transparent stain. Red, blue, green, yellow, walnut or flat black or white. $40.

14 • *Children's Workbench* Desk with a top that adjusts in height from 21″ to 28″. $119.50. The swivel chair has an adjustable seat and back. In yellow, red, blue, green, white or black. $45.

15 • *Hammock Master* Double hammock in various multi-color combinations, with hooks and rope. $60.

of material and human talent, and they also wanted to keep prices of furniture down—the answer they came up with was to use recycled materials already produced by industry. The major component of most of their furniture is a highly developed and strong hardboard made from fiber by-products of the lumber industry, reconstituted newspapers and old cardboard boxes. Certain chairs have seat cushions made from finger foam, which was developed as packing material for electronic equipment in the aerospace industry, and other chairs include plain old tire inner tubes. The Hulls also think that people should take part as much as possible in the creation of their own living environment, so they sell plain tubes and foam for people who want to make their own furniture, as well as the finished furniture both painted and unpainted.

The furniture that results from all this is much cheaper than most, much more colorful and much more imaginative. The furniture can come in primary colors and white with parts covered in silvery mylar, or of course it can be painted in any exotic color combination. At the moment the furniture available includes several chairs and sofas that consist of a swoop of hardboard on circles of hardboard, on which you can put various cushioning materials, plain foam rubber, finger foam or cylinder cushions. A three-seat couch comes at various prices, from $54 for an unpainted base with foam rubber to $219 for a painted base with cylinder cushions. Round-end or dining tables, tubular bookcases, plant stands of various heights, children's tables and chairs are all for sale at very low prices, and for a little more there is a tunnel-like bed for a child that is meant to be played on as well—it costs around $100 unpainted and over $200 covered in mylar.

Leathercrafter, 303 E. 51st Street, New York, N.Y. 10022
32-page leather-chair brochure and 24-page handbag and luggage brochure, 50 cents for both.

About thirty leather chairs are shown in this little brochure. Almost all the designs are based on well-known shapes—the director chair, the butterfly chair, the officer's chair, many of them for between $40 and $100. Others are outright copies of the classic modern chairs by famous designers, often at less than half the price of the originals. A couple of chairs for children are shown, and also chair covers, rugs and pillows in steerhide. Pillows start at $15 for a 12″ by 12″ square, and go on to $18 for a 14″ round one.

The Monroe Company, Colfax, Iowa 50054
32-page catalogue, free.

The Monroe Company manufactures folding tables, benches, chairs and coat racks which it sells mainly to schools, clubs and convention centers, but also to party givers. Chairs start at about $4, and tables are from about $15 for a card table to about $60 for a large semicircular desk for several people. A clear catalogue gives full construction details.

Murphy Door Bed Company, Inc., 40 E. 34th Street, New York, N.Y. 10016
Leaflet, free.

The Murphy Door Bed Company is alive and well and still selling Murphy beds by mail. Their beds, which space-savingly fold up flat against the wall with the bed made up, cost from $85 to $154 without mattress, and any mattress can be used. Onto that price you

16

18

20

17

19

16 • *H.U.D.D.L.E.* "Toobs" children's bunk bed at $299 finished with a vinyl covering in red, yellow or blue with white vinyl edging, end supports and interiors painted in white lacquer; unfinished (in natural fiber color), $199. Table and stool set in red, blue or yellow lacquer with a white base on the table: table, $30 ($19 unfinished); stool, $10 ($7 unfinished).

17 • *H.U.D.D.L.E.* Lounge chair: base unpainted, $19; painted, $31; unpainted with foam, $24; painted with foam, $61. Unpainted with cylinder cushion (as in photograph), $69; painted with cylinder cushion, $81.

18 • *H.U.D.D.L.E.* Chrome mylar plant stands: 6″ high, $10; 20″ high, $16; 33″ high, $20; 48″ high, $25.

19 • *Leathercrafter* "The Ambassador" leather-covered Dacron-and-foam mattress pad on buckled leather straps and a polished chrome frame. Black, natural, saddle-tan, gold or tortoise-brown, $450. Matching ottoman, $195.

20 • *Storehouse* Clock with white hands on 13″-diameter black face and white metal case. It operates on one standard "C" flashlight battery. $35.

21

22

23

24

25

26

21 • *Berea College Student Craft Industries* Welsh dresser with open top. 45″ wide, 20″ deep, 72″ high in cherry, walnut or mahogany. (Due to shortage of 4/4 wide walnut and cherry, price quoted at time of purchase only.)

22 • *Cohasset Colonials by Hagerty* Kit to make this reproduction of a chest of drawers (c. 1740) in the Old Ordinary of the Hingham Historical Society, at Hingham, Mass. 34¾″ high, 38″ long, 18½″ wide. $105.95.

23 • *Berea College Student Craft Industries* Hired man's bedside table, 16″ long, 20″ wide, 28″ high, 5″ drawer depth. Cherry or mahogany, $99.50; walnut, $115.

24 • *Berea Student Craft Industries* Butler's desk-chest, 42″ high, 42″ long, 20″ deep, 16½″ by 38″ writing space. Cherry, walnut or mahogany.

25 • *Cohasset Colonials by Hagerty* Kit to make this copy of a Shaker meeting-house table with a ¾″ pine top. 82″ long, 30″ wide, 30″ high; seats eight. $84.95.

26 • *Cohasset Colonials by Hagerty* Kit to make this reproduction of an early-eighteenth century water bench in the Samuel Lincoln house in Hingham, Mass., in clear pumpkin pine, 49″ high, 40″ long. $99.95.

must add transportation from New Jersey, installation (about $16 in New York City and Bergen County, New Jersey), and the price of building a discreet closet and shelves outside, if you want them, to disguise the bed.

Ortho-Comfort Stores, Town and Country Shopping Resort, 2051 East Camelback Road, Phoenix, Ariz. 85016
Leaflets, free.

"Get More Enjoyment Out of Life—Visit Us Today," says the Ortho-Comfort letterhead. "We offer a complete range of products to make you feel better every day of your life." Here you can find back supports, massage pillows with heat, roller-massage chairs ($500 and up), turbo-jet whirlpool baths, saunas and steam baths, and adjustable beds from hand-crank models at about $300 to king-size deluxe at $1,000. "Flat beds are for flat bodies," says Ortho-Comfort.

Scan Co-op Contemporary Furnishings, Inc., 11310 Frederick Avenue, Beltsville, Md. 20705
Catalogue, $1.
Upholstery swatches, $5; refundable.

Scan was recommended to me by a friend who bought a leather couch there several years ago and said that Scan's prices were so much lower than other stores' that it made you mad (at the other stores). I haven't been able to compare prices because I haven't seen the same pieces elsewhere, but Scan's are certainly moderate. Anyway, this firm, which says it was one of the first to import good Scandinavian furniture at reasonable prices, is now the largest retailer of such furniture in the United States. The catalogue that I looked at had far more Scandinavian furniture than any shop I know of in New York, and any Scan pieces that are on sale in other American firms are very likely available only through decorators. Designs are mainly what we think of as contemporary Scandinavian, in teak, rosewood or walnut, but there are also still newer chrome and painted wood pieces. Absolutely everything is covered—sofas, chairs, wall systems, dining room and coffee tables, trolleys and buffets, beds, chests, furniture for children, brilliantly colored shaggy rya rugs, and modern lamps, so this is an excellent catalogue for people looking for Scandinavian furniture.

Strawberry Bank Craftsmen Inc., Box 475, Little Compton, R.I. 02837
Leaflet, free.

Nice fat free-standing "fire pots" (fireplaces) were designed on a potter's wheel and are now cast by hand in silicon carbide. Good substitutes for parlor stoves, fire pots don't get blistering hot and are therefore useful if children are around. They also have a very simple, natural look about them, and come glazed in slate-gray, woodland-brown or smoke-white. You can choose between three models at $290 to $458 in price.

Storehouse, Inc., 3870 Green Industrial Way, Chamblee, Ga. 30341
72-page catalogue. $1.

Robert Currey opened the first Storehouse in Atlanta in October 1969; since then he has opened six more Storehouses and is about to open more. He stores stock imported furniture as well as crafts from Tennessee, North Carolina and Virginia. The first Storehouse catalogue is very much like the Door Store of Washington catalogue—it has reproduction chairs, bentwood, folding chairs like the director's chair, etc., as well as chests and table tops and bases. However, they do differ in having more furniture for children and also several tables and chairs that have a solid country look; a series of wooden chairs with raffia seats is particularly nice. The back of the catalogue shows some lovely country crafts: fireplace brushes, rope hammocks, quilts and a split red-oak wren house.

The Workbench, 470 Park Avenue South, New York, N.Y. 10016
64-page catalogue, $1.

The Workbench has the largest store on the East Coast devoted to modern furniture, and they sell solid, inexpensive things, much of it in Scandinavian-inspired styles made of oiled teak and walnut—not much influence of modern Italian design around here. Sleek chests from Denmark start at about $155, expanding dining-room tables at about $100 and sofas at just over $200, and you can have a walnut or teak bed made to order in any size you want. If you are tired of those woods, look at the butcher-block desks, glass-and-chrome dining tables, and bentwood and Italian cane chairs.

REPRODUCTION FURNITURE

Berea College Student Craft Industries, Box 2347, Berea, Ky. 40403
28-page furniture catalogue, $1.
48-page handcraft brochure, 25 cents.

Berea College was founded by an abolitionist preacher in 1855 and the student body was completely integrated until the passage of a state law in 1904 made integration impossible. Although black students now make up only about one tenth of the student body, Berea has remained committed to low-cost education. Part of this is an extensive labor program in which students earn money in ninety different programs, though the best-known are the student industries where students produce handmade furniture and various smaller handcrafts.

A pleasant, sober catalogue displays very attractive, although expensive authentic Early American and Colonial furniture reproductions in cherry, walnut and mahogany. There are turned-leg and rope-leg dining tables, New England butterfly tables, spinet and butler's chest desks, Welsh dressers, spool and block front chests. Sheraton, caned, and corn-shuck-seat chairs, costing from $105 to $275, and six beds, including the hired man's bed made to fit in the sloping roofed attic where the hired man slept, these cost $230 and up.

Modern furniture can be made to customer's specifications.

Cohasset Colonials by Hagerty, Cohasset, Mass. 02025
32-page catalogue, 50 cents.
36 fabric samples, $3; refundable.

An excellent collection of kits for making seventeenth- and eighteenth-century American furniture. Each piece has been exactly copied from an original in a museum or private collection, and there is an appealing range of graceful and simple pieces for every room: a

27 • *Carl Forslund* Solid-cherry hope chest, 24″ long, 15″ wide, 15″ high. It can be used as a filing cabinet. Light or dark finish. $99.95.
photo Rooks Photography

28 • *Guild of Shaker Crafts* Reproduction of an oval carrier first used in the Hancock and New Lebanon communities. Shaker sisters used them for gathering herbs and carrying fruit, among other things. 15″ long, 11½″ wide, 3½″ high. Natural or stained finish. $18.

29 • *Guild of Shaker Crafts* Reproduction of one of several clocks made by Isaac Youngs, the chief clockmaker at New Lebanon for a number of years starting in 1815. It has an eight-day wind-up movement and is available with glass- or wood-panel lower door. Cherry with light or dark finish, 33½″ high, 11″ wide, 4½″ deep. $138.

fairly easy-looking project is the Colonial mirror, $17, with the molding taken from an early-seventeenth-century courting mirror in the Wadsworth Atheneum, the kit contains single-shock silvered glass to give that hand-blown look, and also handwrought nails. Other small pieces include block stools, candle stands, wall racks and night tables. And for the more ambitious there are desks, chests, cupboards, a lovely assortment of ladder-back and Windsor chairs, and a child's high-chair taken from an original in the Concord Antiquarian Society. Also headboards, and a four-poster canopy bed with posts copied from originals in the Yankee Pedlar Inn for about $111. The kits come sanded and ready to assemble with hardware, glue, sandpaper and stain.

You can also buy pewter reproductions of collector's items, and fabrics adapted from old designs.

Craft House, Williamsburg, Va. 23185
200-page catalogue, some color, $2.50.
Wallpaper catalogue, $8.50 ($6 refundable).

In 1926 John D. Rockefeller, Jr., set up a nonprofit foundation to preserve the historic buildings and a large part of the Colonial capital of Virginia, which Thomas Jefferson had called "the finest school of manners and morals that ever existed in America." By the 1930's so many visitors had asked where they could buy accurate reproductions of the eighteenth-century furniture on display that the Foundation decided to start a program of reproducing appropriate pieces, and made arrangements with manufacturers in several fields. A program was finally arranged whereby manufacturers would take pieces chosen by a Williamsburg representative and make detailed reproductions, which would then be examined and approved or rejected by a team of people from the Foundation and, when approved, would be manufactured and sold with the Williamsburg hallmark.

The large and educational catalogue will fascinate anyone interested in antiques or reproduction furniture and interiors. It contains not only pictures of the multitude of reproductions but also background information on the originals, a history of eighteenth-century furniture and decoration, and also of Williamsburg. Most of the furniture costs from $500 to over $1,000, with side chairs costing just over $200 and partners' desks over $2,000. Cotton, linen, silk and damask fabrics are between $9 and $20 a yard (with some costing much more), wallpaper about $6 a roll. Lights, mirrors, fireplace accessories, candleholders, and a good collection of china and pottery and glass from primitive tavern glasses and wine bottles to elegant air-twist stemware. There is pewter and silver, and for anyone who would just like inexpensive knickknacks, a section called a "Potpourri of Gifts" lists brass trivets and doorstops, decorated tiles, party invitations, note cards (decorated with old recipes, embroideries or Williamsburg sketches), silver wine labels, hand towels and place mats (one with a lovely primitive design taken from a 1660 wallpaper), and kits for making dolls, candles, needlepoint and crewel, and even the buildings of Williamsburg in cardboard.

Carl Forslund, 122 E. Fulton Street, Grand Rapids, Mich. 49502
98-page catalogue, some color, $1; refundable.

A big, glossy and ever so friendly catalogue introduces furniture made by the Forslund family. The business was started by Mr. and Mrs. Forslund in 1935, has blossomed and bloomed and is now run—efficiently, to judge by the catalogue—by the Forslunds' three sons. You can buy everything for the house here from door-stops based on old toys and a bishop's Victorian solitaire game copied from a set found in the English Cotswolds through colored pressed glass, china and flatware to a great deal of stained hardwood furniture in a mixture of American styles and variations on styles. Some of the pieces are listed as exact replicas, while others are described rather like this tea cart: ". . . like no other, it doesn't even faintly resemble either an old or a new one. At the shop, Burt Johnson, master cabinetmaker, and Mr. Forslund took the legs from the Tad Lincoln lamp table, the handle from the washstand, a drop leaf here, a drawer there and all of a sudden, we had Tilly."

Much of the furniture has been adapted from old pieces lent by customers and is named after them: the Rose Marie candlesticks, $20, are copied from a hundred-year-old pair discovered in a north Wisconsin barn by Rose Marie Metcalf; a small folding tea table, $75, was brought in by a doctor from Dekalb, Illinois, who allowed Forslund to copy it as long as they named the piece "Aunt Edie's Tea Table," which they did; the Rose Kibbe drop-leaf table, $320, which extends to 112″, was copied from an old table belonging to the Kibbe family in Michigan and first seen on a Forslund vacation. Furniture is made from hardwoods, and stained cherry or honey color. There is lots to choose from, and the catalogue should please anyone who likes adaptations of old furniture or fanciful ornaments.

Guild of Shaker Crafts, Inc., 401 W. Savidge Street, Spring Lake, Mich. 49456
Catalogue, $1.25.

Guild of Shakers Crafts was started by the Shaker authority Mrs. Edward Deming (Faith) Andrews, who, with local craftsmen, started making careful copies of specific pieces of Shaker furniture. The Shakers believed that their furniture had been designed in heaven and that the patterns had been transmitted to them by angels; this catalogue and the furniture, accessories and sewn goods all have an extremely appealing "modest plainness."

Chests and tables cost between $150 and $300 (there's a beautiful square pine ironing table of the kind that was often used for canning and apple sorting because of its broad top, for $155). Much of the catalogue is devoted to smaller accessories, candle stands, a candle box, a mirror, a towel rack, a spool chest, a sewing table, a spinning wheel, trays, oval boxes, a sugar scoop, brooms, wood rakes, picture frames (these can be made to order), handloomed throws, gardener's coats and ladies' smocks, a child's apron and bonnet, Shaker clothes to fit 9″ and 11″ dolls, inspirational drawings, crewel and needlepoint kits. And in response to many requests, the Guild has produced a decorator kit with fabric samples, paint colors, sample furniture finishes and advice on how to decorate in the Shaker manner. The furniture is also sold through certain Shaker museums.

Martha M. House, 1022 S. Decatur Street, Montgomery, Ala. 36104
42-page catalogue, some color, $1.

Martha House says that practically all the Victorian furniture being produced in the world today is being manufactured in Montgomery, where there are four large factories. Their large catalogue shows chairs, sofas, a few chests, small tables and a headboard based on the heavy ornate Victorian styles which, they say, were originally made for the stately mansions of the aristocratic South. The wood is Honduras mahogany, tables have wood or marble tops, and the upholstered pieces are covered in velvet, brocade, tapestry or brocatelle. Prices run from around $50 for lamps, plant stands and small coffee tables to around $400 for sofas.

Hunt Galleries, Inc., Box 2324, 2920 N. Center Street, Hickory, N.C. 28601
30-page catalogue, some color, with fabric samples, $1.

Traditional sofas, armchairs, loungers and upholstered benches ("decorator-inspired" they say), and many of the buttoned and flounced pieces have a distinct touch of thirties' and forties' Hollywood; indeed, most of the fabric samples seem to look like velvet or damask. Glamorous buttoned bedheads start at $65, small frilled bedroom chairs at about $50, armchairs at about $95 and three-seat sofas at about $370. Frames are made from kiln-dried stained hardwoods, webbing is reinforced with steel strapping so it will not sag, and springs are of steel hand-tied eight ways.

The North Family Joiners, Star Route 70, Box 73-A, Great Barrington, Mass. 01230
Leaflet, free.

A very new firm of cabinetmakers who make extremely high quality meticulous reproductions of Shaker furniture and "other furniture in a simple country tradition" to order. They will reproduce any piece of Shaker furniture to which they have access or will design furniture in the Shaker style to suit special needs. The leaflet shows just a few standard pieces: a pine bench for $30, a cherry-wood trestle table with a natural finish for $400, a painted-pine six-board blanket chest for $125, and a small cherry-wood lap desk, $185. Standards are so high that this small firm will have to remain small and slow, and will probably develop a long waiting list.

Bryan Robeson, Box 757, Hickory, N.C. 28601
30-page catalogue, 25 cents.

Although they say that the family has been in all phases of the furniture business for over fifty years, this firm has been selling furniture by mail for only four. The stock consists mainly of armchairs, love seats, and stained-hardwood desks and coffee tables. Designs are generally freely adapted from antique styles of various countries—there is an Italian dining table that extends to 60″ for $115, a pair of French country bunching tables for $120, a Mediterranean classic love seat in cane covered with loose cushions for $147. Fabric swatches are sent on request, or the furniture can be upholstered in your own fabric.

Shaker Workshops, Inc., P.O. Box 710, Concord, Mass. 01742
32-page catalogue, 50 cents. February.

The Shaker Workshops was started in 1971 by three men, one of whom, a historian, had previously been buying and selling antique houses, and another of whom, an art historian, had been the curator of a Shaker village. The Workshops manufactures reproductions of specific pieces of Shaker furniture, both

30

31

32

30 • *Bryan Robeson* Chippendale library chair; legs of hardwood with walnut, mahogany or fruitwood stained finish. 42" high, 33" wide, 31" deep. $339.50 in top grain leather; $197.50 in vinyl or your own fabric.

31 • *Shaker Workshops* Rocking chairs are an American invention and the Shakers were among the first to reproduce them systematically on a large scale. This Shaker rocker is 40½" high, 21" wide and 18" deep. Finished, $80; in kit form, $49.95.

32 • *Shaker Workshops* Candle table, 25½" high, 17½" in diameter. Ready-made, $40; in kit form, $19.95.

ready-made and in kits, and several pieces can be seen in Shaker museums and villages.

The furniture is, of course, beautiful, delicate and plain. The kits (which cost about one-third less than the finished pieces) contain all the materials needed, including glue, hardware, sandpaper, stain and step-by-step instructions. No sawing or cutting is necessary, and you need just ordinary tools like a hammer and screwdriver. There are three large tables—two drop-leaf at $75 and $95, and a trestle table at $120—benches, stools, rocking chairs and several smaller pieces such as hanging shelves, mirrors, cupboards, candleholders, hurricane lamps and bowls. Also reproductions of Shaker Spirit drawings to hang and on note cards.

The neat and simple catalogue has an informative list of books and pamphlets on Shaker furniture and history, and a short account of the beliefs of the Shakers—who besides having a great respect for work, which they felt was divinely inspired, were pacifists, believers in the equality of the races and sexes, and ecologists.

Sturbridge Yankee Workshop, Brimfield Turnpike, Sturbridge, Mass. 01566
68-page catalogue, some color, 25 cents.

This large firm sells "1000 basic items for furnishing an early American home" in styles which they say are as "authentic in design as we can possibly find," although the general impression the crowded catalogue gives is not that of strict authenticity. There is a certain amount of furniture, including a collection of Hitchcock pieces made from the original Lambert Hitchcock patterns and complete with gold-stenciled designs; side chairs cost just over $80 and chests around $200. Also plenty of smaller things: Early American hardware, hinges, coat hooks, shelf brackets, door knockers and weather vanes, and lighting fixtures: lanterns, wooden candlesticks, ship's sconces, painted ceramic lamps and glass hanging lamps. Mirrors, clocks, pewter, flatware and pressed glass, and framed pictures which include reproductions of old-fashioned plates, and scenes by Grandma Moses and Andrew Wyeth.

GARDEN ORNAMENTS AND FURNITURE

Erkins Studio Inc., 8 W. 40th Street, New York, N.Y. 10018
34-page Garden Ornaments catalogue, free.
Teakwood Bench brochure, free.

Erkins Studio sells a dramatic collection of reproduction outdoor furnishings to add a touch of grandeur to the garden or terrace: statues, fountains, birdbaths and sundials. Small squatting lead frogs for the lily pond are $23; roaring lions, $70 the pair, for the gateway; Watteau shepherds and shepherdesses, $675 each, for the arbor.

If you have simple tastes you'll find some absolutely plain cast stone planters for from about $40, but that's about all. You'll be really happy with this catalogue if you are rich and ostentatious and dream of filling your ground with a profusion of elaborate urns, leaping animals, swooning cherubs and cascading fountains. Everything is lead or stone, and special designs can be made to order.

33

34

35

36

37

33 • *Erkins Studio* "The Seasons" in carved Italian stone, 33″ high. $235 each, or $940 the set.

34 • *The Patio* 13″-high birdbath cast in light gray Pompeian stone. $45.

35 • *The Patio* Garden statues cast in light gray Pompeian stone. 15″-high owl, $25; 18″-high unicorn, $35.

36 • *Sundials* Sundial carved from calcareous limestone that can be left to develop a light gray patina, treated to stay white, or treated to look old. 16″ by 20″. $250.

37 • *Sundials* "The Salem" sundial, cast in solid bronze and hand-finished. 10¼″ in diameter. $35.

38

39

38 • *Taylor and Ng* (see the Household Objects and Gifts section) Stoneware place setting with blue or brown line on iron-speckled white. The high-fired glaze is especially scratch-and-chip resistant. Dinner plate, salad plate, soup bowl and mug, $11.25.

39 • *Taylor and Ng* (see the Household Objects and Gifts section) Cobalt-blue and white "Calico" vitrified English china. Soup/salad plate, dinner plate, cup and saucer, $9.50.

Erkins Studio imports Mendip teakwood garden furniture from England which, they say, is widely used there in parks. Chairs, benches and tables have a straightforward English park look, are constructed with teakwood dowels and a few brass screws, so do not need to be painted, oiled or brought inside in the winter. Benches (with backs and arms) start at about $150.

The Patio, 550 Powell Street, San Francisco, Calif. 94108
Subscription to spring and fall catalogues, $1.

The Patio sells some indoor games and gifts through its fall catalogue, but mainly stocks outdoor games, and furniture and pool equipment that conjures up a luxurious picture of the comfortable California life. Modern white plastic outdoor furniture with brilliantly colored puffy cushions, and Mexican garden statues, are unlike anything I have seen in the East, and floating chairs, tables, ashtrays and coasters look very Hollywood. The spring catalogue is full of people playing Texas Toss, super basketball, pool badminton or volley ball and riding paddle boards, pool buggies and Super Scamper sailboats in shimmering Californian swimming pools.

Sundials, New Ipswich, N.H. 03071
32-page catalogue, free.
Weather-vane brochure, free.

This firm manufactures and sells sundials. The catalogue gives a history of gnomonics (the art of telling time by sundial) and illustrates about fourteen of their owns dials in bronze, brass, iron and traditional styles, some inscribed with sentiments such as "*Tempus fugit*," "I count only sunny hours," or "Grow old along with me, the best is yet to be." Prices for these go from about $8 for a small brass window-sill dial to $100 for a 20″-high equatorial armillary dial. Imported dials are also shown, including reproductions of seventeenth-century dials from Sweden and modern, hand-carved stone dials from France.

For hammocks, see Modern and Miscellaneous Furniture (above).

GLASS AND CHINA

Glass and china tableware is another area where there don't seem to be many American firms producing. The famous glass and china, both modern and traditional, come from Europe, and the inexpensive from Asia. Don't buy expensive imported glass and china without comparing prices with shops in the country of manufacture, as there are dramatic savings to be made on the higher-priced settings and figurines, and some of the European shops are extremely well organized to mail to America.

Baccarat, Inc., 55 E. 57th Street, New York, N.Y. 10022
Stemware brochure, 50 cents.
Giftware brochure, 50 cents.
How to Choose and Use Wine Glasses, $1.
Ceralene China, color brochure, 10 cents.

This famous old French firm boasts of all the kings, emperors, Presidents, maharajas and embassies that have used their crystal glasses, including a maharaja who ordered from them an entire temple and set of furniture made of crystal. However, "fully aware that people do not serve as many wines as they did formerly, or for those who have always preferred the simplicity of a one-course dinner, Baccarat has fully adapted itself to the three-glass table setting in adequate sizes to take care of any situation." Bar accessories are also available, and for the Southern clientele, an iced-tea glass has been added.

The Stemware brochure shows about twenty-four glass patterns from very simple ones, at about $90 for twelve red-wine glasses, to cut but not elaborate patterns, at about $156 for twelve wine glasses. The Giftware brochure shows vases, paperweights, candlesticks and ashtrays, many of them at prices between $10 and $50. In the China brochure, showing Ceralene china made by Reynaud et Cie of Limoges, most of the patterns are reproductions or adaptations of eighteenth-century patterns. Prices are from $27 to $195 per five-piece place setting.

Bennington Potters, Inc., 324 County Street, Bennington, Vt. 05201
12-page color catalogue, 50 cents.

Bennington Potters was started by David Gill after World War II. He didn't know, at the time, that Bennington pottery was also the name of the highly sought-after stoneware produced in Bennington around 1800, and the name has caused numerous misunderstandings with visitors who turn up expecting wares in the old style.

The Gills make sleek, functional modern stoneware that is cast or molded, not thrown individually on a wheel, in three solid colors—white, a light mustard-brownish color and black—and designs are *somewhat* similar to the Finnish Arabia.

Complete dinner, tea and coffee services are made (dinner plates cost about $2.50, and a ten-cup coffeepot about $12), and casseroles and gourmet cookware (snail dishes, corn dishes and bread/pâté pans) and mugs in the same style complement the place settings. Decorative objects include painted animal piggybanks, tiles and trivets, African-influenced face sculptures, candleholders and several small planters.

Centaur Gifts, Inc., 701 Wood Street, Philadelphia, Pa. 19106
60-page catalogue with some color, $1.

The Centaur sells a mixture of imported gifts, most of which are glass or china. Large pieces of pewter (coffeepots, etc.) start at $20, Dutch copper jugs and planters at $7; German salt-glazed stoneware at $16; printed reproduction of old tapestries, hand-printed on linen and cotton, or machine-woven, $36 to $155; West German earthenware beer steins at $11; stone rubbings from China, around $10; and a great deal of glass, including Pilgrim's Cranberry glass, Corning's Creative glass, Spiegelau from Germany, and Iittala from Finland. Centaur intends to add the largest collection of Wedgwood Jasperware offered in a catalogue.

Rosenthal Studio-Haus, H. Bender, Inc., 584 Fifth Avenue, New York, N.Y. 10036
80-page color Rosenthal Studio Line catalogue, $1.50. Christmas color catalogue, free.

If you are too impatient to write to Germany, you can buy Rosenthal's famous and expensive modern china,

40 • *Carl Forslund* (see Reproduction Furniture in this section) About ninety different pieces of this two-hundred-year-old pattern, Mason's "Plantation Colonial," are always in stock, including egg cups, ladles, place mats, salt and pepper shakers. Place setting of dinner plate, salad plate, bread-and-butter plate, and cup and saucer, $11.65.

glass and flatware at higher prices from this shop in New York. All new Rosenthal designs are screened by a jury of seven people, and nothing is accepted unless approved by all seven jurors. Apart from the Studio Line catalogue, which shows the full range of flatware, stemware and china in twelve shapes, each of which can be decorated with several different patterns, the New York shop also produces a smaller free Christmas catalogue with modern gifts from various manufacturers: bar sets, desk sets, glasses, copper sauce pans, candleholders, fondue sets, etc.

Steuben Glass, Fifth Avenue at 56th Street, New York, N.Y. 10022
Catalogue, approximately $4. Christmas.

In the 1930's the Steuben Glass operation was reorganized, and from being an undistinguished and financially unsuccessful firm, became an internationally known producer of crystal. The transformation was mainly brought about by Arthur Houghton, Jr., a great-grandson of the founder of Corning (which owns Steuben), who felt that the glass should no longer be designed by the glassmakers themselves, but by carefully chosen outside designers. He was helped by the fact that in 1932 Corning discovered a new formula that would produce an exceptionally pure and clear crystal without the problems of the greenish or pinkish tinges that various chemicals had previously sometimes given the glass.

A sculptor was brought in as the principal designer, and over the years Steuben has made less functional glass and more expensive "art objects" and "presentation pieces." Presidents Truman and Eisenhower started a tradition of presenting Steuben glass to heads of state, and pieces are in the collections of over seventy countries. A number of different artists have designed pieces for Steuben, and artists as famous and disparate as Jacob Epstein and Cecil Beaton have made drawings to be engraved on the glass. Pieces range from small, smooth animals to pieces with elaborate, stylized engravings. Some functional pieces cost less than $100, but most prices range from $100 into the thousands.

HARDWARE AND BATHROOM FIXTURES

Ball and Ball, 463 W. Lincoln Highway, Exton, Pa. 19341
52-page catalogue, $1.

This family firm manufactures reproduction hardware fittings and publishes a most informative catalogue, with not only advice on what to use where but also historical information about how similar pieces were originally used. Ball and Ball claims that theirs are "brasses for those who know the originals"; they have indeed made hardware copies for most major museums, and last year, chandeliers and andirons for Independence Hall in Philadelphia. The catalogue illustrates furniture fittings including those used on American-made pieces from about 1720 to 1840, "house hardware" (locks, latches, bolts and knobs), brass and glass chandeliers and wall sconces, door knockers and hooks of all kinds, ashtrays, book ends, table lamps, porch lamps, fireplace hardware and doorstops.

Cape Cod Cupola Co., 78 State Road, N. Dartmouth, Mass. 02747
48-page catalogue, 25 cents.

Cape Cod Cupola makes not only cupolas but also cast-aluminum mailbox signs for under $10, three-dimension post signs, and a whole lot of weather vanes from aluminum silhouettes at under $20 each to full-bodied copper vanes, made in molds more than a hundred years old and hand-hammered, at prices between $90 and $400.

Garden Way Research, Charlotte, Vt. 05445
Fireplace equipment leaflets, free.
Cart leaflets, free.

Garden Way has designed and manufactured several tools to solve common fireplace problems: tongs that are neither too heavy nor too flimsy, and have three gripping points to hold odd-shaped logs; a long puff poker which you blow down when starting or reviving a fire—it's an old Chinese idea and means you don't have to bend over (the Garden Way manager says it's the only tool he uses regularly at his own fireplace); and a canvas sling which is both a carrier and a log rack (you put it on a wrought-iron frame) so that you don't have to bother to unload and you won't get wood chips spilled on the carpet in the process. The above tools cost about $15 each, including postage. For about $23, there is a new patented fireplace grate with movable log supports which is designed to cure smoky fireplaces, burn round logs and odd kinds of wood better, and, therefore, cut firewood costs. There are various letters from satisfied customers (with their complete addresses; I always feel suspicious when vague locations are given).

P. E. Guerin, Inc., 23 Jane Street, New York, N.Y. 10014
54-page catalogue, $1.

Importers and manufacturers of sumptuous hardware since 1857, they are, as they say, "style and quality leaders in decorative brass and bronze." They have never willfully discarded a pattern since they were founded, so now have over fifty thousand styles on their books, any one of which can be had on special order. They will also reproduce antique pieces from customer's samples or create new ones to customer's designs.

The catalogue shows bathroom fixtures with taps in the shapes of birds and dolphins, and spouts in the shapes of swans and turtles, soap dishes like leaf-strewn shells, and mirrors with frames as elaborate as those around old oil paintings. Prices for basin sets start at about $160. Building hardware ranges from gleaming modern doorknobs at about $17 to fantastic cremornes with brass rods for about $125, and at the end of the catalogue there is a collection of small but very stately metal and glass coffee tables at about $763 and up.

Horton Brasses, Box 95, Nooks Hill Road, Cromwell, Conn. 06416
42-page catalogue, $1.

This is another family firm that makes reproduction brass fittings for antiques. The catalogue has the various products divided into styles; first Hepplewhite pulls and escutcheons, then Queen Anne, then Chippendale, and later on comes Victorian hardware. There is also a small selection of hinges, latches, lock parts, bedbolt covers, casters, bellow nozzles, and unlike the other hardware shops, they have knobs in porcelain and wood as well as brass, and latches and hinges in iron. Books on American furniture are sold, and Goddards polishes.

Portland Stove Foundry Co., 57 Kennebec Street, Portland, Maine 04104
Leaflet, free.

Has nostalgia a future? Portland Stove Foundry Co. makes Franklin stoves from the original patterns that "warmed the hands and hearts of men great and small since this country was founded." And a heart-and-hand-warming sight their leaflet is too. In addition to parlor, kitchen and boat cook stoves and heaters, there are five fireplaces, which come in porcelain enamel of all colors. One of the fireplaces, "The Eagle," based on patterns from 1742, is decorated with American symbols: whale-oil lamps, New England pine trees, flags and eagles. You can get an extra pair of brass eagles for the top too, and the doors shut to make a closed stove. Prices are between $87 and $500.

Sherle Wagner, 125 E. 57th Street, New York, N.Y. 10022
Large color catalogue, $2.

Burt Lancaster, Barbara Hutton, Princess Grace and the Maharanee of Baroda all have Sherle Wagner bathrooms . . . What's more, the Maharanee of Baroda bought her gold-plated dolphins and cherub fixtures, marble counters and hand-painted washbasins by mail. "Until recently," says a Sherle Wagner press release, "gold faucets were merely shaped like swans or cherubs, or snail shells; marble tubs were set off by crystal chandeliers and handcarved Louis XVI *chaises percées* . . . Now Sherle Wagner uses marble as an art form for the bathroom with shell-shaped washbasins handcarved in onyx standing on an onyx fluted pedestal, with bath faucets of malachite and gold, or other real jewels, like amethyst, Tiger Eye, rose quartz, rock crystal and lapiz lazuli . . . Sherle Wagner 'the man with the Midas Touch' designs and manufactures bathroom fixtures, accessories and hardware whether the mood is rococo or contemporary"—though what Sherle Wagner calls contemporary is what we call rococo. Anyway, in an astounding catalogue you'll see the gold-plate, silver-plate and solid-brass taps and faucets, decorated bowls with background colors to match the fixture of any other manufacturer at around $100 each, revolving units to hide the toothpaste and soap at around $100 each, gold-plated or silver-plated towel bars and rings, paper holders, soap dishes (mostly shaped like shells), reeded and bamboo benches, knobs, pulls, hardware and medicine cabinets, often co-ordinated so that everything in the bathroom matches.

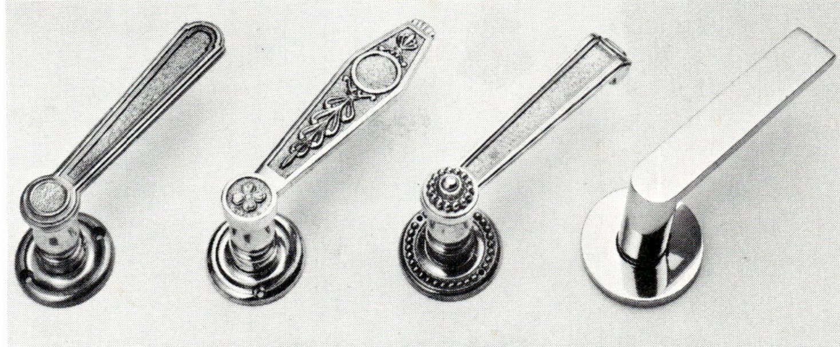

41

42

43

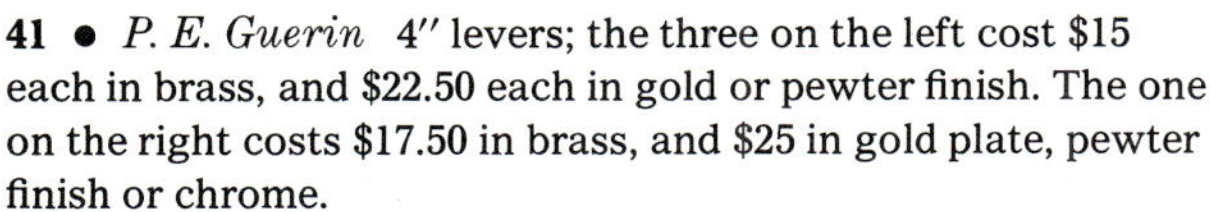

41 • *P. E. Guerin* 4″ levers; the three on the left cost $15 each in brass, and $22.50 each in gold or pewter finish. The one on the right costs $17.50 in brass, and $25 in gold plate, pewter finish or chrome.

42 • *Portland Stove Foundry* Reproduction of one of the earliest Pennsylvania stoves of Revolutionary days. Brass rosettes and top corner ornaments are supplied, and accessories are available. $289.95.

43 • *Sherle Wagner* Hand-painted wash basins with matching faucets, new designs by Sherle Wagner. Basins, $176; matching faucets with 24-carat gold plate, about $258.

44 • *The Crossroads of Sport* Service plates with reproductions of old English golf prints. A set of six plates, each with a different print, $60.

HOUSEHOLD OBJECTS AND GIFTS

Abbey Press, St. Meinrad, Ind. 47577

Annual subscription to three Christian Family color catalogues, 35 cents. January, April, September.

The Abbey Press was started almost a hundred years ago by St. Meinrad Archabbey, a Benedictine monastery which published a small amount for its own use. Over the years the press has gradually stopped publishing strictly Catholic literature, and especially within the last three years appealed to a much wider market with goods that express a more general Christian message—or even just a vague humane with-it concern.

The catalogue illustrates a small and often humorous collection of presents, but the most unusual products are the graphics—fantastic glowing colors and striking modern designs should delight anyone who likes to spread a bit of cheer, or a worthy thought. The posters are the most inspirational—for around $2 each they colorfully announce that "Peace is not needing to know what will happen next" and that "Life is a mystery to be lived, not a problem to be solved"—but you can also make your own mobile with printed circles. Each mobile kit costs 75 cents and has six printed circles on themes such as "Good vibes," "Happy day," "Peace" or "Love" or "Good news" which exhort in pink and orange "Take time to smell the flowers" and in blue and yellow "Seize the day." Plenty of cards, writing paper, fold-and-mail notes—some are simply the outlines of flowers in one brilliant color on another, others boldly express such sentiments as "I have often had to eat my own words and on the whole I have found them a rather wholesome diet" or "Isn't it good to know you've got a friend." The catalogue has pages of gifts for teen-agers, and plaques for children's rooms—this is obviously a terrific place for presents for them.

Ajello Candles, 484 Route 17 North, Paramus, N.J. 07652

For the 12-page color catalogue, please send four 8-cent stamps.

The Ajello family has been making candles since 1775, and has made them for "the world's most famous and discriminating people" including American Presidents, Queen Elizabeth and, in 1921, an 18′ one for Enrico Caruso. There are white, odd-sized, long-burning dinner candles, and painted novelty candles in animal shapes, Raggedy Ann and Andy, President Nixon and Agnew; special-occasion candles for weddings, birthdays and anniversaries (the last two marked to be burned down each year—and then every ten years in the case of anniversary candles); and seasonal candles for spring, Easter, Valentine's Day and Christmas. But the most typical Ajello candles are the heavily ornate Venetian and antique candles decorated with flowers and fir cones around the base and painted in deep red or green. Prices go from $1.50 to $14.50 for a birthday or anniversary candle with your name or names on it. Candles can also be made to special order.

J. D. Browne, Ghirardelli Square, 900 North Point, San Francisco, Calif. 94109
Brochure, 25 cents.

They tell me they run a marvelous small retail operation on Ghirardelli Square in San Francisco. They also publish a small brochure with gadgets and gifts such as an automatic golf scorer, $8.50; a kit with six tools which lock into the handle of a hammer, $11.50; an electric pencil engraver, $8.50 (recommended by the police to engrave your name and address on anything stealable); a key chain with a buzzing alarm timer, $6, etc., etc. They also have a leaflet called "J. D. Browne's Index to Europe's Finest Writing Instruments," which illustrates seven especially distinguished ball-point and fountain pens.

The Candle Mill, East Arlington, Vt. 05252
44-page catalogue, 25 cents. Spring, fall.

The Candle Mill is a two-hundred-year-old grist mill which houses a large collection of antique candle molds. Candles made from some of the molds are sold in the mill, and so are candles made by other New England craftsmen, as well as candles imported from over twenty different countries. The candles from the old molds are plain and elegant; there are also real bayberry candles, dripless beeswax candles, and solid pillar candles, as well as candles in jugs, crocks and pots, candles in swans, and candles that float. Local craftsmen paint candles with scenes of sunsets and rainbows, or bury flowers inside that glimmer when the candle is alight. And from Germany there are Berte Hummel candles with the famous children decorating them. Many of the candles are animal-shaped, and there are several for Christmas as well as plenty of holders, from a small wooden mouse to a large fruit centerpiece to be put around the biggest candle, 5½″ in diameter. Supplies for making your own candles and soap are also sold, and so are some toys and gifts.

The Crossroads of Sport, Inc., 5 E. 47th Street, New York, N.Y. 10017
48-page catalogue, 50 cents.

Crossroads sells original works of art and limited-edition prints of hunting and fishing, offering a large selection of traditional paintings of waterfowl, upland birds, sporting dogs. Not the kind of prints that can be bought in many stores, these are far more expensive and go from a watercolor of a pheasant's head for $60 to an oil painting, "Covered Bridge," by the noted American illustrator Eric Sloane, for $5,000. Prints in editions of 450 or 1,000 are less expensive, costing between $40 and $75, but these, too, cost more than many traditional English and American graphics.

The Crossroads of Sport also sells gifts of interest to sportsmen: a set of six glasses, each decorated with a different antique decoy, cost $17.50; eight dessert plates with African animals in color, $30; lamps, clocks, wastepaper baskets, place mats and figurines are all decorated in the same vein; and a large selection of old and new books on hunting, fishing and golf is stocked.

The Downstairs, 5718 Roeland Drive, Shawnee Mission, Kans. 66205
8-page catalogue, 25 cents.

Line drawings illustrate old-fashioned decorative objects for the house that have been hand-painted in the primitive, stylized flower patterns typical of the Pennsylvania Dutch. Small mirrors, wall candleholders, spoon and plant holders cost between $6 and $17 each, and you can also order birth certificates, marriage certificates or plaques that announce "This is the kitchen of . . ." with names and dates that you choose.

Nan Duskin, 1729 Walnut Street, Philadelphia, Pa. 19103
24-page Christmas catalogue, $1.

Nan Duskin—women's ready-to-wear shop with Delman, Gucci and Valentino boutiques, a small department of luxury goods for men, a well-known jewelry department, and a price range of moderate to "the sky is the limit"—publishes a Christmas-gift catalogue. The gifts include such things as gold-plated key rings with whistles attached; bone-china Christmas-tree ornaments; chrome spray-can containers from Italy (to take the advertising out of the kitchen or bath); hand-painted tortoise-shell bicycle baskets; Gucci leather bags and wallets; Valentino belts and wraps; cashmere sweaters; mink cardigans; flowing "night time gowns" and robes; and one or two at-home dresses—last year in brilliant red with a floor-length cape for $125.

Finland Design, Inc., 816 Lancaster Avenue, Bryn Mawr, Pa. 19010
Catalogue planned, free.

So far, this retail shop for modern Finnish goods has only sold Fiscar scissors and gorgeous but expensive Opa stainless-steel hollowware, by mail. However, a catalogue is being prepared which will offer an all-round selection of modern Finnish goods; glass, Marimekko cotton fabric (brilliant colors and big designs), handwoven woolens, the Fiscar scissors, stainless-steel hollowware and cookware, plastic home accessories and furniture, Aalto birch stools and tea trolleys, candles and lamps. As Finnish-designed goods are so lovely, and not gathered together in any other shop in this country or in any catalogue that I know of, this is a useful source.

Flagman of America, Inc., 27-29 Chestnut Street, Hartford, Conn. 06120
Brochure, free.

This firm manufactures flags and sells flagposts and parade equipment. A small brochure shows national flags, ecology flags and message flags for boat owners (a witch on a broomstick is an "All in Fun" flag signifying that wife is ashore . . . hmm . . .). They will also make flags on special order for cities, groups and individuals. Prices for outdoor flags start at about $5.40 for a 2′ by 3′ Stars and Stripes and about $14 for 3′ by 5′ state flags.

Greek Island Ltd., 215 E. 49th Street, New York, N.Y. 10017
24-page catalogue, free.

Greek Island has been importing clothes, jewelry and things for the house from Greece since 1963. Many of their goods such as needlepoint and copperware they get from the National Welfare Organization, which has tried to raise handicraft production above the "dreary tourist level"; handwoven spreads, table mats and fabrics they get from Vienoula on Mykonos; earthenware from the Ikaros factory in Rhodes; modern jewelry from Athens, and old jewelry not from Greece at all but from Turkey. The goods aren't the real back-to-the-land crafts, but have been chosen and often designed for the "sophisticated U.S. consumer" (to quote the president). Looking through the well laid out catalogue, I see woven wall hangings, needlepoint cushions ($30 and up), pottery owl wine cups, bronze statue of Athena charioteer ("Very important-looking piece"), glass monster fish from Turkey, "paperweights or table objects," a bird-shaped candle snuffer, copper casseroles, glass *taverna* carafes, and turn-of-the-century terra-cotta roof-line tiles from torn-down buildings, $20 each. You can use them as doorstops, garden ornaments or as "yet another simply nice to have around thing," says the catalogue.

Hammacher Schlemmer, 147 E. 57th Street, New York, N.Y. 10022
Free catalogues, published five times a year. Special food catalogue and Plummer-McCutcheon catalogue.

Started 125 years ago, this well-known specialty store makes a point of selling expensive gadgets for people who have everything, though they also have a large selection of perfectly sensible though generally higher-priced items for the home and kitchen. If you are looking for a golf-ball alarm clock or a parking-meter lamp, then this is the catalogue for you, though you may not want your children to glimpse the electric merry-go-round for children's room, bar or swimming pool ($2,750) or the wondrous hot-dog cart ($1,395).

It is possible to shop at Hammacher Schlemmer without feeling that you are in an imperial court on the eve of a well-deserved revolution, but this requires looking into the back pages of the catalogue. There you will find a very good selection of kitchen appliances at the same prices charged by other stores, and an array of gourmet foods, eccentrically priced, some slightly cheaper than others listed in this book, others at close to twice the price of their competitors.

Hammacher Schlemmer has absorbed two other old New York specialty stores—Plummer, whose specialty is fancy china, silver and glass, and McCutcheon, known for its linens. A joint catalogue is now issued with a wide choice in both these categories, but remember that these are the very areas where buying from abroad can save you the most money, so some comparison shopping should be worth most consumers' while.

Haverhill's, 137 Utah Avenue, South San Francisco, Calif. 94080
64-page catalogue, some color, free.

Haverhill's specializes in smart gifts, sometimes specially made and imported for them alone. A good selection on the whole, mostly clean-cut and sleek designs with quite a few gadgets for the affluent and things that I haven't seen anywhere else (or at least not everywhere): a solar cooker to cook skewered food by the sun's rays, $10; picnic flatware in a neat case, $13; handsome screenprinted onion and potato bags, $6; an enormous kite stamped with huge numbers, $11; and the best-looking collection of coffee-table games around. There are also little gadgets such as a map measurer, and hand-hemmer stitcher and electric scissors. Most of the prices are between $5 and $20, but you can also get pieces of modern furniture, movie equipment and a ridable electric model of a 1932 Chevrolet for $1,099.95.

Hayfields Studios, Inc., E. Deering Road, Deering, N.H. 03244
Color leaflet, free.

George and Ruth Wolf make things for the house with painted decorations copied from old originals—the art was brought to the West from the Orient by the East India Company in the 1600's and years later became popular in New England. The Wolfs make lamps with bases in the shape of sap buckets, planters, candle sconces in metal and painted in red, green, mustard or dark blue with the stylized flower designs in a combination of the same colors and gold. A Chippendale mirror and small table are also made.

Hoffritz for Cutlery, 20 Cooper Square, Dept. K-2, New York, N.Y. 10003
48-page catalogue, $1.

This chain of retail stores publishes a well-organized and beautifully photographed catalogue of cutlery and gifts. Strong and handsome knives, shears, scissors, peelers and crackers of every description are laid out in tempting no-nonsense rows. You are bound to find something you've been looking for (I was delighted to see wooden fondue forks that have the tremendous advantage of never getting too hot and burning your tongue). Here's what you'll find, and plenty of choice within each category: bar sets and accessories, kitchen cutlery (which covers a lot), servers, gadgets and tableware, weather instruments, optical equipment, mirrors, personal care (mustache scissors, beard brushes and automatic massagers), manicure implements and sets, tool sets, hunting and pocket knives, and gardening tools.

Hunting World, Inc., 16 E. 53rd Street, New York, N.Y. 10022
116-page general catalogue, $1.
Bronzes by James Clark catalogue, $2.

Influenced by the current interest in conservation of the species, Hunting World doesn't have too much to do with hunting any more, and mainly sells expensive gifts for the sporty and equipment for travelers. Deerskin bags from Spain (only twenty-five are made each month), elephant-skin purses from Italy, and Jet-Black Royal Long Grain Morocco briefcases from France (these for $850) are displayed amid English police whistles, Bond Street gun cases, English game, and fishing diaries and safari clothes from Africa.

There is also a catalogue for limited-edition animal bronzes by Dr. James L. Clark (Director Emeritus of Preparation and Installation, American Museum of Natural History); most of the bronzes cost between $1,500 and $2,000.

Jennifer House, New Marlboro Stage, Great Barrington, Mass. 01230
64-page catalogue, 25 cents.

Housed in the red-painted barns of an old farm, Jennifer House describes itself as New England's American marketplace, and says it sells "Distinctive Gifts for Gracious Living . . . Gracious Giving," which means, in fact, reproductions of old clocks and telephones, coin banks, turn-of-the-century trade signs, pressed glass and cigar-store Indians, as well as imports of pewter, brass boxes, bentwood furniture and English Staffordshire china—fifty-five-piece sets for about $65.

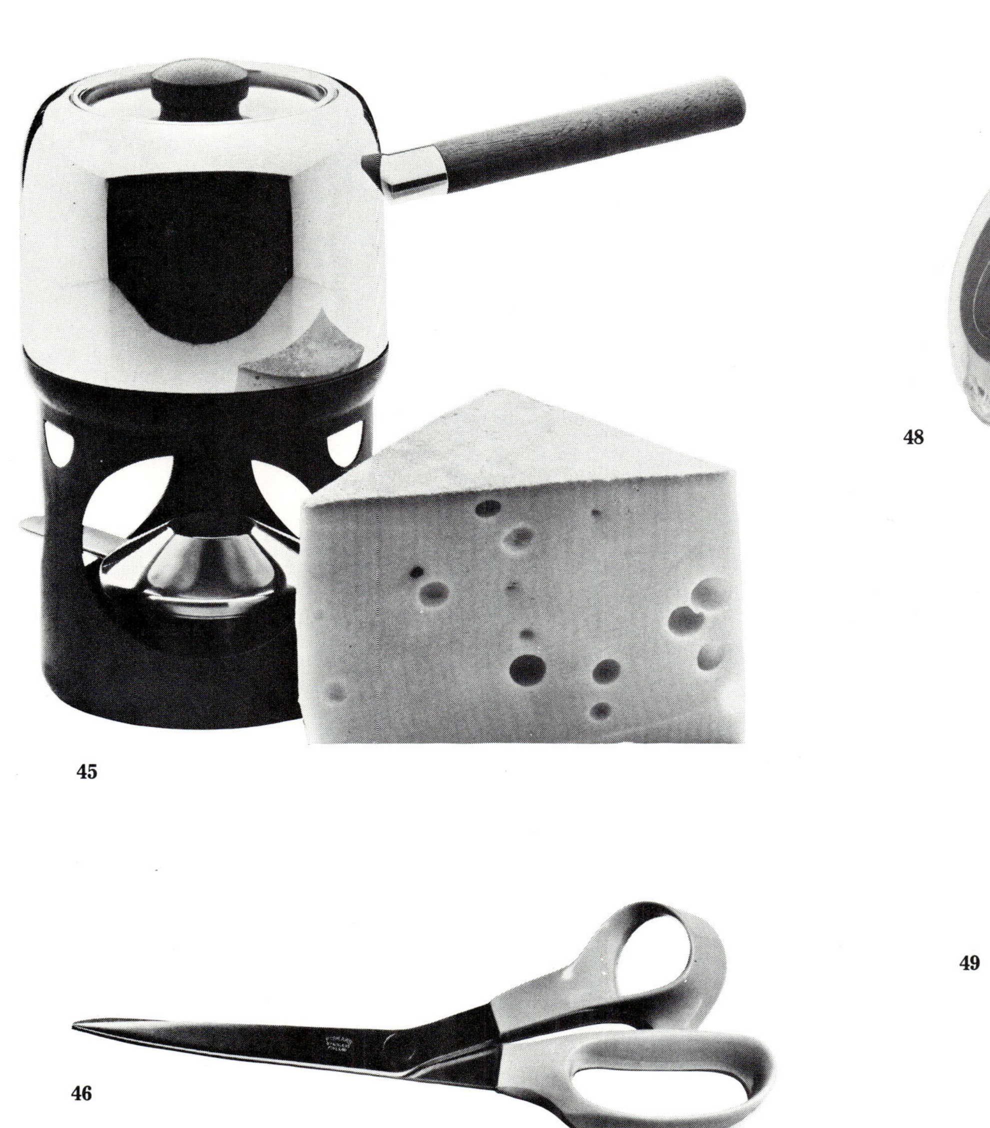

45

46

47

48

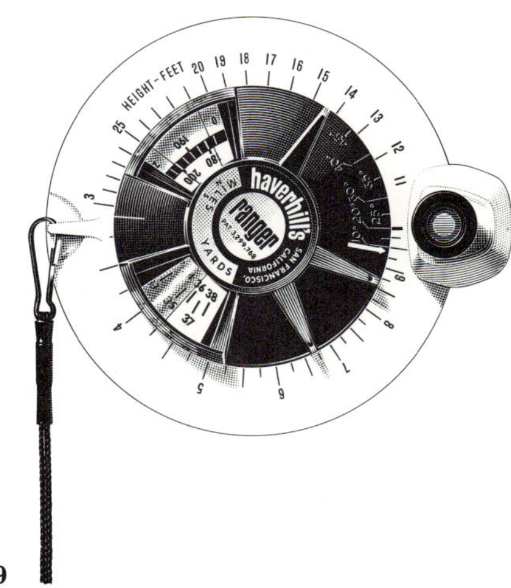

49

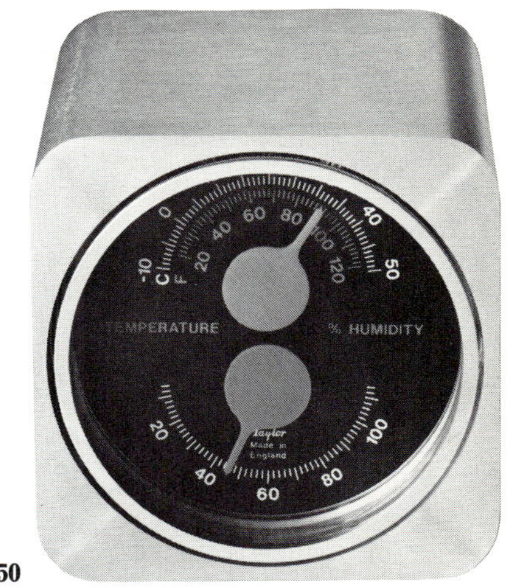

50

45 • *Finland Design* Fondue set, designed by Timo Sarpenava. $39 postpaid.

46 • *Finland Design* Lightweight scissors, manufactured by Fiskars. $7.95 postpaid.

47 • *Greek Island* Glass monster-fish paperweight, about 3″ long. Blue glass with yellow and white design. $4.75 each.

48 • *Haverhill's* Wind-up "Monaco" shaver that was taken to the moon by Shepard and Roosa on Apollo 14. Self-sharpening. $22.95.

49 • *Haverhill's* "Ranger" measures distances from 6″ to almost as far as the eye can see, in yards, nautical miles, statute miles and other units. $24.95.

50 • *The Kenton Collection* A thermometer-hygrometer gauges the temperature and humidity. Has a 3¼″ square anodized aluminum case. $35.

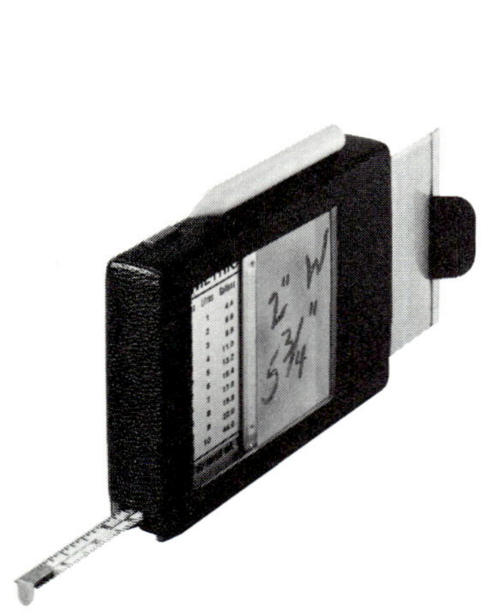

51

52

53

51 • *The Kenton Collection* Pocket-sized retractable ruler with magic pad and pencil for writing down measurements. In a leather case, $3¼'' by 2½''. $10.

52 • *The Kenton Collection* Thermos that keeps 26 oz. of liquid hot or cold for twenty hours. $18.

53 • *The Kenton Collection* Kit to make a paper model of Jerusalem, 12'' square when finished. $5.

The Kenton Collection, P.O. Box 34257, Dallas, Tex. 75234
Color catalogues, free.

A new mail-order gift firm that is owned by the Kenton Corporation, which also owns Cartier, Mark Cross, Georg Jensen and Valentino. In fact, if you write to any of those firms for a catalogue, you'll be sent the Kenton Collection catalogue. This is one of the most design-conscious gift firms, and the extraordinarily handsome catalogues with stunning color photographs and crisp white paper make the sleekly modern gifts unreasonably appealing. The gifts for adults and children, many of which cost between $5 and $30, though some cost over $100, are well chosen from among the goods sold by the Kenton Corporation-owned shops, but there are also many other things that can only be bought through the catalogue.

In the catalogues I looked at, the Kenton exclusives (available in this country only through the Kenton catalogue) included: a mahogany Chinese yardstick with brass-nail markers, $10; a Russian hand-painted lacquer box, $50; and a 7'-high acrylic aquarium with a pump, filter light and magnetic brush for $375. And there was a kit of paper and markers for children to draw on, with the promise that Kenton would imprint the two best drawings on 10'' plastic plates, and also a decorative ant farm in natural pine with a round window for $17.50. This year, at least, Georg Jensen Christmas cards were on sale at half price after Christmas.

The Left Hand, 145 E. 27th Street, New York, N.Y. 10016
24-page catalogue, 25 cents.

This catalogue of supplies for the left-handed is very considerately printed (what is back to front to the rest of us) so that the pages can be properly turned with the left hand. The president of this shop, June Gittleson, a member of the oppressed minority herself, says that she started The Left Hand about three years ago so that her fellow sufferers would have somewhere to find more easily manageable utensils. Left-handy supplies include pens, playing cards and address books, scissors, steam irons, cameras, watches, guitars and things for sports people such as fishing rods and reels, golf clubs and baseball mitts. And to stop all the agonizing twisting is the most asked-for utensil of all—the left-handed can opener, about $3, followed by the counterclockwise screwdriver (made for The Left Hand in Italy) and the left-handed potato peeler. And just for a bit of encouragement there are lefty sweat shirts, and mugs ("Left-handed Drinkers Unite"), and posters of legendary lefties such as Michelangelo's "David," Charlie Chaplin, two of the Beatles—guess which. Helpful books on golf, needlepoint, knitting and teaching left-handed children are available too.

Propinquity, 8915 Santa Monica Boulevard, Los Angeles, Calif. 90069
Gift brochure, 25 cents.
Supplementary antiques mailing, free.
Caftan brochure, free.

"Come back, now, to the past, come back to nostalgia, come back to Propinquity," says the brochure in one of its few earnest passages. The rest is a clever, camp invitation to join the "ever swelling ranks of those who revel in the recent past," though lovers of more modern baubles are certainly catered to as well. Along with the bamboo plant stands, pub mirrors, high-wheel bicycles, antique bentwood, advertising art, soda-fountain furnishings and movie memorabilia, you'll find buttons and books, candies and candles, Mickey Mouse and Raggedy Ann pillows, and a thoroughly inspired collection of oddities for the "panic stricken last minute gift list."

54

Shopping International, Inc., 777 Shopping International Building, Norwich, Vt. 05055
48-page color catalogue, 25 cents. January.
64-page color catalogue, 25 cents. July.

This large firm puts out colorful catalogues of inexpensive imports from over thirty countries, and says that goods are chosen to show something of handicraft and cultural traditions. In fact, although most of the imports are in distinctively "local" styles, they tend to look mass-produced, and the most interesting things are less ethnic-looking—modern jewelry, household objects and Christmas decorations. Other goods that have been shown in recent catalogues include alabaster book ends, Florentine trays and leather handbags from Italy, music boxes and porcelain figurines from Germany, note cards and cow bells from Switzerland, engraved bases from Sweden, and shifts and gowns from Japan, Pakistan and China; also "the first significant selection of Chinese handicrafts from the People's Republic of China." But unfortunately here, too, mainly the kind of cloisonné and soapstone goods that we have been getting from Hong Kong have been chosen, rather than the simpler and more unusual things that more choosy firms have imported. Prices are low.

55

William Spencer, Creek Road and Conestoga Lane, Rancoca Woods, N.J. 08060
200-page black-and-white catalogue, 35 cents.

The Spencer catalogue doesn't start promisingly, with fiberglass cupolas, Colonial wood signs and ornamental switch plates. But as one continues, past the ornamental mailboxes and sundials, through the hitching posts and patio accessories, a strange feeling of fascination for these copies of old American hardware begins to set in. By the time I'd reached the ornamental knockers, I was beginning to weaken, and when I reached the copies of cast-iron toys, old-fashioned circus wagons and fire engines, I was nearly won over, the very high price of these reproductions ($52 for a hook-and-ladder company) being the only drawback. After that, my resistance to the mechanical coin banks and reproductions of clocks and furniture had more or less disappeared, though I couldn't help wondering if an antique captain's chair would really cost much more than the $77 charged for a reproduction. Whether you'll actually buy anything from the catalogue depends, I suppose, on how you feel about expensive cop-

54 • *Propinquity* Mickey-Minney pillow, $7.50; book ends, $8; Mickey Mouse alarm clock, $15. The other pieces are Mickey Mouse memorabilia, of which a changing selection is always on hand.

55 • *Propinquity* Advertising pieces and memorabilia: paper pickle sign, $1.50; Union Leader tobacco tin, $25; Dan Patch tin, $15; Excelsior ice-cream tray, $35; Campbell soup mugs, $2.50; Y-B cigar cutter, $57.50.

56 • *Taylor and Ng* Bamboo bird cages from China, 17″ high, $42; 25″ high, $88. Blue and white bird feeders, $1.50 each. The cages can be used for soft-billed birds or plants.

ies of once-inexpensive originals; but the catalogue is fun to go through.

Takashimaya, Inc., 509 Fifth Avenue, New York, N.Y. 10017
Leaflets, free. Available November through March.

Takashimaya is a branch of a chain of famous Japanese department stores. Their Fifth Avenue branch stocks such Japanese specialties as bonsai trees, kimonos, *byobu* screens and Japanese dolls, but their Christmas leaflet has a general assortment of inexpensive gifts. Only a few of them have an obvious connection with Japan. The leaflet I looked at had a kit to make greeting cards with leaves and paper, $5.50, a *kiri gami* (paper cutting) kit, wood-block calendars, cotton Happi coats, Mikimoto cultured pearls, a wok cooking pan, and then the kind of practical gifts you might find in any American store—thermos bottles, travel bags (made of "chemical leather"!) and plexiglass boxes.

Taylor and Ng, 651 Howard Street, San Francisco, Calif. 94105
22-page brochure, 25 cents.

"Very subtle, very simple, very ecological," says Taylor and Ng of their brown carton gift wrap, which also goes for their wares—a graceful collection of household implements in wood, clay and steel, many of them to do with eating. This year's brochure has a movable wok, six pots planted with Chinese vegetables, wood and bamboo steamers from Taiwan, some really beautiful knives for slicing from Japan, a Mongolian fire pot with brass skimmers to retrieve cooked food, and other things, most of them beautifully basic. People who have seen it tell me that Taylor and Ng is one of the most attractive shops in the country.

The Vermont Country Store, Weston, Vt. 05161
96-page catalogue, 25 cents. Spring, fall.

The Vermont Country Store was started by Vrest Orton, a writer who gave up "affairs of state"—the Pentagon, among other things—to go back to Vermont and make an old-fashioned country store like the one his father and grandfather had owned. "I wanted it to have the same 19th century counters, shelves and kerosene lamps," he says. "And most of all I wanted it to have the same kind of merchandise: New England foods, store cheeses and crackers, bolts of calico cloth, kitchen knives and cooking forks, and the atmosphere redolent with an evocative potpourri of wood smoke from the pot-bellied stove and of tobacco, peppermint sticks, freshly cut cheese, roasting coffee, nutmegs, cinnamon sticks and so many other nostalgic things I remembered." Mr. Orton, who has also helped preserve the Village of Weston, and persuaded various friends to start local museums, managed to find old shop fixtures, including some of his father's, and set about choosing his stock. "I selected only what I liked. Instead of cheap plastic, it had to be made of old-fashioned substances like iron, brass, glass or wood. Furthermore, it had to serve some useful purpose in the home. And lastly it had to be in good taste." The result is that the stock is well above the standards of most "country stores," which Vrest Orton dismisses anyway as "imitations." The catalogue illustrates soaps, foods, toys, kitchen utensils, etc., mostly useful, and when old things are reproduced, they are the good plain old things, not the gimmicky ones.

57

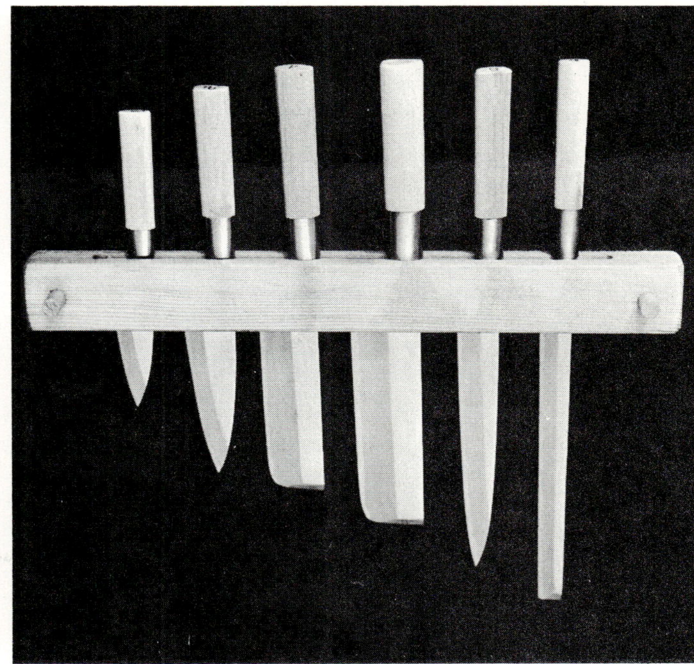

58

59

57 • *The Vermont Country Store* Reproduction of early-American cookie molds. The man and woman cost about $10 each; the two on the right, about $12 each.

58 • *Taylor and Ng* Japanese cutlery set, six traditional knives. *From left to right:* 1 and 2 *funayuki* general-purpose knives for fruits, vegetables and fish, 3 and 4 *usuba* for slicing and mincing vegetables, 5 *sashimi* for slicing raw fish, and 6 *takotiki* for octopus (or meat). Set with 24″ rack, $37.85.

59 • *Taylor and Ng* *Left:* Wood and bamboo steamers; you can steam three kinds of food at once (steaming minimizes loss of vitamins, etc.). $18.50. *Right:* A pot and colander all in one. When the spaghetti, vegetable, fish or fowl is cooked, you simply lift it out on the strainer. $9.25.

Weston Bowl Mill, Weston, Vt. 05161
40-page catalogue, 25 cents. Christmas mailing.

This seventy-five-year-old mill is still turning out old-fashioned wooden things for the house. If you'd like a handsome wooden pail, it's yours for $7.50, a well bucket is $8.50, and lovely plain pine sugar buckets in assorted sizes start at $3.75. They are up to 13½″ high and can be used to store food, or almost anything else. You can also get pastry boards, chopping blocks, carving boards, candleholders, spoons, bellows, racks and shelves, spoons and scoops, and many other things.

Women Enterprises, Inc., 242 E. 50th Street, New York, N.Y. 10022
Leaflet, free.

WE was created by women who met in the women's movement and had ideas about what they would like to do but couldn't do in their jobs or businesses. They were incorporated in June 1972, and so far, products include Christmas note cards with a feminist wreath, and writing paper adorned with "Political Power to Women," "Memo from a Liberated Woman," or "Women of the World Unite," which was printed by one of the members. There is a $15 watch with the women's liberation symbol and the word "Sister," and a T-shirt in black and gold (the original feminist colors) saying "Sisters of the Susan B. Anthony League" ($3.50), both of which are designed by WE but made by regular manufacturers, and EcoloGel cosmetics made by a woman to un-pollute your pores and un-clog your complexion. Regrettably, WE is as vague about the ingredients of these cosmetics and what they really do for you as less ideological firms are about theirs.

Yield House, Department 262, North Conway, N.H. 03860
Catalogues, 25 cents. Spring, fall.

"Friendly pine" in nostalgic, vaguely Early American styles is the specialty of Yield House, and they say that much of it goes to customers in the Midwest. The catalogues overflow with antiques, old phone centers, record-file end tables, stereo-tape lazy Susans, and planters in the shape of spinning wheels, quite a lot of them available as kits. Also antique-styled clocks, wall plaques, personalized signs, tinware to stencil, and lots of oddities. And buried amid the Americana, a few completely different things such as a modern Italian plastic kitchen timer, a cowhide log carrier, or a enormous cage for gerbils or mice (billed as "posh pet apartment playground").

KITCHEN UTENSILS

Bazaar de la Cuisine International, 7-16 149th Street, Whitestone, N.Y. 11357
80-page illustrated black-and-white catalogue, free.

Kitchen utensils are now among the easiest of specialized wares to buy by mail, and the newly ambitious chef who discovers that she suddenly needs all sorts of pans she never had, can write away to several firms for a complete selection. The Bazaar de la Cuisine is a relatively new firm whose thorough catalogue includes a wide choice of copperware, including some very handsome copper molds, heavy aluminum pots and pans, woodware as well as stainless cookware, a full range of Sabatier knives, etc. In other words, everything for cooking and a number of lovely objects that make kitchen decorations in themselves.

Bazaar Français, 666 Sixth Avenue, New York, N.Y. 10010
50-page large illustrated black-and-white catalogue, free.

Established in 1877, le Bazaar Français is a family firm now in its fourth generation which specializes in imported French copper cooking utensils, which it sells under its own brand name, 666. As with its competitors, the Bazaar Français catalogue offers an extremely full range, not only of French copperware, but of earthenware, tinware, wood and aluminum kitchen tools and Le Creuset cast-iron ware. They also offer a rare retinning service.

If you are planning to buy a whole batch of equipment, a complete *batterie de cuisine*, as the French call it, it's probably worth your while getting several of these catalogues, both to compare prices and also to see what you really need. There are obviously more tools here than you would have guessed by yourself. The Bazaar Français catalogue for instance lists, under potato, "bag sets, ballers, baskets, peelers and ricers." There are lemon graters, squeezers, strippers and zesters. Prices can be very high. A duck press, should you be tempted to buy one, costs $250, but other items, such as the heavy steel frying pans, are very reasonably priced from $4.50 up.

A thorough index and complete illustrations make this a particularly useful catalogue.

Board and Barrel, Larimer Street, Larimer Square, Denver, Colo. 80202
Brochure, free.

A large brown sheet has stylized line drawings of the functional kitchen goods made of natural materials that Board and Barrel sells. A glass-and-wood spice rack is exclusive to the shop, but although the other things are not unusual, they make a very appetizing showing collected together like this: copper bowls, wooden spoons, whisks, wine racks, Evangel pottery from Albuquerque. And for other parts of the house: rope hammocks from Pawley Island, South Carolina, and sheepskin pillows and rugs (rugs in sizes up to 6′ by 6′ for $144).

The China Closet, 6807 Wisconsin Avenue, Chevy Chase, Md. 20015
34-page catalogue, free.

A handsome little catalogue, not as professional as some of its bigger competitors, but nonetheless offering a pleasant choice of attractive and original kitchen utensils and related items. Here are the usual Sabatier knives, Creuset pots and the like, but also a number of less easy-to-find items, such as French steel and aluminum flatware at $4.40 a four-piece setting, a number of molds for pâté, meat loaf and ice cream, and a very nice little Swedish kitchen scale for $6.95. The China Closet also sells some handsome lucite accessories, such as cookbook holders and a knife rack that holds and sharpens seven knives. Among their other hard-to-find offerings are some attractive and inexpensive chil-

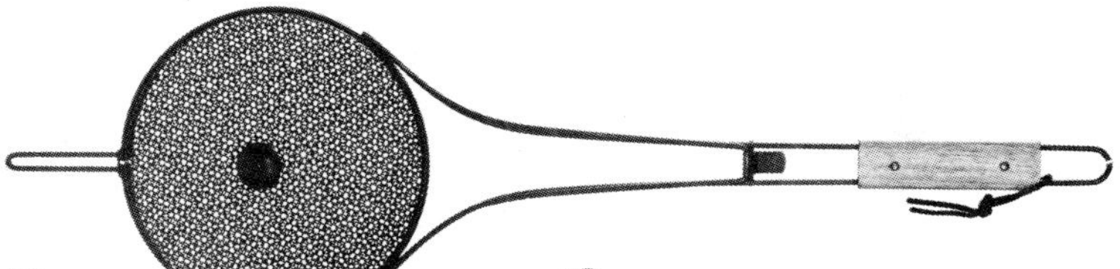

60

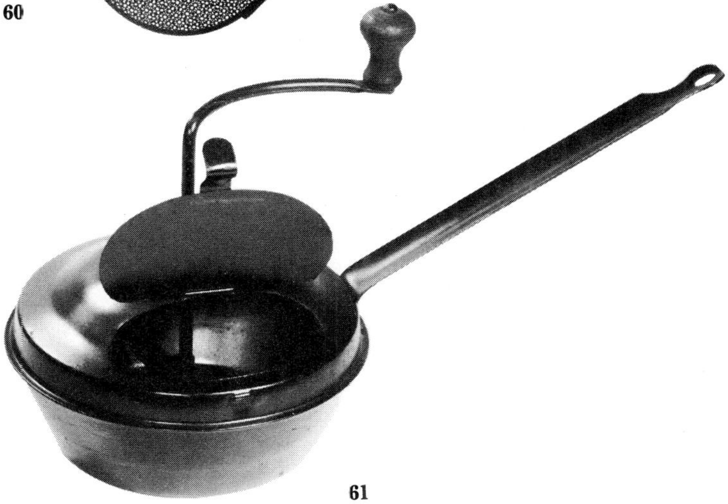

61

62

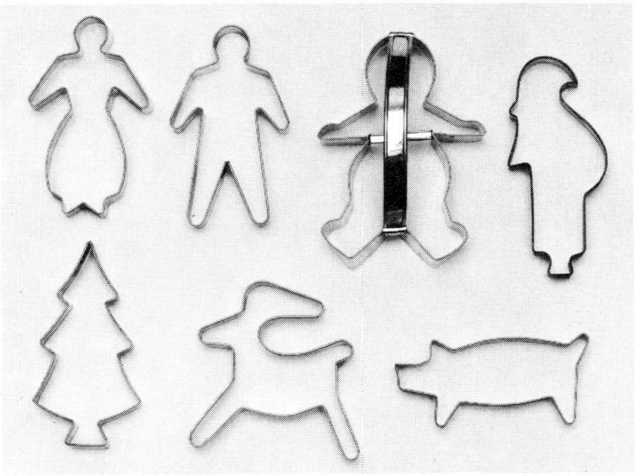

63

64

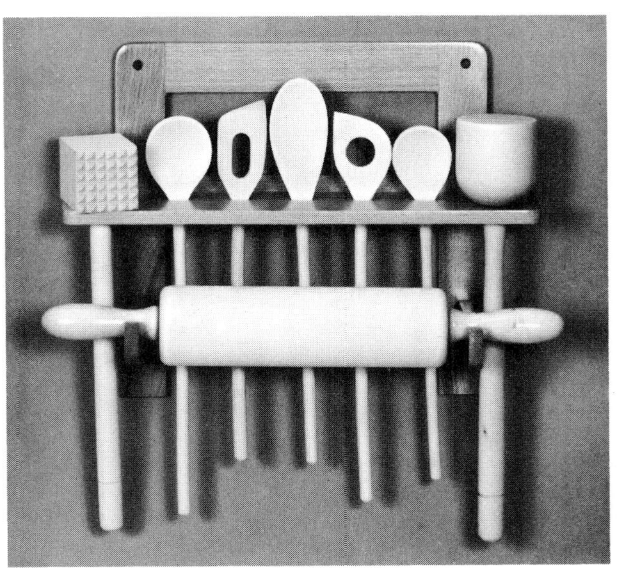

65

60 • *Levkar by the Barrel* Popcorn popper, 2-qt. capacity. $7.95.

61 • *Levkar by the Barrel* Coffee roaster, 2-lb. capacity, for gas or electric stove. $11.95.

62 • *Colonial Gardens Kitchens* Italian oil can enables you to control the amount of oil you pour and prevents dripping. 24-oz. size, $6.25; 42-oz. size, $7.98.

63 • *Levkar by the Barrel* Cookie cutters: gingerbread woman, gingerbread man, snowman or gingerbread man, Santa Claus, Christmas tree, deer, pig (size roughly 2½″ by 4½″), 79 cents each.

64 • *The Vermont Country Store* (see the Household Objects and Gifts section) English reproduction of an antique coffee grinder. $14.
photo Tom Ward, Inc.

65 • *Levkar by the Barrel* Nine-piece kitchen set: rack with rolling pin, meat hammer, vegetable masher, twirler, pointed spoon, round spoon, pointed mixing spoon, straight-edged mixing spoon. $16.95.

dren's plates and mugs, such as four porcelain animal mugs for $2.95, and a number of silver items that I hadn't seen elsewhere and which were again distinguished by their good design and low prices.

Colonial Gardens Kitchens, 270 W. Merrick Road, Valley Stream, N.Y. 11582
80-page illustrated black-and-white catalogue, free.

Colonial Gardens specializes in American regional kitchenware and lists a number of very useful items that other catalogues don't have. They have a modern version of the old-fashioned ice-cream maker, $18.95 for the hand operated 4-quart freezer, $33.95 for the electric version. They have a nice cast-iron corn-bread skillet that will cook eight wedges of corn bread, for $3.95, and a home flour mill for $15.95 that grinds a pound of corn or oatmeal in a minute. Nutmeg graters, sourdough mix, griddle weights, apple parers are among the other helpful offerings. The catalogue also has a selection of continental kitchenware, but the American items are the reason for which I would get their catalogue. There is also a broad selection of American and European foods.

Lekvar by the Barrel, H. Roth and Son, 1577 First Avenue, New York, N.Y. 10028
56-page catalogue, free.

Lekvar by the Barrel offers a wide range of special kitchen utensils with a particular emphasis on the extraordinary paraphernalia needed by the meticulous pastry chef. Their illustrated catalogue devotes a page to decorating tubes, another to "special drop flow tubes" that make attractive flower decorations with one press. There are pages of molds for ice cream, chocolate and coquilles St. Jacques, pans for making *madeleines* (the delicious French answer to Danish pastry), assorted boilers, steamers, broilers and a veritable universe of cookie cutters in every imaginable shape. There is also a wide selection of coffee mills and grinders (including that old-fashioned kind you hold in your lap), coffee makers, copperware and a unique selection of wooden implements. An excellent selection for more specialized needs, though not as complete as and general a choice as some others listed here.

The Maid of Scandinavia Co., 3245 Raleigh Avenue, Minneapolis, Minn. 55416
240-page color catalogue, 50 cents.
One year's subscription to Mail Box News, $3.

A big catalogue of such fantastic supplies for making spectacular cakes, pies, tarts and cookies that it's enough to coax one into the art of cake decorating. Besides molds, icings, edible and inedible decorations illustrating every hobby and interest, there are books to tell you how to proceed, aids to correct possible disasters, and festive novelties such as sugar babies, chocolate coins, decorated sugar, candy pebbles, crystallized violets and edible glitter. Plenty of party supplies and plates, napkins, invitations, favors, etc., which can be printed to order—so this catalogue is useful not only for inveterate cake decorators, but for anyone who cooks for children or who likes giving parties with frills.

Mail Box News is a little monthly magazine with recipies for fabulous-looking cakes—the cake of the month in the issue I looked at was a Monopoly board, and there were articles on readers' recipes, cakes from Finland and Sweden and "Cakes for Kids."

Manganaro's, 488 Ninth Avenue, New York, N.Y. 10018
16-page catalogue, free.

Manganaro's, whose speciality is Italian food, is described in detail in the Food section, also offers a number of specialized kitchen utensils of particular interest to those who want to make pasta, etc., at home. Since most suppliers show a marked bias toward France, you should look at this catalogue for various cheese graters, tomato strainers and noodle makers. There is an impressive machine which looks like a small printing press and will make noodles in eight different thicknesses ($29.95).

You can make ravioli either by using a small cast-aluminum device that looks like an ice-cube tray, for $4.75, or buy the big ravioli master that mass produces the requisite dough squares ($29.95). Manganaro's also sells various small espresso machines, using either the steam, drip or electrically powered steam, a home version of the kind used in espresso bars. The first two are very reasonably priced, $5.75 for a six-cup steam machine, and $4.25 for the drip kind. The electric is somewhat more expensive, at $14.50 for three cups, $21.50 for nine.

Paprikas Weiss, 1546 Second Avenue, New York, N.Y. 10028
64-page illustrated catalogue, annual subscription $1.

Paprikas Weiss, an excellent source of kitchen utensils, specializes in the needs of Middle European cooking, but offers a good general selection. They have such unique items as a wide choice of wooden coleslaw cutters, spaetzle machines (to make dumplings) and poppy-seed grinders. There is a lot of woodware, such as rolling pins and meat tenderizers, and aluminum stock pots, bakeware and meat grinders. There is also a full range of French copperware, and since these can be so expensive, it is worth getting the catalogues from the various shops and comparing their prices.

LIGHT FIXTURES

Aladdin Industries, Inc., P.O. Box 7235, Nashville, Tenn. 37210
12-page catalogue, free.

Aladdin makes very good kerosene lamps to be used if you have no electricity, when it fails or simply for atmosphere. You can get the equivalent of 100 watts on these lamps, which come in brass or aluminum in models for the table, wall or to hang. Prices are about $25 to $31.

Authentic Designs, 139 E. 61st Street, New York, N.Y. 10021
64-page catalogue, $1.

Careful re-creations and adaptations of Early American light fixtures are made here. Each fixture is made by one man and to a large extent made by hand, the brass arms are individually cut, bent and shaped by the same methods that were used two centuries ago, and the wood is turned by hand. The metal parts are solid brass and the woods are those most often used in eighteenth- and nineteenth-century America: maple, birch or poplar. The lights are for electric bulbs but can also be ordered for use with candles. Most sconces cost between \$25 and \$50, most chandeliers between \$150 and \$300.

DB Design, Charlotte, Vt. 05445
Brochure, free.

This firm sells two kinds of lamps. One is a round globe on a square base; you can get the globe in any one of nine colors and the base in any one of seven colors for about \$15. The other lamp "combines the ancient art of paper folding with 20th century plastic technology," to quote the brochure, and is one basic geometric shape made of hand-folded rigid vinyl plastic in a variety of colors, and comes in a hanging, table or floor version at prices from \$26 to \$56. This one is designed by DB (David Bredemeier) himself.

Heritage Lanterns, Sea Meadows Lane, Yarmouth, Maine 04096
16-page catalogue, 75 cents.

Twenty-three copper lanterns are handmade in traditional early-Colonial shapes. They are electrified and can be used indoors or out. Most prices between \$40 and \$100.

King's Chandelier Co., Highway 14, Eden, N.C. 27288
88-page catalogue, 50 cents.

This family firm designs and assembles chandeliers from imported Czechoslovakian crystal, and uses *no* plastic parts. About fifty magnificent chandeliers and sconces in crystal, and some in brass, cost between \$40 and \$700, with most between \$200 and \$400—they are illustrated in a catalogue which is interspersed with letters from happy customers, and photographs of historic homes in which the chandeliers are hung. There are also some chandeliers made in strass crystal, an especially brilliant patented Austrian lead crystal previously only used in strass costume jewelry. These cost more—between \$160 and \$800.

George Kovacs, Inc., 831 Madison Avenue, New York, N.Y. 10021
40-page catalogue, 50 cents.

One of the few stores in New York where really modern lamps are sold, George Kovacs, Inc., started out in 1961 by importing lamps, but has now become one of the largest manufacturers of lamps and lighting fixtures in the country. They say that lights should be "simple, inconspicuous, unpretentious and tasteful"; consequently, although the lamps are very modern-looking, they are almost always basically restrained arrangements of squares, cylinders and circles in black, white or shiny chrome. Prices run from about \$15 (what Kovacs calls *very* easy on your pocketbook) for plastic Danish-designed shades to assemble yourself to \$135 for a solid standard lamp with a rectangular polished chrome base and rectangular white shade that takes up to 700 watts. In between there are all sorts of basic standard and table lamps with absolutely simple metal or wood bases, discreet cylinders for background lighting, spidery desk lamps and squat wall lamps—most of them at prices between \$40 and \$80.

66

67

68

66 • *Authentic Designs* Twelve-arm chandelier with center of maple and the rest of brass; 24″ high, 21″ in diameter. \$265.

67 • *Authentic Designs* Solid-brass chandelier 16½″ high, 12″ in diameter, with 2′ of suspension chain and a ceiling canopy. \$75.

68 • *Aladdin Industries* Aluminum kerosene-only hanging lamp with a 14″ shade. \$39.50.

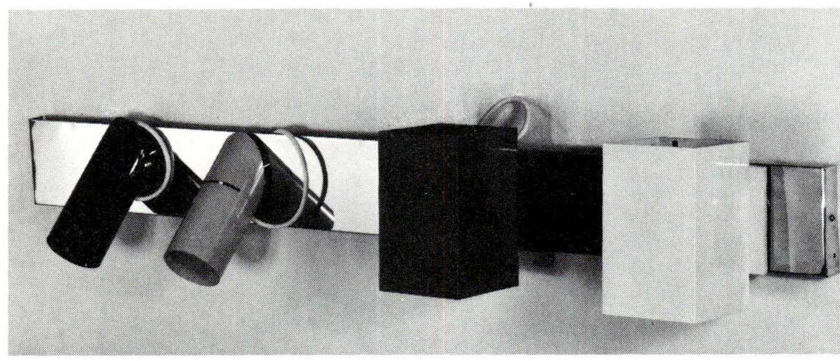

69

70

69 • *George Kovacs* "Zonking Place," polished chrome strip, 48″ long, 4½″ wide, which can be fixed to a wall horizontally or vertically, $29.50. Lamps that can be magnetically attached (as many as you want)—the two on the left in white, red, yellow, or black, $17.50; the two on the right, $29.50.

70 • *George Kovacs* White plastic ceiling lamp, 18″ high, 16″ wide. $70.

Lampland, 579 Sixth Avenue, New York, N.Y. 10010
38-page catalogue, some color, 35 cents.

Another source for modern lamps, not quite up to Kovacs' standards but here the prices are a bit lower; as with Kovacs, there are a lot of cylinders and globes, mostly in shiny or brushed chrome or in bright colors—more color here than at Kovacs'. One lamp which is a 6″ ball for a table or wall costs $16 in color and $20 in chrome; a tall graceful floor lamp that throws light up to the ceiling, providing an indirect light for the rest of the room, costs $55.

Traditional Glass Studio, 233 W. 7th Street, Eugene, Oreg. 97401
Color leaflet, $2.

The Traditional Glass Studio produces stained-glass lampshades in styles copied from, or inspired by, the shades designed in the 1880's by Louis C. Tiffany. Each of the shades is made from art glass cut and leaded by hand, and each one is signed by the person who made it, and then registered. Prices mostly between $40 and $200.

Earl Unger, 817 New York Avenue, Martinsburg, W.Va. 25401
6-page catalogue, free.

A West Virginia craftsman makes an odd collection of small lamps in styles varying from a lamp with a base made from a one-gallon utility can for $6.50 to a plastic-and-chrome "office" lamp with three movable black-tinted bulbs for $34. Earl Unger also sells adapters to make jugs and fruit jars into lamps.

LINEN

Chrisalem Sheets by Malerich, 2158 Charlton Road, St. Paul, Minn. 55118
Price list, free.

This firm makes dainty custom sheets in pale colors—light blue, pink, peach, primrose and cream nylon with nylon-lace trimming on the top sheet and pillows, or embroidered sheer trims and insertions. The sheets don't need ironing, and Malerich says that in spite of their fragile appearance, they are very durable. Each set costs between $33 and $48 according to size, and consists of a fitted bottom sheet with elastic all the way around, a flat top sheet and two pillow cases. As the sheets are made to order, they can fit any bed, and can have various color combinations. Blanket covers are also made.

Norman Dine Sleep Center, Wuensch, 33 Halsted Street, East Orange, N.J. 07018
29-page catalogue, free.

People who aren't up to making their own fitted sheets for odd-size beds can buy them here. They are rather expensive, starting at about $8 for medium-size beds, but the sleep center will make top or bottom fitted sheets in Sanforized percale in any shape or size, including bunk-size (which I always have a problem finding) for children or diagonal boat bunks. "Sinfully luxurious" washable satin sheets in black, lilac blue or red are also for sale, at $9 and up.

Jean Gale, Inc., 535 Madison Avenue, New York, N.Y. 10022
Leaflet, free.

Jean Gale sells clothes for girls and ladylike linens: Swiss-embroidered and monogramed sheets with pillowcases to match start at $15 for a twin-size sheet and $9 for a pillowcase. Hand-painted with flowers, placemats in plasticized shantung or leatherette cost $2 each, and there are also matching sheets, towels and blanket covers embroidered and monogramed.

Porthault, 57 E. 57 Street, New York, N.Y. 10022
94-page color catalogue, $1.

For some reason that I don't understand, Porthault is beloved of the rich and the grand. The catalogue starts with a dreary 8′ tablecloth made for the visit of H.M. Queen Elizabeth to the Elysée Palace in France, and continues with an equally dreary 86′-long cloth made for the 2,500th anniversary of the Persian Empire; you can have either of these made for you at unspecified costs. Table sets in linen, embroidered voile and appliqué voile start at about $130. There are completely matching sets for the bathroom, including washing mitts, cosmetic bags and bath robes, which cost in the vicinity of $200 if you buy one of each and more if you have them monogramed. Bed sets start at around $100 and wallpaper matching the linens is available, and a flowery plasticized fabric for kitchen or bathroom wallpaper. There is also linen for babies and children, and several smaller things such as lobster bibs for under $20, as well as a special luxury soap powder to wash your purchases with.

PEWTER

Colonial Casting Company, 443 S. Colony Street, Meriden, Conn. 06450
Leaflet, 25 cents.

After making molds for other manufacturers for many years, Colonial Casting Company decided to make some for themselves and use them. They now make a small collection of cast-pewter reproductions: Stark and Strong Early American plates, scalloped "old English" Colonial plates, early-eighteenth-century goblets, Early American tavern mugs, and spoons cast from the original. A 3″-high rum cup costs $11; candlesticks start at $18.50 a pair, and plates at $6.

For more pewter, see Cohasset Colonials, Craft House, Williamsburg, and Sturbridge Yankee Workshop under Reproduction Furniture; Jennifer House under Household Objects and Gifts; and Centaur Gifts under Glass and China; all above, in this section.

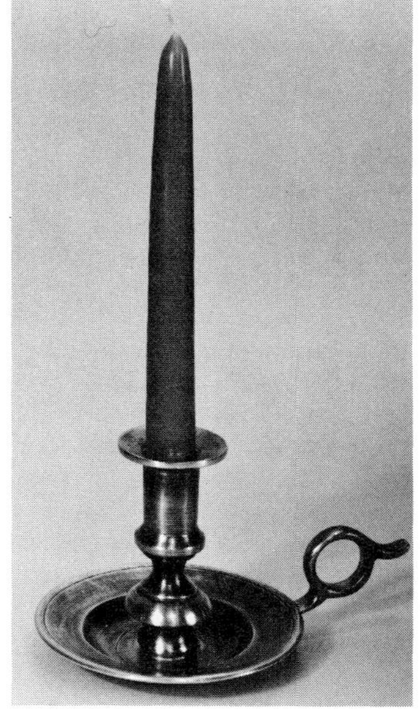

71 • *Colonial Casting Company* A few pieces from a collection of antique reproductions.

RUGS AND TAPESTRIES

Casa de Mexico, Box, 411, Donna, Texas 78537
Price list, 50 cents; refundable.
Polaroid photographs of specific items, 50 cents.

This small firm sells mainly old Western and Mexican antiques, but also has a few small rugs, made in Mexico. Rugs made of cowhide and goat hair, cloth-faced underneath, go up to 4′ by 7′ at $35. Mexican Indian woven rugs have light backgrounds with patterns in red, turquoise, yellow, black and blue; they cost $10 and are about 2′6″ by 5′.

The Fringe, 5600 Walnut Street, Pittsburgh, Pa. 15232
No catalogue.

A weaving studio that sells wall hangings and weaves wall hangings to order at customer's request. Prices are between $100 for a small piece of under 3′ by 4′ to about $500 for one of around 5′ by 6′. Most styles are highly textured abstracts, but I have also seen a Madonna and Child embroidered in metal thread on blue silk, for ecclesiastical use. The Fringe will enlarge and work on a design of yours (they have done this for several churches), or you can tell them what size and colors (with swatches) you would like, and for an advance of $30 (to be put toward the price of the hanging) they will send three sketches in color.

Charles W. Jacobsen, Inc., 401 S. Salina Street, Syracuse, N.Y. 13201
Catalogue, free.

Charles Jacobsen, author of an extremely useful book, *Checkpoints on How to Buy Oriental Rugs*, has been shipping Oriental rugs on approval for thirty years and says he has never had a customer write in with a single complaint. This firm sends descriptive lists of new Oriental rugs at prices from $125 for small ones to over $1,000, and used rugs, semi-antique, and antique—definitions of all these terms are carefully given—in fact, the catalogue is worth getting if you're thinking of buying an Oriental rug without knowing much about them, for these definitions alone. After looking at the catalogue, you fill out a form describing the kind of rug you want, size, price range, background color and type of pattern (floral, geometric, all over). Jacobsen then sends you (with a hand viewer if you have no projector) color Kodachromes of specific rugs you have asked for, plus others in sizes you are interested in. And with the Kodachromes comes a complete article and history of the different types of weaves. Finally, Jacobsen hopes you will ask them to send selections on approval. They pay the shipping costs both ways and add: "If by any chance you did not buy from a shipment, we would not feel bad. Our table of experience tells us that our shipping charges are a small item."

Reedcraft Weavers, Beulah, Mich. 49617
Price list, free.

Cotton rugs and place mats are woven by hand here "in the best tradition of American handweaving, without the use of fly shuttle or power devices." The rugs are washable, reversible and inexpensive; sizes go from 20″ by 20″ at $5 to 2′6″ by 5′ at $20. The design is a very small zigzag and diamond pattern, which comes in either white and pale colors, or else black, white and dark colors. The rugs are also available in solid off-white, and stairway runners can be made to measure. No illustrations.

Tapestry Associates, 300 Central Park West, New York, N.Y. 10024
Color slides, $1.

Tapestry Associates sells signed modern tapestries by appointment and by mail. Designs are gorgeously colored abstracts that look almost like paintings. Prices go from $35 to $150 per square foot, depending on the technique and material, with modern Aubussons costing about $110 per square foot. As 3′ by 5′ is a typical size, the prices are at least in hundreds of dollars. When asking for slides, it is important to give details of the price range you are interested in, and the size of the space you want to fill.

KITS

Coulter Studios, Inc., 138 E. 60th Street, New York, N.Y. 10022
28-page color brochure, $1.
Card with yarn samples, 50 cents.

Coulter Studios sells kits to make rya rugs and pillows imported from Sweden. The catalogue shows twenty-two rugs and eighteen pillows in abstract designs and mainly deep reds, blues and purples. The shaggy rugs are made by knotting yarn through a canvas backing, and they need no special equipment but can be made while you sit comfortably in an armchair, following a working chart if you have bought a ready-made design, though Coulter Studios encourages its customers to design their own ryas. Prices go from about $40 for a kit to make a 2′ by 3′ rug, to about $240 for a kit to make a rug 6′6″ in diameter. Kits include backing, yarn, needles, graph and instructions.

W. Cushing and Company, North Street, Kennebunkport, Maine 04046
New catalogue planned; ask about the price.
"The Rug Hooker, News and Views," bimonthly magazine, $1.25 single issue, $5 for a year's subscription.

This firm supplies everything for making hooked rugs: patterns, hooks, cutters, frames, wool, shears, instruction books, and it manufactures Cushing's "perfection dyes" which are used for batik and tie-dye, as well as by weavers and rug hookers. The large catalogue illustrates patterns, not kits, for hooked rugs, and the range is very wide—animal, plant, nautical and scenic designs are inspired by Blue Willow plates, Pennsylvania-Dutch designs, crewel embroidery and even a thirteenth-century Persian bowl in the Metropolitan Museum. For people with staying power there are designs for hall runners and stair carpets. "The Rug Hooker, News and Views" is a friendly little magazine for ardent rug hookers, with letters, from readers, and sections such as "Help! Answers to Hooking Problems" and "Ask Anne, Answers to Dying Problems" and articles such as "Orientals—How to Select and Use Colors."

72

73

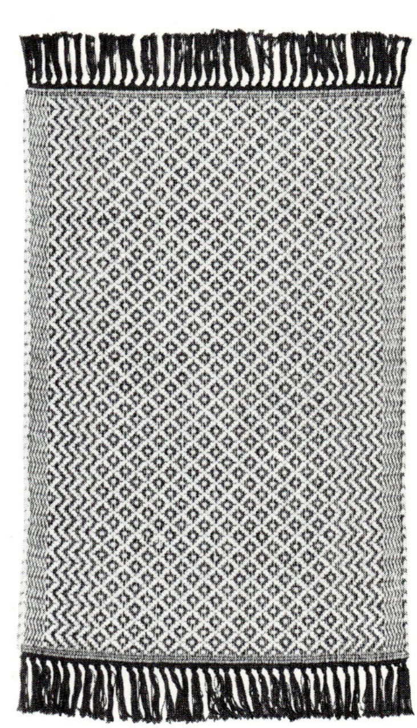

74

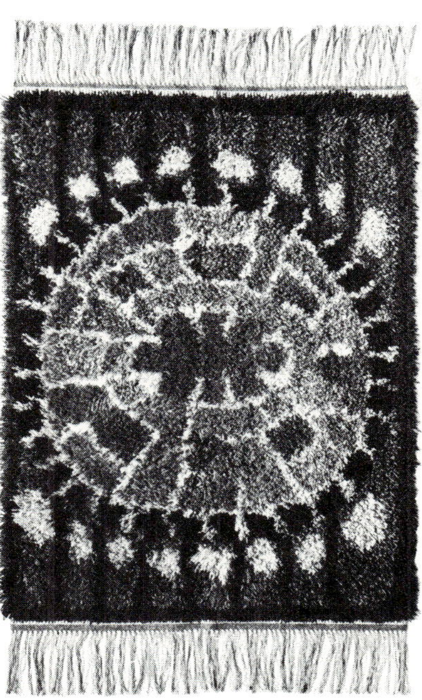

75

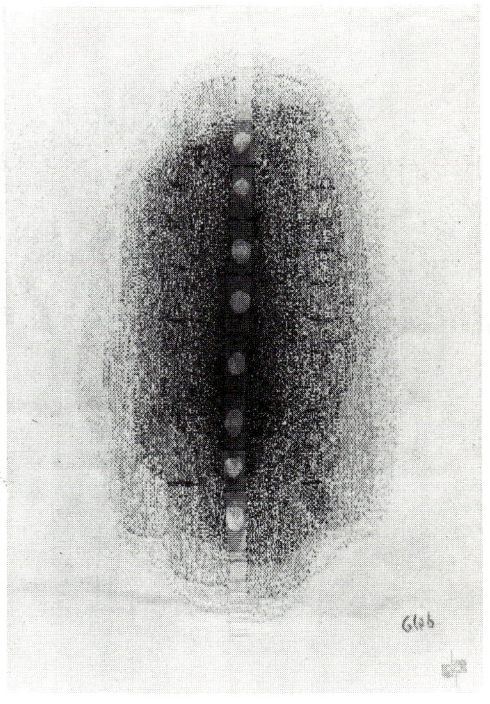

76

72 • *Charles W. Jacobsen* Four-panel prayer Saph, main colors camel, red, ivory and navy-blue. This rug measures 3′ by 8′ and costs $275. It is also available in single panels in sizes from 2′ by 3′ to 6′ by 8′.

73 • *Charles W. Jacobsen* A Mishkin rug made in northwest Iran copying the geometric design of Caucasian rugs. Blue, green, rose, ivory, beige, brown and gold are the main colors. A 3′ by 5′ costs from $150 to $225, depending largely on the quality.

74 • *Reedcraft Weavers* Handwoven cotton rug in sizes from 20″ by 20″ at $5 to 2′6″ by 5′ at $20.

75 • *Coulter Studios* Kits to make this rya rug, "Dalby Hage," are available in several sizes starting at 32″ by 41″ for $66.50. Main colors are greens and golds, but they can be changed to almost any other combination.

76 • *Tapestry Associates* Tapestry "Gleb" in orange, woven with a technique similar to the one used at Aubusson, but with more texture. Signed, in an edition of six, $3,860.
photo P. L. Buer

Heritage Hill Patterns, c/o Barbara Zarbock, Box 624, Westport, Conn. 06880
18-page catalogue, some color, $1.

Barbara Zarbock runs this firm herself and says that as she isn't bound up in red tape, she gives faster service than larger organizations. Her catalogue illustrates about seventy designs painted on burlap or monk's cloth for making hooked rugs. Some of the designs are small complete rugs, others are 14" or 18" squares which can be used as pillow cases and foot stools, or put together to make a rug as large as you like. The designs are neither traditional nor abstract but what Barbara Zarbock describes as "timeless": animals, plants and birds are illustrated with varying degrees of realism, and a group of "geometrics" (regular designs based on snowflakes), flowers and a quilt are especially suitable for joining together to make a large rug. Paternayan yarns are sold separately, and there are instructions in the catalogue for using hand hook and punch needle.

Shillcraft, 106 Hopkins Place, Baltimore, Md. 21201
24-page color catalogue, free.

Complete kits for about twenty-four hooked rugs with brightly colored English yarn. The designs are mostly floral, but there are one or two inspired by Oriental patterns. Also about twenty-four kits to make children's rugs, including several Walt Disney rugs showing Mickey Mouse, Donald Duck, Dumbo, Pinocchio, et al. Price for a kit just under 2′ by 4′ is $30.

Woolcraft, Inc., P.O. Box 747, Islington, Mass. 02090

Woolcraft is the exclusive distributor in America of rug kits from the well-known English firm Patons. The rug styles and colors are very standard indeed, nothing here to shock or surprise. This is how the catalogue describes them: "Traditional designs, based on classical Oriental rugs . . . floral designs derived from English and American furnishing traditions and abstract styles of Scandinavian design." There are three catalogues; they all come with yarn samples.

24-page color catalogue, Patons Rugs to Make at Home, 25 cents.

About fifty kits to make hooked rugs. Each kit consists of a stenciled rug canvas, pre-cut wool, latch hook and everything needed to bind the edges. Supplies can also be bought separately. Price for a rug 2′3" by 3′6" is about $30.

28-page color catalogue, Patons Classic Oriental Rugs, $1.

About eighteen hooked rugs loosely based on Oriental patterns, in sizes from 3′ by 3′ for $36 to 4′ by 8′ for $122. These kits can also be sold with charts instead of stenciled canvases, which makes them less expensive, especially in the larger sizes.

44-page catalogue, some color, Stitched Rug Charts, $2.

This catalogue has the actual charts for twenty-six stitched rugs, together with directions for buying the right amount of yarn. These rugs are stitched the way needlepoint is, but the yarn and canvas are considerably thicker. Many of the patterns are made up of triangles, circles, squares and lines.

For more rug-making kits, see Needlework in the Hobby and Professional Equipment section.

15
JEWELRY & SILVER

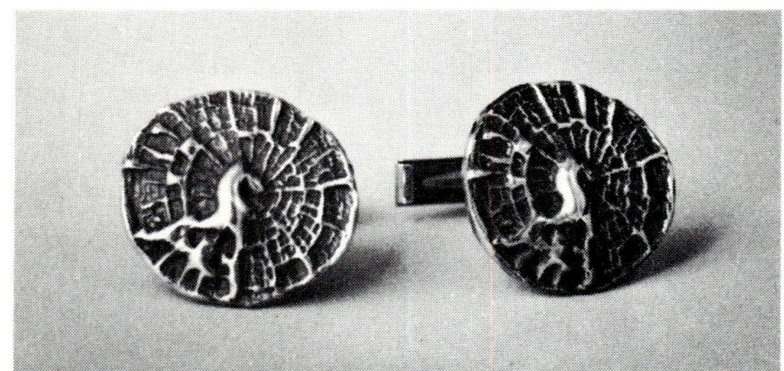
1

2

3

4

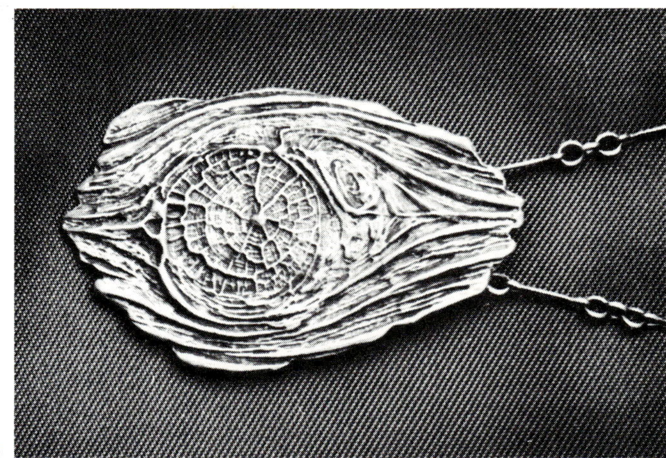
5

6

7

1 • *The Craft Shop at Molly's Pond* Sterling-silver cuff links, "Steed of Myths and Dreams." $20.

2 • *The Craft Shop at Molly's Pond* Sterling-silver ring, "Novae Stellae." $25.

3 • *The Craft Shop at Molly's Pond* Sterling-silver tie tacks: balsam-tip, wood-knot, Mucrospirifer, $6.50 each; starfish, $8.

4 • *The Craft Shop at Molly's Pond* Sterling-silver wood-knot tie clip, $8; sterling-silver wood-knot cuff links, $20.

5 • *The Craft Shop at Molly's Pond* Silver wood-knot pendant and chain. $32.

6 • *The Craft Shop at Molly's Pond* Silver cast from a Mucrospirifer fossil, Devonian period: key chain, $15; cuff links, $18; tie tack, $6.50.

7 • *The Craft Shop at Molly's Pond* Long beech-fern silver pins. Small, $12; medium, $16; large, $20.

Aladdin House Ltd., 648 Ninth Avenue, New York, N.Y. 10036
48-page brochure and color cards, $1.

Aladdin House, which specializes in selling artifacts and antiquities by mail, also makes jewelry reproductions in sterling silver and 14-carat and 18-carat gold based on jewelry that they own. They have quite a few replicas based on Byzantine crosses at between $16 and $50 in silver, and $45 up in gold, as well as rings, earrings, tie tacks and cuff links based on various Egyptian and Roman symbols and charms. Prices for these range between $13 and $30 for silver, and $25 and $195 for 14-carat gold.

Amulets and Talismans Ltd., 33 Christopher Street, New York, N.Y. 10014
24-page brochure, 50 cents.

"May the Udjat of Ra guide your smooth passage to the kingdom of Pharos" blesses the cover of this brochure, and much of the jewelry inside is what the store calls "metaphysical, i.e., archeological." In sterling silver or 18-carat gold, there are pendants and rings in the symbols the ancient Egyptian astrologers gave the ruling planets; chain-link bracelets with occult charms; "Om" (the primal chant) rings; infinity, Yin-Yang, and Chinese good luck, Ky, Star of David, the Legendary Hand of Fatimah, Ankh, Scarab, Eye of Ra, and even lucky-horseshoe and modern crucifix pendants. Also various scarab, lovers'-knot and collage-of-amuletic-symbols rings.

For the less mystically inclined, there are eight gold and silver chains, and also some very simple, modern jewelry. Chains start at $10 for silver, many pendants are between $10 and $20, but prices go as high as $355 for 18-carat gold lapis-lazuli cuff links.

The Craft Shop at Molly's Pond, U.S. 2, East Cabot, Vt. 05647
12-page brochure, free.

Luella Schroeder designs and makes sterling-silver jewelry by hand. The pieces, which are in small editions, are made by a variety of techniques: some are forged, others are cast, and others are cut, hammered and soldered. Patterns are often based on wild plants in Vermont: there are pins in the shapes of three different kinds of fern, medallions decorated with wild flowers, and earrings in the shapes of balsam-fir tips and wood knots. There are also tie tacks modeled after starfish and leaping trout, and cuff links based on fossils. Prices for sterling silver go from $6 to $25, and some of the pieces can be made in gold to order.

Desert House, 3514 E. Grant Road, Tucson, Ariz. 85716
24-page catalogue, 25 cents.

The president of Desert House says the firm goes to Indian reservations and buys jewelry directly from the craftsmen and traders, but since the price for the genuine article seems to "rise on a straight upward curve," they also stock manufactured turquoise and silver from factories in the Southwest. A neat brochure illustrates a few handmade silver, turquoise and coral rings and earrings that cost between $23 and $175, and magnificent Navajo squash-blossom necklaces for $350 to $450. There is also plenty of factory-made silver and turquoise jewelry under $10, and copper under $5.

8 • *Desert House* Indian-style necklaces made from imported coral beads. *Left:* single strand of Cupolini coral (twig shapes) with shell hishi, $39.95. *Center:* tube coral combined with shell hishi, $35. *Right:* double strands of Cupolini coral and shell hishi, topped off with silver beads, $79.95.

9 • *Desert House* Typical sand-cast sterling-silver belt buckle made by Navajo craftsmen for a 1½" belt. $49.95.

10 • *Desert House* Typical sand-cast silver jewelry, made by hand. A mold is carved into a piece of volcanic pumice and filled with molten silver, then filed and polished. *Left to right:* turquoise and silver key ring, $17.35; coral ring, $65; Navajo turquoise cluster ring, $65; double-nugget turquoise ring, $70.

11

12

11 • *Desert House* Typical handmade silver bracelets. *Top left:* silver and turquoise bracelet, $22.95. *Top right:* silver and coral, $75. *Bottom left:* turquoise and silver, $47.50. *Bottom right:* silver and turquoise, $175.

12 • *Desert House* Typical Navajo squash-blossom necklaces. As with all the handmade Indian jewelry, *no two pieces* are identical, so when you order a piece it will not look exactly like the one photographed. *Left:* "Princess," $450. *Right:* "Little Princess," $350.

Mignon Faget, 716 Dublin Street, New Orleans, La. 70118
Leaflet, free.

An ex-art student designs a witty collection of suede and leather bags and clothes, and by mail she sells her jewelry. An exotic leaflet shows glistening silver and gold shells on gleaming black bodies. The jewelry is all modeled realistically after sea creatures: for between $12 and $40 there are sterling-silver sea-urchin rings, sand-dollar cuff links, baby-snail earrings; and pendants of moon snail, cockleshell, clamshell and Venus clamshell on suede ties or silver chains. For $50 to $85, hand-rolled leather belts have heavy silver buckles in the shapes of shells or crab bellies. Most pieces are available in 14-carat gold at prices from $90 and up.

Greek Island Ltd., 215 E. 49th Street, New York, N.Y. 10017
24-page catalogue, free.

Greek Island, a shop that imports an assortment of things from Greece, has quite a lot of jewelry in their catalogue—long worry-bead necklaces, curly metal arm bands, and an assortment of jingly earrings and necklaces for under $20.

Shopping International, Inc., Norwich, Vt. 05055
48-page color catalogue, 25 cents. January.
64-page color catalogue, 25 cents. July.

Among the other decorative imports in these large catalogues, there is always an inexpensive and varied selection of jewelry—mosaic from Italy, enamel from Austria, wood from Germany, pewter from Norway, and silver from Israel. Mostly under $20, and plenty for under $10.

Tom W. Thomason, 400 San Felipe, N.W., Albuquerque, N.Mex. 87104
Leaflet, free.

Mr. Thomason designs and makes rather massive, rough jewelry with or without precious stones, in silver, gold and platinum. He has a degree in fine arts from the University of Mexico, his work has appeared in quite a few shows, and he sells through shops in New York, Washington, San Francisco. By mail, he makes jewelry to order at prices from $150 and up. For a fee of $10 he will send several designs from which you choose one and return the designs to Mr. Thomason with a third of the price as down payment. If you don't like the finished piece of jewelry you get your money back, except for the $10.

Tiffany and Co., Fifth Avenue and 57th Street, New York, N.Y. 10022
Gift catalogue, $1, October.
How to Buy a Diamond brochure, 50 cents.
Christmas-Card and Stationery catalogue, free. September through December.

Tiffany's is run by Walter Hoving, who doesn't believe in giving the public what it wants, because the public doesn't know what it wants. Luckily, Mr. Hoving knows what it should have—good design—so at Tiffany editorial board meetings no one is allowed to say, when discussing stock, "Will it sell?" They must say, "Is it new? Is it exciting?" Tiffany's refused to frame Bay of Pigs calendars in Lucite for President Kennedy; whether or not they approved of the Bay of Pigs, they

13

14

15

13 • *Mignon Faget* Sterling-silver belt buckles on hand-rolled soft suede or smooth leather. Belts, from the top: sea urchin, sand dollar, male crab belly, female crab belly, double scallop, double cockle, at prices between $50 and $85. Available to order in 14-carat gold.
photo Christopher R. Harris

14 • *Mignon Faget* Sterling-silver pendants on suede ties. *Top:* large cockleshell. *Bottom:* large scallop shell. $48 each. Available to order in 14-carat gold.

15 • *Greek Island* Hand-hammered metal bib choker in gold or silver finish. $20.

certainly didn't approve of Lucite (Kennedy came back and asked for silver). They rejected a large order for $50,000 worth of diamond rings for a pro-football team because Tiffany doesn't think that gentlemen should wear diamond rings.

Well, Tiffany's taste isn't perfect—whose is?—but it's not that bad. The Christmas catalogue shows, besides very expensive modern jewelry, modern silver, including quite a few little things for under $25, and some unusual china and glass. The Christmas cards in the card brochure are mainly reproductions of paintings or very discreet modern designs.

Unique Products, Callicoon, N.Y. 12723
Leaflet, free.

Little mimeographed sheets illustrate small pieces of silver jewelry, small animal scatter pins and larger stylized stars and fish pins with bits of abalone or copper, and children's and adults silver and abalone rings, all for under or around $5. But apparently Unique Products' most popular product is its sterling-silver thimble, which comes in three styles: with a satin finish, with abalone or "antique." The cost about $5 each, and they can be engraved—they make good keepsakes, says Unique.

Western General Store, Box 14348, Opportunity, Wash. 99214
20-page catalogue, 25 cents.

This firm sells perfectly pleasant factory-made "Western Design" and Indian-style jewelry in sterling silver, turquoise (genuine and simulated), and copper, aimed at the under-thirties. Most things cost less than $10.

For more jewelry, see the Handicrafts and Museums sections.

16
MUSEUMS

As museums in America have become more important, so have their shops. What were once small stands selling a few slides and postcards have grown into what are often the best art galleries and bookstores in town. Posters, reproductions, local and imported crafts have all been added, and in some cases, such as New York's famed Brooklyn Museum store, the result has been an internationally famous emporium of exquisite and otherwise unfindable folk items from all over the world.

With the growth of the stores, their facilities for selling by mail increased. Several now publish lavish illustrated catalogues and advertise in national magazines. Many more have excellent lists of their wares which have gained a local reputation but are still largely unknown outside their area. Most are worth looking into, particularly at Christmas for their cards, engagement calendars and art reproductions. But it is also worth keeping an eye on such items as exhibit posters, often issued by the smallest of museums. Many of the graphics sold at $10–$20 these days are not limited and numbered editions but the equivalent of these museum posters, which can sometimes be bought for as little as $1 each. Several museums also sell original works, such as lithographs, which they have commissioned and which can be an excellent way to get around high gallery prices (for instance the Los Angeles Museum).

The museums are also sources of reasonably priced reproductions of American antiques. I've often suggested that foreign visitors go to New York's Metropolitan Museum for its lovely silver and glass. Many museums, too, such as the American Indian, are beginning to act as outlets for current craft items, a vital help both in keeping the crafts (and the craftsmen) alive and in giving us all a chance to buy the lovely and all-too-rare things that our culture has produced and that our stores have neglected for so long.

Brooklyn Museum, Gallery Shop, Eastern Parkway, Brooklyn, N.Y. 11238
Christmas brochure, 25 cents.
Lists of books from the Museum Bookshop and Museum Publications, and a special list of art books for children, free.

If prizes were to be given to stores, the Gallery Shop would be one of my first candidates for an award. It is in many ways a model museum store and shows what can be done, both for the museum goer and to encourage craftsmen, here and abroad. Started in 1954 by Carl Fox, the shop began by selling toys from other countries but soon expanded into its present vast collection of some thousand toys from all over the world as well as handicrafts and folk arts from sixty-five countries. Fox went on to the Smithsonian, where for a while he established an equally grand series of stores which was, unfortunately, discontinued. What could have been an exciting extension of the Brooklyn experiment was severly curtailed and the stunning displays of artisanry and high art that Fox gathered are gone now, leaving behind only a small selection and all-too-many plastic replicas of the Apollo rockets.

This means that the Brooklyn Gallery is now, with the exception of the UN Gift Store, the country's leading source of relatively inexpensive handicrafts of a sort that, for the most part, commercial establishments have lacked the taste or imagination to stock. Now under the direction of George Mangini, the Brooklyn Gallery stocks items which, to quote them, range from "Russian dancing bears, spinning tops from Kentucky, hand puppets from Germany, Czech cornhusk dolls, whistles from Yugoslavia, and Japanese kites, as well as festival masks, woven rugs, wall fabrics and tapestries, silver jewelry, shoulder bags, glass and 19th century Persian pots and lacquer boxes."

It should be stressed that unlike those of other museums, the Brooklyn's offerings are all original, whether contemporary or early-nineteenth-century. Their prices are also extremely low and this is a marvelous place not only to buy things for your children but to let them do their own shopping. A miniature German tea service is only $2; Indian brass animals are $1.60; German teddy bears cost as little as $1.90 for a 4″ model, $2.90 for a 7″ model; an Inuk Eskimo doll costs $2.25; and a terra-cotta ceramic pig from Guatemala is all of 80 cents. Given such a choice, why ever buy the plastic ephemera that is so stridently pushed on television?

There is an equally exciting variety for grownups: Cambodian silver boxes shaped like exotic fruits or animals, $6.90; Italian coral or coral-and-silver bead necklaces, $12.50; hand-blocked cotton scarves from India, $1.60; Pakistani beaded bracelets for $1.75; traditional Russian lacquer wood boxes, $22; or a handwoven Indian rug, 43″ by 84″, for $15.

Obviously I could go on forever, and the best thing to do if you possibly can is to visit the shop itself. But if you can't, the catalogue gives you a tantalizing sample.

The Brooklyn Museum bookshop offers a choice of Christmas cards and reproductions, largely reflecting the museum's emphasis on Americana. I suspect that among its most popular posters are those issued for the Norman Rockwell exhibit, and two of his paintings, "The Dugout" and "Tattoo Artist" (I assume there is no need for me to describe these basic artifacts of American culture), are available in full color for only $2.

The museum's own publications are also available, as well as a very helpful little list, prepared with the Brooklyn Public Library, of art books for children which can also be purchased from the bookshop.

Chesapeake Bay Maritime Museum, St. Michaels, Md. 21663
Leaflet, free.

This waterside museum, which preserves a Chesapeake Bay harbor, complete with ships and buildings, has a shop devoted to maritime history which also sells the work of local artisans. Among the items it can sell by mail are books, notepaper and Christmas cards with nautical motifs. Their most interesting offering, however, is Chesapeake boat plans, which can be used for model building or for framing. Sloop, log canoe, bugeye, skipjack and pungy are all available, for $1, plus 50 cents' postage.

Dwight D. Eisenhower Library, Abilene, Kans. 67410
Price list, free.

The Eisenhower Library offers a number of books and mementos of interest to admirers of the late President and of the Presidency itself. In addition to the books written by Eisenhower and some about him, there are note cards showing scenes of Eisenhower's life, inaugural medals in gold wash and bronze, at $4 and $5, and assorted other items, such as Franklin D. Roosevelt's Portfolio of Navy Prints at $2.

Everson Museum of Art, 401 Harrison Street, Syracuse, N.Y. 13202
Price list, free.

The Everson Museum is far from being one of the country's best-known museums, but its price list contains some interesting items. The museum's own catalogues include publications on ceramics, which are a specialty there, and some unusual publications on American art, including a 64-page history of American Ship Portraits and Marine Painting ($3) which sounds like an excellent present for any sailing buff. The museum also offers catalogues from other museums, a useful service, and a number of very reasonably priced reproductions and posters. A 16″ by 24″ poster (black and red on sand color paper) for a Tantra art exhibit for only $1 seemed a special bargain—though I say "seemed," since the price list is unillustrated.

Fogg Art Museum, Harvard University, Cambridge, Mass. 02138
Price list, free.

Harvard's Fogg Museum is one of the country's most impressive university art galleries and one of the few with its own publication program. It is these catalogues that the museum sells by mail, and students and collectors may be interested in some of them. They reflect the particular strengths of the Fogg and range from a study of *Chinese Painting of the late Ming period* for $12.50 to a 14-page pamphlet on *Ben Shahn, as Photographer* for 50 cents. The publications are particularly strong on contemporary America and Asia and on classical antiquity but include individual publications, such as one on Turkoman rugs, which may interest people with very specific collecting needs.

Huntington Library, San Marino, Calif. 91108
Reproductions, Slides, Postcards, Christmas Cards, Notepaper, Photostats and Publications catalogues, free. (Send long stamped, self-addressed envelope.)

This famous California institution sells its own publications, reproductions of paintings in its collections, and the like. Among its publications are some lovely items that I've seen nowhere else and which I assume are available only from the Huntington. These include a number of facsimiles, selling for only $1 each, of such items as *Davy Crockett's Almanac* and two collections of poems and letters in manuscript, the former containing eighteen poems, from Robert Burns to Robinson Jeffers, and the latter twenty letters, from such varied authors as Robert Frost and George III. Other facsimiles, of particular interest to children, are copies of an 1800 edition of *Cinderella*, an 1805 version of *Old Mother Hubbard*, a *Pictorial Primer* for children, and so on. There is also a charming reproduction of Lafcadio Hearn's *The Boy Who Drew Cats*, a Japanese fairy tale illustrated by Yasu Komiya. The library's publications center on English and American history and on letters with special emphasis on California. These are, for the most part, on the nineteenth century but include such unexpected modern topics as *History of the Jews of Los Angeles*.

Library of Congress, Information Office, Washington, D.C. 20540
Brochure and price lists, free.

Although the Library of Congress does not have a store as such, it sells a number of items similar to those

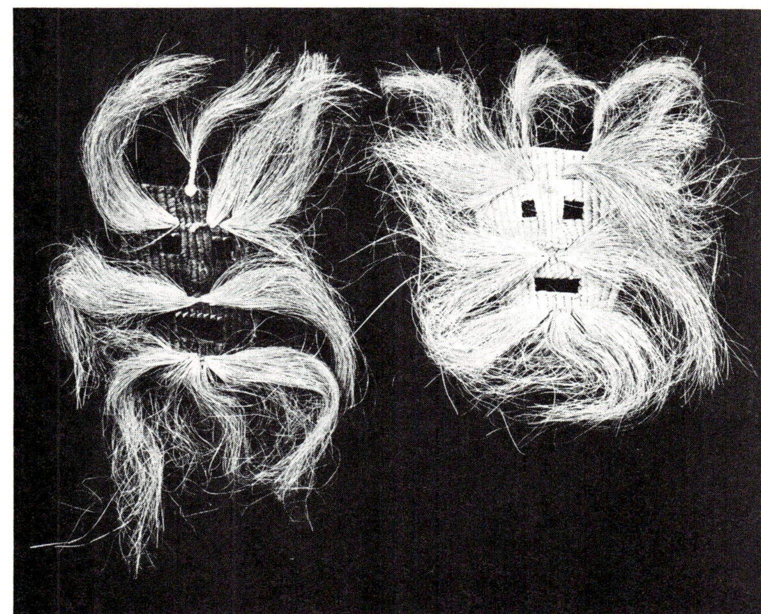

1

2

3

1 • *Brooklyn Museum* Mexican sisal mask in assorted colors, 9″ plus beard. $3.90.

2 • *Brooklyn Museum* Bronze alloy plaque of Buddha, Siam. 14″ high. $12.90.

3 • *Brooklyn Museum* Nineteenth-century embroidered silk pendants from the People's Republic of China, 2″ in diameter. Each one is unique. $12.90.

available from museums, and it has an extraordinary catalogue of American folk recordings and records of poets reading from their own books. (These are listed separately in the Music section, below.)

The Library's selection of greeting cards includes a very handsome group of Christmas cards, many based on woodcuts in its collections. In addition, there are a large number of cards without greetings, bearing no Christmaslike illustrations, which are intended for use as notepaper the year round. These include charming Japanese sketches, a handsome sixteenth-century Venetian zodiac, and a fifteenth-century woodcut of storks that would make a nice little birth announcement. The Library's prices are those that prevailed in the now inflation-ridden cities sometime ago and cards go from 10 to 25 cents, sold in packages of at least ten of one design.

The Library also publishes a number of facsimiles and books. Among these is a booklet containing reproductions of Lincoln's Gettysburg Address and Paul Revere's engraving of the Boston Massacre, printed in color, both for $1.50. A facsimile of Captain John Smith's map of Virginia, 16″ by 19″ is only $1.75, as is the facsimile of the first page of Genesis from the Gutenberg Bible, reproduced in black with the opening words in red and with capitals and ornamentation in red and blue. The Library also issues a list of its publications, many of which are free or available at nominal cost.

Los Angeles County Museum of Art Bookshop, 5905 Wilshire Boulevard, Los Angeles, Calif. 90036
Price list, free.

The Los Angeles list is still at the stage which many similar museums passed some years ago, but there are among the relatively few items in its list several that are well worth considering. The museum's own publications are the featured offering and include a number of very valuable publications that you may not be able to get elsewhere. These fifty titles range from studies of Afghan, Indian and Nepalese art to a study of the first 150 years of American printmaking. In addition to these, the museum bookstore stocks over three thousand titles in the arts and will accept special orders for any book *or reproduction* in print—this last being, I think, a unique service.

The original prints and posters commissioned by the museum, however, strike me as being its most interesting offering. Still in print are Man Ray's "Reclining Woman," a three-color original lithograph, 20″ by 26″, signed and numbered in an edition of 100 copies, for only $100. There is also an Oldenburg "Symbolic Self-Portrait with Equals," an offset lithograph in an edition of 300, for $175, and a black-and-white aquatint by Leonard Baskin, "Masaccio," in an edition of 100, for $100. Posters, such as a Calder copy of the original silkscreen commissioned by the museum, are $12.50. To show how much more reasonable museums are in their prices, one can compare the Baskin lithograph, which is on sale in a leading New York gallery for $150.

Metropolitan Museum of Art, Fifth Avenue and 82nd Street, New York, N.Y. 10028
72-page color Christmas catalogue, 25 cents.
Catalogue of sculpture reproductions, free.
Price lists of slides, postcards, books, needlepoint kits, free.
Color catalogue of reproductions of paintings, free.

The Metropolitan may be the country's most famous museum; it is certainly the one that has best organized the sale of its publications, reproductions, etc. Each year has brought a broader choice or items, most of which are exclusive with the museum.

The major catalogue is its annual Christmas one, in which it presents its most popular items with professional lushness. The 1972 catalogue started with 22 pages of the museum's famous Christmas cards (which are changed every year), very handsome reproductions that are models of good printing. Then came reproductions of fine porcelain, which the museum offered for the first time: a lovely flowered Meissen plate for $17.50, and a copy of a plate made in 1760 for Peter the Great's daughter, for $50, both copies made by Haviland of Limoges. For people who like collecting plates, this would be a far more interesting purchase than all the annual and Christmas plates now being sold.

The museum's most famous copies have been of Early American glass, cut-glass decanters, pitchers, etc., following the American styles that flourished around 1820. Four glasses and a decanter sell for $50; a small, amber-colored pitcher for only $8.75; four tumblers and a decanter in a sunburst pattern, $27.95. Also available from a later period are a blue sugar bowl and creamer, tumblers, bowls, lovely dolphin candlesticks, all from the mid-nineteenth century.

In addition to glass, the museum was one of the first to offer reproductions of ancient jewelry, and here again, their selection is splendid. A gold lion-mask ring from Luristan (1000–800 B.C.) sells for $7.85 (gold finish over silver); a Frankish three-serpent brooch from the sixth or seventh century for $13.50; Byzantine crosses for $9.50, and lovely large belt buckles and similar ornaments ranging from $4.50 to $29.50—all fantastic bargains as well as exquisite objects.

Finally, the museum offers an engagement calendar each year and now also publishes a handsome address book, $2.75 and $4.95, respectively, both with 40 pages of color.

The separate catalogue for sculpture reproductions includes some charming and inexpensive pieces, my children being especially fond of the three Jerboa mice from the Twelfth Dynasty ($3.95) and the various hippopotamuses, also Egyptian ($5 up). The reproductions are mostly from the Ancient Middle East, including a number of lovely cups and wine jugs but there are also some remarkable bronze copies of some of the treasures of the Cloisters, but these are far more expensive: $150 for a medieval falcon, but it is made of bronze with traces of gold mounted on a block of Belgian black marble.

My favorites are the classically simple copies of Paul Revere coffee spoons in sterling silver for $5.50, the kind of wedding present I wish I'd gotten. The museum also offers some copies of Shaker tables; a number of needlework kits based on pre-Columbian textiles, selling from $16.95 to $39.50; and a very nice selection of its own designs of notepaper and cards, the latter bearing Kate Greenaway illustrations for a Victorian alphabet book. In other words, there is an enormous variety of well-chosen reproductions, ranging from the moderately priced to the very expensive.

The museum also issues an illustrated catalogue of its very handsome color reproductions and also has lists of slides, postcards and various packets of special interest to schools (or to parents). Educational discounts are available to the former, but unfortunately not to the latter.

4

5

6

7

8

9

10

4 • *Metropolitan Museum of Art* Early-American glass, reproduction of one of the most famous designs from the Sandwich glasshouse: the Dolphin candlestick in emerald green. Mid-nineteenth century. 10⅝″ high. $17 single; $34 the pair.
photo David Fletcher

5 • *Los Angeles County Museum of Art Bookshop* Poster for an exhibition of American printmaking with an engraving by Paul Revere, 30″ by 20½″. $5.

6 • *Metropolitan Museum of Art* Ancient Egyptian wall calendar, 12″ by 17″. Illustrated with a different magic symbol and a text of explanation for each month. December unfolds to a 3′ picture of a mummy case. Eight full-color illustrations, five duo tones. $3.95.

7 • *Metropolitan Museum of Art* Early-American blown glass, reproductions of rare examples of small three-mold wine or cordial glasses (c. 1820). Height 4⅛″. Boxed set of four glasses, $35; boxed set of four glasses with decanter, $50. Also sold separately.

8 • *Metropolitan Museum of Art* Reproduction cast in stone, from a mold taken direct from the original sculpture of an Egyptian owl, Ptolemaic period, 332–330 B.C. It can be hung from an attachment on the back. 4⅛″ by 4¼″. $12.50.

9 • *Metropolitan Museum of Art* The museum's first reproduction in fine porcelain is a 9¼″ plate from the royal porcelain factory at Meissen (c. 1725–40). Decorated with Chinese flowers and butterflies in seventeen colors; molded basketweave border. $17.50.

10 • *Metropolitan Museum of Art* American glass, Thistle plates, reproductions of lacy glass plates of the 1830's—the repeating pattern may have been inspired by Halley's Comet, which appeared in 1835. A boxed set of four plates, $18.75.

11

12

13

11 • *Museum of the City of New York* Cast-iron reproduction of a circus calliope (c. 1896). 15″ long; colors red, gold, black and white. $39.50.

12 • *Museum of the City of New York* Pollock's Redington Toy Theater, $10 (with plays: *Jack in the Beanstalk* and *Aladdin*).

13 • *Museum of the City of New York* Reproduction of a map of New York and Brooklyn (1877). 27″ by 48″. $5.

Mission Houses Museum, 553 S. King Street, Honolulu, Hawaii 96813
Brochure, free.

This museum preserves three early-nineteenth-century Protestant missionary houses, which are a national historic landmark, and has a gift shop that stresses local Hawaiian products, "including items relating to the whaling trade and the South Pacific." The shops carry an extensive selection of books for children and adults on Hawaii, and a number of locally made gifts. These include a missionary doll, outrigger canoes, Hawaiian hand puppets and several native versions of checkers and bowling. The local *kukui* nut is used to make jewelry, chokers and pendants selling for $1.50, and a lei made of thirty of the polished nuts sells for $18. Of particular interest are a number of rarer items, specially made, about which you must write for particulars. Scrimshaw is available as jewelry for men and women, earrings, cuff links etc. Feather leis are available, as are shell leis made of the very small and delicate shells from the island of Nihau. Profits from the shop help further the Mission Houses' educational programs in Hawaiian schools.

Museum of the American Indian, Broadway at 155th Street, New York, N.Y. 10032
Lists of slides, specialized monographs, cards, free. 86-page list of books about Indians, 50 cents.

This is the largest Indian museum in the world and offers a wealth of material not only on North American Indians but on those of Central and South America. As might be expected from a museum of this kind, much of its activity is directed toward schools and specialists, and its collection of slides is an extraordinary document in itself. The extensive book list is both a basic bibliography and a catalogue of titles that may be bought from the museum itself. There are also scholarly lists of monographs, leaflets, and the like.

Unfortunately the museum's lovely craft store does not issue a catalogue, since its holdings are all one of a kind and thus constantly changing. However, if you know pretty much what you would like in the way of basketry, kachina dolls, masks, pottery and other craft items from all the Americas, the store encourages you to write with your inquiry and they will tell you what they stock and at what price. No reproductions are sold, and obviously buying from the museum is a sure guarantee of authenticity.

Museum of the City of New York, Fifth Avenue at 103rd Street, New York, N.Y. 10029
Price list, free.

The Museum's small shop has always featured a delightful collection of reproductions of Americana, and though it has, unfortunately, no catalogue, its offerings are nonetheless worth considering. Among the items I found most interesting were a reproduction of a ship's decanter, made of clear lead crystal, for $10, and some charming Friesland tiles, 5″ by 5″, made in Holland, in blue-and-white or multicolored of birds, animals, people, flower, fruit or patterns, at $4.50 or three for $10. Delft tiles are also available, showing figures from the Dutch colonial period and costing $3 for a 4″ square tile and $5 for 6″ square. Also from Holland are lovely handcrafted wooden meat boards, using seventeenth-century designs and measuring 18½″ by 8″.

More recent Americana includes a $6 kit for making

an old-fashioned doll, including the hand-tooled wooden parts and material for its clothes. Patterns for making soft toy animals are also available, $1.50 for a kitten and $3 for larger animals. The finished toys cost $6 for toys 1′ high and $3.50 for the kitten, half the size. Ante-bellum paper dolls—a family of four, copies from the 1860 *Godey's Lady's Book,* cost $1.50 for four sheets, and a group of reproductions of old mechanical banks are also available, starting at $19.50 for a Tammany and going up to $37.50 for Uncle Sam or Jonah and the Whale.

Among the items relating to New York history are a 1776 map of New York, in its original colors, for $2.95 and a later, 1877 version for $5. For medallion collectors, the museum struck a commemorative of its fiftieth anniversary, available in bronze for $15, silver for $100 and gold for $500.

Museum of Fine Arts, Department 751, 479 Huntington Avenue, Boston, Mass. 02115
48-page color catalogue of cards and gifts, 25 cents. Annual.
48-page black-and-white catalogue of books, 25 cents. Annual.

Though not as large as the Metropolitan's, the Museum of Fine Arts shop has always been an exciting and original place for me (I also have memories of their restaurant selling the best brownies I've ever eaten). As with all museums, their catalogue offers a wide selection of cards, though with a stronger emphasis on Oriental and Early American art, two of the museum's strongest points. There is a selection of jewelry reproductions similar to the Metropolitan's, but also a substantial offering of sculpture reproductions, Greek, Roman and Etruscan heads and statues, some as little as $6.50 (for an old Egyptian head) to $100 for a T'ang pottery horse. Unique to the museum are its splendid reproductions of classic American silver: a lovely, lithe letter opener adapted from a Paul Revere skewer, for $11.50 (an ideal murder weapon for a genteel mystery), and a marvelously simple spouted cup by Joseph Richardson, Jr., 2″ high, for $55. There is also an Ebenezeer Moulton pitcher dating to 1810, for $90, and a Benjamin Burt beaker for $37.50. These are custom-made and require three weeks for delivery, but are well worth the wait, for their evocation of the severity and simplicity of American craftsmanship of the Revolutionary period.

While this illustrated catalogue includes a charming array of lesser gifts ranging from matchboxes to jigsaw puzzles, the most welcome addition for many may well be the needlework section. The museum has shown great imagination and taste in its choice of needlepoint and crewel patterns from its collections. Rather than the usual, often banal designs, they offer a stunning DeStael painting, bright as a Braque, and unfortunate only in its high price, $75. There is also a lovely adaptation from a Hiroshige drawing of a grasshopper, and morning glories ($55), and a detail from a *No* costume design at the same price. Two needlepoint designs, for $38 and $40, are based in a Braque detail and on a Persian bowl. There are some very inexpensive crewel-embroidery kits, based on the traditional plant motifs dating from early-eighteenth-century Ipswich, Massachusetts, at $8 each, as well as larger crewel designs from the same period ranging from $14 to $22. As with the Metropolitan, museum members get a discount, and it may be worth your while becoming a mail-order member.

14

15

14 • *Museum of the City of New York* Reproduction of a two-sided jigsaw puzzle with a Currier & Ives print on each side: "Fashionable Turn-Outs in Central Park" on one side, "Central Park–Winter" on the other. $4.

15 • *Museum of Fine Arts* Reproductions of ancient figures. *Left to right:* Mercury, Greco-Roman, in bronze, 6½″ high, $25; Hermes with a ram, 12½″ high, $35; bronze head of warrior, Etruscan, 525-500 B.C., 5¼″ high, $8.50; bronze dancing woman, Etruscan, 525-500 B.C., 5¼″ high, $18.50; standing girl, Italic, c. 200 B.C., 8″ high, $18.50.

16 • *Museum of Fine Arts* Gold- and silver-plated jewelry made from reproductions of ancient coins, amulets and ornaments. Earrings, pins, cuff links, tie clips and pendants at prices between $3 and $7.

Museum of Modern Art, Publication Sales Department, 11 W. 53rd Street, New York, N.Y. 10019
40-page color Christmas catalogue, 25 cents. Available each September.
Postcard, slide, reproductions and publications lists, free.

New York's Museum of Modern Art was one of the first museums to offer a wide range of materials for sale to its members and to the general public, and has also been the first to commission new artwork systematically, both for its annual Christmas cards and for various objects that it has produced and sells. As a result, the museum offers a number of items reproducing some of its famous holdings and other works that are less familiar but appear to be very popular as well.

The museum's very handsome Christmas catalogue shows this mix even in its colorful Christmas cards, some of which are by Picasso, Derain and Calder but others which are more pop, such as Thom Klika's "Santa Claus Is Coming to Town." All the cards are very attractively presented but tend to be more expensive than those from other museums, the cheapest being 30 cents and others going up to 50 cents. Some Christmas cards can be transformed into tree decorations or mobiles—one a silver star at 75 cents; the other, again by Klika, centering on a gay rainbow, $1.50.

The museum's objects are not copies of pieces in the collections, which in part I regret, since it would be marvelous to have a place where one could buy, for instance, some of the items in its collection of good industrial design, but are decorative and often amusing metal or plastic objects. Among the most popular are a pair of chrome-plated aluminum hearts that sell for $10. The most expensive item is a multiple sculpture in an edition of 100—"Kinetic Circle," by Phyllis Mark, gold plate on aluminum, for $95. This is as good a place as any to note that museum members get a 25 percent discount, so the saving on this piece would pay for a year's membership (about $20 for an individual).

Other items tend to be less expensive, such as a set of forty plastic blocks, Konnecto, which allow you to construct your own sculptures or a series of interlocking transparent colored discs, each for $2.50.

The museum sells a number of reproductions of its most popular and famous paintings, such as Rousseau's "The Dream" or Van Gogh's "Starry Night," at $7.50 each, and has a very extensive list of postcards and of color slides (these at 60 cents each). A few of the museum's attractive posters are still available, for prices that range from $2 for a sepia-and-white announcement of the Arget photograph show to $10 for Robert Indiana's red, white and blue poster for *Four Americans in Paris* or the full-color with silver Jackson Pollock poster. As with other museums, the annual engagement calendar, this year devoted to food, is the perennial bestseller.

Finally a word about the museum's excellent books and pamphlets, all available by mail and still among the country's best bargains in art publishing. In addition to such famous volumes as *Picasso in the Collection of the Museum of Modern Art* ($15) and *Four Americans in Paris* ($7.95) or *The History of Photography from 1839 to the Present Day,* there are a number of less known but extremely attractive illustrated volumes and limited editions. The Ben Shahn *Partridge in a Pear Tree* at 95 cents is often used as a Christmas card, but there are equally handsome little volumes by Shahn, Calder, Frasconi and others from 95 cents up. The museum's publications list has details of these as well as the older, basic titles on painting, sculpture, photography, architecture, film, industrial design, crafts and art education. No museum in the world, I believe, has such an extensive publication program and its books and pamphlets have set a high level which it would be marvelous if other institutions could emulate.

The New York Public Library, Sales Shops, 42nd Street and Fifth Avenue, New York, N.Y. 10018
62-page color catalogue, 25 cents. Annual.

What was once a modest sales counter with Christmas cards has blossomed into two very imaginative stores, one at the main library, the other in the new Lincoln Center Library of the Performing Arts. As a result, a number of delightful cards relating to theater and dance history have been added to the library's earlier offerings. Among these exclusive items is a series of giant, 6″ by 9″, postcards reproducing old theater posters featuring the Duse, Ethel Barrymore, Maude Adams and a very abandoned Eva Tanguay, showing a surprising amount of leg. There is also a set of ten cards with black-and-white drawings of more modern actors and actresses—Judith Anderson, Katharine Cornell, Lunt and Fontaine—though to the younger generation these distinctions may seem dubious.

The library's cards, which come without greetings or can be imprinted with your own name, include some lovely bits of Americana, such as a Currier & Ives print of ice skating in Central Park or a Thomas Nast sketch of Santa. There are many classic images drawn from the library's collections, including a number of illustrated manuscripts, seventeenth-century German and Italian engravings, a charming William Blake sketch, and others, many at 10 cents and none more than 20 cents. The library also, appropriately enough, sells bookplates, for practically nothing: a box of 50 for $1, five boxes for $3, and ten for $5, probably the only item in this book still available for a penny. The bookplates include several suited for children and others relating to the theater, the sciences, horticulture, and other special interests.

In addition to cards, the catalogue lists some charming reproductions of old children's books, including a Kate Greenaway coloring book and a volume containing fifty-three full-color Currier & Ives reproductions that can be cut out and mailed. A number of books on the theater are also available, as well as some of the library's own publications.

There are also some twenty pages of toys, games, statuettes, etc., including a number of old favorites such as a wild-flower card game, Beatrix Potter posters, some charming and inexpensive musical jewel boxes, etc. An excellent place to check for inexpensive children's presents, which combine those rare qualities of good taste and the ability to enchant children as well.

Norwegian-American Museum, 502 W. Water Street, Decorah, Iowa 52101
Price lists, free.

This museum shop was one of my favorite discoveries, for it showed how national interest has grown in crafts and customs that, a few years ago, one would have assumed would disappear from the American scene. The museum itself (under the patronage of King Olaf V of

17

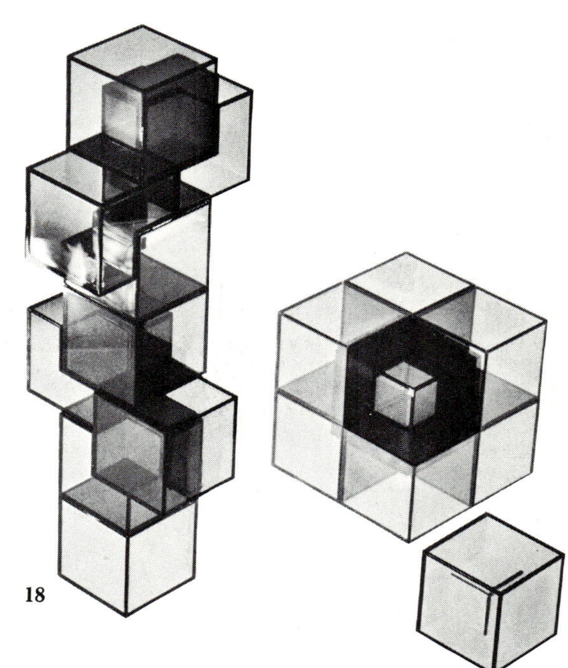

18

17 • *Museum of Modern Art* Playing cards designed by Bruce Blackburn, standard size. $5.

18 • *Museum of Modern Art* "Equivocations," designed by Betty Thomson. Eight incomplete molded cubes and one complete cube can be arranged in various ways or made into one 4″ cube with the ninth cube in the center. $20.

19

20

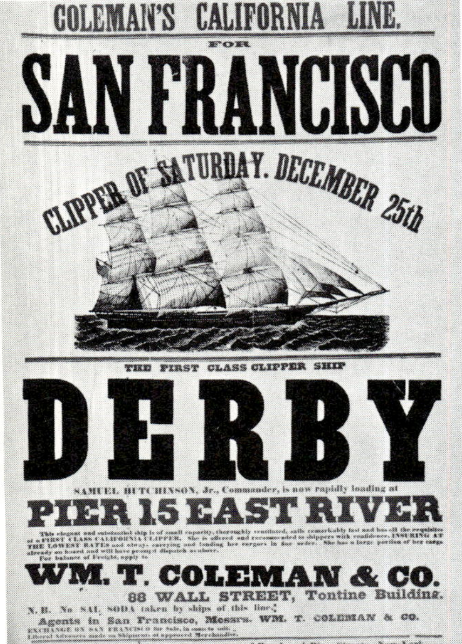

21

22

23

19 • *Whitney Museum of American Art* Reproduction of "Early Sunday Morning" by Edward Hopper, 23″ by 37″. $5. *photo Geoffrey Clements*

20 • *Whitney Museum of American Art* Circus poster by Alexander Calder. Main color, yellow; 22″ by 30″. $5.

21 • *Peabody Museum of Salem* Reproduction of broadside in black, red and white, 34″ by 22½″. $3.

22 • *Peabody Museum of Salem* Liverpoolware reproduced by Wedgwood from originals in the museum's collection. Larger jug, 6½″ high, $25; smaller jug, 5″ high, $13.25; bowl with compass rose inside and ship and verse outside, 7¼″ in diameter, $25; cup with picture of sailor's departure and verse, 2½″ high, $3.50.

23 • *Peabody Museum of Salem* Collotype reproduction, hand-colored, of a scarce engraving by Abel Bowen of the U.S. frigate *Constitution,* launched in 1797. 18″ by 23″. $7.50.

Norway) is ninety years old, but its craft shop is only seven years old and has in recent times had difficulty keeping up with the demand for its Norwegian craft specialties. The most interesting of these are the Klostersom kits, which include the canvas, yarn, needle, pattern and instructions needed for a technique similar to needlepoint. The results are very charming pillows, table runners, tote bags, and the like, decorated in traditional Norwegian patterns. The kits cost from $4 to $8 for a pillow 15″ square, real bargains. The museum also publishes a number of works on *rosemaling*, a traditional style of painting objects with intricate patterns (see Hobby section). A packet of three sheets of designs for this is available, as are various reproductions and notepapers with the designs. A *Pioneer Cook Book*, compiled by museum volunteers, is also available. What a shame that such museums don't exist for each of the immigrant groups that came to America.

Peabody Museum of Salem, Sales Desk, 161 Essex Street, Salem, Mass. 01970
Illustrated brochures, free.

The Peabody Museum's offerings are the nicest gifts for sailing buffs that I have seen, and faced with its choice of prints, it is hard to decide which are the most pleasing. The Peabody has several categories of reproductions. First are color prints of originals in its collection, reproductions for the most part of nineteenth-century oils and watercolors. A lovely, romantic portrait of the U.S. frigate *Constitution* reproduces a scarce 1817 engraving, and is hand-colored. Clipper ships, brigs, the Northern Whale Fishery, the *Daphne* attacking a monster sea serpent are all subjects, ranging in price from $7 to $25 for the ship *Poland* burning at sea, 18¼″ by 24½″. These prices are for unframed prints, but framing can be arranged through the museum. In addition to these, the museum offers color plates from *Marine Paintings and Drawings*, 10″ by 13″, framed at $6 each, $1 more for postage. Color plates from the Chinnery catalogue are $1.50 each or $5 framed. Other reproductions include a lovely, stark broadside or sailing notice of a clipper bound for San Francisco, black, white and red, measuring 34″ by 22½″, for $3. Christmas and note cards, a list of books and pamphlets and back numbers of the Peabody magazine, the *American Neptune*, are also listed.

Finally, the museum has for sale a number of very attractive plates, bowls, etc. Exclusive with the museum is a set of twelve plates made by Josiah Wedgwood and Sons to commemorate the 150th anniversary of the East India Society. Each plate shows a different Salem vessel and is 10½″ in diameter. The set costs $90, or $8.50 each, plus postage. Also from Wedgwood are Liverpool-ware reproductions: a bowl with a compass rose inside for $25; cups; a small pitcher for $13.25 or $16.50; and a striking jug with a black ship on it, 6½″ high, for $25.

Philadelphia Museum of Art, P.O. Box 7646, Philadelphia, Pa. 19101
34-page color catalogue, free.

This museum shop is another example of growth and expansion in recent years and the handsome catalogue includes a number of things not to be found elsewhere. As with all museums, it starts with Christmas cards based on the museum's holdings, which are extremely varied and include a number of nostalgic nineteenth-century American engravings by Thomas Nast and others, as well as some delightful American primitives. (I particularly liked a nineteenth-century locomotive for 20 cents.)

The museum's Americana is also very well represented in its painting reproductions, which include a lovely "Noah's Ark," by Edward Hicks, for $15, and a Winslow Homer watercolor, "Gloucester Schooner," for $10. The museum also has a nice line of boxed notes, some of which are available without greetings and thus usable year-round. Several are based on Early American quilt or sampler designs and are extremely attractive.

Given today's interest in needlework, the choicest item from Philadelphia is its new needlepoint kits, Bargello patterns adapted from an English 1841 sampler and available in various colors as small purses or eyeglass cases ($10 each or $18 for a matched set). These would seem perfect presents for beginners or for the vast number of teen-agers who have taken up needlework. The shop also offers sampler packets of design tracings that can be used for pillows, belts and other accessories, for 75 cents each.

In addition, there is a small choice of handsome jewelry. I particularly liked the reproductions of sixteenth- and seventeenth-century French keys made into pins and pendants for $5 to $6.50, as well as some pendants based on, of all things, Japanese eighteenth- and nineteenth-century sword guards, a marvelous transformation of swords into not-quite plowshares from the City of Brotherly Love. Finally, the museum offers stained-glass reproductions: a rose, quail, duck or unicorn, ranging from $13.50 to $20.00, sold with a loop that allows you to display the glass on your window, or presumably to fill in the gaps in your own stained glass if your house has one of those turn-of-the-century stained-glass doors or borders.

Whitney Museum of American Art, 945 Madison Avenue, New York, N.Y. 10021
Price lists, free.

The Whitney does not offer as much for sale as other New York museums but it does have a very nice selection of its own exhibition posters, which it sells at extremely reasonable prices, as well as a good selection of reproductions and postcards. The posters cost from $5 to $15 and include such attractive subjects as the museum's exhibits of Frankenthaler, Gottlieb, Motherwell, American Naïve Painting, Albers' Homage to the Square, and Calder's Circus. For anyone interested in modern American art as such, rather than in collecting prints and original works of art, these are excellent value. The museum also sells a series of "Save Our Planet" posters, costing $10 or $15, plus $2.50 postage, by a number of artists. Roy Lichtenstein has done "Save Our Water," Georgia O'Keefe "Save Our Air," Steichen "Wilderness," Calder "Wildlife," Buckminster Fuller "Cities," and Ernest Trova "People."

The museum's reproductions are also reasonably priced and feature its most famous American painters, Bellows, Gorky, Hopper, Marsh, Pollock, Prendergast and others at prices that go from $1 for Bellows' "Dempsey and Firpo" to $16 for Pollocks "#16." The museum also issues a price list of its postcards.

When ordering by mail, please add $1.50 for postage.

* * *

It's worth mentioning that all these museum catalogues play, inadvertently, a secondary role of guide to the museum collections themselves. In reading through them, I became aware of the things available in many cases just a few hours away from home. It's one of the ironies of American life that the very people who would go to a European city partly to visit its museums don't even think of driving two hours to see an equally rich display in a neighboring city. Going through these catalogues, you may find yourself deciding to do more than mail in a coupon.

17
MUSIC

INSTRUMENTS GENERAL

BAGPIPES

The Wandering Piper, 167 Newbury Street, Boston, Mass. 02116
Price list, free.

The Wandering Piper specializes in bagpipes but it sells more than an instrument, it deals in a way of life. Obviously, bagpipe enthusiasts are not just interested in music but in re-creating Scotland, its rituals and traditions. As a result, this price list soon moves from bagpipes to the accompanying costumes and equipment: plaids, jackets, hose, bonnets, spats, brooches, insignia, chevrons, and the like. Books and records are also available, but the price list includes pictures of appropriate garb so that you can see where your garter flashes or dirk should go.

The bagpipes themselves can cost as little as $165, and Spanish pipes, similar to the Scottish ones, can be bought for $78. Clansmen drums are available from $120 up, but the accessories and costumes can easily cost far more than the instruments, an Argyle jacket with vest costing $95.

Other Scottish products are also available—jewels, glasses and a great many books on Scottish regiments and clans. Parts and repair needs are also available, from sealing wax for reeds to new pipe bags.

BAND INSTRUMENTS

Carroll Sound, Inc., 351-53 W. 41st Street, New York, N.Y. 10036
14-page catalogue, free.

Carroll specializes in sound effects and percussion instruments from the world over and many of these *outré* objects are available only from them. The sound-effect section is probably of more limited interest—instruments to make dog barks, lion roars, cricket sounds and chicken clucks are all available, as well as machines that give the impression of men marching (to ward off muggers?) or wind and storm (to authenticate a telephoned excuse?). But while one can think of various uses for the sound effects, there is a clearly defined audience for the extraordinary range of percussion and other instruments sold by Carroll. Here are temple bells, Chinese tom-toms and gongs, Chinese lutes, flutes and mandolins, Indian bamboo flutes and other Indian instruments ranging from the flute-like been and tumbi to the zither-like swarmandel. From Africa come thumb pianos, steel drums and log drums, and from Israel copper and calfskin drums useful for all Near Eastern music. Somewhere between sound effects and musical instruments are Carroll's last offering—whistles, auto horns and brass-bulb horns. A very different kind of store.

Rhythm Band, Inc., P.O. Box 126, Fort Worth, Tex. 76101
62-page color catalogue, free.

Rhythm Band, Inc., is the country's largest manufacturer of elementary musical instruments and has a thorough catalogue which it mails to schools, but which is also available to individuals. While many of its listings, such as the rhythm bands, are of interest only to schools, or to very large families, there are a great many instruments which parents or children may wish to send away for. Soprano recorders start at as little as $1.50, and go up to $75 for bass recorders. There are all sorts of drums, timpani, maracas and other simple instruments, and some lovely tom-toms costing $14.95 up. The company also sells an instrument called the ChromAharp, Resonator bells and other instruments with which I'm not familiar. But for the most part, these are the familiar instruments of childhood, from a xylophone for $2.95 to electric guitars and pianos, ukeleles, student guitars from $19.95 up, and master guitars from $59.50.

FLUTES

Shakuhachi Flutes, Monty H. Levenson, Route 1, Hilltop Drive, Willits, Calif. 95490
No catalogue.

Monty Levenson has been making Japanese Shakuhachi flutes for the last two years, getting many of his orders from a letter he wrote to the *Last Whole Earth Catalog*. The flutes he makes are available for $10, $15, $25 and $35 (the prices depending on the material), plus $1.50 for postage. All the flutes have a range of about two octaves, and various records are available to demonstrate what their music sounds like. Levenson publishes a small handwritten pamphlet about the construction of the flute which he sells for the steep price of $3.25, and is at work on a beginner's manual, but each flute comes with a free explanatory leaflet and bibliography.

HARPSICHORDS, SPINETS, CLAVICHORDS

B & G Instrument Workshop, 318 N. 36th Street, Seattle, Wash. 98103
18-page price list, 50 cents.

B & G supplies harpsichord parts and hopes in the future to do the same for clavichords. Jacks, jack slides, pins, music wire, felts and bushings are all available at discount prices. So are keyboards, soundboards and the larger parts. Various kits are also sold, for keyboards, but kits are not available for the harpsichord as a whole. However, B & G says that all the parts needed are listed in their price list and that buying these separately is still cheaper than kits available elsewhere.

B. W. M. Benn, Harpsichords, 4424 Judson Lane, Minneapolis, Minn. 55435
8-page black-and-white catalogue, 25 cents.

Mr. Benn, his wife and some outside help have been making harpsichords for eight years, turning out some five to ten instruments a year, built from scratch in their own shop. Benn harpsichords are based on the eighteenth-century instruments, which were built with very thin soundboards and with lighter construction and stringing. They make spinets, virginals, clavichords, as well as single and two manual harpsichords. Benn says that their prices are below the European, but here Benn refers to harpsichords sold in the

United States, since prices in Europe are still considerably lower. Price, however, is obviously not the sole consideration in buying something as complex and delicate as an instrument of this sort, and anyone contemplating such a purchase should look at the various possibilities offered. For a five-octave bentside spinet Benn charges $900, clavichords are $950, and two-manual harpsichords $3,900.

John Shortridge, Harpsichord Maker, Route 2, Box 41a, Purcellville, Va. 22132
Leaflets, free.

John Shortridge was curator of musical instruments at the Smithsonian Institution when he resigned to devote himself to the making of harpsichords, which he now does with his wife, from his most appropriate address. The instruments he makes are, he feels, "perhaps the most authentic and exact copies of specific antique instruments available." They are sold direct to the customer, who commissions the exact model he wishes. There is, at present, a waiting list of three years for these rare harpsichords. Shortridge is now specializing in seventeenth-century models and makes French, Italian and Flemish harpsichords as well as German clavichords from that period, and a later French model. Prices range from $1,200 for the clavichord to $4,800 for the two-manual harpsichord based on a French 1770 model. Other two-manuals cost $4,100, with a single-manual Italian instrument costing $2,350. The harpsichords have received high praise from the press and are included in some of the country's major museum collections.

1 • *John Shortridge* Copy of a 1652 French harpsichord of Claude Jacquet, Paris. $4,100.
photo Hill Murray Photo

Robert S. Taylor, 8710 Garfield Street, Bethesda, Md. 20034
Brochure, free.

Taylor is the American importer of the harpsichords, spinets and clavichords made in Germany by Kurt Sperrhake. This is a one-man operation, the instruments being on display in Taylor's home and sold directly to customers. As a result, his prices are lower than those charged for any similar, famous-make harpsichords if you are buying in the United States.

Taylor's brochure shows ten different instruments. Clavichords cost about $1,150, spinets about $1,200, and one-manual harpsichords about $1,900. Two-manual harpsichords are considerably more. (These prices are very rough estimates because of the fluctuation of the dollar as this book goes to press.)

Zuckermann Harpsichords, Inc., 160 Sixth Avenue, New York, N.Y. 10013
16-page catalogue, free.

Zuckermann has been building harpsichords for seventeen years and selling kits since 1959, and says that "there are probably more Zuckermann harpsichords and clavichords in existence than the total of all other kinds both ancient and modern combined. And all, or almost all, of these were built by amateurs." The kit is very carefully made and Zuckermann says that it is easy to assemble, assuming you enjoy doing this kind of work. If by any chance you fall short, Zuckermann will help by letter or phone or replace any part that you may have damaged.

The Flemish harpsichord complete costs $420 or $495, but kits cost $195 and $270 for the cabinet parts, and $170 for the musical parts. A concert harpsichord

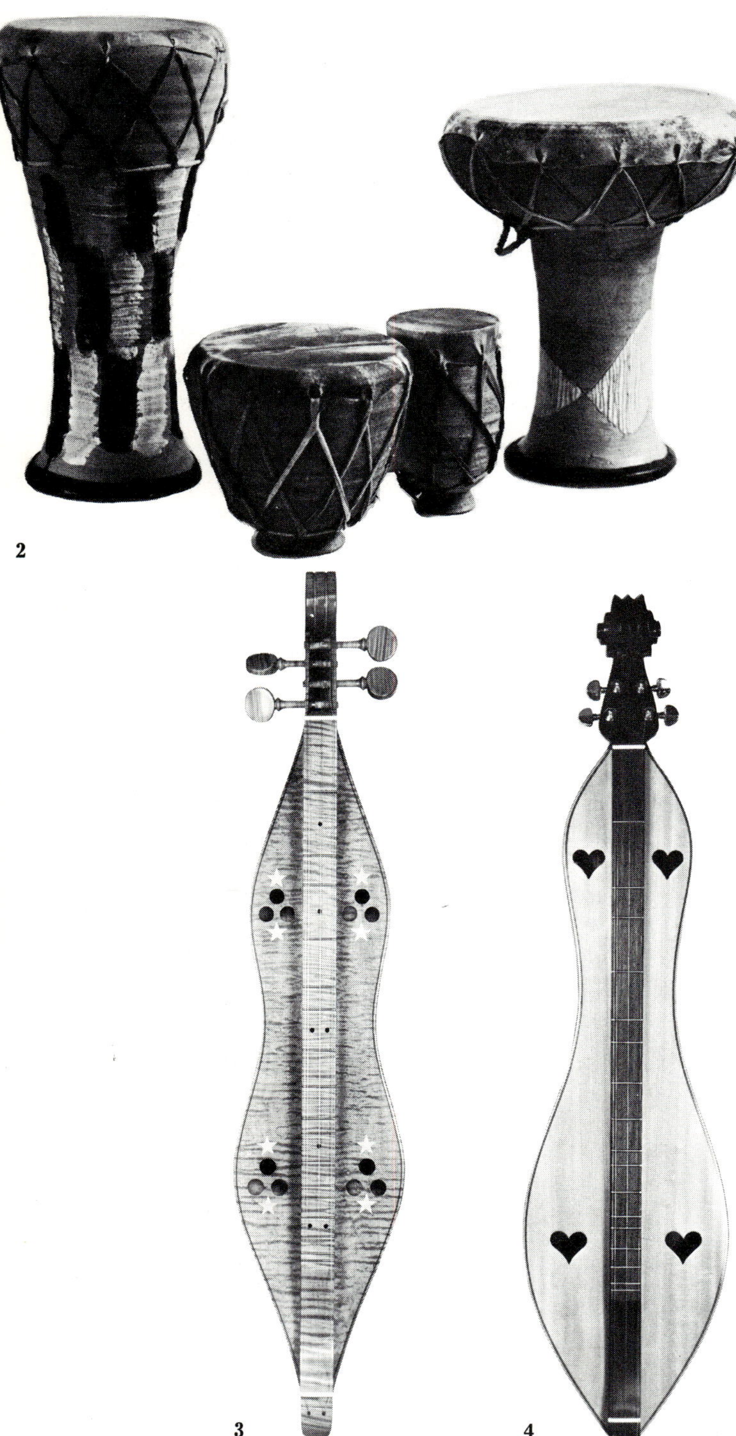

2 • *Ceramic Drums Left to right:* Dumbeg, 15″ high, $18.75; 12″ high, $15. Moroccan bongos, $17.50. Timbali, 14″ high, $18.75; 11″ high, $15.

3 • *Dennis Dorogi* Mountain dulcimer, Star model, 36″ high, 7½″ across, 3½″ deep, made of curly maple with hand-carved pegs, ivory nut and bridge. $175.

4 • *Dennis Dorogi* Mountain dulcimer, 36″ high, 9″ across, 3½″ deep, made of East Indian rosewood with gold-plated Grover Rotomatic tuning machines, ivory nut and bridge. A mellow and resonant sound. $300.

costs $675, and $200 more for a two-manual. The cabinet parts, second keyboard and musical parts for this model cost $375, $200 and $180, respectively. A small clavichord II costs $250 for the complete kit. Full information on shipping and charges is included.

RECORDERS

Koch Recorder, Haverhill, N.H. 03765
Brochure, free.

William Koch was the first American to make recorders up to the standards of European craftsmen, and since his death in 1970 his son has carried on after him. Koch recorders are held in high esteem; still, they continue to be the least expensive of the fine recorders you can get in America. They are available in cocobolo wood or native black cherry, tenors and basses are also made in black birch, and altos and sopranos in maple. A two-section soprano recorder is only $10, with three-sections $21. Alto recorders cost $30, tenor $39, and bass $100.

FOLK INSTRUMENTS

Appalachian Dulcimer Corp., 232 W. Frederick Street, Staunton, Va. 24401

A. W. Jeffreys, Jr., with his family, is the corporation listed above. Jeffreys started making dulcimers for his friends and soon found himself selling to customers throughout the country and the world. A letter of inquiry will bring a photo of one dulcimer and current price, which includes instruction booklet, carrying bag, noting bar and pick.

CapriTaurus Dulcimers, P.O. Box 153, Felton, Calif. 95018
Brochures, free.

CapriTaurus' name derives from the compatible birth signs of the two brothers who own it, and their specialties are dulcimers and thumb pianos. They say that their prices are lower than the usual and that their kits are even more reasonably priced, since they mill their own wood. Dulcimers in hardwood laminate cost from $59.50 to $74.50, and "solid"-hardwood models cost from $100 to $150. Kits cost $22.50 for mahogany, $27.50 for mahogany and spruce, and $33 for walnut and spruce. Various books, records and accessories are also available.

Ceramic Drums, 2719 Stuart Street, Berkeley, Calif. 94705
Leaflet, free. (Send stamped, self-addressed envelope.)

Two potters started making ceramic drums based on Middle East and African drums about three years ago. They have added different shapes, sometimes based on designs by customers, and now are going to add more—tube drums and Persian drums, and also a Chinese ceramic flute called a *tsun,* which they believe is unobtainable in America. Drums are unglazed, painted with slip, and made the traditional way with water-soluble glue and lacing. The drum heads are rawhide goatskin. A set of three low-standing table drums costs about $34.

Dennis Dorogi, Dulcimers, Ellicott Road, Brocton, N.Y. 14716
Catalogue and pamphlet on mini-psaltery, 25 cents.

Dennis Dorogi's instruments are extremely handsome examples of craftsmanship and have, in fact, been exhibited in museums. Prices range from $75 for the cheapest model, made entirely of cherry wood, to $300 for more expensive woods. Dorogi also makes psalteries, the Biblical instrument that is part of the harp family, as well as cases for his instruments.

The Dulcimer Shoppe, P.O. Box 110, Highway 9 North, Mountain View, Ark. 72560
Leaflet, free. Published twice a year.

The Dulcimer Shoppe not only sells a selection of their own dulcimers but also stocks a large number of related items, such as dulcimer records, books about the instrument, and a number of instruments not made in their shop. Their dulcimers range in price from $68 to $120 and up for instruments made to order, but most of their models are priced at $85 to $87.50, depending on whether you want banjo or violin pegs. This is the price of their most popular models, made of walnut and having four strings. There is also a make-it-yourself dulcimer kit, containing all the necessary parts, for only $31.95 plus postage.

Among other instruments for sale are recorders, melody flutes, kazoos and jew's-harps, the last only 95 cents for the small model and $2 for the large. There are also kits for making a fretless five-string banjo ($50), and an Ambira kit, which makes a Westernized version of the small African thumb piano ($5). Finally, even non-music lovers may be interested in the Ozark clog doll, a foot-high loose-limbed doll that dances on a paddle in time to your music ($8.95, including postage and handling).

Here, Inc., 410 Cedar Avenue, Minneapolis, Minn. 55404
Price list, free.

"Here, Inc. was started in 1968 to provide jobs for minority people who were circumscribed in job opportunity." Looking for items that could be manufactured easily and without a major investment, the group began to make dulcimers and then gradually discovered that making kits as well made even better sense. Their price list now includes a variety of folk instruments, sold either finished or as kits. A $20 kit makes a teardrop dulcimer that can be bought for $45 finished, the $28 kit makes a $60 finished dulcimer, etc. Psalteries are available for $40 or $50, with kits at half these prices, and a thumb piano is available for $5 (only in kit form). They have banjos and bancimers (dulcimer fretted banjo) for $45 and $85; also various booklets and spare parts. Finally, imported acoustical guitars of all kinds are available, from $125 up (including case), but $1 (credited to your purchase) must be sent for additional information about these.

Hughes Company, 8655 W. 13th Avenue, Denver, Colo. 80215
Catalogue, free.

Hughes specialized in kits that allow you to make dulcimers, Irish harps, balalaikas and similar instruments at home. Hughes was the first to manufacture such kits and the large assortment is popularly priced, dulcimer kits starting as low as $7.95, with the finished instrument costing $19.95. Other dulcimer kits are more expensive, and the "Musicians model," with a more delicate tuning system, costs up to $25.95. A hammered dulcimer, which is closer to a harpsichord, can be made from $23 to $37. Irish harps and sitars also come in kits starting at $25. Guitars start at $10 and go to $25, and the traditional Russian folk instrument, the balalaika, costs roughly the same. All these instruments are available completed, for considerably more, or assembled but needing a final sanding and finishing, for slightly less. Only the simplest tools are needed to assemble the instruments, and Hughes calculates that time needed ranges from four to five hours for a small dulcimer to forty to fifty hours for a guitar.

Homer C. Ledford, 125 Sunset Heights, Winchester, Ky. 40391
Leaflet, free. (Send stamped, self-addressed envelope.)

Homer C. Ledford has been making dulcimers since the age of nineteen, while at college and while a teacher of industrial arts. Seven years ago he started making dulcimers full time. He makes walnut dulcimers, starting at $67 for one with three strings. He also makes a traditional sweetheart "courtin'" double dulcimer for two people to sit opposite each other, one playing the melody and the other the harmony. And in 1971 he invented the dulcitar, which can be used as a dulcimer or a guitar—both the double dulcimer and the dulcitar are made to order and cost $150 each. Homer C. Ledford is also available as an after-dinner speaker/entertainer, when he plays mountain ballads and shows his handmade instruments.

F. Proffit, Jr., Route 2, Todd, N.C. 28692
No catalogue.

"A small business (one employee—me!)," says F. Proffit, Jr. Frank Proffit Senior was the traditional folk singer, ballad singer and maker of dulcimers who is credited with saving the song "Tom Dooley," and encouraging the current interest in traditional music. His son also loves the "simple and beautiful creations of common folk" and makes hourglass-shaped dulcimers and fretless banjos in the old way from local hardwoods. You can get a California dulcimer, yes—he says—but it just won't have the same sweet and beautiful tone. Prices: about $95 for a three-string dulcimer, and $92 for a fretless banjo.

Robinson's Harp Shop, Mount Laguna, Calif. 92048
Leaflet, free.

Here you can get plans to make harps or kits to make them, or finished but unassembled or finished and assembled harps—Irish, Paraguayan or mini-concert. Plans cost $5 to $15, kits $100 to $450. Some of the harps are highly decorated, or you can get decoration ideas and designs if you'd rather decorate them yourself.

Roy Scott, 2747 Woolsey Street, Berkeley, Calif. 94705
Brochure, free.

Scott sells handmade and individually decorated thumb pianos. The smallest (12-key) instruments cost $10 and larger ones are available, up to an 18-key model for $20. The larger instruments have deeper tones and more volume, the smaller tend to sound more like music boxes.

Stewart-MacDonald Manufacturing Co., Box 900, Athens, Ohio 45701
Catalogue and supplements, 25 cents.

Banjos and banjo parts are the specialty of this firm. Its Eagle Banjos are $150 for the low-cost model, $295 for the more expensive—both somewhat higher in a resonator model. Parts, for repairs or for those building their own, which are usually hard to come by, are here available in great detail, as are accessories such as arm rests, cases, polishes, etc. The same are also available for certain related instruments, such as guitars and mandolins.

HISTORIC INSTRUMENTS

MerryField Meadows, Star Route A, Inthelium, Wash. 99138
Leaflet, 25 cents.

Edward Merrifield started making instruments seven years ago when he wanted a lyre harp and couldn't find one. He likes to make unusual instruments that are no longer available, and he carves them and inlays them with mother-of-pearl. He makes a small lyre harp for $200. All other instruments are special order, prices on request.

The Renaissance Gilde, Water Street, Cambridge, Wis. 53523
Brochure, free.

This unique enterprise was established to provide "good, playable, authentic lutes and other historic stringed instruments" for performers of early music. Basing their endeavor on meticulous research and, judging from the photographs, extraordinary workmanship, they make various kinds of lutes in three qualities. The chamber instruments are the least expensive; the Consort incorporates more intricate design and finer woods; and the Soloist is their all-out special. A Renaissance/Elizabethan lute costs $425, $775 or $1,350, depending on the category. All instruments are sent out on approval, and a trade-in allowance on your old lute is possible.

PRINTED MUSIC

G. Schirmer, Inc., 609 Fifth Avenue, New York, N.Y. 10017
Catalogues:
Band and Orchestra Music, free.
Musical Literature, free.
Musical Classics—Opera Librettos, free.
Organ Music, free.
Piano Music, free.
Vocal Music, free.

Schirmer's is the country's best-known music store and the above list of sheet music and books about music gives you some idea of how comprehensive their stock is. The store also sells records and "all things musical," but for mail-order buyers the music catalogues may be its most useful service. The Vocal Music catalogue alone is 100 pages long, covering music both sacred and secular. Here is more Sigmund Romberg than I realized was still in print, as well as the expected classics and an astonishing number of songs that I'm sure I've never heard before. The listing of Musical Classics has scores for piano, vocal, organ and instrumental, while the list of books (Musical Literature) includes elementary texts, advanced works of theory and more general books on music.

Spanish Music Center, 319 W. 48th Street, New York, N.Y. 10036
Brochures and price lists of music and records, free.

My letter to this firm brought me a vast amount of literature, much of it centered around the guitar: books of instruction, music for solos, duets, guitar and voice (you can play "Greensleeves" on the guitar, as well as Bach, Dowland and Vivaldi), not to mention the dozens of others listed in 24 packed, mimeographed pages. Also available is a large selection of records from Spain, with Zarzuelas and flamencos galore, Latin American records and the Center's own catalogue of records, selling 12-inch LP's for as little as $2.95 and $3.95. A very thorough offering that I should imagine would liven up classroom study of our neighbors to the south, quite apart from the natural audience of aficionados of Latin music.

RECORDS

Records are available at two totally different price scales. On the one hand many stores, particularly in towns where there is little competition, sell records at the manufacturer's list price. At the same time, a large number of stores and mail-order businesses sell the same records for much less. Even there, prices vary and can be even lower during special sales, etc. To complicate matters further, stores will stock special imports, discontinued records, and the like, at even different prices.

Clearly, if you buy only a few records, complicated price comparisons are not worth-while. But if you are building a serious collection, then it is worth getting on the mailing lists of some of the firms listed below. In addition to this, it is worth following the ads, particularly in the Sunday *New York Times*, of the special sales announced by such firms as Sam Goody, Inc.,

5

6

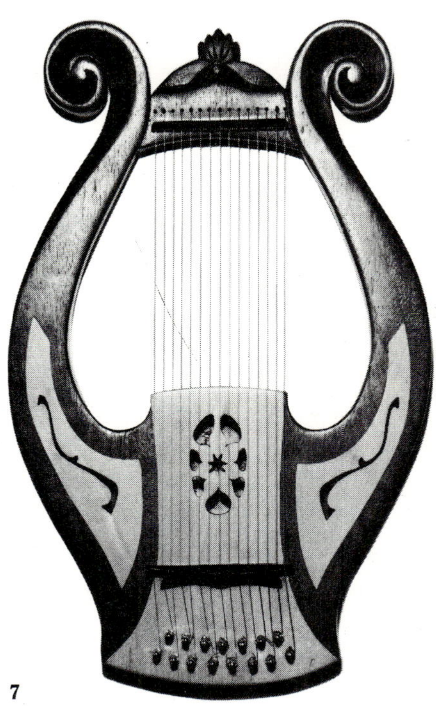

7

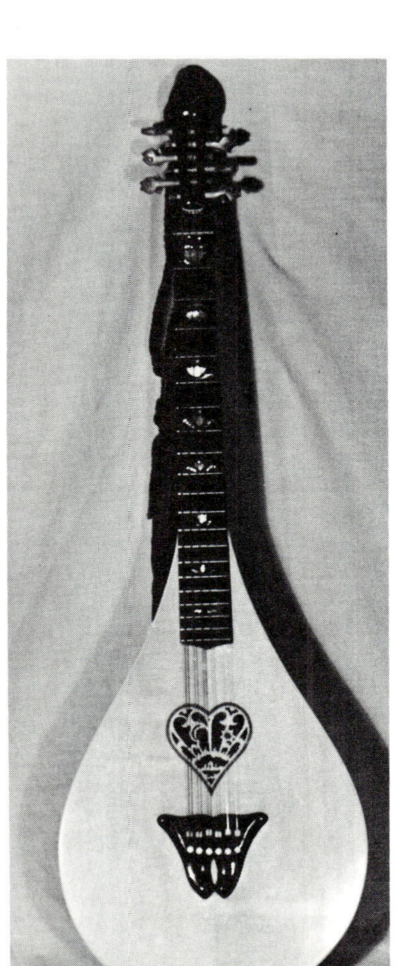

8

5 • *Robinson's Harp Shop* Tara Irish harp, 60″ high, available completed, carved and decorated, $695; completed, decorated but not carved, $550; in kit form, completed but unassembled, $350; in kit form, shaped but unsanded and unfinished, $250.

6 • *Roy Scott* Thumb piano, 8″ high, 5″ wide, 1⅛″ deep. $14.95.

7 • *MerryField Meadows* Lyre harp carved from a solid block of mahogany with mother-of-pearl inlay on the back, carved hollow on the front with a spruce soundboard. $200.
photo Reichner Studio

8 • *MerryField Meadows* Guitar carved in the shape of a swan was made by special commission for the singer Donovan. The back is carved hollow from a block of mahogany and has a rosewood bridge and fingerboard; the latter is inlayed with mother-of-pearl. The swan's eyes are set with fire opals. Similar guitars can be made to order, price upon request.

9 

10 

9 • *Indian House* Pueblo songs of the Southwest recorded live at the 48th Inter-Tribal Indian Ceremonial in Gallup, New Mexico. $5.

10 • *Indian House* One of two records of Taos Round Dance songs, recorded at Taos Pueblo, New Mexico. Each record has sixteen songs. $5.

46-35 54th Road, Maspeth, N.Y. 11378, and Marboro Books, 131 Varick Street, New York, N.Y. 10013. Goody's comprehensive firm, stocking all records, normally sells at a good discount and will send you the big Schwann catalogue of records and tapes, and the Harrison tape catalogue for 75 cents each. Marboro's specializes in remainders, as it does in books, but will occasionally sell new records at varying prices.

These firms sell only new and current records. There are a number of firms specializing in out-of-print and occasionally secondhand records. These, too, are listed in this section.

Chesterfield Music Shops, Inc., 12 Warren Street, New York, N.Y. 10007
Price lists, free. Issued four to six times a year.

Chesterfield is one of a number of firms specializing in record sales by mail. It is one of the largest and oldest in the field and will send you its price lists several times a year, once you send them your name. They have a number of exclusive, imported items and sell records in all fields of music and the spoken word. If you plan to buy seriously by mail, it is worth your while getting on several such mailing lists and comparing prices as well as the extent of the stock ordered.

House of Oldies, 267 Bleeker Street, New York, N.Y. 10014
32-page price list, $1.

"World Headquarters for out-of-print 45's" says the price list of the "oldest oldie shop" in New York. The store specializes in rock-'n'-roll oldies, LP's and 45's, with over a million titles in stock, five thousand of which are listed in the closely packed price list. The price list also reproduces the Cash Box Top 100 from the "early years," 1963 on. The store also stocks rhythm and blues, 1950 pop and sound tracks. Whether it's "Abba Dabba Honeymoon" with Debbie Reynolds or "Zoom Zoom Zoom" with The Collegians, or any of the fourteen titles starting with "Teen-age" or "Teenager," the 50's and 60's are all here on 45's. If you've outgrown your collection, the House of Oldies will consider buying from you.

Indian House, P.O. Box 472, Taos, N.Mex. 87571
Leaflet, free.

An anthropologist and his Indian wife make first-rate hi-fidelity recordings of North American Indian music. The Isaacs recommend their records for Indian study programs at all levels. They say that children can easily learn the social dances and especially enjoy the strong rhythms. At more advanced levels, the songs contain information about Indian history. Records cost about $5 each and have been very well reviewed.

Library of Congress, Music Division, Recorded and Sound Section, Washington, D.C. 20540
Price lists, free.
A full catalogue, "Folk Music," is available from the Superintendent of Documents, Government Printing Office, Washington, D.C. 20540, for 40 cents.

During the Depression years, John and Alan Lomax and their associates went through the United States recording our folk music and folk tales in much the same way that photographers from the Farm Security Administration recorded the visual aspects of American rural life. The result is one of the monuments of American history, a unique attempt to capture a vital aspect of life that came just in time and left us all a heritage that might otherwise have been lost. Though the Lomaxes' efforts are known to many who have a serious interest in folk music, relatively few people know that many of these original records are still available from the Library of Congress and that they have been supplemented by several other programs, including a major one of recording the music of the American Indian. The Library's brochure lists the contents of each LP, which sells for $4.95, and there are Afro-American spirituals, blues and game songs, work songs and calls, as well as a marvelous record of religious songs and actual church services. White work songs include songs of anthracite miners, railroad songs, songs of Michigan lumberjacks, sea songs and chanties, cowboy songs and cattle calls from Texas, Mormon songs and folk music from Wisconsin.There are also several records from Latin America, folk music from Venezuela, Mexico, Puerto Rico and Afro-Bahia (Brazil). Indian music starts with recordings from the Smithsonian's cylinder collection, recorded from 1910 to 1930, and goes on to music recorded, mostly in the 1940's, by Iroquois, Papago, Sioux, Piute, Pueblo, Choctaw, Apache and other tribes, including various dances, love songs, lullabies, war songs and a Navajo song commemorating the flag raising on Iwo Jima in World War II.

The Library also has an extensive catalogue of spoken recordings, based for the most part on its famous poetry readings. Here, again at $4.95 each, are America's best-known poets reading their own work: Eliot, Cummings, Frost, Jeffers, Tate, Auden, Lowell, Aiken, Rukeyser, Snodgrass, Roethke—just about all the names you'd expect, though curiously stopping short of Ginsberg, Ferlinghetti, and other, still-unestablished poets. There is also a two-record interview with H. L. Mencken, and two records of poetry in Spanish by Salinas and Mistral. An excellent list, which hopefully will in time be extended to cover broader areas of American and other poetry.

11 • *Music Minus One* Volume One, a rhythm background record of eight popular songs for any musician or vocalist to sing or play along with. Comes with a music book containing melody line, chords and lyrics. Each song is transposed for all instruments. $6.98.

Music Minus One, 43 W. 61st Street, New York, N.Y. 10023

64-page annual catalogue, free.

I had seen some of these records in stores and always liked the idea of being allowed to play the role of the missing soloist, but I didn't realize the extent of the Music Minus One catalogue. Some fifty to sixty new records are issued each year, and you can write both for the annual catalogue and a semiannual newsletter. Music Minus One seems to have an enthusiastic following of current musicians, as well as listing Albert Einstein and the King of Siam among its former customers. In addition to its repertory of sing-along and play-along records, Music Minus One produces a number of specifically instructional records, helping students of various instruments at different levels, from rank beginner to advanced.

The Record Album, 254 W. 81st Street, New York, N.Y. 10024

Price lists, free. Issued every month or two.

This store, which describes itself as specialists in out-of-print records, deals primarily with classical and popular 78's, though they have a small stock of standard LP's and 45's. They will try to supply specific records that you are looking for, but also issue mimeographed lists of records in all areas of music, specifying the condition of the record and charging accordingly.

Prices range from a Soviet recording of the Bolshoi Opera's B. Ivanov singing Tchaikovsky's Mazeppa aria for $2.50 to records like Maria Neweth singing "Pace, pace, pace, mio Dio" from *La Forza del destino* for $20. Most records, however, are in the $3 to $8 bracket. The Record Album is also interested in buying fine vocal collections, should you decide to turn in your old Victrola for one of those new machines.

Thomas J. Valentino, 151 W. 46th Street, New York, N.Y. 10036
Price lists, free.

"From a cat's meow to a lion's roar—from a pistol shot to a world war" is not only this firm's motto but a description of its product, long-playing and 78-rpm records that provide sound effects and other special recordings. Valentino's index is, as a result, an extraordinary document in itself, from pigs squealing to seals barking, coyotes howling or crowds shouting, toilets flushing or lions being restless. If you want a boat whistle, you can choose between the *Queen Mary's* or a river boat's; guns are available in every variant, as are drums, doors and police cars. Because each effect is relatively brief, the contents of the records are mixed and some labels read like short stories—Running upstairs, body falling downstairs, knocking on door, garbage truck in one sequence—and I wonder whether some old radio programs weren't written with the Valentino catalogue as inspiration.

More homogeneous arrangements are also available, records of calliope or silent-movie music, carousels, fife and drums, bugle calls, music boxes. If you are thinking of making your own film, or planning a theatrical production or simply need help in remembering those old, familiar noises, Valentino's albums, at $5 each, offer all sorts of opportunities.

STEREO EQUIPMENT

If you are prepared to take trouble to assemble a stereo system from the best components at lowest possible cost, check with several discount firms for each component, as prices differ considerably between companies. Check also with the Hong Kong firms on components small enough to come by parcel post. Hong Kong prices on turntables (Dual and Garrard, for instance) are often almost a third lower than American discount prices after paying postage. If you buy components from another state, you avoid paying state tax, which goes quite a way toward paying shipping costs. *The Stereo Directory and Buying Guide* ($1.85, including postage) is published each October by Ziff-Davis Service Division, 595 Broadway, New York, N.Y. 10012, and gives manufacturers' list prices (don't trust blindly the list prices discount firms give; they are sometimes inflated). Stereo magazines carry advertisements from discount houses, most of which don't publish price lists, but here are a few that do.

Boston Audio Corp., One Discount Drive, E. Randolph Industrial Park, Randolph, Mass. 02368
16-page catalogue, free.

Stereo components, stereo furniture, tape units and car players.

Midwest Hi Fi, Box 567, Ellsworth Industrial Park, Downers Grove, Ill. 60515
List, free.

A very short list of components and suggested combinations.

Olson Electronics, 260 S. Forge Street, Akron, Ohio 44327
180-page catalogue, with some color, free.

A very large catalogue is published by this chain of over seventy electronics stores. Not only stereo components are listed, including Olson's own "Teledyn" and "Olson" brands, but also car accessories, amateur radio gear, walkie-talkies, telephone accessories, tools and hardware, etc.

Radio Shack, 2617 W. Seventh Street, Fort Worth, Tex. 76107
180-page color catalogue, free. September.

This chain of 1,700 stores sells components and ready-made electronic home-entertainment products to music lovers, hobbyists and experimenters in electronics. They manufacture, or have manufactured to their own specifications, most of the goods they sell, which are sold at prices that are about the equivalent of discount prices for similar goods with better-known brand names. Stock covers ready-made stereo systems, tape and cartridge decks, radios, walkie-talkies, intercoms and also a wide range of kits, some of which make more esoteric gadgets, such as metal detectors, smoke detectors, lie detectors, and equipment for the car such as automobile alarm systems, auto analysers and ignition systems.

Stereo Warehouse, Inc., 782 Higuera, San Luis Obispo, Calif. 93401
30-page catalogue, free. New ones published about every three months.

By far the most helpful, the Stereo Warehouse catalogue lists a fairly small number of components and recommended systems, but gives background information on why each model has been chosen. They say that their customers are mainly college students or anyone who is really "into music," and this is what they say about themselves: "We offer an alternative to people who are plagued with local retail stereo shops which have a poor selection, exorbitant prices, tend to push one or two particular brands, and who don't really know what they're talking about when it comes to stereo equipment. You see, music is important to all the people here at the Warehouse—we're all young (the average age being 23) and music is interwoven with our lifestyles, therefore, we know stereo equipment intimately."

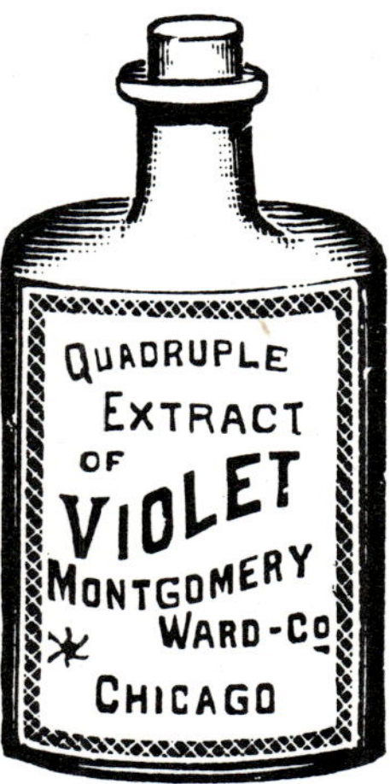

18
PERFUME & COSMETICS

1

2

3

1 • *Caswell-Massey* Cucumber cosmetics made by Caswell-Massey for over a century–Sarah Bernhardt used the night cream with elder flowers in the 1880's. Night cream, 4 oz., $3; cold cream, 4 oz., $3; face lotion, 3 oz., $2; emulsion, 3 oz., $2.

2 • *Caswell-Massey* ½ oz. musk oil, $3.50; ½ oz. ambergris oil, $4.75; civet oil, ½ oz., $4; Holy Smoke, ½ oz., $5.

3 • *Hové Parfumeur* Horoscope perfumes and *eaux de toilette* packaged with the signs of the zodiac. 4 oz. cologne, $3.75; 8 oz., $7.25.
photo Stuart Lynn

Capriland's Herb Farm, Silver Street, Coventry, Conn. 06238
Price list, 10 cents.

Caprilands, which provides everything for the herb gardner including luncheon programs to which guests are begged to wear gardening clothes and flat heels, also sells supplies from its own gardens to make fragrances. Lavender, lemon verbena, frankincense, myrrh, etc., for sachets; rose petal and orris root for potpourri; Zanzibar cloves and spice mixture for pomanders. The owner, Adelma Simmons, says that her own little mimeographed book *The Little Book of Fragrances* ($1) is popular. It describes and gives a history of several herbs and spices with informal advice on how to grow them and what to do with them. You can also buy herbs and teas, and artemisia Christmas wreaths made of herbs and flowers, which cost about $8 each.

Caswell-Massey Co. Ltd., 518 Lexington Avenue, New York, N.Y. 10017
100-page catalogue, $1. Spring, fall.

George Washington, Captain Kidd and Edgar Allan Poe are among Caswell-Massey's former customers, and the present owners of this historic apothecary shop are determined not to lower the tone or allow elegant things to die. In their hands, Oral Hygiene Aids and Medicine Chest Necessities become essential accessories of a gracious life. After a look at the Caswell-Massey catalogue you don't just grab the toothpaste any more, you select Email Diamant from France, Pasta del Capitano from Italy or Aronal from Switzerland, and you apply it with an imported black-boar-bristle bone-handle toothbrush; you pick your teeth with Le Negri goosequill toothpicks from France, and stick your dentures in with Eucryl plate fixative from England. If the bad-breath ads have been getting to you, you foam away your worries with Caswell-Massey's foaming mouthwash made from aromatic oils. You shave with a straight razor sharpened on a horsehide strap imported from Scotland, dab your cuts with an English styptic pencil (it won't crumble like an American one), comb your hair with a handmade natural-horn comb (never mind the charming way it warps), brush your hair with an English hardwood brush and smooth it down with Chandrika Brahmi Hair Oil from India.

In addition to an astonishing variety of unguents and instruments for pampering, preserving and perfuming yourself, you'll find quite a few things here that you'll have trouble finding anywhere else, among them: mustache wax, lavender smelling salts, chamois nail buffers, cosmetic vinegar, and snuff.

P. Fioretti and Co. Inc., 1470-72 Lexington Avenue, New York, N.Y. 10028
Price list, free.
Perfume price list, free.

The small, dark shop looks ancient, but this firm was in fact started in 1929 when it made fruit-flavoring extract and fruit-flavored syrups for the Italian coffeehouses in Greenwich Village. Now, besides concentrated flavors which are exported, Fioretti makes the ingredients for do-it-yourself perfume. "Why throw money away . . . live modern . . . do it yourself," they say. Floral essences cost about $4 an ounce, and fixatives about $4 an ounce too. Oil of musk, bath oils, bottles and atomizers are also sold. P. Fioretti's letter to

4

5

6

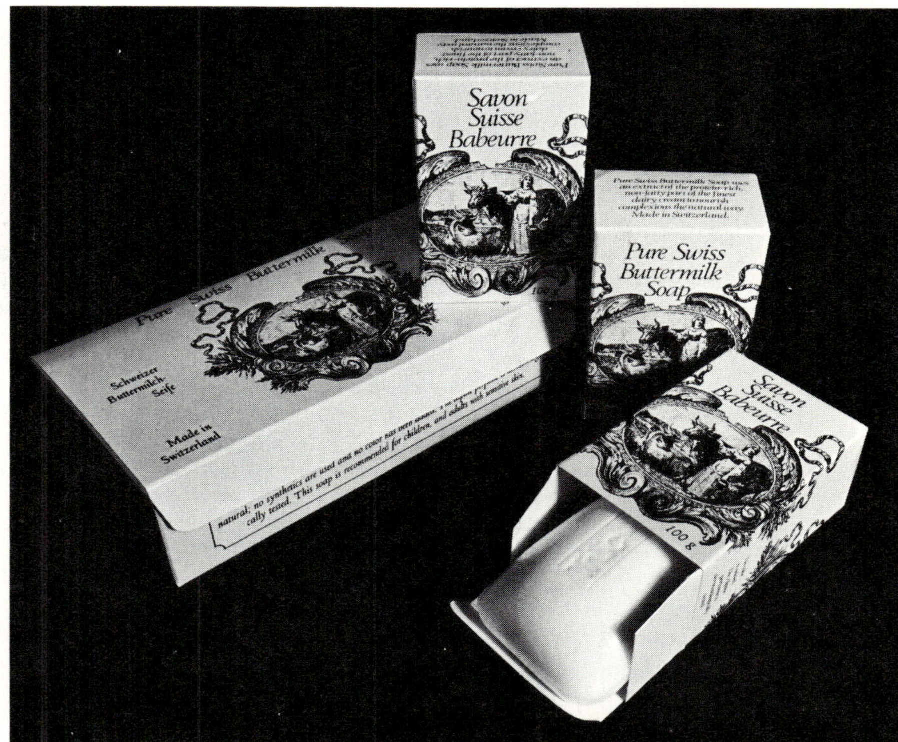

7

4 • *The Soap Box* Maize-meal soap, single cake, $1.35; box of three, $4.

5 • *The Soap Box* Indian flower soap, a popular, heavily scented German soap with twenty different ingredients including palmarosa oil, floral essences from India, balms and resins from Indonesia, and oil of cinnamon from Ceylon, in a nineteenth-century box. Single bar, $1.25; box of three, $3.75.

6 • *The Soap Box* Almond-oil shampoo, $2 per bottle.

7 • *The Soap Box* Swiss buttermilk soap. A very mild soap, good for people with sensitive skin. Single cake, $1.25; three cakes, $3.75.
photo Christopher S. Johnson

me ends with a wistful note: "The expansion of our business could have continued with the participation of the young generation of our family, but it didn't work out that way on account of other interests on their part."

The Herbary and Potpourri Shop, P.O. Box 543, Orleans, Mass. 02653
Brochure, free.

Started in 1941, this shop originally devoted itself exclusively to culinary herbs but has since branched out to develop other uses for herbs. A leaflet on insect-repellent herbs, for instance, is available for 15 cents, and a brochure on "Creating Potpourri" ($1.15) is a helpful guide to using some of the supplies sold by the shop. Dried herb seasonings are also available, as well as culinary herbs and seeds for planting. Among other items available are sachets, wreaths, pomander kits, and various soaps and cosmetics using herbs and other organic properties.

Hové Parfumeur, 723 Toulouse Street, New Orleans, La. 70130
16-page brochure, free. Fall. Summer supplement, free. Spring.

A seductive pink brochure, illustrated with flowers, cherubs and 1890's ladies clutching fans, lists over fifty perfumes made in an old Spanish house in New Orleans—the closest thing to Paris, anyway. The business was started in the 1930's by Mrs. Alvin Hovey-King and has been owned and run by the women of the family ever since, meanwhile gathering a faithful clientele, many of whom have bought here for thirty years. If that, and the fact that the perfume, at $7.35 the ounce, is about a quarter of the price of French perfume, doesn't persuade you to buy American, maybe the "petite samplers" will. For $3.50 you can try any four floral perfumes or any four New Orleans blends, or any three men's colognes. Besides the many perfumes, you can buy bath and body oils, candle oils, sachets, solid perfumes, and oils for making rose jars, sachets and potpourries at home.

Meadowbrook Herb Garden, Route 138, Wyoming, R.I. 02898
Catalogue, 50 cents.

Meadowbrook is the only American distributor of Dr. R. Hauschka's cosmetics from West Germany. A Meadowbrook leaflet says that "Hygienic care of the skin combines a proper inner attitude as well as an outer cosmetic program. By inner attitude we understand a healthy way of life in its universal sense and meaning. This includes wholesome nutrition, sufficient sleep, bodily activity, and an adequate amount of sun." For your insides, to supplement the daily diet or to use occasionally as tonics, there are "elixirs" prepared from wild flowers or organically grown fruits, uncooked and with no preservatives: gentian to help the digestion, rowan to harmonize the metabolism, rose hip to prevent colds, elderflower to detoxify the body, and rose petal to stimulate and calm the body at the same time. For outer application there are "natural" cleaning creams, herbal lotions, hair lotions, foot-bath concentrates, blackthorn-flower massage oil, and citron, lavender, rosemary and pine-needle bath concentrates.

Robert Perfumer, Inc., P.O. Box 45, Jackson Heights, N.Y. 11372
Price card, free.

The president of the firm says that from 1916 on Mr. Robert was the Kenneth of his day and was known by the catch phrase "Robert Makes You Beautiful." Now only a humble card lists perfume at about $14 an ounce (about half the price of French perfume bought in America), toilet water and cologne, and bath oil, dusting powder, etc., with names like "Lady of Leisure" and "Thinking of You."

The Soap Box, Box 167, Woodstock Hill, Conn. 06218.
68-page catalogue, free. October.

A beautifully produced catalogue illustrates more exotic soaps than you could ever imagine. We have all heard about the food soaps: almond, buttermilk, cucumber, oil of lemon, etc.; and the flower soaps: violet, magnolia, gardenia, geranium, etc.; but what about fresh grass, brown sugar, St.-John's-wort as ingredients? Or lime and glycerine, oil of myrrh and patchouli (with the clinging scent)? Tempting, elegantly packed soaps of all sorts have been found or made by this firm (if you want to bathe in the sea, try milk of lily and coconut, good for salt water. If you know any children, give them Alice in Wonderland Soap printed with Tenniel's illustrations). All the soaps are triple-milled and based on natural ingredients—although the Soap Box says that natural ingredients are no better for you than artificial, just infinitely more agreeable. Most soaps cost around $1 per cake. And equally exotic are the creams, lotions which contain glycerine and turtle oil or rosewater, and the shampoos—lettuce, mink and almond oil (all beautifully packaged, unlike most shampoos). Here you can also find luffa (vegetable sponge), brushes, a prize-winning travel toothbrush, and a toothpaste made from the "toothbrush tree" in Africa.

19
PETS

1

2

3

1 • *Duncraft* Bird feeder for suet.

2 • *Duncraft* One of the twenty-four bird feeders for sale.

3 • *Felix—The Katnip Tree Co.* Canvas-covered scratching post for cats. About $5.

Audubon Workshop, 2907 McArthur Boulevard, Northbrook, Ill. 60062
48-page brochure, 25 cents.

Over seventy feeders, houses and baths for birds are on sale here at prices between $1.25 for a chickadee goldfinch feeder and $100 for a twenty-four-nest martin house. Most of the houses are made of wood, many of them designed to foil squirrels and pigeons, many designed to attract special birds, and there are also some feeders called "bird theaters" for attaching to the window sill, with a glass roof to protect the birds and food from rain and snow but enabling you to watch them. Books, with a gourmet selection of bird food and binoculars, and kits to make feeders and houses are available, and for $4.50 there is a bird lover's starter kit, with a feeder kit, a wren-house kit and a booklet called "Know Your Birds."

Duncraft, 25 S. Main Street, Penacook, N.H. 03301
24-page brochure, 25 cents.

Plastic and metal bird feeders are made and sold here. There are twenty-four models, besides post and hanging feeders, some for seeds and some for suet or bread, as well as feeders to clip onto window sills, and one to stick to the wall by suction. Binoculars, bird books and wild-bird seed are also on sale.

Dusay, P.O. Box 24407, New Orleans, La. 70124
32-page catalogue, 25 cents.

This astonishing catalogue shows a complete line of useful accessories for dogs and cats; leashes, car beds, brushes and clippers, medicines, "no mate tablets," and a special spoon for giving medicine. There are lots of helpful little solutions to any dog problem. However, the catalogue also shows goods for people who have gone far along the road toward turning their dog into a baby substitute: doggie pajamas come with a pomponned nightcap; "Our Puppy's Baby Book" comes in pink or blue; and the Pet High Chair enables doggie to join you at meals. And for people who want to dress up their dog there are collars with bow ties, a powder-pink Dacron dotted-swiss granny gown, complete with mobcap, and a collection of doggie hats and sun glasses, "Ivy League" hat to "Calypso" trimmed with colorful fruit—maybe mummy and daddy can find hats to match.

Fabulous Felines, Inc., 113 Lexington Avenue, New York, N.Y. 10016
Price list, free.

Anyone who wants a classier cat than those advertised in profusion on neighborhood notice boards should apply to Fabulous Felines, which has been in the business for twenty years and whose owners are authors of *The Fabulous Feline* (a book) and the Cat section of the *Encyclopaedia Britannica.* An impressive price list includes guarantees that come with the cat and the news that for the lifetime of your cat you can call Fabulous Felines at any time of the day or night for a free consultation. They sell Abyssinian Ruddies, Burmese, Himalayan, Persian and Siamese. Prices start at $85 for Siamese—except the golden ones, which are $115, and go up to $300 for silver-colored Abyssinian Ruddies.

Felix—The Katnip Tree Co., 416 Smith Street, Seattle, Wash. 98109
Brochure, 15 cents.

This useful brochure gives cat-care advice and lists standard things such as portable cages, nail clippers, harness leash and a come-and-go door. It also illustrates a scratching post covered with a heavy barklike canvas instead of carpet, on the grounds that the harder substance will wean a cat away from softer carpet and upholstery fabric. And there is an ingenious "mousie house" with a disappearing mouse to give a cat a chance to work off its chasing instincts. Plenty of unsolicited testimonials of thanks for these and other goods exclusive to this firm appear in the back of the brochure.

Satra's Purr Palace, Route 1, Elkhorn, Wis. 53121
Brochure, free.

A "palace of giftdom" for people who are mad—very mad—about cats: cat calendars, cat jigsaws, cat candles, cat magnets, cat seals (imported from Germany), cat tape-measure covers, cat pencil sharpeners, cat memo pads and cat books. Also one of two things actually *for* cats, such as a cat napper bed and a denim bag full of toys.

Stromberg's Chicks and Pets Unlimited, Box 717, Fort Dodge, Iowa 50501
48-page pet catalogue, 50 cents.
48-page poultry book, some color, $2.50.

This firm, whose catalogue is full of encouraging maxims such as "Pets Provide Much Pleasure and Pride!," "Have Fun—Variety Is the Spice of Life!" and "Encourage Hobbies Early in Life to Make a Happier Future," breeds fowl (a million chicks a year) and sells pets. The poultry book shows lots of aristocratic-looking chickens, some that lay extra large eggs, some that are delicious to eat, and others whose great appeal is that they will be admired by friends and neighbors—there is an impressive choice of breeds. Exotic ducks, geese and turkey are also illustrated, and their virtues and histories are recounted in detail. There's a page of pigeons with the exhortation to "raise pigeons for pleasure—they are a wonderful hobby" and a page of game birds "Be a REAL SPORTSMAN—Raise a few game birds!" It all looks so easy that it's tempting.

As for the pet catalogue, Stromberg's says that "a youngster with hobbies and pets is happy and rarely a delinquent." To keep him happy and rarely deliquent there are coati-mundis, jaguarundis, kinkajous and cackler midget honkers, not to mention the chow chow dogs, Himalayan cats, mynahs (better talkers than most parrots), Mexican burros and skunk kittens. And for the happy child's parents there are peafowl and African crowned cranes to add dignity and charm to the lawn or estate. The catalogue is conveniently full of photographs of these superior pets, with the prices underneath, cages, houses, baskets and even caskets are listed, and so are all the books and other little things you need. In fact, I'm sure that by the time you've finished looking through this persuasive catalogue, you'll be availing yourself of the Special Birthday Gift Service and sending someone a black bear cub with your card.

4

5

6

4 • *Stromberg's Chicks and Pets Unlimited* Bourben Red turkeys. About $35 a pair.

5 • *Trefflich's of West Broadway* Baby leopard, $1,250. Price of other leopards on request.

6 • *Trefflich's of West Broadway* Baby elephant, $4,500. Price of other elephants on request.

Three Springs Fisheries, Lilypons, Md. 21717
48-page color catalogue, 50 cents.

This inspirational catalogue of water-garden supplies also has fish, and plenty of advice for would-be aquarium owners. Exotic fish are shown in full color, fish collections, plants, and other supplies, are listed and their special uses are described. You can even get scavengers like bullfrogs, and pets like alligators and monkeys. All livestock is shipped by the mysterious "Three Springs patented method."

Trefflich's of West Broadway, Inc., 141 W. Broadway, New York. N.Y. 10013
Mimeographed price list, free.
The largest firm of animal importers in the United States sells mammals, birds, reptiles and puppies from Africa, India, Brazil, Singapore and Thailand to zoos, circuses, carnivals and private buyers.

They sent me a very messy mimeographed price list, but as Henry Trefflich says that prices change from day to day, you can avoid the list if you know what you want. Many of the animals on the list are obviously for professionals: "One breeding pair of Grant's zebras, $4,000"; "Elephant, 5′, female, can be lead, fond of crowds, $2,750; F.O.B. Ohio"; "One orangutan, male, 351 lbs., Sumatrian, tame, perfect condition, $2,500." Among the nonvenomous and rear-fanged snakes, front-fanged venomous snakes, polar bears and pumas, there are all sorts of mild monkeys (South American ones from $25 to $85), miniature horses, tortoises, lizards and frogs, South American birds and decorative waterfowl that make more suitable pets.

20 SERVICES

BOOKBINDING

Classic Bindery, Box 572, Mendham, N.J. 07945
Leaflet, 25 cents.

This firm was set up by a husband and wife who were appalled at the prices they were asked to pay when they wanted their own books bound. They investigated and found that binderies, as opposed to retail stores, charge very low prices. They found a bindery in Brooklyn that they liked and decided to specialize in arranging binding by mail at moderate prices. (As far as the Farrellys know, the Classic Bindery is the only firm that does hand-binding only by mail.) The binding can be in cloth, one-quarter leather binding or full leather binding, and styles are traditional with marbleized end papers and the title and author's name stamped in gold. Besides books, the Classic Bindery binds magazines, playbills, cookbooks, scrapbooks, newspapers and letters. Cloth bindings cost from $10 to $16 according to size, and bindings with leather in them from $15 to $80, according to size and style.

CHAIR CANING

Veterans Caning Shop, 550 W. 35th Street, New York, N.Y. 10001
No catalogue.

If you are not up to recaning your broken chairs yourself (see the Hobby and Professional Equipment section for supplies), write to this shop, which will tell you how much they charge for caning, rush work and fixing splint seats.

COMFORTER REPAIRS

J. Schachter, 115 Allen Street, New York, N.Y. 10002
Leaflet, free. Satin swatches, 35 cents.

"Our specialty is the RECOVERY of used, worn DOWN COMFORTERS," writes William Schachter, and "although our trade is slowly becoming extinct, we get stronger each year." When a customer's old comforter (or eiderdown or quilt—same thing) comes into the shop it is torn apart and the old fabric is thrown away, then the wool or down is sterilized, refluffed by machines, and power-blown into the new comforter, which is interlined with down-proof nylon. Customers can have quilts remade with their own fabric or sheets, and in any size or shape, even round—experimental work undertaken. Prices start at $36 for a 64″ by 84″ quilt in customer's fabric.

EMBLEMS

Scottish Imports Ltd., 174 Grant Avenue, San Francisco, Calif. 94108
Occasional leaflet, 25 cents.

Besides importing tartan fabric, kilts, sweaters and Scottish jewelry, this firm has a stock of Scottish clan and family pocket emblems and Irish shields embroidered in gold and silver. If your name isn't on their list, Mrs. Hughes, a member of the Heraldry Society, will search for the coat of arms of your family and make an emblem. Special designs are also made to order for schools, clubs, trade associations, etc. Send a sketch or tracing of the design you want, give an idea of the quantity, and Scottish Imports will quote a price.

ENGRAVING

Elgin Engraving Co., 940 Edwards Avenue, Dundee, Ill. 60118
16-page brochure, free.

Elgin Engraving Co. will engrave your name or initials on "the world's most unusual gift," an ordinary-size pin which arrives in a blue pouch, for $1, or four thumbtacks for $1.50. More usefully, they will engrave door plates, door knockers, combs, coat hangers, shoe horns, book marks, screwdrivers, luggage tags, and plaques for almost anything you are likely to lose or want to identify, such as cameras, golf bags, umbrellas, scissors, hats and glass cases. Most prices are below $5.

GLASS

The Pairpoint Glass Company, 851 Sandwich Road, Sagamore, Mass. 02561
No catalogue.

This firm, which has been making crystal by hand since 1861, sells only through their factory blowing room (open to visitors Monday through Friday) or by mail. As most of their sales are of custom pieces, they have no catalogue, so you can't easily buy their hand-blown lead crystal without a factory visit. However, you can order pieces to be made for you by mail as Pairpoint specializes in engraved presentation glass, and they also have a matching-service in which, for example, they replace broken chandelier parts, such as candle cups and bobêches, complete with original cutting and engraving.

HANDBAG REPAIRS

Modern Leather Goods Repair Shop, 11 W. 32nd Street, New York, N.Y. 10001
No catalogue.

Send in a handbag that needs repairing and this firm will write and tell you how much it will cost; send in a check and they start work.

METAL REPAIRS

M. J. Dotzel, 402 E. 63rd Street, New York, N.Y. 10021
No catalogue.

Specialists in metalwork, this firm repairs pewter and other metal objects, makes liners for containers and rewires chandeliers. Customers send in goods for an estimate.

NEEDLEPOINT MOUNTING

Modern Needlepoint Mounting Co., 11 W. 32 Street, New York, N.Y. 10001
Leaflet, free.

The leaflet gives details of this firm's needlepoint mounting service. They will mount customer's work onto almost anything, common requests being for handbags, tennis-racquet covers, telephone-book covers.

RUG CLEANING AND REPAIRS

Kent-Costikyan, Inc., 305 E. 63 Street, New York, N.Y. 10021
No catalogue.

Specialists in cleaning and restoring (reweaving) French and Oriental rugs. Customers send in their rugs and Kent-Costikyan replies with an estimate of the cost of whatever the customer wants done. Cleaning costs from $25, and repairs cost anywhere between $50 and $500.

Pattison-Bolson Rug Service, Inc., 29-15 38th Avenue, Long Island City, N.Y. 11101
No catalogue.

Specialists in cleaning and repairing Oriental rugs. Customers send in rugs and receive an estimate of the cost of repairing or cleaning.

SIGN CARVING

Swan's Island Design Studio, P.O. Box 98, Swan's Island, Maine 04685
Leaflet, free.

This design studio carves to order simple and distinguished signs, mainly lettering for shop signs, estate signs and sternboards for boats, but also figurative sculptures. At the moment, signs cost $4 per colored letter and $7.50 per gilded letter, plus the cost of materials, but prices vary with the size of the lettering and the complexity of the design.

1 • *Silhouette Studio* Recent examples of Natalie Garvin's work. If you send a clear side-view snapshot and $3.75, she'll cut your silhouette.

SILHOUETTES

Silhouette Studio, 52 Woodhouse Avenue, Wallingford, Conn. 06492.
No catalogue.

Natalie Garvin is one of the few scissor artists, or silhouette cutters, left in the country—she thinks there are about thirty professionals now. The young don't seem to be taking it up, she says, and the older ones are dying off. She hopes, however, that an increase in the popularity of silhouettes will cause more people to take up the art. (The National Portrait Gallery, London, had an exhibition of Victorian silhouettes in 1972.) For $3.75, plus postage, she will cut your likeness and mount it on a plain white card; for $5.50, including postage, she will cut your likeness and mount it on a hand-cut 5″ by 7″ card. In both cases you must also send a *clear* side-view snapshot.

SPINNING

Bartlett Yarns, Inc., Harmony, Maine 04942
Brochure, price list and yarn samples, 25 cents.

Bartlett Mill was started in 1821 by the Bartlett family to service the farmers in the area. Although it is no longer owned by the same family and now customers live far and wide, the owners continue to spin customers' own yarn to order, and think that they must be one of the few firms doing it in the United States. They spin it into 1- to 4-ply yarn and charge around $1.90 per pound of yarn. They also sell weaving yarns and rug yarns, and have rug patterns, a few illustrated on their brochure and a lot listed on an unillustrated price list.

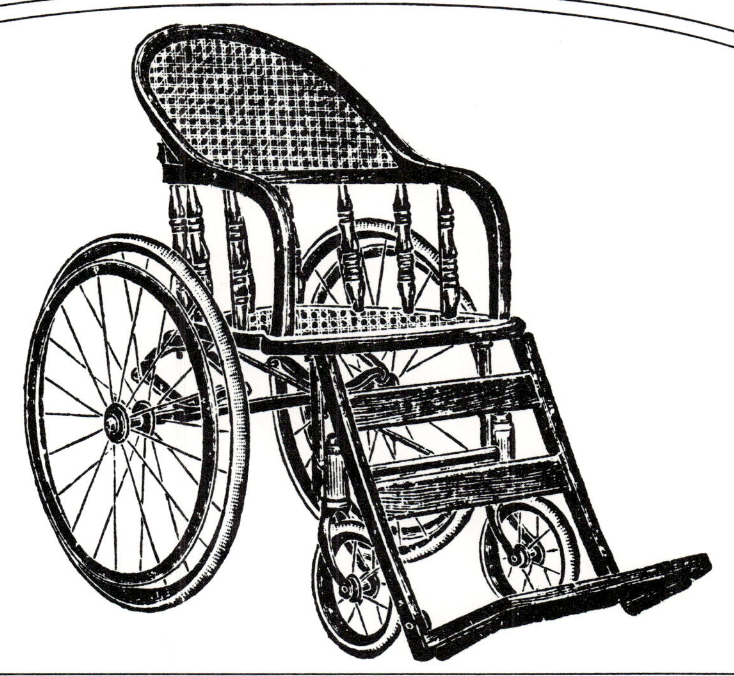

21
SPECIAL NEEDS

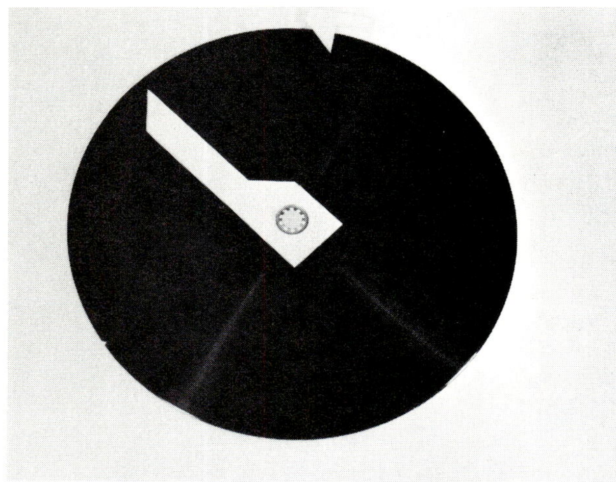

1

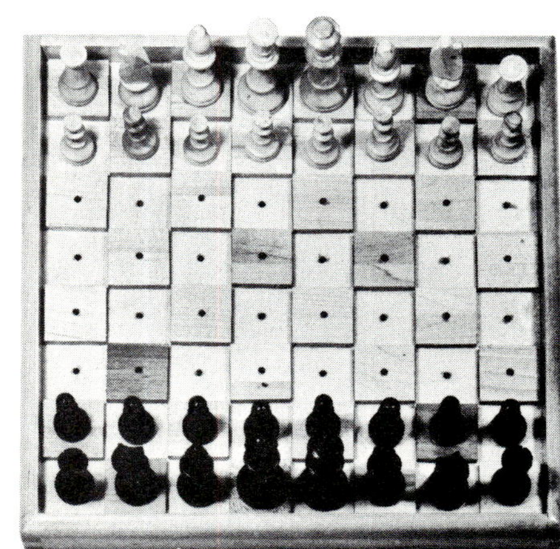

2

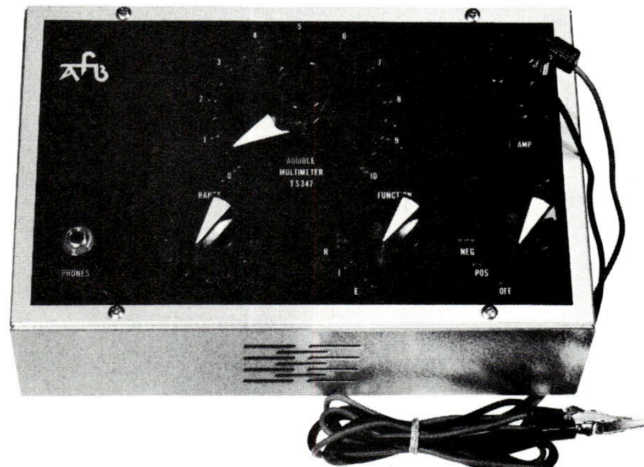

3

1 • *American Foundation for the Blind* A circular slide rule for multiplication, division and logarithmic computations. Molded in vinyl plastic, 10″ in diameter, complete with Braille and inkprint instructions. $4.50.

2 • *American Foundation for the Blind* Chess set: board with raised and lowered squares. Men have metal pegs which fit into holes on board. Colors distinguished by having flats sanded on the white. $9.50.

3 • *American Foundation for the Blind* Audible Multimeter designed for use by technicians and hobbyists to give accurate tactile readings. $145.
photos Richard J. de Rosa

The Arthritis Foundation, 1212 Avenue of the Americas, New York, N.Y. 10036
23-page self-help pamphlet, free.

The foundation publishes and distributes a pamphlet for people with arthritis entitled "Home Care Programs in Arthritis—A Manual for Patients." It contains helpful information on exercises and suggested ways of doing certain activities which may help to relieve arthritic pain. In addition, there are ideas for adapting chairs, bathtubs, etc., so that they will be easier to use by the arthritic person. The pamphlet contains a small list of companies which manufacture products of special interest to the handicapped. The foundation hopes to come out with an expanded version of this self-help manual in the near future.

American Foundation for the Blind, Inc., 15 W. 16th Street, New York, N.Y. 10011
Aids and Appliances brochure, free. Catalogue of publications, free.

The American Foundation for the Blind runs a nonprofit mail-order service selling commercial, adapted or special devices to help reduce the problems arising from blindness. Their catalogue is available in Braille or inkprint and has aids to help the blind or partially sighted: writing equipment, sewing aids, travel aids, music aids, games, watches, and all sorts of things for the kitchen: a specially chosen frying pan, a dispenser to measure teaspoonfuls, a "flame tamer" for people who have trouble keeping the heat or gas or electric fires low enough to prevent burning.

The catalogue of publications contains a list of both free and priced publications available, most of them for families, teachers and professionals who deal with blind people, but sources for Braille and talking books are also given.

They are preparing an *International Catalog of Aids and Appliances for the Visually Impaired* ($2), which should be ready by the time this book is published. It will list aids from all over the world, plus manufacturers' or distributors' addresses and prices.

Science for the Blind, 221 Hill Rock Road, Bala-Cynwyd, Pa. 19004
Leaflet, free.

A nonprofit organization with a $10 annual membership fee that develops and sells sophisticated aids to its members. Besides instruments to help with technical work, there are low-cost ham radios, tape recorders, disc players and cassettes, as well as free monthly taped periodicals such as *Radio Digest* (a collection of articles about ham radio chosen from electronic and ham-radio magazines), *Timely Topics* (nontechnical scientific material taken from publications like *Time* and the *New York Times*) and selections from *Consumer Reports.*

National Association of the Deaf, 905 Bonifant Street, Silver Springs, Md. 20910
Book list, free.

This organization gives a great deal of advice on aids for the deaf and where to get them, including all sorts of signaling devices. They stock a few books on communicating with the deaf, and have a book which has proved to be extremely useful to people—not only the deaf—who are learning English, *A Dictionary of Idioms for the Deaf.* It was designed to supplement existing school dictionaries and to explain English phrases that cannot be understood from the definition of the separate words.

Cleveland Orthopedic Company, 3957 Mayfield Road, Cleveland, Ohio 44121
50-page catalogue, free.

This firm sells living aids for physically handicapped and convalescent people and I daresay no need is left out. There are all kinds of bathroom and tub aids—elevated toilet seats, tub safety rails and special soap holders, to name a few. There is also a large assortment of self-help devices, such as extension arms, cigarette holders and remote-control switches. For recreation there are specially chosen games, and for eating there are many specially designed utensils, gadgets and accessories to make both eating and cooking easier. The selections include products for all ages from child to adult.

Constructive Playthings, 1040 E. 85th Street, Kansas City, Mo. 64131
170-page catalogue, some color, $1.

This large catalogue of toys and equipment from many manufacturers includes six pages of aids to learning for mentally and physically handicapped children, and also marks toys among the general selection which are especially suitable for the handicapped.

FashionABLE, Rocky Hill, N.J. 08553
24-page catalogue, 25 cents. Spring, fall.

FashionABLE was started by a woman who became partially paralyzed and realized how much the physically handicapped are in need of special clothing and products for daily living. Specially designed and made clothes, and a selection of gadgets that would normally be sold in a variety of shops, are listed in this catalogue, which is intended for disabled people living at home rather than in institutions. There are aids for dressing, including a gadget for people who can't tie bows, and for cooking and eating, bathing and cleaning. The stock is not at all the same as Cleveland Orthopedic Company's, which is more for institutions and has more recreation equipment. Both catalogues are definitely worth sending for.

Shalik's Rehab Aids, Box 826, Miami, Fla. 33143
Leaflet, free.

Shalik's sells small aids to help the disabled living at home, specially concentrating on people who have had strokes. There are several arm slings, and a few aids for eating, washing, tying shoelaces, etc., with one hand.

Vocational Guidance and Rehabilitation Services, 2239 E. 55th Street, Cleveland, Ohio 44103
12-page catalogue, $1.

This organization puts out a catalogue of clothing and a few aids for the chronically ill and disabled. All items are functionally designed—dresses with special closings for women with limited manual dexterity, wrap-around slips for women with limited overhead arm movement, carry-alls for wheelchairs, special clothes for children in braces, to name a few. They are more than eager to do custom orders. The organization also plans to come out with a catalogue for the Sunbeam Shop, a retail outlet for products made by the handicapped.

4

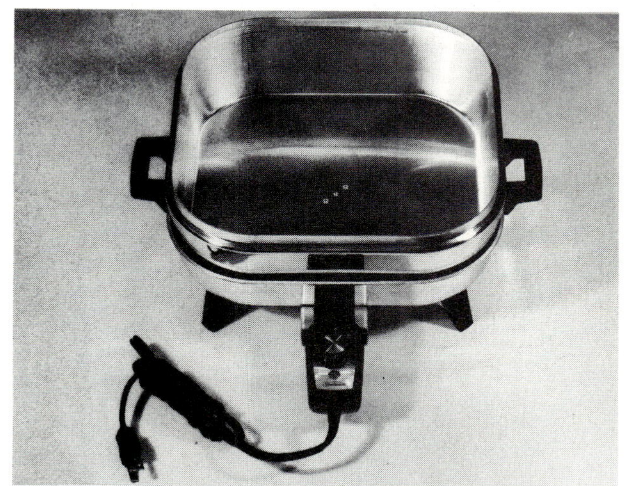
5

4 • *American Foundation for the Blind* The AFB has a large number of Swiss-made watches with every dial in Braille and inkprint. Prices from $16 to $300.

5 • *American Foundation for the Blind* Sunbeam skillet with control. A buffet-style frying pan with protective feet so that it can be used at the table. When the automatic heat control has been removed, pan can be completely immersed for cleaning. $23.95.
photos Richard J. de Rosa

Better Sleep, Inc., New Providence, N.J. 07974
24-page catalogue, free.

A firm that is devoted to furthering the comfort of insomniacs and bed-pressers (as lazy boys were called in Dr. Johnson's day). If you have trouble getting to sleep, there are lots of helpful hints in this catalogue (such as a diagram of the ideal position for easiest relaxation), or try the earplugs, sleep mask, foot warmer or "Sleep Mate" ("which gives a rhythmic, tranquil sleep-inducing sound that blocks out noises"). If you don't have trouble sleeping, wear the anti-snore mask and give someone else a break. For just relaxing in bed you'll find back supports ("throw away those extra pillows"), blanket supports to keep the blankets off tender feet, pillows to use when you go to bed in curlers, and pillows guaranteed to stop you waking up with "impressed wrinkles" on your face. For relaxing in the bath there are three different bath pillows, and a "soaker's Delite"—a rubber cap that fits over the overflow valve so you can get a nice deep bath; also a bath lift seat (about $8) to help you get out. And if, when you've staggered out of the bath, you want to fall asleep again in a chair or the car, you'll find a good assortment of little pillows to help you do that.

Norman Dine Sleep Center, Wuensch, 33 Halsted Street, East Orange, N.J. 07018
30-page catalogue, free.

More aids for insomniacs. Norman Dine, whom *Time* magazine called "the dean of beducation," claims to have solved over a million sleep problems over the past thirty years, but besides pillows and noise drowners for better sleep, the catalogue lists all sorts of gadgets for people who spend waking hours in bed: trays with pockets for books, bags to keep things that tuck into the mattress, stands to enable you to read while lying down. Italian carved headboards, round king-size beds, push-button beds and exercise machines of all sorts are for sale.

Sleep-Learning Research Ass'n, P.O. Box 24, Olympia, Wash. 98501
32-page catalogue, free. Leaflets, free.

"Everything for the experimenter," says this catalogue offering recorders, tapes and books for those who wish to experiment with sleep learning and sleep therapy. The catalogue explains the principles of learning while you sleep, and then offers "The Amazing Electronic Educator!" and other devices, as well as related items such as the Mystic Pentagram that allows anyone to become a "Psychic Reader." Once you have your under-pillow speaker, the courses offered are rather tame: understanding the new math, weight reduction, self-confidence, the facts of love and life for teen-age girls, as well as complete books on records, such as *The Basic Writings of Emerson* and others clearly best listened to while asleep. Various other courses are also available, suitable for sleep or periods of wakefulness, covering such suggestive areas as Hypnosis for Bowlers, or less worldly areas such as Psychic Development.

Survival Associates, P.O. Box 8, Old Chelsea Station, New York, N.Y. 10011
Brochure, free.

Probably the most unique response in this book to our polluted environment is this two-women firm established to sell air-pollution masks to people who wish to protect themselves against air pollution and also demonstrate their concern. Now that weather forecasts regularly tell you whether urban air is acceptable or not, you may have wondered what you are supposed to do when the air outside, particularly in the morning rush hour, is unbreathable. Survival's masks, it claims, will protect you against 90 percent of most of the contaminants in the air, though there is little that can be done about carbon monoxide or dioxide short of wearing a special mask whose canister must be replaced every two hours. A single-cartridge mask costs $12 and is good for about 500 hours of bad air, after which a replacement filter for $5 is necessary. For people with special breathing problems or those who have to jog or bicycle in a polluted atmosphere, the dual-cartridge mask at $22 is recommended. The Survival brochure includes some horrifying data on air pollution, the diseases it causes and a few of the things you can do to render their product unnecessary.

22
SPORTS EQUIPMENT & CLOTHES

GENERAL

Abercrombie & Fitch Co., Madison Avenue at 45th Street, New York, N.Y. 10017
Spring catalogue, March. Outdoor Sports, May. Fall catalogue, August. All free.
Christmas catalogue, $1. October.

When Ezra H. Fitch and David T. Abercrombie, both of them sportsmen, started their shop in 1892, they ignored the usual practice of keeping merchandise neatly on the shelves and set it up as though in use, pitching tents and installing equipment around the floors. They saw to it that salesmen became familiar with the rods, reels and firearms by actually using them, and they decided on a policy of putting quality before price, which made Abercrombie & Fitch the most famous sports-goods store in the world, and a supplier to every American President from Theodore Roosevelt on.

However, although Abercrombie & Fitch still has an enormous range of the most expensive American and imported equipment for most sports, and although Abercrombie's says "the spirit and the guiding policies of its founders remain alive in the hearts and minds of the organization," sportsmen who send for their catalogues will be disappointed, for in recent years the catalogues have shown mainly medium-priced casual clothes, and their Christmas catalogue is a fairly typical classy gift catalogue with clothes, silver-plated jugs and goblets, indoor games, what they call "executive gifts" (desk sets, clock radios, etc.), exercise equipment, Braun kitchen appliances, with just a few of the things illustrated related to sports—skis, guns and animal-decorated cuff links.

But Abercrombie & Fitch (which now has several branches around the country) does an enormous amount of business by mail, both domestically and to customers abroad, and at this writing plans to publish a catalogue of sports equipment (in May 1973), and if it is successful, will publish it regularly every year, probably in May. Apart from that catalogue, people interested in equipment for any sport should write to them direct; they say they will find anything not in stock—in recent years they claim to have sold most things to do with the outdoor life, from collapsible bathtubs to chain-mail shirts for oil workers in the Colombian jungle working in poison-arrow territory.

Eddie Bauer, P.O. Box 3700, Seattle, Wash. 98124
46-page color catalogue, free. Issued three times a year.

Among the most interesting mail-order catalogues are those concentrating on clothes and equipment for the more adventurous sports: hunting, fishing, exploring, camping. The two major firms in this field are Eddie Bauer and L. L. Bean, each at opposite ends of the country, though they have some distinguished competitors. Both Bauer and Bean grew from being small outfitters to very big businesses (though Bean is still family-owned, while Bauer is now owned by General Mills), which means that they are able to manufacture a large part of the goods they sell. Bauer makes half of what it sells or has it made to their specifications. The major Bauer speciality is based on the goose: insulated garments and camping equipment and now home furnishing, all using goose down, are their most interesting offerings.

Bauer designed the World War II flyer's suits, using goose down, and likewise has supplied the clothing for many polar expeditions. The Bauer catalogue starts with pages of variants on this theme, offering parkas, shooting coats, light jackets, etc., reassuringly labeled as being comfortable for temperatures ranging from −40° to 65° above, and ranging in price roughly from $40 to $80. Bauer also offers goose-down boots and bonnets, and a rather frightening-looking face mask, ideal for skiers, snowmobilers, et al. Equipment of all kinds for these sports are another Bauer specialty, but the firm also offers a full range of leisure wear, even selling Harris Tweed jackets and other more citified outfits, which are of less interest.

Bauer sells a wide range of boots, shoes, socks, underwear and other cold- or wet-weather clothing. They have a larger selection, I would guess, than Bean, and in the areas where I compared prices they are consistently more expensive than their Eastern competitor. If, however, you are planning to buy a whole wardrobe for yourself and your family, you should get both catalogues, since each offers quite a few exclusive items.

Bauer also has a full range of camping and exploring equipment and has used its goose down to insulate a number of very warm-looking sleeping bags. For home use there are also a number of goose-down pillows and comforters, those marvelously light and incredibly warm bed coverings so widely used in northern Europe, though these are far more expensive than the ones you can buy direct from Europe. Should anything happen to any of these goose-down furnishings, Bauer maintains a repair service for any item it has sold you. As with Bean's, swatches of sample materials are available for many of the goods.

Bauer stresses its complete and unconditional guarantee, which ensures money back on any purchase with no restrictions whatsoever.

L. L. Bean, Inc., 454 Main Street, Freeport, Maine 04032
60- to 120-page catalogues, free. Issued four times a year.

L. L. Bean is something of a national institution, and its famous catalogue was one of the inspirations behind the *Whole Earth Catalog.* Over half a million customers throughout the country and the world buy through this exceptional document, and over the years Bean has become a multimillion-dollar business.

In part, this is because more and more people have become caught up in the kind of outdoor life—camping and exploring as well as hunting and fishing—for which Bean provides the necessary equipment. But I suspect that a great many people have written in simply because Bean's clothing is sensible, well made and often a real bargain. When my husband wanted a winter coat the other year, any number of people suggested that he write in for Bean's Great Coat, a lightweight pile-lined coat that seemed both warm and reasonably priced at $53.50. Likewise, Bean's chamois cloth shirts, made of cotton flannel, compare favorably with Viyella shirts of a similar nature and are cheaper here ($8.35) than Viyella is in England. I mention price because Bean's products seem to me to be as good as any that can be bought in this country, and yet their cost is much lower than at New York's famous men's clothing stores. Though the main emphasis in the Bean catalogue is on the clothing, shoes, boots, coats, etc., needed by men on hunting expeditions and the like, the firm offers a wide choice of "civilian" clothing and items that women will want as much as men. Mocca-

2

1

3

4

5

6

7

1 • *L. L. Bean* Chamois cloth shirt, made of wind-resistant cotton flannel, thickly napped on both sides. Made extra full with long sleeves, long tuck-in tails and two buttoned pockets. Forest-green, tan, bright-red in sizes 14½ to 19. Free samples of the fabric available. $8.85 for men; $8.75 for ladies.

2 • *L. L. Bean* Allagash hat with a 3″ wide brim as a protection against rain and sun. The crown contains a mosquito net which covers face and neck. Olive-green in men's sizes, 6¾″ to 7¾″. $11.

3 • *L. L. Bean* Maine hunting shoe, originally developed in 1912. Uppers are of supple top-grain cowhide, chemically treated in the tanning process to resist water for life. Bottoms are of ozone-resistant rubber with cushioned inner soles. The outer sole of crepe is permanently vulcanized to the vamp and has Bean's own non-slip chain tread. Tops come in three leg sizes and different heights, prices $18.50 to $30. Similar shoes for women cost $20.75.

4 • *Gokey* Botte Sauvage pull-on boots, cut from Brazil ski-grain oil-tanned leather and of genuine moccasin construction, have hand-sewn vamps, middle soles attached by machine, and are quarter-lined. Made with heel counters and steel arches for good support and have non-slip soles and heels. Men's sizes 7 to 12 in C, D and E widths; other sizes and women's sizes to order, all $60.

5 • *L. L. Bean* Blucher moccasins with oil-tanned brown ski-grain uppers and true moccasin construction with hand-sewn toe piece. Blucher style lacing for snug fit at heel and arch. Non-slip rubber sole with molded arch support. Men's sizes $15; women's, $12.50; boys', $13.75.

6 • *L. L. Bean* Bird Shooting Pants, briar-resistant all-wool reversed whipcord, with extra strong leather-trimmed pockets. Legs are cut full for rough walking. Waist sizes, 30″ to 50″; inseams 29″, 31″ and 33″. Color: forest-green. $26.85.

7 • *L. L. Bean* Travel bag, can be carried by hand or over the shoulder. Made of cotton twill outside and inside, and bonded to a middle layer of rubber for resistance to moisture with leather trim. Two large outside compartments. Green with tan trim. $24.50.

8 • *James Bliss* Machine-washable PVC gear bags in yellow and blue, blue and white, or red and white, 25″ high, 9½″ in diameter. $14.95. *photo Photography Incorporated*

sins for either sex, for instance, cost $11; nylon shells—light, waterproof sports jackets—just under $10; trousers between $10 and $30, etc. For those living in very cold climates there is a wide choice of warm underwear originally designed for Antarctic explorers—down-insulated jackets, Balaclava helmets, and similar gear—while for the summer, they offer an ingenious undergarment that is said to make you feel much cooler.

Bean's catalogue devotes nearly half of its space to sports and camping equipment: fishing rods, flies, and the like; waders and special boots; canoes and lightweight motors; back packs, sleeping bags, tents, axes and knives, all are listed in great variety. Whether for real expeditions or backyard cookouts, the catalogue is an excellent guide. Indeed, it's hard to think of an excuse not to consider writing in.

Gokey Co., 21 W. Fifth Street, St. Paul, Minn. 55102
Catalogue, free. March, August.

Some people leap out of cars and chase other people across town to find out where they got their Gokey boots. Other people leave Gokey to their friends in their wills, and so many people write Gokey emotional thank-you letters about at last having comfortable feet that Gokey throws most of the letters away.

Gokey has made "roughing boots" for over a hundred years, snakeproof boots, and a whole range of handmade shoes and boots for men and women. Prices range from about $11 for canoe moccasins to about $90 for their famous snakeproof boots (worn daily by the men who work in the Florida snakepits . . .).

Besides their own boots and shoes, Gokey sells clothes, shoes and sports equipment by other top American and foreign manufacturers.

Herter's, Inc., Department 51, Waseca, Minn. 56093
660-page annual black-and-white catalogue, $1.
120-page catalogue, free.

"The authentic world source for fishermen, hunters, guides, gunsmiths . . ." The cover of Herter's catalogue goes on to list a huge number of potential customers, and given their vast catalogue, it is difficult to imagine any outdoorsman whose interests are not touched upon. Hunting equipment is the most important item and close to 250 pages are devoted to every kind of rifle, bullet, sight and targets as well as reloading tools and dies, of which Herter's states it is the world's largest manufacturer. Bows and arrows follow the rifles, with over forty very full pages starting with sets for youngsters and going up to powerful hunting bows.

An equally complete fishing section covers two hundred more pages, listing such specialties as Herter's fly-tying kits; feathers, fur and hair for lures; hundreds, if not thousands, of fishhooks ("the largest stock in the world"), and of course rods, reels and nets sold separately or in kits.

Other offerings are not as incredibly complete, but there is a good selection of down-lined clothing, at prices that compare well with other leading shops. Herter's seemed definitely less expensive than Bauer and competitive with Bean, though each firm has a number of exclusive items that can't be readily compared.

Herter's also has a large range of snowmobiles, with machines costing as much as $882, plus shipping and crating. The firm also makes parts for snowmobiles and sells related equipment, such as snowshoes, etc. Herter's is known for its low prices, and wherever comparisons have been possible, their goods have certainly turned out to be among the less expensive available. A large number are made for Herter's, and in the areas of the greatest strength (i.e., hunting and fishing equipment), I should think theirs would be a basic catalogue.

Moor & Mountain, 67 Main Street, Concord, Mass. 01742
48-page catalogue, free. Spring/Summer and Fall/Winter.

Moor & Mountain was started six years ago by two young businessmen seeking independence and country life and has grown to a firm that sends out 100,000 of each of its catalogues. The two men who run the firm personally select and test the equipment they sell, and some of it—the back packs and canoeing tents—have been designed by them. They try to keep their catalogue as simple and easily understandable as possible and "try to pre-select based on function and to impart the rationale for our choices." As a result, the catalogue has some very helpful copy on, for instance, chosing cross-country skis, etc. Clothes and equipment for skiing, hiking and boating predominate. A number of items are manufactured for Moor & Mountain, including back packs and sleeping bags, cooking utensils and down clothing. Among the brand-name items carried are Tyne canoes, kayaks from England and Norfell tents.

P & S Sales, P.O. Box 45095, Tulsa, Okla. 74145
96-page catalogue, free. Issued three times a year.

This small but thorough catalogue offers a selection from various manufacturers of equipment for camping, hunting and fishing. Prices seem to be competitive and the choices reasonable, with a few pages devoted to most areas. Not for the specialized sportsman looking for the widest selection, but a handy list which supplies customers throughout the country.

Port Canvas Company, Dock Square, Kennebunkport, Maine 04046
12-page brochure, free. Spring, fall.

Port Canvas Company was started six years ago "on a worn shoestring in the belief that there was a need for rugged, simple canvas products of old-time quality and workmanship." Details of the materials used and the methods of manufacture are given in the brochure; the goods, which are indeed rugged, simple and handsome, are available in navy-blue, Breton-red or natural. There are bags of various kinds—for hockey, tennis or ski gear, and a lovely red, white and blue bag for ski boots or ice skates, $12; seaman's duffels; a canoe bag to tie to the thwarts of a canoe; an artist's portfolio (which can also be used as a suitcase); and a brush holder that rolls up like a tool kit, $7. A few hats, heavy sweaters, a jacket and some foul-weather gear from Norway are also sold, and so is canvas by the yard.

ARCHERY

Kittredge Bow Hut, P.O. Box 598, Mammoth Lakes, Calif. 93546
196-page catalogue, 25 cents.

Kittredge sells archery equipment, primarily to those who hunt with bow and arrow, and this catalogue, which they call "the Archer's Bible," is a strange mixture of modern-day technology and equipment that calls earlier civilizations to mind. Most of the equipment is clearly deadly and includes razor-sharp arrowheads that guarantee a "good blood trail." Bows range widely in price, some costing as much as $140, though various kits and bow-and-arrow-building materials are also offered. In addition to the wide range of arrows, quivers, and the like, the catalogue lists related outdoor equipment—knives, camping equipment, game calls and scents—as well as ten pages of books on archery.

Besides issuing a very thorough catalogue, Kittredge offers personal help, advice on the best equipment within certain budgets, advice on what to buy to go into back country, etc. It's an approach which obviously works, since last year Kittredge received close to eighty thousand orders from all over the world.

BICYCLING

Metropolitan New York Council, American Youth Hostels, Inc. 535 West End Avenue, New York, N.Y. 10024
24-page black-and-white equipment catalogue and 24-page travel catalogue, free to members.

If you are a serious cyclist, joining American Youth Hostels may make sense, even if you don't plan to join any organized activities. Membership is open on a family basis for those who no longer qualify as youths. The American Youth Hostels catalogue contains just about everything a cyclist may need, except for the actual bicycle, which it is assumed you have. Sleeping bags, back packs, rain gear, camping utensils and various kinds of bike equipment are all available. This last includes saddlebags, cycling jerseys and shirts, various repair tools, and accessories ranging from pumps and taillights to chain and locks. American Youth Hostels has been selling these things for twenty years, well before the recent cycling boom, and as a result has had great experience not only in supplying cyclists but in designing a great many of the items which they sell exclusively. Because they sell as a service to their members, their prices tend to be reasonable and their accessories give value for money. Membership is only $5 for those under eighteen, $10 for those over, and $12 for families.

BOATING AND CANOEING

James Bliss & Co., Inc., Route 128, Dedham, Mass. 02026
288-page annual catalogue, $1.

"Everything marine" states the catalogue cover, and it is hard to imagine anything, short of the boats themselves, that is not listed in this encyclopedic volume. Bliss caters primarily to a yachting crowd, judging from the pages devoted to cruising accessories, yacht-club signals, logbooks, guest registers, and the like. But there are also full selections of more serious items: searchlights, pumps, marine paints, and hundreds of spare parts, tools, nautical hardware, etc. Illustrated in detail, the catalogue serves as a guide to the five Bliss stores or to mail order, where Bliss promises same-day service.

Defender Industries, Inc., 255 Main Street, New Rochelle, N.Y. 10801
160-page catalogue, 75 cents.

Defender's *Marine Buyer's Guide* is a comprehensive catalogue for the serious boat owner—for someone who actually repairs and even builds his own boats and needs both the hardware and the raw materials involved. Defender is "the principal source for dynel and polypropylene in the United States of America as well as leaders in the fiberglass field." Their catalogue includes instructions on the application of fiberglass and resins, as well as directions for building a fiberglass boat. Paints, finishes and the equipment for applying them are also listed, as well as pages of ropes, cables, hardware and everything else that goes into a boat, some manufactured by Defender, others coming from other manufacturers.

The catalogue also lists a number of lamps, bells, etc., but for the most part emphasis is very much on the meat-and-potatoes of boating, with nary a captain's cap in the whole book.

Folbot Corp., P.O. Box 7097, Charleston, S.C. 29405
50-page color catalogue, free.

Folbot manufactures a line of light, kayak-like boats that can be used for white water, fishing and surfing or with sails. The boats vary in price from $59 for a junior pre-fab up to $330 for the largest boat, these being the factory prices. In addition to a wide range of models, all sorts of accessories are also available from Folbot.

The Fulton Supply Co., 28 Fulton Street, New York, N.Y. 10038
20-page annual catalogue, free.

Clothing for amateur sailors is the specialty of this firm, with goods, mostly imported, looking both utilitarian and stylish. Scottish oiled wool sweaters at $35 are featured, but a less expensive, local turtleneck is available for $15.95. Norwegian waterproof clothing costs only $15.95 for trousers and $18.95 for a parka. A slicker for girls is $4.99, French sailing gloves cost $6.95, and so on. A nicely varied and unpretentious selection at reasonable prices.

Goldberg's, 202 Market Street, Philadelphia, Pa. 19106
200-page annual catalogue and 6 "mini-catalogues" of sale items, $1.00.

Goldberg's has been selling boating supplies for thirty years and claims to be the country's largest firm in its field. They have stores in New York and Philadelphia, but clearly, much of their business is done by mail. Their large, thorough catalogue is businesslike and serious—"no gadgets, just 'real' items," they wrote me. Some is built to the store's specifications; much is ordered in bulk. Starting with nylon rope, the catalogue centers on basic equipment and hardware, including electronic equipment, but does not have boat-building supplies as such.

Hans Klepper Corp., 35 Union Square West, New York, N.Y. 10003
24-page color brochure, free.

Hans Klepper has been making folding boats in Germany since 1907. And the brochure lists folding boats and kayaks, rigid fiberglass kayaks, accessories for the boats and for looking after them, tents, books and touring guides, and an impressive "partial list of the historically famous ventures in which Klepper Foldaways have played an important role." Prices start at about $275 for a one-man touring kayak, but their most popular double-seater, the folding, unsinkable *Aerius* (first to complete an Atlantic crossing, selected for exhibit in the Museum of Modern Art, honored by Design for Sport), costs about $440.

Leisure Imports, Inc., 104 Arlington Avenue, St. James, N.Y. 11780
Color brochures, free.

Leisure imports inflatable canoes and dinghies made in France by Pennel et Flipo, which is apparently the world's largest manufacturer in this field and supplier to Jacques Cousteau. The boats they make are attractive, inexpensive and, Leisure states, very durable. "Constructed of 20 guage, vinyl-urethane . . . they will last five to eight years with good care." The boats are very light, the heaviest weighing 19 lbs., and their strength is attested to by their use in several American white-water schools. The inflatable canoes go from $34.95 for a 6′3″ child's canoe to $99.95 for the large (10′6″) two-man canoe. The dinghies range from $19.95 for a child's boat to $59.95 for a two- to four-man dinghy (7′6″). Various accessories, pumps and air mattresses are also available.

Luger Industries, Inc., 3800 W. Highway 12, Burnsville, Minn. 55378
80-page color catalogue, free.

Luger has been selling boat kits for the last twenty years to people who have never built a boat before and have no special tools—so any problems were ironed out long ago, they say. The parts of the boat are delivered absolutely finished and are fitted together and "chemically" welded by you in exactly the same way that factory boats are assembled. Luger says that many of the boats can be made by one person alone, while some of the larger boats need two people to position the heavier pieces, and seven or eight people to turn the hull over.

Luger boat kits were recommended in the *Whole Earth Catalog* by someone who had used a kit. He said that the quality was very high, though it took him three times longer to make his boat than Luger predicts, and he thought that the accessories (windows, galley hardware, etc.) were mediocre and overpriced—better buy these from a mail-order discount dealer, he said. The point of these kits is, of course, to save money, but Luger says that if you want, you can also make certain modifications which would be terribly expensive on factory-made boats. Prices start at about $240 for the sailing boats and about $900 for the powerboats. There are also two houseboats, and the latest innovation is "bare hull" kits for even greater economy. With these you get just the fiberglass parts and plans and instructions for making your own wood parts. Prices for these start at about $240 for a 14′ sailboat.

Old Town Canoe Company, Old Town, Maine 04468
28-page color catalogue, free.

Old Town manufactures and sells canoes, kayaks and powerboats. Its pack canoes range from $250 for an 11′11″ 35-lb. Carleton model to $375 for an 18′ 75-lb. Chipewyan. Sailing canoes are more expensive, costing $795 for a 16-footer, but sailing equipment can be purchased separately which can convert a standard canoe for $300. Wood and canvas are available at higher prices. In addition to these, Old Town makes duck boats, one-man pack canoes, covered craft, white-water canoes and kayaks, these last coming close to the canoe prices. Six different powerboats are also sold by Old Town, ranging in price from $2,195 for a 17′8″ Shrike to $11,250 for the most expensive, Atlantis, some eight feet longer. A full line of accessories, paddles, oars, vests and various items of clothing are also available.

Henri Vaillancourt, Mill Street, Box 199, Greenville, N.H. 03048
No catalogue.

A strictly one-man operation, Henri Vaillancourt makes Malecite birch-bark canoes by the same processes that Indians have used since time immemorial. Each one takes a month to make (but there's a waiting list), and prices are between $400 and $600, according to size. He also makes fancily carved Indian-style paddles for about $40, and can make canoes and paddles to your own design.

West Products Corp., 140 Greenwood Avenue, Midland Park, N.J. 07432
192-page catalogue, free.

West's catalogue of marine supplies emphasizes its own products, and two thirds of their business come from the sale of items they've manufactured or licensed. West's marine rope is one of the firm's best products, at prices which they call 50 percent lower than its competitors', since it is sold direct. Anchors, chains and other items of hardware are also featured. West life rafts are available for sale or rental and cost $685 if bought. Life vest, preservers and related equipment are also listed.

At a less serious level, West sells a wide assortment of quietly chic, utilitarian clothing as well as storm suits and other all-weather wear. Just about all the other accessories that one can think of are listed in this serious and attractive catalogue, and as usual, there are a number of items that struck me as suitable for every-day use: a handsome duck carry-all for $6.50 and small duffle bags for $13.95, for instance, or the virgin-wool storm turtlenecks for $12.95. The Swedish nautical blankets at $22.95 also struck me as being as useful at home as on a cabin bunk.

For nautical pictures, decorative objects and gifts, see the firms listed under Models in the Collecting section.

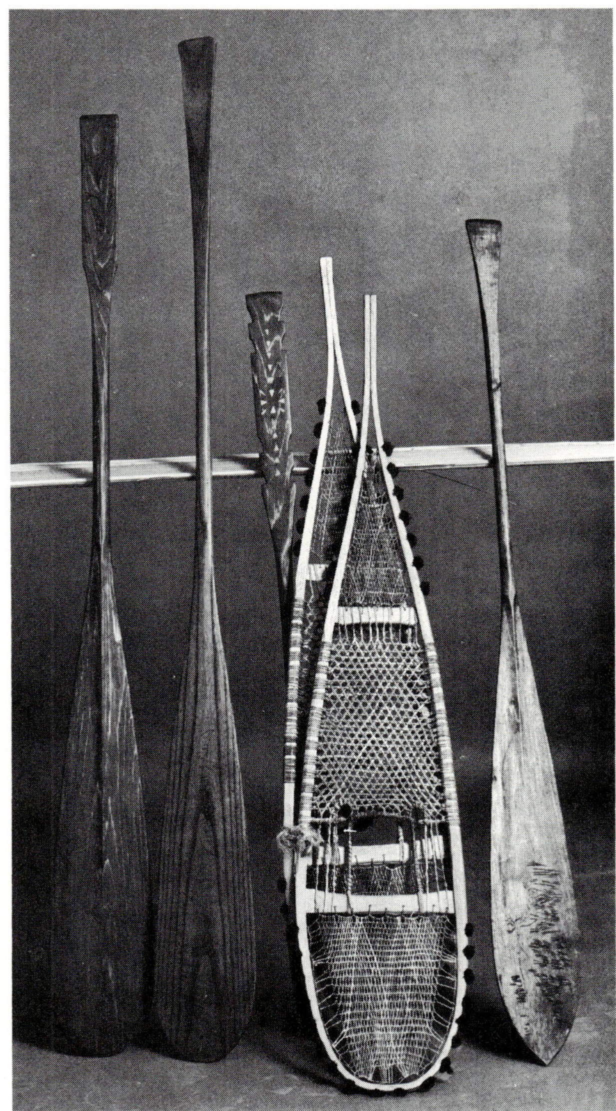

9 • *Henry Vaillancourt* Paddles in Malecite Indian style—cedar, $25 each; hardwood, $40. The paddle behind the snowshoes has a bone inlay design on the grip which is $15 extra on the hardwood only. The paddle on the right of the snowshoes has incised line decoration on the blade, and the paddle on the extreme left of the snowshoes has leaf-and-vine incised design on the grip, no extra charge. The snowshoes are webbed with deerskin rawhide and are northern Indian in style. $100 per pair.
photo Richard Nash

10 • *Don Gleason's Camper's Supply* Pack baskets of ash made by American Indians. 18″ high, $13.95; 20″ high, $15.95; 22″ high, $17.50.

11 • *Don Gleason's Camper's Supply* Basta toothbrush. The handle can be filled with toothpaste and a little can be released each time you brush your teeth; it holds two weeks' supply. $2.

12 • *Holubar Mountaineering* Children's Highland parka, down-filled with standing down-filled collar and down-filled pockets with Velcro closing flaps. There is an adjustable drawstring at the waist and a pre-set snap band which sews behind the collar for attaching the optional down Highland hood. Children's sizes 6, 9, 12. $17.95.

13 • *Don Gleason's Camper's Supply* Pocketknives with blades of Buck quality steel, brass liners and non-slip grips. The measurement is for the longest blade: knife with 2″ blade, $7; 2½″ blade, $12; 3″ blade, $15; 3¼″ blade, $18.

14 • *Don Gleason's Camper's Supply* Dog pack enables a dog to carry his own food. In waterproof coated nylon with leather reinforcements on corners and two compartments. Size, 9″ by 10″ by 4″ on each side. $20.

15 • *Don Gleason's Camper's Supply* Sleeping pad system. Sack is stuffed with clothing to make a pillow during the night; during the day the pad goes into the sack with room for the sleeping bag, also making a weatherproof bundle. Foam pad, $7.50; stuff sack, $2.90.

16 • *Don Gleason's Camper's Supply* Air mattress weighs only 20 oz. and has individually inflated cells. 22″ by 46″ inflated, $3.90. Air pillow snaps to the mattress providing more length, weighs 4 oz., $1.60.

CAMPING AND HIKING

Antelope Camping Equipment Mfg. Co., 21740 Granada, Cupertino, Calif. 95014
16-page catalogue, free.

Ed Goddard, the owner of Antelope, started making back packs in the fifties when his son became a tenderfoot scout and he learned to make nonwelded frames for children, which would grow as the children did. From these beginnings grew a firm that now makes some 2,500 frames and bags each year, in five sizes that are particularly geared to the needs of the young. The firm makes everything listed in its catalogue: frames and kits, straps, knapsacks and pack bags, sleeping-bag cases and other such accessories.

Camp and Trail Outfitters, 21 Park Place, New York, N.Y. 10007
24-page black-and-white catalogue, free. Winter, spring.

Camp and Trail sells equipment from various manufacturers and is thus a useful place to compare offerings. Prices seem reasonable, with sleeping bags available for as little as $55 for a medium-size goose-down-filled "Icelandic special." A wide variety of tents is available, priced at from $90 for a simple nylon two-man tent to $252 for a two-man "Himalayan tent." Camp and Trail stocks many of the Sierra Designs items as well as those by Alpine Designs, North Face, and other firms. Parkas, snowshoes, back packs, climbing boots, and other hiking, camping and mountain climbing supplies are also listed.

Frostline Kits, P.O. Box 2190, Boulder, Colo. 80302
32-page color catalogue, free. March and September.

Frostline makes do-it-yourself kits of lightweight camping equipment and down-insulated clothing. The material is pre-cut, all the raw materials are provided and the customer saves considerably by supplying the labor himself. Sleeping-bag kits are available from $44.95 up, and Frostline also has kits for quilts, comforters and pillows to be used at home, the only catalogue that I have seen offering this. A twin-size comforter costs $39.95 and a king-size $56.95, far less than it would cost to buy these ready-made here and even less than abroad.

Jackets, coats, parkas and ponchos are also for sale, a tundra goose-down-lined jacket costing $26, trousers $19.95, parkas $8.95. Kits are also available for children's sizes in most of these. In addition to clothing, Frostline has kits for packs and frames, and tents—a Kodiak two-man tent costing $64.95. An excellent catalogue which allows you to make expensive outdoor equipment at very reasonable prices.

Don Gleason's Camper's Supply, Inc., P.O. Box 86, 9 Pearl Street, Northampton, Mass. 01060
162-page annual catalogue, 25 cents.

Gleason's very complete catalogue focuses on camping in normal climates and has a wide choice of the kind of equipment that a family would need on a summer vacation, rather than equipment for Arctic exploration. The catalogue starts with propane-gas-fueled camping kitchens, goes on to camp stoves and lanterns, and even has a section on portable toilets and similar accessories for those who like to camp in comfort.

A special feature is the tent section, some thirty pages devoted to tents of every kind, with a thoughtful introduction for the new camper. Gleason's has a special line of lightweight nylon tents and various cabin tents that are the size of small houses. They also sell a "Pop-Tent" that will sleep four and can, the description assures us, be put up in ninety seconds.

In addition to these, many of which seem ideally suited for a child's night out in the backyard, there is a good selection of camp beds, cots, camping chairs and other furniture that makes good sense for the home. Much of the cooking, toasting and grilling equipment can also be used at home.

Holubar Mountaineering, Ltd., P.O. Box 7, Boulder, Colo. 80302
64-page Holubar color catalogue, free.
32-page Carikit catalogue, free.

Holubar is a manufacturer of camping and light backpacking equipment whose specialities are goose-down-filled parkas and sleeping bags, but who also sells a full range of camping equipment. Their parkas start at $33 and their goose-down-filled garments start at $27. More ambitious pieces of clothing, including down-filled trousers, are also available, for $110. Their sleeping bags start at $68 and go up to $167 for the expedition model. Hats, gloves, shirts are also available from various manufacturers. Holubar also makes a number of tents, a two-man expedition tent, for instance, costing $110. Various items of camping equipment are also for sale, cooking utensils, lanterns, trail food, etc. In addition, Holubar has a range of mountain-climbing equipment and shoes.

The Carikit line features sew-it-yourself kits, in which all the material is precut and ready to be sewed by the customer. Parkas, hoods, boots, mittens, sleeping bags, even a tent are all available in this form.

Kelty Pack, Inc., 1801 Victory Boulevard, Glendale, Calif. 91201
38-page annual catalogue, free.

Kelty is a leading manufacturer of packs and mountaineering equipment and the catalogue lists all its offerings in these fields. Their back pack is their most famous; the frames cost $25 and up, while the pack bag costs $21 and up. Various accessories are all listed as well as Kelty's own tents, day packs, sleeping bags, clothing and camping equipment, cooking utensils, stoves, and the like. Among the various special items is a special, light (12-oz.) cycle-hiker, suitable for bikes or short hikes.

The North Face, P.O. Box 2399, Station A, Berkeley, Calif. 94702
32-page color catalogue, free.

A reputable manufacturer of high-quality backpacking and mountaineering gear, the North Face publishes a very good descriptive catalogue of its own products and a few things made by other firms. Sleeping bags, tents, packs, clothes and some accessories are listed.

17

18

19

17 • *Kelty Pack* Cycle hiker, a new lightweight pack designed for bike trips or an all-day hike carrying light but bulky items. There are two compartments—the larger one is designed for books, sweaters and rain gear; the smaller one for a lunch box, camera and swimsuit. The bottom is 12½″ by 15½″, and the pack is 15½″ high. $9.95.

18 • *Kelty Pack* Tioga, extra large back pack with a suspension system that permits pack weight to be supported almost equally on front, back and sides of pelvis. A buckle which virtually eliminates waist-strap slipping, yet allows easy adjustment of waist-strap tension and retains the quick release of Kelty standard buckles. The upper compartment is completely open to allow packing of bulky odd-sized items, while the lower compartment with a flap-protected zipper gives quick access to items needed. Available as follows: 15¼″ wide and three lengths—medium length 18½″, volume 2,600 cu. in.; large length, 22″, volume 3,300 cu. in.; and extra large length, 24″, volume 3,500 cu. in., $65.

19 • *Smilie* Nesting camp pots of heavy-gauge aluminum with deep sides and flat bottoms. Each pot, including the cover and handle, will nest one within another from 1 quart to 14 quarts. They all fit into a standard kayak or pack box except the largest (14-quart) size. Prices run from $5.60 for the 1-quart size to $9.95 for the 14-quart.

The Smilie Company, 575 Howard Street, San Francisco, Calif. 94105
64-page catalogue, 10 cents.
16-page camp-food catalogue, 10 cents.

The Smilie Company has been in the camp- and trail-equipment business for over twenty years, and unlike its competitors, is strongest in the smaller items that are needed for any expedition. Here are cooking kits, nesting pots, camping frying pans and coffeepots, and all sorts of related material that can be used both away from home and also in your own backyard. I found their baked-enamel coffeepots, a 16-cup size for $3.50 and a 35-cup size for $3.95, very attractive in the way simple utilitarian objects are, and something that might fit into a kitchen as easily as a campsite. The same is true of their plastic coffee cups, at 29 cents each, and their very handsome 2½-gallon aluminum bucket, $2.95. Smilie also has a range of bottles and canteens, eating utensils, camp stoves, etc., as well as various compasses, first-aid items, lanterns, axes, camp beds and tools, etc. In addition to these, Smilie makes its own camp foods, listed in a separate catalogue.

Pack frames and back packs, sleeping bags, air mattresses, tarps and tents are also available, many of the tents being by Sierra Designs. Standard Wall Tents are made to order, the tents themselves (poles are extra) ranging from $50.45 for an 8′ by 10′ to $121.50 for a 14′ by 16′. Rucksacks, snowshoes and items of warm clothing, these again by Sierra Designs, are also listed, as is a good selection of books. The strongest item here is the area guidebooks for California and neighboring states.

For more camping equipment, see listings under Mountain Climbing, Skiing and Exploration in this section.

DOG SLEDDING

Nordkyn Outfitters, P.O. Box 24572, Seattle, Wash. 98124
Price list, free.

Nordkyn was started by Ray and Ruby Thompson, who were pioneers in the Alaskan North and lived by trapping for fur and meat. From their use of dog sleds came the knowledge that led to a number of books on "mushing," as the use of dog sleds for sport is called, and practice in using the equipment that Nordkyn sells. This includes sleds, harnesses, ganglines, dog packs for hiking, and related equipment for winter sports. Nordkyn is proud of its Montgomery sleds, which sell from $150 for the recreational model to $200 for transport sleds. Their leaflet shows exactly what you'll need for anywhere from one dog to five, and has a chart for ordering harnesses which shows you how to measure your dog. Various books are available, aimed particularly at the beginner.

FISHING

The Fly Fisherman's Bookcase, 138 Grand Street, Croton-on-Hudson, N.Y. 10520
Catalogue, free.

This catalogue combines a listing of books on fishing with a catalogue of tackle and other fishing equipment. The book section is extensive and offers substantial discounts of at least 10 percent and often more. The equipment section prides itself on the severe testing of the items listed, stating that each is "personally tested" and that "if any product, regardless of name or reputation, proved to be of inconsistent quality, we have dropped that item . . ." The Fly Fisherman offers Vince Cumings and Pezon et Michel rods, the latter imported from France. Hardy cane fly rods and reels are among the other brands featured, and there are a number of other famous names listed, many at considerable discounts; a Pflueger reel listing for $16.70, for instance, sells here for $11.50. Another speciality is fly-tying equipment and materials. A custom-made fly-tying bench is offered for $13.95, and various kits are also offered, as well as the various raw materials. Though this is a smaller catalogue than most, the items listed seem competitively priced and are obviously aimed at the serious fisherman.

The Netcraft Company, 3101 Sylvania Avenue, Toledo, Ohio 43613
170-page catalogue, free. Issued four times a year.

The Netcraft Company has been selling fishing equipment exclusively by mail for thirty years and sends out some 200,000 catalogues a year. Their listings include the most famous brands as well as harder-to-find items, and about a third of their space describes do-it-yourself projects. Netcraft feels its prices are "very competitive" and the company prides itself on its speedy processing of orders. The Netcraft catalogue starts, appropriately enough, with a number of net-making kits, and goes on to list such items as a cork kit, for lining tackle boxes, spinner-making kits, grommet kits, etc. Here is a very extensive selection for sportsmen who enjoy making or repairing their equipment. Pages of parts are listed, allowing you to make your own terminal tackle, assemble rods, etc.

Ready-made equipment is also available in every category, as is a small collection of boat motors and related accessories. But clearly, the most exciting items are the do-it-yourself components.

The Orvis Company, Inc., 50 River Road, Manchester, Vt. 05254
128-page color catalogue, free. January and September.

The Orvis catalogue ranks with Bean's and Bauer's as among the most famous in the field of outdoors equipment, and like these, has gone from its early speciality to cover other areas, such as clothing, which can be of general interest. But fishing is still very much at the heart of Orvis' activities, "Makers of fine Fishing Tackle since 1856." Orvis rods, manufactured in Vermont, are still their most famous product and the current catalogue lists some seventy-five models. Their Wes Jordans, made of impregnated bamboo, cost $235, and extras, including a leather case, can bring the price up to $292. Other bamboo rods start at $91. Glass rods, of course, are much less expensive and start as low as

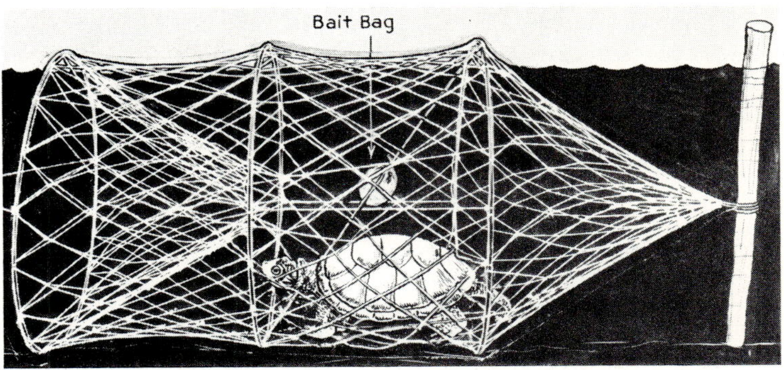

20

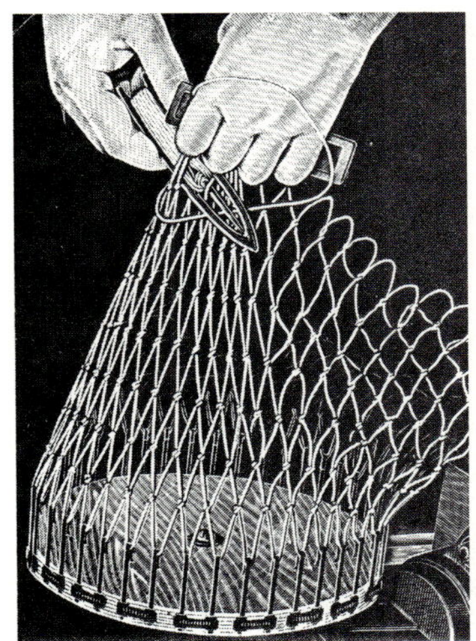

21

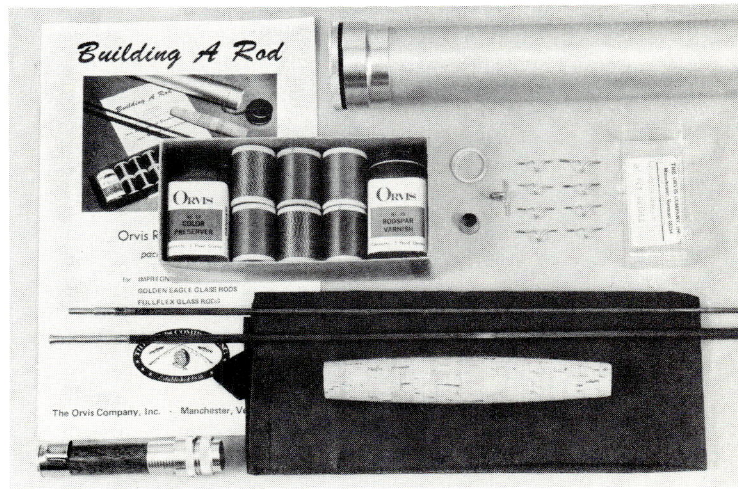

22

20 • *Netcraft* Netcraft's own version of the turtle trap; comes with complete instructions for setting and baiting. Under $10.

21 • *Netcraft* Net-making tools and instructions; the net-making wheel makes uniform meshes for landing nets, fish bags, turtle traps, etc. Instructions come with the wheel, which costs under $5, but beginners are advised to also buy the pamphlet *Popular Netcrafts* ($1) which gives instructions for making a lawn hammock, among other things.

22 • *Orvis* Battenkill impregnated bamboo fly-rod kits. First-grade bamboo blanks with ferrules mounted, formed cork grip, first-grade walnut reel seat, all hardware, supplies and instruction booklet (including diagramed guide spacings), with sack and Champion aluminum rod case. $87.50. *photo William Cheney Rupert Studios*

$31. However, you may wish to buy one of Orvis' rod-making kits, which will produce a bamboo rod for $65 or $87.50 and glass rods from $21.95.

The most stunning visual part of an Orvis catalogue is the pages of color plates devoted to flies, 209 in the current catalogue, available singly or in assortments, such as the trout selection, containing fifteen basic flies for $10. Fly-tying materials are also available.

Orvis also has a wide selection of clothing and related equipment such as waders, fishing vests, creels, and a vast array of special items such as fly threaders, clinch-knot tyers, and the like.

In addition to this, Orvis stocks out-frame tents, back-packer tents and back packs, light canoes, inflatable boats and other camping equipment. The canoe weighs under 25 lbs. and is 11′ long, made of cedar, and costs $295, plus shipping. The inflatable boat can hold two men, weighs 18 lbs. and costs $65. A wide variety of clothing is also available, including Orvis' famous duck-hunting camouflage outfits. The seventeen pages of sports clothes include goose-down vest and jackets, fishing trousers, hunting shirts and boots and Orvis' featherweight rainwear. Various gifts and accessories complete this very attractive and thorough catalogue.

MOUNTAIN CLIMBING, SKIING AND EXPLORATION

Akers Ski, Andover, Maine 04216
18-page catalogue, free. August.

Akers specializes in cross-country ski equipment, with some ski-jumping equipment, and the owner says that when he first opened eleven years ago, there was very little demand for touring equipment, whereas now it makes up 75 percent of his sales. Almost all the skis, boots, clothes and accessories have been imported from Scandinavia, and two books are on sale about Nordic touring.

Eastern Mountain Sports, Inc., 1041 Commonwealth Avenue, Boston, Mass. 02215
240-page color catalogue, $1.

The huge Eastern Mountain Sports catalogue is probably the most comprehensive in the fields of camping, skiing, mountain climbing and related sports, and it is certainly one of the basic catalogues that a serious purchaser should have on hand. "We believe that this book is one of the Bibles of our industry," EMS states, in asking for reader response, and their book is both thorough and useful (a comprehensive section on ecology, for instance, has a long discussion of legislation on the preservation of recreation areas, as well as a number of specific suggestions as to what hikers and others should do).

EMS is a major supplier of skiing equipment and its catalogue devotes twenty-four pages to skis, poles, wax and other accessories. Skis range in price from $36 for the least expensive light touring models to $80 for the most expensive racing skis, with children's skis available from $10.95 to $19.95. Many catalogue sections have a helpful table of details so that you can immediately see which brands will be listed, what their specifics and prices are. Thus you can see at a glance that packs range from $6 to $49.50, or that down-filled parkas are available from $32 in EMS's own make to $87 for an Alpine Designs expedition model. All sorts of clothing is available, from socks and long underwear to ponchos and parkas, all jauntily modeled by various bearded, mustachioed and otherwise very modern and natural-looking types, something I've only seen in California catalogues. Apparently, as far as the rest of the country is concerned, young people look as they did fifty years ago, and while bearded gentlemen may exist, they should not be photographed, certainly not in long woollies.

One of the strongest EMS fields is mountain climbing and they list extensive selections from Chouinard, SMC, Forrest, Interalp and other manufacturers. The result is a very full, comparative listing. Snowshoes, kayaks, "orienteering equipment," tents and sleeping bags all have similar sections, each listing various brands.

In addition to this, EMS has several services that I have not seen elsewhere. Much of the equipment can be rented: tents, sleeping bags, skis, stoves, climbing equipment are all available for periods ranging from one to three days to twelve to fifteen. Adult touring skis, for instance, can be rented for $4.25 for the minimum period, $9.45 for fifteen days and $1.30 for each additional five days thereafter; in this case, a deposit of $15 is required.

On the other hand, EMS also encourages group purchasing and offers substantial discounts to pooled orders. Certain items (excluding clothing) are eligible for a sliding discount, starting at 5 percent for purchases totaling $150 to 40 percent if you buy $9,600. Given the price of this much equipment, a small group ought soon to be able to get as much as 15 or 20 percent by buying $600 or $1,200 worth of equipment.

The Great Pacific Iron Works, P.O. Box 150, Ventura, Calif. 93001
72-page black-and-white catalogue, $1.

This firm began as Chouinard Equipment Company in 1965 and is now the manufacturer and distributor of high-quality mountaineering equipment for technical rock and ice climbing. Its catalogue is one of the handsomest I have seen, showing a sensitive appreciation of the environment and of the beauty of classical tools. The seriousness of their commitment is clear from the beginning of their catalogue, which discusses the deterioration of the climbing environment that has come about from the increased popularity of the sport. Concern is also expressed about "moral deterioration. Armed with ever more advanced gadgetry and techniques the art of technical climbing is becoming so degraded that elements vital to the climbing experience . . . are being submerged . . ." The equipment in the catalogue tries, therefore, to stress the climb itself: "The fewer gadgets between the climber and the climb, the greater is the chance to attain the desired communication with oneself . . . and nature. The equipment offered in this catalogue attempts to support this ethic." An impressive preamble to any catalogue.

The pages that follow are an illustrated treatise on climbing, showing the relevant Chouinard equipment: carabiners imported from Germany, hexentrics (metal chocks), stoppers, rope and webbing, as well as hammers, crampons, boots and a section on ironmongery that includes such exotic-sounding items as rups and bugaboos. There is also a section called Sortware fea-

23

24

25

26

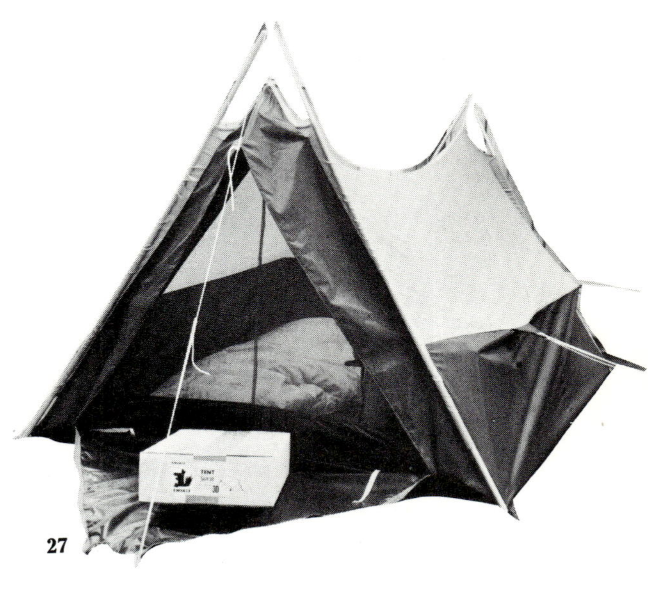

27

23 • *Recreational Equipment* *Left:* all-purpose parka of Cascade 60/40 cloth, moderately water-repellent and breatheable. Generously cut to fit over other clothes and lined with nylon in the upper body, sleeves and hood for added wind resistance and ease of dressing. It has two chest-high fleece-lined hand-warming pockets, two lower zippered patch pockets, and an inner drawstring at the waist. Colors: crimson, navy, sage-green. $22.95.
Center: superlight rain parka, exceptionally waterproof, of a new fabric of polymer resin with lightweight nylon taffeta and with no seams at the shoulders for the rain to penetrate. Colors: navy, lobster-red and spruce-green. $19.95. *Right:* wilderness parka made of Cascade 60/40 cloth, nylon-lined in the upper body and sleeves and hood with an integral hood. Four front bellows pockets with snap closures, and a map pocket inside the drawstring at the waist. Colors: crimson, navy and sand. $32.95.
photo Keith Gunnar

24 • *Frostline Kits* Kit to make Tundra jacket for men and women, for coldest conditions. The outside is of 1.9 oz. Ripstop nylon quilted to a taffeta interlining and stuffed with prime northern goose down. Large insulated pockets are covered with flaps and closed with concealed zippers. There are nylon knit cuffs and a drawstring at the waist. Weight, 2 lbs. 2 oz. Colors: navy-blue, medium-blue, forest-green and orange. Price according to size, $26 to $28.50.

25 • *Frostline Kits* Kit to make this down sweater for men and women. The lightest of the jackets is made of 1.9 oz. Ripstop nylon insulated with prime northern goose down. The pockets are down-filled but without flaps, the high down-filled collar has snaps for an optional hood. Colors: navy-blue, medium-blue, forest-green, red and orange. Price according to size, $15.95 to $17.50.

26 • *Eastern Mountain Sports* Dhaulagiri sleeping bag with 11″ total loft, 6½″ above the body, which means that most people should be comfortable in a tent to 50 degrees below. EMS says that it's the warmest regularly produced sleeping bag, as far as they know. Regular size fits people up to 5′11″, weighs 5 lbs. 3 oz. and costs $120. The large fits people up to 6′7″, weighs 5 lbs. 11 oz. and costs $130.

27 • *Eastern Mountain Sports* A sew-it-yourself kit to make Le Manoir tent, complete with patterns and all necessary supplies. A high-altitude tent which, because of its very light weight (6 lbs. 14 oz.) and two-man size, can be used for summer back-packing. The tent is 7′ 5″ long with pull-outs, giving 18″ high vertical side wall space. Triangular entrance with nylon-coil zipper closure at the front and a large zippered window at the rear. Mosquito netting on all openings. $69.95.

28

29

30

28 • *Recreational Equipment* *Left:* Optimus 11-lb. larger stove, uses white gas, pump provides faster starting. In a metal box which folds to 7″ by 7″ by 4½″. $24.95. *Center:* Optimus 8R, newer-design stove which is completely integrated in a metal box. Easy-to-fill tank pops out front when open, and the stove has a self-cleaning device built in. Folded size is 5″ by 5″ by 3″. $12.95. *Right:* Optimus 80, compact white gas stove in a box that opens to form a support for a small pot. Box size 3¾″ by 5½″, the stove is 5″ high. No pumping is required for starting or maintaining the stove. $10.95. *In the front* is Svea 123, a compact Swedish stove which burns white gasoline with no pumping required. Stove is 5″ high with built-in windscreen, wire pot supports and a small pot which inverts to form a cover. A pot lifter is included. $12.50.

29 • *Recreational Equipment* Sigg Tourist Cooker, a lightweight aluminum nesting cook set for use with Svea 123 stove. It includes a 2½-pint pan, a 3½-pint pan, a lid that will serve as a pan, stove base and wind protection. Set nests to 4¾″ height, 8¼″ in diameter. $18.50 with stove; $9.75 without stove.

30 • *Recreational Equipment* Nesting billies, a set of lightweight aluminum pails, 1, 2 and 3 quarts with lids that serve as plates or frying pans. Wire handles. Svea stove fits inside 1-quart pail. $7.50.
photos Keith Gunnar

turing harnesses, slings and various items of clothings, such as cord knickers, mitts, packs, hats and glacier glasses. Mountaineering periodicals and films on a rental basis are also available. This lovely and impressive catalogue has a Japanese print as its cover and its style brings to mind books such as *Zen and the Art of Archery*, works which show that expertise in the minutiae of a sport can lead to far more than hitting a target or getting to the top of a mountain.

Recreational Equipment, Inc., P.O. Box 22088, Seattle, Wash. 98122
34-page color catalogue, March and September, free.

REI is a consumer co-op, started in 1938 by a group of Seattle climbers and hikers who wanted to import climbing gear from Europe at lower prices. Reorganized as a Rochedale type of co-op in 1958, the group now has 320,000 members and seems to operate much like a university co-op, paying back a dividend based on purchases. Much of REI's material is manufactured locally to its specifications and under its control, with prices that REI feels are very low for the quality involved. Joining REI costs only $1, by the way, and also entitles you to join their tours and charter flights, most of which leave from Seattle, though a number go from New York.

REI sells a wide variety of brightly colored and attractive parkas starting at $28. Shirts, pants, skiwear and other items of clothing are all available, as well as a separate line of goose-down clothing.

Skis and ski equipment are another major offering, some made by REI, others from a variety of manufacturers here and abroad. The cheapest REI beginner's skis are $24.94, though even cheaper models are available in the Norwegian Tronderski brand, whose cheapest touring skis are $20. Far more expensive models are also available—Rossignol skis, for instance, going up to $200, and Kneissl up to $180. Ski sets, including poles, tie straps, etc., are also available, as are various waxes and accessories.

REI also has a wide variety of back-packing, climbing and camping equipment, and their summer catalogue has a very full choice, some of it manufactured for REI, some by others, and some imported exclusively by REI, such as a very handsome line of rucksacks, the French Sacs Millet. In addition to tents and air mattresses and related camping equipment, REI also sells Grumman aluminum canoes and Chestnut canoes, either in wood and canvas or in fiberglass, these last being the cheapest at $244 for a 16′ boat, but none higher than $344 (for a Chestnut canoe of roughly the same size).

Sierra Designs, 4th and Addison Streets, Berkeley, Calif. 94710
32-page annual color catalogue, free.

People who use Sierra Designs camping equipment recommend it highly. Parkas and sleeping bags are among their most famous products, and their 60/40 Parka is so handsome that I was tempted to get it for everyday wear. The 60/40 refers to the blend of cotton and nylon from which it is made, and is apparently very water-repelling. The 60/40 Parka costs $42 and comes in various good colors, as do all of Sierra Designs products (where else can you get purple sleeping bags?). Their most popular sleeping bags, mummy bags, are lined with goose down, seem extremely well built and come in three models, the lightest costing $85 for a regular size and their most popular model, the "200," costing $100. The Sierra catalogue is filled with excellent detailed information on the construction of these bags, and in this respect too, theirs is a model catalogue.

In addition to other models of the above, Sierra also sells ponchos, cagoules (a variant of the poncho), wool shirts, hats, mitts, jackets and other items of clothing. They stock a selection of mountain-climbing equipment, some of it Chouinard, cooking equipment, bike packs and a full line of white-water boats and accessories, which are listed in a separate brochure. They also sell tents for two or three people, selling from $112 to $155. If you wish to try to make sleeping bags or tents yourself, you can buy materials from Sierra Designs, which will sell you fabrics, down, zippers, etc.

The Ski Hut, 1615 University Avenue, Berkeley, Calif. 94703
62-page color catalogue, free. Issued every spring.

The Ski Hut is an importer of quality, mountaineering, back-packing, skiing and hiking equipment, and its handsome and extensive catalogue lists products from a wide variety of sources as well as their own "Trailwise" label. The Trailwise expedition parka, consisting of two separate down-filled jackets, costs $88. Their trail parka costs $32, and their down vest $23. Some attractive items of clothing, suitable for everyday wear as well, include Clarke's crag hoppers (English wool knickerbockers), for climbing or looking like a 1930's gentleman, $30. Irish fishermen's sweaters cost $47, a Bolivian alpaca poncho, $35, etc. The imported items are handsome and sophisticated, and are for the most part all-purpose. More seriously athletic is a line of mountaineering boots, and related footware. The Ski Hut also has a full selection of cookware, various camping foods, packs, compasses, books and related items, including a very comfortable-looking kiddie pack for $16.

In addition to these relatively civilian goods, the Ski Hut has a good selection of sleeping bags, climbing equipment, skis, snowshoes and knives. Some of these are made by Trailwise, others are generally available.

31

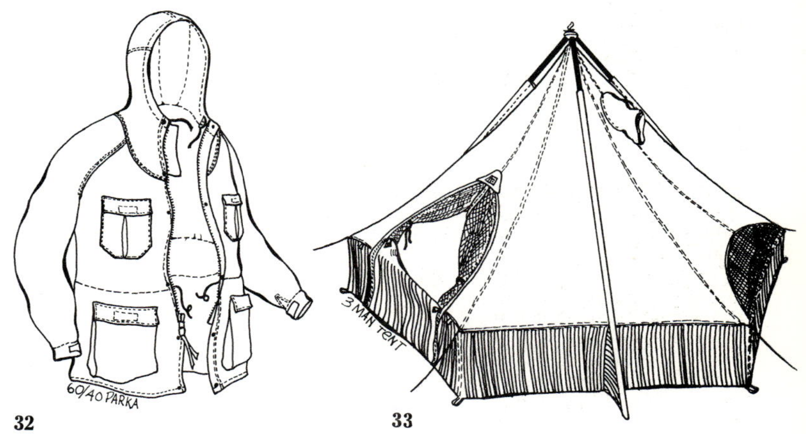

32 33

PARACHUTING

Parachutes, Inc., Orange, Mass. 01364
128-page annual black-and-white catalogue, free.

Parachutes, Inc., distributes the sport parachuting equipment made by the Pioneer Parachute Co. of Manchester, Connecticut, selling to wholesalers and to individuals by mail. In addition, Parachutes, Inc., will arrange for lessons, charging $55 for a complete first jump course, but only $11.50 for each subsequent jump. Their catalogue lists all the equipment needed, which goes well beyond the obvious, for you also need boots, helmets, etc. You can buy a complete kit for anywhere from $455.90 to $1,027.60, or you can buy the items separately, the cheapest chute costing $225. Besides the essentials, this very thorough catalogue lists all the other extras needed, as well as a number of books on parachuting, special photographic equipment and a full complement of maintenance tools and supplies.

31 • *Parachutes* Para-Commander Canopy, the choice of the U.S. team, the U.S. Army team and PI instructors since 1964. Recommended for parachutists who have at least fifteen jumps with steerable canopies. $357.

32 • *Sierra Designs* 60/40 mountain parka is fully lined and has four front pockets closing with Velcro, which can be operated easily with mittens. The entire back of the parka from waist to neck is a pocket for carrying a sweater or other large items. The hood draw cord and leather sliders are on the inside facing, so the loose ends will not whip the face in a high wind. Colors: navy, green, orange. $42.

33 • *Sierra Designs* A lightweight tent particularly good for back-packing families; it is called the three-man tent but can accommodate four with some crowding. A six-sided tent with tripod pole arrangement, a large door closed with zippers and a mosquito door, also zipper-closed. Two vents in the peak, plus two zippered windows for ventilation. In the center of the tent floor there is a 38″ zippered cook hole. Net pockets set at the top of the lower side wall to hold small things. Peak height, 58″; packed size, 8″ by 22″. $159.50.

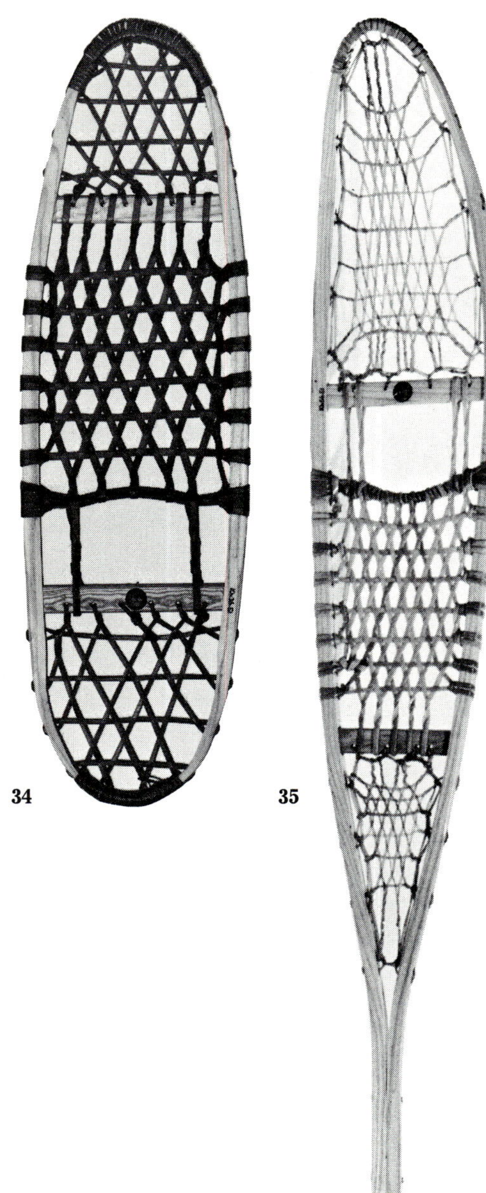

34 • *Vermont Tubbs* Green Mountain Bear Paw, a versatile snowshoe that is good for beginners. Designed especially for New England winter conditions and best in wood and brush. Supports weight of up to 225 lbs.; measures 13″ by 33″. $40. *photo Sanders M. Millens*

35 • *Vermont Tubbs* Alaska Trapper, a long narrow snowshoe with a 10″ tip up on the toe, excellent for deep light-powder conditions. In spite of its length, it is easy to walk on and often used for racing. 10″ by 56″. $43.50.

RIDING

H. Kauffman and Sons Saddlery Co., 139-141 E. 24th Street, New York, N.Y. 10010
72-page black-and-white catalogue 50 cents. Issued twice a year.

"Fine English saddlery and riding boots" says the letterhead of this family firm established in 1875, in what was once a horse-auction gallery in the heart of the horse market, an area I didn't even know New York ever possessed. Kauffman sells everything related to horseback riding, down to veterinary supplies, but while they sell Western bits, saddles and clothes, the bulk of their offerings is for the classic English style. "Hunt appointments," reads one page, including hunting horns and silk hunt lashes, and of course flasks and a sandwich case made of the finest leather. All the clothes that one can imagine going with these accessories are also offered: tweed riding jackets, jodhpurs, riding hats (including silk top hats for the more formal hunts). Needless to add, saddles, spurs, girths, bridles, etc., are all listed, many of these last being imported from England.

In addition to this, Kauffman has special racing equipment, including jockey's outfits, polo requisites, all the items needed for grooming, and even blacksmith supplies. There are also several pages of books related to all aspects of horsemanship, and various gifts for children and adults with riding motifs. The catalogue index states that Kauffman carries a large number of items not listed, but after looking up "Underwear, riding" and "Vacuum cleaner, horse," I can't imagine what else there might be to order.

Miller Harness Co., Inc., 131 Varick Street, New York, N.Y. 10013
96-page catalogue, $1; refundable against first purchase. Issued every spring.

Like Kauffman, Miller is a major supplier of riding equipment, with a similar range, such as formal riding clothes, Marlborough riding boots and shoes from England, accessories, etc., but Miller has a larger selection of saddles, listing a number from America and Europe. Prices, however, seem roughly the same. Miller also has a more extensive choice of such relatively technical items as protective equipment, treatment books, schooling and breaking equipment, and the like. As with Kauffman, there is a selection of Western saddlery and appropriate clothing, along with grooming and stable equipment and the materials needed by those who own horses as well as ride them. Both stores have very similar offerings, though on the whole, Miller seems to have more for the horse and Kauffman more for the rider. If you're undecided as to who should have priority in your household, its probably best to have both catalogues.

SNOWSHOES

Beck Outdoor Projects, P.O. Box 3061, South Berkeley, Calif. 94703
4-page catalogue, free.

Beck's is a mixture of Old World craftsmanship and modern America, for their specialty are snowshoe bindings and crampon straps made of neoprene nylon. Started a few years ago with $100, the firm prides itself on the fact that all of its equipment is handmade and that their models were developed by them. Beck will also do custom work. Their snowshoe bindings cost $7.00 a pair for standard sizes, up to 11, and $11 for a special model. Their crampon straps are four for $5.25, $6 for the professional model.

Vermont Tubbs, Inc., 18 Elm Street, Wallingford, Vt. 05773
Brochures, free.

Vermont Tubbs has been making snowshoes for over a hundred years but reports that in the last few years its business boomed and its work force has increased tenfold. Tubbs snowshoes are made of New England white ash and are available either in rawhide or in neoprene, which "while not as aesthetically appealing . . . resists snow building and, as a result, is comparatively lighter." The shoes come in several models, ranging from $36 to $44, and children's versions are also available. Tubbs also sells bindings and other accessories, including a book on snowshoeing.

TENNIS

Stephen J. Ferron, Inc., 55 E. 44th Street, New York, N.Y. 10017
20-page catalogue, free.

Ferron's is the country's oldest store specializing in tennis and related sports, and sells all the clothing and equipment required for these games. Their most famous item is the Ferron power bat, a racquet made to their own specifications and strung to your own preference (the store makes a point of selling no pre-strung racquets). The frame costs $26 for the regular model, $18 for the lighter, with stringing costing $10 to $20 depending on whether you choose nylon or the more expensive lamb gut. Ferron's also stocks the major brands of tennis and squash racquets, though here again, their own power bat is available. Badminton and table-tennis racquets and sets are also available. In addition to the actual equipment, Ferron's has a large stock of classic tennis clothing, the sweaters, dresses, shoes, and so on, all in immaculate white, many made specially for the store. Hats, neckties and similar extras are also offered.

TENTS

Eureka Tent and Awning Co., 625 Conklin Road, Binghampton, N.Y. 13902
32-page catalogue, free.

Eureka is a leading tent manufacturer, selling its products both under its own names and under the private labels of some of the country's major suppliers of camping equipment. The catalogue, as can be imagined, lists every kind of tent imaginable, from vast Adirondack Cabin Campers, which can be as large as 10′ by 8′ or 12′ by 9′, to small bivouac tents intended for youngsters. Eureka has a number of other family-sized tents, mountain tents, wall tents and various explorer tents. They also sell tepees, which follow exactly the originals of the Plains Indians. Eureka also sells tent accessories, chairs and cots, sleeping bags and cooking utensils and accessories.

Nomadics, Star Route, Box 41, Cloverdale, Oreg. 97112
Leaflet, 25 cents.

The man who started this firm, which makes tipis and tipi kits, writes: "Lived in a tipi for six months in conditions that ranged from 102 to 12 degrees and two inches of snow (for months). Tipi proved to be a brilliant shelter—plenty comfortable. We experienced its time-tested worth, but modern manufacturing had not done it justice. We decided to make one ourselves with much finer materials and workmanship.

"Since our first tipi, made in January, 1971, we have made over 800. Our operation remains 'home industry' scale. Tipis are cut in the loft of our barn. Our horses (seventeen) are below. The sewing of the tipis is done by wives of the local farming families. They sew in their own homes.

"We are evolving into a self-supporting private high school in which making tipis is part of the curriculum. Gardening, horsemanship and ranch maintenance are other integral parts of a student's life."

The good handwritten leaflet gives detailed descriptions of the tipi (which is based on the Sioux design with the Blackfoot and Cheyenne improvements) and of the methods of manufacture and materials used. Prices for kits of pre-cut materials, ready to be sewn on home sewing machines, start at $121 for a 16′ cover, and $180 for a 22′ cover in marine-treated Terrasol. Ready-made covers cost $172 for a 16′ and $247 for a 22′. Duck canvas and Acrilan kits are also for sale at higher prices.

See also listings under Camping and Hiking in this section.

23
TOYS & GAMES

1

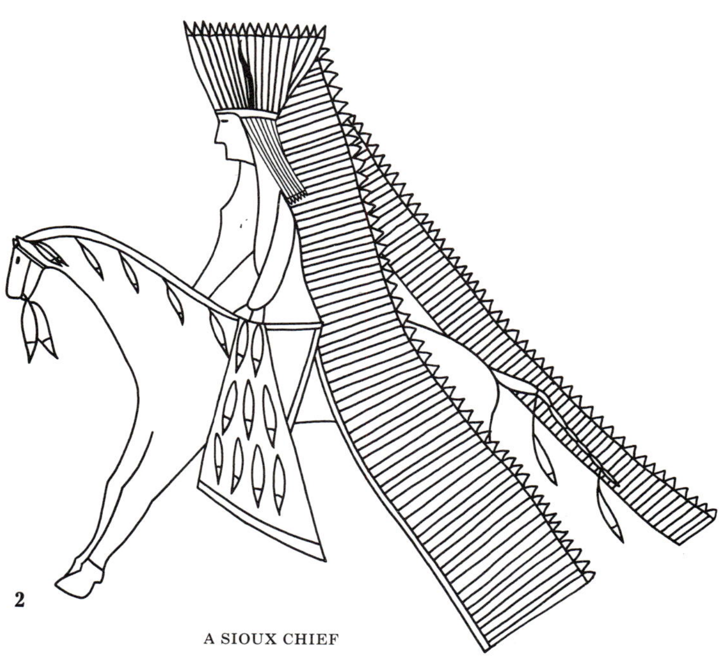

2

A SIOUX CHIEF

1 • *Child Life Play Specialists* Swing with a rubber seat that holds the swinging child securely and will not hurt any child who gets in the way. Ropes are adjustable and come with hooks and hitching rings. Swing can be used inside or out. $7.50.

2 • *Bellerophone Books* An adaptation of American Indian art for coloring from *A Coloring Book of American Indians.* $1.50.

Bellerophon Books, 153 Stuart Street, San Francisco, Calif. 94105

20-page brochure, free.

Fifteen complicated coloring books, "all from superbly amusing historical sources," cover subjects like the Renaissance, Chaucer, the Old and New Testaments and a medieval alphabet. The designs are small and intricate but look smashing after some judicious work with felt-tip pens, and are demanding enough for adults; in fact, a friend of mine has colored more pages of *The Greeks* than her ten-year-old daughter. There are also educational paper dolls—Queen Elizabeth I, and Henry VIII and his wives; and *Old Christmas,* by Washington Irving, with illustrations by Walter Crane and Ralph Caldecott, "superb as a gift for those who should have more than a Christmas card, but less than a Cadillac."

Brentano's, 586 Fifth Avenue, New York, N.Y. 10036

48-page color catalogue, free.

For years known as one of the country's leading bookstores, Brentano's has in recent years begun to sell all sorts of things, and their catalogue contains a great many gifts for grownups. If you are interested in cribbage or the latest variant of Scrabble or a game using tarot cards, this is a good place to look. Here are all sorts of puzzles, word games, three-dimensional tick-tack-toes, and various chess and checker sets including a three-dimensional chess set which should keep anyone busy for days. Brentano's version of games is relatively traditional, specializing in such old-time favorites as backgammon, jigsaw puzzles, and the like. There are also a number of needlework kits, terrarium and other more hobbyish offerings. The rest of the catalogue lists current books, prints and records, of the sort that major stores feature in their ads around Christmas time.

Childcraft Education Corp., 52 Hook Road, Bayonne, N.J. 07002

48-page catalogue, some color, free.

Although not quite as impeccably tasteful as Creative Playthings (below), Childcraft makes the same kind of modern "educational" toys in clear colors and clean-cut designs, and their prices are sometimes a couple of dollars lower than Creative Playthings'. The catalogue is divided into several sections: "First Toys" for babies up to about the age of two, with finger exercisers, crib toys, crib mobiles and an animal quilt for a baby to lie on the floor on—it has textures to feel and floppy pieces to pull and chew; "Put Together Toys" with colorful puzzles of various kinds and big beads to thread; "Block Play" with several kinds of blocks and construction sets, as well as trains, road signs and animals to use with block constructions; "Let's Pretend" has puppet theaters and disguise kits; "Housekeeping" has child-size wooden kitchen appliances, pots, pans, house-cleaning set, doll's beds; "Active Play" has various jumping and rocking inventions, as well as throwing games such as wall quoits and mini-basketball. Finally there are large "Learning Through Fun" and "Science" sections, which have counting-number and word games, and science and nature study supplies, various terrariums and greenhouses, a luminous star finder, a crystal-growing kit and a kit to make a weather station, and other absorbing equipment. There are plenty of toys in this catalogue I haven't seen before, and most of them look interesting.

Child Life Play Specialties, Inc., 55 Whitney Street, Holliston, Mass. 01746
24-page catalogue, free.

Child Life designs and manufactures a very well made collection of wooden play equipment which should keep any child amused and healthily exercised. It is mainly for outside, although one or two things such as a slide and a doorway gym are for indoor use. There are several swings for children of all ages, including babies and toddlers; the cheapest is the monkey swing for $5, which is a single rope with a wooden seat and includes a hook and hitching ring "for tree or basement rafter." One swing, "Leapin' Lena," for inside or out, has rubber straps instead of ropes, so you can bounce around on it. Slides, seesaws, rocking boats, punching bags and sandpits are available, and all sorts of climbers and jungle gyms at prices from $24 and up. Also several playhouses and a tree house, and a space trolley for $35; it's one of those contraptions like a ski lift—you sling it between two trees and skim along on a rolling seat. You can save about 20 percent of the price on many pieces by buying them in kit form and assembling them yourself. An amiable letter in the catalogue from a Harvard Ph.D. says that although the writer is a certified mechanical idiot capable of turning the most elementary household task into a costly disaster, to his utter amazement he found the task of assembly rather pleasant and the end product absolutely splendid.

Constructive Playthings, 1040 E. 85th Street, Kansas City, Mo. 64131
170-page catalogue, some color, $1.

This big catalogue illustrates toys, games and supplies mainly for schools, but it will be extremely useful for parents because it is just about all-inclusive, and anyone who wants to simplify life can get almost everything for children of all ages here. All the things usually stocked by toy shops are here in quantity: dolls (including a boy doll with a penis), doll carriages, trains, farm sets, animals, puzzles, board games, books and records, larger equipment such as furniture, seesaws, dollhouses, playhouses and puppet stages—also supplies for various activities: scissors, papers, pastes, crayons, paints, several different kinds of clay and modeling materials, musical instruments, science equipment, animal cages and an aquarium or two.

There is also lots of equipment for parents who want to help children with schoolwork—from the earliest games that teach recognition of numbers and letters and time through "Action-Fraction" games to sets of charts and cards of simple science experiments. An invaluable catalogue.

Creative Playthings, Princeton, N.J. 08540
96-page color catalogue, 25 cents.

Creative Playthings, *the* "educational" toy manufacturer, publishes a catalogue which they now, somewhat pretentiously, call a "Guide to Good Toys." In fact, it's pretty much like the old catalogue, but with a short essay consisting of observations about children and toys that are stale news to any alert parent. I'm also not convinced that Creative Playthings toys are any better for children than other toys now generally available. They *are*, however, *much* more pleasing to the discriminating parental eye. A shelf full of "creative playthings" is a glorious sight to behold, and any parent who enjoys toys and likes strong basic shapes,

3

4

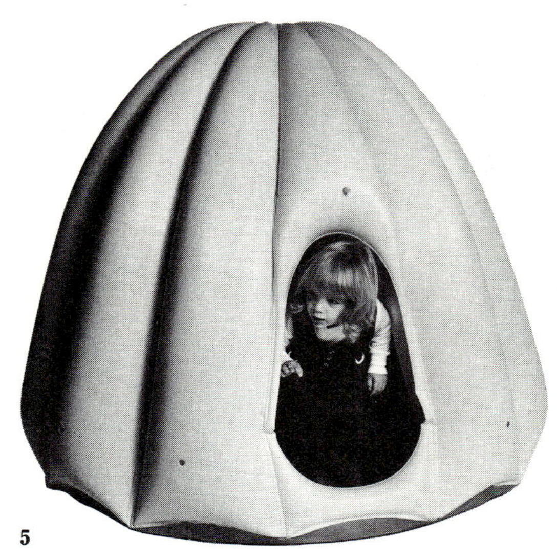

5

3 • *Creative Playthings* "Anyway Racer." Driver's face gives the direction. 9½″ long. $4.50.

4 • *Creative Playthings* "Star Blocks." Twenty see-through plastic shapes for building and mixing colors in red, blue, amber and clear. 2″ long. $4.95.

5 • *Creative Playthings* Inflatable igloo, 50″ high. $39.95.

6

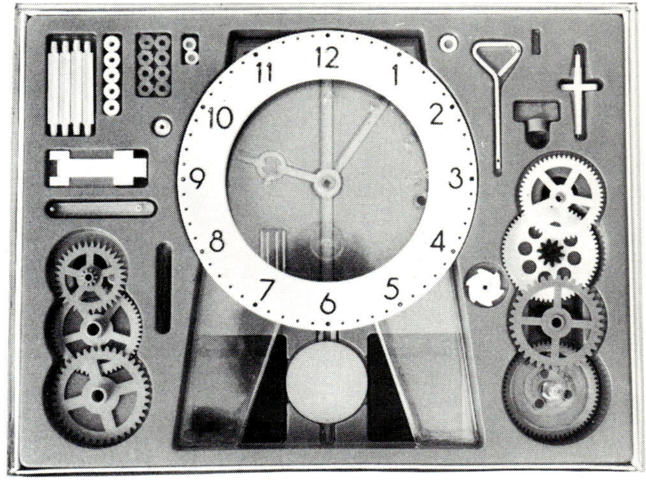

7

8

9

10

6 • *Dollsanddreams* Handmade puppets by Etienne Delessert, $10 each. Picture books by Etienne Delessert: the top one is $4.95, the bottom one $5.95. Baby in a basket, $2.25; gingham dolls (mother and father), $3.25; set of three vehicles, $2.95.

7 • *Dollsanddreams* Plastic kit to build a clock that works $10.

8 • *Dollsanddreams* *Left:* coloring books, 50 cents each. *Right:* cardboard dollhouse to be colored and constructed, $3.50. Watercolor paints with brush, $2.50.

9 • *Dollsanddreams* *Top and left:* colorful plastic bath toys, $2.50 each. *Right:* leather-and-wood teething rattle and ring, $2.95.

10 • *The Enchanted Doll House* Exclusive handmade Goose Hollow Enchanted doll dressed in pink gingham dress, bonnet and parasol with white apron and black high-button shoes. Yellow, black or red hair. 18″ high. $20.

gleaming natural wood and primary colors should certainly send for the catalogue, which is temptingly designed.

Besides their own simple and beautiful versions of most basic, nonmechanical toys for children up to the age of about ten, they have lots of toys and equipment for babies (this is an unbeatable place to find presents for newly borns) and all sorts of their own inventions: unbreakable, bendable mirrors for toddlers, colorful tubes, cylinders and lids to play in the bath with, a carrying box with four compartments, each fastened with a different kind of lock, and handsomely printed puzzles and board games.

The firm now has dealers all over the country; the catalogue gives their names and a toll-free number to call to find out which your nearest shop is. It also suggests that if you don't live near a shop, or the shop you live near doesn't have what you want, you should buy by mail from Princeton.

Dollsanddreams, 454 Third Avenue, New York, N.Y. 10016
Leaflet, free. Christmas season only.
A neat little leaflet shows a very fetching collection of toys for young children. The one I looked at had beautifully simple teething toys and rattles, furry animals, handmade puppets, a build-a-clock set, kits to make cardboard dollhouses and an English village, Sasha and Gregor dolls, crayons and paints, marvelously colored plastine modeling clay, and stocking stuffers—almost everything except the Sasha and Gregor dolls costs less than $10. This looks like a good place to polish off a gift list quickly and painlessly.

Edcom Systems, 145 Witherspoon Street, Princeton, N.J. 08540
22-page color catalogue, free. Booklet "EY," free.
Edcom is run by many of the people who started Creative Playthings. They put out a lovely catalogue of Christmas decorations and small toys (listed in the Christmas section, above) which gives details of various educational toys they sell for babies up to the age of one year, and manuals for their parents on how to help babies "achieve their full potential." The idea of starting to worry about full potentials so soon is off-putting, but the toys look harmless enough—wooden chime mobiles, bath boats and harbor, a turning hourglass module, and a squeeze bulb that sends colored liquid along a plastic pipe. The booklet "EY" describes two cribs with built-in learning modules, one at about $150 and the other at about $300.

The Enchanted Doll House, Manchester Center, Vt. 05255
38-page catalogue, 50 cents. Fall.
The Enchanted Doll House is an 1812 Colonial house full of imported, handmade or out-of-the-ordinary toys, books and games. The specialty is, of course, superior dolls and dollhouses. The dolls range from original rag dolls at $6.50 through realistic baby Victoria "just home from the hospital" to distinguished Madame Alexander Renoir and Degas girls at $15 each, and a Gainsborough girl in lace over taffeta with a tulle-trimmed straw hat, which, in spite of costing $55, sold out last year. There are four classic dollhouses to choose from, two little hand-painted Vermont carrying houses sold here only, and an unpainted pre-cut kit to make a small dollhouse for $20. Dollhouse people and furniture in several styles are also available.

Federal Smallwares Corp., 85 Fifth Avenue, New York, N.Y. 10003
52-page color catalogue, 25 cents.
A fascinating catalogue of small imports, most of them for under $3. This is a really good place to find unusual party favors and presents. Magic Rainbow pencils write in four colors at once; Kate Greenaway matchboxes open to reveal tiny animals; coloring books have old-fashioned postcards to be mailed after they are colored; crayon soap can be used to write on bath and tiles and then washed away; and a handsome peasant family can be made from a construction-block set. Besides the old and the odd (like the porcelain foot creamer—it pours through the toe), there are furry toys from Germany and brightly colored educational toys, reproduction china dolls, books and jigsaw puzzles. And, at slightly higher prices, the specialty: handmade dollhouse furniture in antique styles: a little pedestal desk has cubbyholes, a drawer and a quill pen; a brass bed has a striped mattress; a fireplace has bellows, brass-colored andirons, and a gold-metal clock with glass dome.

Virginia Frosteg, Box 367, Pelham, Ga. 31779
Leaflet, 25 cents.
Virginia Frosteg makes an exceptionally nice three-way doll, which she sells for about $12.50. At one end is Little Red Riding Hood in a red mobcap, and if you turn her upside down you find either grandmother or the wolf, depending on whose face you cover with the blue gingham mobcap. My daughters have a Red Riding Hood three-way doll that they are very fond of, but when we compared the two we all preferred Virginia Frosteg's version, even though it doesn't have the tiny buttons and lace that the girls like, for the faces on her version are especially agreeable.

The Fun House, P.O. Box 1225, Newark, N.J. 07101
64-page brochure, free.
The Fun catalogue features magic tricks, novelties and souvenirs, which should be just the things for children's parties. There is nothing dazzlingly new, just the old deluxe squirt camera, rubber hot dog and relighting birthday candles, and the Talking Toilet, "Wildest Party Idea of the Year. When a guest sits on your 'John' seat a laughing voice says 'Hey! I'm working down here.'" Also patches, mini-posters, crazy labels, etc.

The Game Room, P.O. Box 1816, Washington, D.C. 20013
80-page catalogue, free.
This catalogue, which lists about four hundred humorous gifts, is intended for adults who are young at heart but will fascinate older children, and if you are not too squeamish, will be a good place to get them presents. My ten-year-old daughter spent several days poring over the catalogue, ordered herself a bedside mat that looks like a hundred-dollar bill and asked me to get her several more things for her birthday. Here is what she says: "This catalogue is a laugh every two minutes. They list over three hundred items. Among them they have W. C. Fields banners—'Who took the cork out of my lunch?' And you send them a picture of friend or foe or your dog or anybody, and for about $5 you can

11

12

13

14

11 • *The Enchanted Doll House* Big-sister and little-sister dolls, wearing blue cotton dresses with organdy collar and lace-edged bloomers. Big sister, 20″ tall, $16; little sister, 14″ tall, $13.

12 • *The Enchanted Doll House* Exclusive handmade Goose Hollow Family dolls. *Left:* papa and girl on sofa, mama and boy behind. *Right:* grandma and grandpa on sofa, and daughter behind. $20 each.

13 • *The Enchanted Doll House* Colonial dollhouse with wallpaper, removable curtains and storage space. The outside is painted in high-gloss white enamel with blue shades. 34″ long, 26″ high, 18″ deep. Shipped knocked down with all holes pre-drilled and ready to assemble. $65.

14 • *The Enchanted Doll House* Steam engines with all-brass steam sections, fitted with safety valves and safe-burning fuel lamps. Finished in black, red, green and polished brass. *Top:* steam tractor with self-aligning front wheels and reversing-speed regulator; exhaust steam comes from the chimney. $35. Lumbar wagon $9. *Lower left:* small steam engine, $13. *Lower right:* superheated twin-cylinder steam engine has a 6.5cm flywheel stop cock, whistle, water-level plug and safety valve, also fuel lamp and filler funnel. $33.

get an 8″ by 10″ jigsaw with the photograph printed on it. Or you can get a headline or a coffee mug with your name printed on it. Or maybe you'd prefer a set of Mother posters; for instance, they have a 'Don't squeeze the toothpaste from the middle of the tube' one."

Go Fly A Kite Store, 1613 Second Avenue, New York, N.Y. 10028
Leaflet, 25 cents.

This small shop has the biggest collection of kites in the world and puts out a super leaflet with pictures of about thirty of them—eagles, centipedes, dragonflies, bats, fish, hawks and dragons—colorful, shiny and very decorative when out of action, in fact, if lazy you could just hang some of them on the wall and look at them. Many of the paper and plastic kites cost under $5, and most of the cloth kites cost under $20, but prices can go up as far as $105 for a king-size silvery dragon. Several books on how to build and fly kites are for sale.

Learning Games, Inc., 34 South Broadway, White Plains, N.Y. 10601
Leaflets, free.

This firm sells three products, one of which is a beginner's chess set which, they say, is the only beginner's set officially endorsed by the United States Chess Federation. Each piece is a flat square with the name of the piece and the moves it can make written on it. Another thing they sell is a Cuisinaire home mathematics kit for adults to help children with math. The kit contains the rods which symbolize different numbers according to length and which are widely used in schools now; *Modern Mathematics Made Meaningful* is a guidebook for parents and teachers to both traditional and new math; and a series of activity cards for the parent to use with the rods alone first or with a child of kindergarten to ninth-grade age. The chess set and the home-mathematics kit cost $15 each. Learning Games is planning to put out a Geoboard Kit intended to introduce children to the basic concepts of geometry.

The Little Doll House, Stockbridge, Mass. 01262
Leaflet, free.

Six cloth dolls are handmade copies of old dolls or Kate Greenaway illustrations; each one is 12″ tall and costs $12.50. The Little Doll House says: "Only the finest quality fabrics, ribbons and laces dress the dolls, and are easily removed with the tiniest snap fasteners . . . every doll is fully guaranteed for perfect craftsmanship." Lady Goodey is dressed in an 1850 ante-bellum velveteen or taffeta dress, bonnet and purse, with petticoat and lace-trimmed pantalets, while Little Girl Goodey is in an organdy or cotton printed dress and bonnet, and Little Horatio (a Kate Greenaway doll) wears a corduroy or velveteen suit over a ruffled shirt, and comes with a hoop and stick. The Little Doll House restores antique dolls and will dress them in correct period costumes.

The Mallet and Peg Shop, Washington Road, P.O. Box 90, Woodbury, Conn. 06798
24-page catalogue, 35 cents. September.

About thirty-six plain wooden toys are made by the Mallet and Peg Shop. Little 9″ cars cost $2.50, while air-

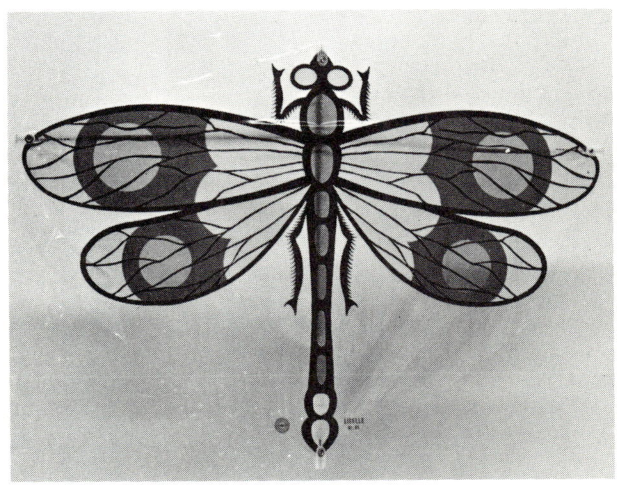

15 • *Go Fly A Kite* Kites at 60 cents, $3 and up.

planes, fire trucks, dump trucks, bulldozers, steam rollers, steam shovels, paddle boats and tug boats and a doll's bed are all under $10. A cradle, a kiddie car, an ironing board, a wheel barrow and a 4′8″ train are for sale at higher prices.

Mary Meyer Mfg. Co., Inc., Mary Meyer Station, Townshend, Vt. 05353
Color leaflet, 10 cents.

Mary Meyer moved to Vermont in 1944 because the pace was slower than in the city. Today the pace is about the same but, they say, the problems—traffic, congestion, pollution—are miles away and Vermont "is one of the finest places in the world to live, work and enjoy life along the way." The small color leaflet shows 9″ plush animal hand puppets and a saucy collection of people hand puppets: sailor, doctor, nurse, fireman, policeman, king and queen. As most puppets seem to be fairy-tale characters, these might be a nice change. Each one costs about $4, including postage.

Milo Products Corporation, Grantham, Pa. 17027
Leaflet, 25 cents.

Dado blocks were designed and are sold by this firm. They are flat birch-plywood pieces with cutouts along the edges so that they fit into each other and can be used for making structures of various sorts. Mainly suitable for schools and play groups, since they are expensive—$16 for twenty-four (with a discount for institutions). Various testimonials from teachers who have used them come with the leaflet saying that dados are good with two- to five-year-olds.

The Montgomery Schoolhouse, Inc., Montgomery, Vt. 05470
Leaflet, free.

This new firm makes wooden toys for young children and sells by mail a "Beach and Sandbox" series. Trucks, trains, cars, bridges, tunnels and wharfs are made from wood and preserved with a finish of linseed oil, which also gives a nice golden color. Most of the toys cost between $2.50 and $7, and a collection of these should keep a child very entertained on the beach or in the sandbox setting up and changing around various scenarios.

The New York Doll Hospital, 787 Lexington Avenue, New York, N.Y. 10021
No catalogue.

This well-known old store, in spite of its grand name, is just a couple of rooms up a narrow flight of stairs. The rooms are, however, crowded with rows and rows of antique dolls in all sizes and shapes staring blankly out at the intruder. Antique dolls are bought and sold here, but the hospital also fixes broken dolls and toys by mail.

The Rainbow, 9640 Santa Monica Boulevard, Beverly Hills, Calif. 90210
68-page catalogue, free, but 50-cent contribution welcome.

This extraordinary shop has so many virtues that it is hard to know where to begin. It was started by a couple whose daughter had cancer, which made them realize that there was a great need for a treatment center on the West Coast. With intelligence and imagination they started the Rainbow Shop to earn the enormous sums needed. They found 250 members who each put up $100, they formed a craftsmen's council that commissioned goods to sell, started workshops to teach people in the community how to make the goods, and found volunteer buyers to stock the shops with other things around the country. All work for the Rainbow is voluntary and *all* profits go into a fund for the treatment of children's cancer. Although $65,000 worth of goods was sold in the first six months, the Rainbow people want to earn $100,000 per year and would like to see similar stores start up around the country run by local volunteers.

The Rainbow is particularly pleasing because in addition to the good intentions, imagination and brains have created a first-rate shop. The goods are really lovely—there are excellent imported toys, such as the Fischertechnik building set, the Kaj Bojesen wooden toys from Denmark, appealing household things such as scales from Italy and brilliant potholders from South America, but also wittily designed needlepoint kits, tote bags, toy bags, puppets, rag dolls, picture sweat shirts and notepaper that you won't see anywhere else. Also scientific experiments, project and crafts books, games and many other things that must be available in other shops, but I haven't seen them elsewhere.

Rombins' Nest Farm, Fairfield, Pa. 17320
52-page catalogue, 25 cents.

Rombins' Nest Farm sells Americana and Pennsylvania-Dutch-style gifts, but so many of them will please children that this seems a good place to list the catalogue. There are small china ornaments, bird pictures, animal notes and a collection of cast-iron reproductions of old toys, including a pageful of animal and people banks for under $5, and a sensational group of mechanical banks that move when you deposit a coin—children dance, monkeys tip hats and Uncle Sam waggles his whiskers, these for around $30. Also some really charming cornhusk dolls, including cornhusk angels and a very limited supply of cornhusk crèches.

Rural Arts and Crafts Association, P.O. Box 227, Parkersburg, W.Va. 26101
14-page color toy catalogue, $2; refundable.
Quilt catalogue planned, $2; refundable.

This is a two-hundred-member co-operative which is active in ten counties in western West Virginia. It was set up with the help of the Office of Economic Opportunity to promote traditional Appalachian skills and provide economic help to poor-area residents, mainly the elderly. The toy catalogue is illustrated with color snapshots and shows a really charming collection of patchwork animals at prices between $6 and $16, and also some non-patchwork cloth dolls such as Raggedy Ann and Andy for $8 each, and a plush kangaroo with a baby in her pocket for $12. A quilt catalogue is being prepared and will be available by the time this book is published.

Otto Schmidt and Son, A Division of the Mead Corporation, 2 Allwood Avenue, Central Islip, N.Y. 11722
32-page catalogue, some color, 60 cents.

Otto Schmidt supplies schools with games, art supplies and equipment, but is also willing to sell to anyone else who is interested. Their catalogue is fairly professionally oriented, with expensive construction games, mathematical aids, learn-how-to-write charts, and step-by-step art projects, but it also illustrates some children's furniture that might be good for home use. Brightly painted animal shapes serve as rocking seats, desks and crawl-through games for children, ages two to eight. They are shipped flat, ready to be assembled (two of them are small enough to mail), and they cost between $20 and $26.

Dick Schnacke Mountain Craft Shop, Route 1, Proctor, W.Va. 26055
Leaflet, free. February.

An arty brown sheet introduces the old American folk toys made by Dick Schnacke and fellow craftsmen in Appalachia. The toys are simple and very appealing, many of them involving skills and patience that should keep you busy for hours. There is a whimmy diddle to rub, a flipper dinger to blow, a mountain bolo to swing and a buzz saw to twirl, not to mention an old-fashioned top to spin—sixty-three toys altogether and new ones are added each year. Practically all of them cost less than $3.

16 • *The Rainbow* Handmade puppets: Raggedy Ann and Andy, $3 each. Indian princess, gingerbread man, rabbit, $2 each.
photo E. K. Kaufman

F. A. O. Schwarz, 745 Fifth Avenue, New York, N.Y. 10022
Catalogue, some color, free. Spring/summer.
96-page catalogue, some color, free. Fall/winter.

F. A. O. Schwarz claims to be the oldest and most famous toy store in the world, though now it is more than a store—it's seventeen stores throughout America that stock between ten and twelve thousand different toys from all parts of the world. It hasn't lost its storybook toy-shop quality—you just step inside the Fifth Avenue store and you are surrounded by luxurious banks of expensive giant furry animals, whirling mechanical toys, tinkling music boxes, and elaborately dressed dolls. Every traditional toy for children of all ages is here, and the large catalogue goes through dolls and their clothes, dollhouses, Steiff plush toys, painted wooden toys, rocking horses, board games, bigger games such as table tennis, children's typewriters, art supplies, battery-operated cars, Dinky toys, construction sets, craft kits, woodwork sets, nature and science sets, electric trains, phonographs, walkie-talkies, farms and forts, bikes, pedal cars, outdoor equipment, sports equipment, puppets and fancy dress. They stock most famous foreign and American makes and carry all the name toys like Raggedy Ann, Snoopy, Joan Walsh Anglund and Mickey Mouse. In short, it's the rather expensive dream of many a covetous child and adult. Schwarz says that opera singers playing the toy pianos and automobile magnates working the toy cars are a common sight, and King Hussein bought one and a half truckloads of toys here a few years ago.

Johnson Smith Company, 35075 Automation Drive, Mount Clemens, Mich. 48043
80-page catalogue, free.

The old Johnson Smith catalogue of tricks and novelties has already passed into history, being reprinted like the Sears, Roebuck. Modern times, however, have caught up with the company, and like its address, its psychedelic cover shows that times have changed. It is only in the last pages of the catalogue that we find those old favorites, the imitation gold teeth and fake "amazingly realistic" vomit, the flavored rubber chocolates and squirt flower, the lifelike rubber masks and

17

18

19

17 • *Vermont Wooden Toy Company* Green Mountain Choo Choo. 53″ long, 9¼″ high. Engine, tender, boxcar, lumber car and caboose, $60. The circus car (second to last) is sold separately, with a giraff, for $15.

18 • *Vermont Wooden Toy Company* Vermont lumber truck with lumber, 12″ long. $8.

19 • *The Workshop for Learning Things* Construction set with 637 unfinished pieces. $445.

accompanying gory horror rubber feet that are such staples of American life. Here the present blends imperceptibly into the past. The beatnik disguise ("real gone, man") and the realistic sideburns ("wear them for those special occasions") are obviously helpful to those who have found the transition to modernity exceptionally difficult. The hippie wig could be worn with the vampire fingernails and the giant comic ears to put off an undesirable suitor for one's daughters, and no doubt rubber dollars, bitter toothpicks and dribble glasses are as useful now as they ever were.

The rest of the catalogue is a mixture of household items, gadgets and novelties that are somewhat less inspired but may turn out to be useful. Where else can you get two thousand standard tickets, consecutively numbered as at the movies, etc., for $2.50—helpful for your amateur magic shows or possibly as a different present for children. Among the laser pistols, powerful (though secondhand) electric generators and professional electric rock polishers nestles an offer that gives the mail-order shopper the thrill of a magical mystery tour, the surprise excursions that railroads used to offer: A SURPRISE PACKAGE for only $1. Be a sport, urges the catalogue, take a chance and get a surplus bargain. Or, if you feel exceptionally sporting, order the Special Extra Value Package for $2.95, which may contain several items. If you look carefully, some of the old magic is still there.

Toy Review, 383 Elliot Street, Newton, Mass. 02164
Sample issue, free. Four issues per year, $2.

Toy Review is a cross between a magazine and a catalogue. It has news, information and short articles about toys and children's activities (in the extra large Christmas issue I saw, there were articles on Halloween parties, "the traveling child," toys you can make, an easy recipe for cookies, etc.), and reviews of toys and books by readers and the magazine staff, though the reviews are mainly the observations of parents whose children have used the toys rather than thorough and extensive testings. The reviews are useful because a very wide variety of toys and educational aids for children of all ages have been found and described; however, Toy Review sells some of them so the write-ups can't claim to be entirely disinterested. I should think that anyone involved in looking after children would find it well worth sending for a sample copy, although the Toy Review gives no hint (beyond the manufacturer's name) as to where to buy the toys that the Toy Review doesn't sell—a serious setback to mothers of young children who have neither the time nor the energy to set out on major hunts for specific toys.

Vermont Wooden Toy Company, Old High School Building, Waitsfield, Vt. 05673
34-page catalogue, 25 cents.

A really nice collection of unpainted wooden toys for young children. This company says that it tries to build safe and beautiful toys that will last—no nails, screws, staples or plastics that could hurt a child are used and they omit paint and artificial finishes because they want their toys to "taste as good as they look." If one of the toys should break, it can quickly be fixed by a parent with a tube of glue—being someone with a pile of complicated broken toys in the closet, I like that bit. About fifty toys altogether, from babies' rattles and wooden beads to chew, through cars, boats, trucks with blocks, hobby horses, airplanes and doll carriages to a box sled. They're expensive, though; most of the best toys are between $10 and $20.

Weston Bowl Mill, Weston, Vt. 05161
40-page catalogue, 25 cents. Christmas mailing.

This mill manufactures mainly small wooden things for the house, but the catalogue also shows some inexpensive wooden toys painted in primary colors: a truck, a car, a train, five boats, a wooden whistle, a 5-lb. bag of unpainted building blocks for only $1, a 4-lb. bag of wood parts to make things with for only $1.50, and two bucket chairs for children—one, a musical rocking chair, for $25.

The Workshop for Learning Things, 5 Bridge Street, Watertown, Mass. 02172
34-page catalogue, 50 cents. Spring.
Book list, free.
List of Courses for Teachers, free.

At this six-year-old center, teachers and other educators take courses and work out new programs and materials to be used in schools. Their catalogue is very pleasantly written, and the goods they develop and sell look genuinely workable and exciting—useful for enterprising parents who would like to work with their children, as well as for teachers. The Workshop's newest and biggest idea is "cardboard carpentry." Working with three-layered cardboard, which they say is very strong and much easier to work with than wood, teachers and children together have made all sorts of terrific things: storage cubes and shelves, tables, chairs, desks, wagons, slides, playhouses, dollhouses and puppet stages. Tools for working the cardboard as well as an instruction and plan book ($2) are available. Not only should making the equipment be enjoyable and instructive, but normally expensive things like playhouses and dollhouses should become possibilities. Some storage units are on sale ready-made.

The center has also worked on photography in the classroom and has several photography kits for taking and then developing photographs without water and in a light room. A family camera kit, complete with three cameras and instruction book, costs $22. Specially developed microscopes ($9 and up), mechanical building kits, construction kits, playground things, sand sieves and a sand-and-water table kit, soapstone-carving kits, and a printing-press kit are also sold. But look at the Kelsey printing catalogue (the Hobby and Professional Equipment section, above) before buying a press here. Although this one is said to be especially easy for young children to use, the Kelsey kits are much cheaper.

World Wide Games, Inc., Box 450, Delaware, Ohio 43015
34-page catalogue, free. September.

Solid wooden games for children and adults are made here by people who not only love games but also think they're good for you. The Baileys, who started and still own the firm, have worked as recreation leaders, and travel around demonstrating their games and training other recreation leaders. They say that their games are often used in hospitals and in clubs for rehabilitation as well as by people who just like games. There is a fascinating collection from all over the world: "fast and noisy" box hockey from modern America; devilishly difficult Hindu pyramid puzzle from ancient India; Devil's Needle and Tangram puzzles from China; and Shisima, brought back from the Meshack Imbunya family who live near Kaimosi, Kenya. After immersing myself in the catalogue, I can sympathize with the man who went to Africa, and in the old colonialist spirit, moped so much without his table cricket game that he had the Baileys send him another, air freight. There are lots of games for under $5, other larger ones for around $40, and if you get carried away and set up a whole games room, you can buy yourself a rolling games cabinet which was built "because of popular demand and friendly insistence."

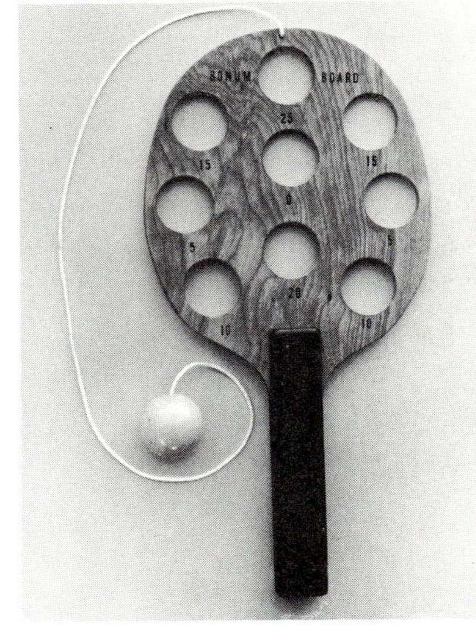

20

21

20 • *World Wide Games* Bonum Board, a paddle that apparently originated in America around 1880 when the paddles were decorated by wood burning. Two games can be played by one person or several. You can either try to get the ball into the holes with the highest numbers, then count the points, or you can go around the paddle getting the ball into each hole with as few tries as possible. $3.95.

21 • *World Wide Games* Adi board for an ancient game that is still played in Ghana today, indoors with a board, outside with holes in the earth and seeds. It is one of an ancient family of games played in Africa, Asia and the islands of the Pacific. Black walnut board with natural finish, cloth bag of marbles and instructions. $11.95.

INDEX

ABOUT THE AUTHOR

MARIA ELENA DE LA IGLESIA was born in Madrid in 1936, and attended Dartington Hall School and Newnham College, Cambridge, England, from which she was graduated with honors and where she also received her M.A. degree. She has written articles for *The Times* (of London) and is the author of two children's books, *The Cat and the Mouse* (1966), and *The Oak That Would Not Pay* (1968), both of which were published by Pantheon Books. She is also the author of *The Catalogue of Catalogues*, the complete guide to shopping abroad by mail. She is married to publisher André Schiffrin and they live in New York City with their two daughters, Anya and Natalia.